IN THE WAKE OF FIRST CONTACT

IN THE WAKE OF FIRST CONTACT

The Eliza Fraser Stories

KAY SCHAFFER

Department of Women's Studies
University of Adelaide

Published by the Press Syndicate of the University of Cambridge
The Pitt Building, Trumpington Street, Cambridge CB2 1RP, UK
40 West 20th Street, New York, NY 10011–4211, USA
10 Stamford Road, Oakleigh, Melbourne 3166, Australia

Printed in Australia by Brown Prior Anderson

National Library of Australia cataloguing-in-publication data
Schaffer, Kay, 1945– .
In the wake of first contact: the Eliza Fraser stories.
Bibliography.
Includes index.
1. Fraser, Eliza Anne – In literature. 2. Fraser, Eliza
Anne – In art. 3. Australian literature – History and
criticism. 4. Literature and history – Australia – History.
5. Race in literature. 6. Women and literature –
Australia – History – 19th century. 7. Literature,
Modern – History and criticism. 8. Aborigines, Australian,
in literature. 9. Aborigines, Australian – First contact
with Europeans. 10. Australia – History – 1788–1851 –
Historiography. I. Title.
A820.9351

Library of Congress cataloguing-in-publication data
Schaffer, Kay, 1945–
In the wake of first contact: the Eliza Fraser stories / Kay Schaffer
p.   cm.
Includes bibliographical references and index.
1. Australian literature – History and criticism. 2. Fraser, Eliza
Anne – In literature. 3. First contact of aboriginal peoples with
Westerners – Australia 4. Literature and history – Australia–
History. 5. Australian Aborigines in literature. 6. Race in
literature. 7. Women and literature – Australia – History – 19th
century. 8. Literature, Modern – History and criticism. 9. Fraser,
Eliza Anne – In art. 10. Australia – History – 1788–1851–
Historiography. I. Title.
PR9605.7.F73S33 1995
820.9'351–dc20   95–17890

A catalogue record for this book is available from the British Library.

ISBN 0 521 49577 6 Hardback

Production of this book was assisted by the
South Australian Government through the
Department for the Arts and Cultural Development.

Indexed by Meryl Potter

Contents

Illustrations

Maps

Figures

Preface

In May 1989, I slumped back in my chair at the Sorbonne, attempting to disguise my stunned surprise after hearing that the lecture I had been invited to give had been cancelled. Little did I know that the acute frustration I was feeling would result in my writing the book you are about to read. It has had an interesting genesis.

I was in France at the invitation of two universities, Paris III (Sorbonne) and Toulouse-le-Miral, to lecture to their post-graduate students in the Literatures in English program. My book, *Women and the Bush: Forces of Desire and the Australian Cultural Tradition*, had just been launched in Australia and was due for publication in Europe. I was on study leave and on my first trip to Europe. I had been invited, with the assistance of the Australia Council, to give lectures at emerging Australian Studies Centres in some twenty universities in the United Kingdom and Europe while overseas and to present an overview of the book. I took delight in the opportunity.

French universities taught very little Australian literature at the time. At the Sorbonne, for example, Patrick White's *A Fringe of Leaves* appeared on the syllabus (as the only Australian novel) perhaps once every three years. When the novel was taught in Europe, lecturers and students tended to focus on a comparison between the historical antecedents of the novel and their fictionalisation, about which I knew nothing. Nonetheless, I had responded to the invitations with enthusiasm, and promised to deliver a lecture entitled 'Australian Mythologies: Ideas of the Feminine in Patrick White's *A Fringe of Leaves*'. I imagined that it would not be too difficult to utilise the frameworks from *Women and the Bush* to provide a point of departure for the *Fringe of Leaves* lecture. Any further research necessary for the paper could be managed in between lectures and other research activities in the three months prior to my arrival in Paris.

Upon rereading the novel, however, I realised that I had made a serious error in judgement. *Women and the Bush* had examined the democratic nationalist notions of Australian national identity and how they had evolved across a range of cultural forms (particularly historical and literary texts, film and the media); the ways in which these forms and their institutional supports (from sociology, history, literature, politics and popular culture) evoked concepts of 'femininity', particularly in regard to landscape representation; and what effects these representations might have on actual (white) women in Australia. Finally, the text employed deconstructive strategies to challenge the myth of Woman/women in regard to two key short stories, one by Henry Lawson ('The Drover's Wife') and one by Barbara Baynton ('The Chosen Vessel'). Patrick White barely rated a mention. He appeared on page 17 in a list of modernist writers from the 1950s who challenged the democratic nationalist canon of Australian works, the perspective with which I was preoccupied. His novel is inspired by a shipwreck and 'captivity' of a white woman (his Cornish Ellen Gluyas) amongst indigenous peoples on what is now called Fraser Island; it proceeds from a set of modernist assumptions and critiques about what it means to be Australian that are very different to those of the democratic nationalists.

Clearly, if I were to impress my French audience, I had some work to do. I set myself to the task. Because the first questions Europeans tend to ask about the novel are: 'Is it true?' or 'Did it really happen?' I began to plan some archival research in London, Derbyshire, Edinburgh, and the Orkney Islands, hoping to examine the differences between what was known of the actual historical event and the ways in which it was transformed by White. Along the way, I examined the varied, but universally enthusiastic, critical reviews of the novel by Australian and overseas critics. At the same time, I was dismayed by the stereotypic characterisation of femininity and the harsh depiction of Aboriginal characters in the novel. I worried particularly about the act of cannibalism in which Ellen and her hosts engaged at a taut and fragile moment in the narrative, a moment elided in most of the critical reviews. This led me to ponder, from a post-colonial perspective, modernism's fascination with 'the primitive'. With these issues in mind, I began to structure the paper; I thought of it as a contained, short-term, interesting project directed to a particular goal.

My stunned response in the office of my professorial host in Paris occurred when he advised me that, contrary to his previous letters, he now did not want me to deliver a lecture to his post-graduate students on Patrick White's novel, *A Fringe of Leaves*, as he had not been able to include the novel on the syllabus. Rather, he said, he hoped that I might introduce students to what I believed they should know before reading their first piece of Australian literature. A daunting project, especially when presented to me at 3 p.m. for a 5 p.m. lecture! I had just spent the last two days in Paris confined to my hotel room, rewriting the lecture, restructuring and timing it carefully, articulating it clearly into a tape recorder, and practising my introduction with a sprinkling of French. This, in the city of the Eiffel Tower, the Louvre, the Beaubourg, and other Parisian enticements. I had resisted them, all for the sake of the lecture which was now not going to take place. In fact, I had spent the greater part of my non-lecturing time in Europe researching the woman and the legend which provided the historical basis for White's fiction.

The frustration was exacerbated a week later upon my arrival in Toulouse for what I believed to be a Friday lecture to post-graduate students on the novel, only to find a note on the door of the *U.E.R des Langues Littératures Civilisations Etrangères et de Linguistique, Section d'Anglais*. It informed students that the department was closed for the day in preparation for a weekend conference, to which students were not invited. I was to give a paper at the conference – but it concerned Henry Lawson and Australian nationalism, not Patrick White nor Eliza Fraser. I left France never having delivered the paper. But the research had provoked my interest. The inability to articulate my early speculations or share my growing enthusiasms with a scholarly audience – *any* audience – meant that I returned from study leave with a feeling of unfinished business and a project which is only now nearing its end.

So, I would have to say that I never intended to write this book; I never chose the topic, nor the area. Rather, it chose me. And once chosen, the relationship held.

Authors develop complex relationships with their objects of study. We get to the end not only by intellectual interest and dogged determination, but by weathering the emotional highs and lows, as well. Often this particular relationship which I have had with my elusive Eliza held only tenuously, attached to my tenacious curiosity. It carried me through many more months of intermittent archival work over a five-year period in Sydney and Melbourne, London and Kew, Derbyshire, Edinburgh, the Orkney Islands, and Sri Lanka. As well, extensive work was carried out on my behalf by archivists in New Zealand and South Africa, in search of further traces (never found) of the 'real' Eliza Fraser and her fictional avatars. The historical dimension of the project presented an interesting set of intellectual conflicts. It tested my delight in and commitment to post-modern perspectives against my considerable affection for and skill at historical research; it tested my knowledge that there is no 'real' person to be found in the archival materials which mark a life against my keen desire to know more about the actual woman and the times in which she lived.

I had confronted this dilemma before. In 1984, after having engaged in doctoral research on Katharine Susannah Prichard for some three years and toyed with the idea of writing a critical biography using the techniques of psychohistory, I abandoned the project. In an article in which I examined the attendant problems of biographical work, I wrote of the need to handle historical projects differently:

> Recent post-structuralist and French Feminist theorists have challenged [histori-cal] notions of the individual. They suggest a new point of departure . . . To say something different one needs to read both the woman and the text [her bio-graphic traces] as signs, traversed by the various discourses and contradictory codes of meaning. To do so restores to the woman, and to the text, a plurality, a multiplicity of meanings, a diffuse diversity. A deconstructive reading subverts attempts to reduce the woman/text under the master's critical gaze, a gaze which narcissistically reflects back the critic's identity while it obscures that of the object.[1]

Why, then, I asked myself, was I once again engaged in a historical/ biographical project? What was so enticing about primary research in dusty archives? I knew I was in pursuit of fool's gold but I could not resist it, despite my inability to turn up any more information on this mysterious woman than that contained in the few books and articles previously published con-cerning the event. One night, after a twelve-hour session at the Public Records Office, Kew, in a concerted effort to conquer the problem, I dreamt of being an archival librarian digging a dirt floor with a shovel. The shovel continued to hit unyielding stone below the floor. It stymied my work. I listened to the dream: I shifted my perspective and abandoned the libraries, but not the endeavour.

The pleasurable aspects of the project expanded considerably during sev-eral 'on-site' visits. I wrote the first draft of what was to be the aborted Paris paper in Stromness in the Orkney Islands in April 1989. I recall several bleak, stormy days of sitting at a window of an upper-storey room facing the grey sea, only four houses down the cramped flagstone laneway from the stone cottage in which Eliza Fraser had lived with her husband, Captain Fraser, and their three children prior to her departure with the Captain on their fatal voyage to the antipodes. It was in the Stromness Museum that I first read *The Rescue of Eliza Fraser* (1986) which had been prepared by Neil Buchanan and Barry Dwyer for the Fraser Island Historical Society's 150-year commem-oration of the shipwreck. That text makes a well-reasoned effort to reconcile dilemmas presented by a number of contradictory reports of the event. It tests documentary evidence against the authors' considerable knowledge of local history and topography in order to get closer to the 'truth' of 'what really happened'. I began, however, to see the contradictions in the texts as signs of the making of 'colonialism's culture', to use Nicholas Thomas's suggestive phrase. I began reading the documents as sites for the production of colonial knowledge and power relations, as exercises of power whereby women, escaped convicts, mutinous seamen and indigenous peoples all came under (and at the same time resisted) the imperial/colonial gaze.

Upon arrival back in Australia, I made several trips to Fraser Island where, whipped with sunshine, sea air and sand, and assisted by a number of enthusiastic local historians and environmentalists, I retraced the locale of the shipwreck of the *Stirling Castle* in 1836 and the fate of its crew. I became conscious of other layers of meaning connected to the history of the event, concerning environmentalism, Aboriginal mythology, and contemporary political and historical perspectives. Often there was exhilaration as, with my friends, I traversed up and down the coast, over wilderness trails and up to lookouts, around lakes, across swamps and lagoons, in what is now a stunningly beautiful World Heritage area. I became increasingly familiar with the territories which before Eliza Fraser's arrival had belonged to the Badtjala, Gabi-Gabi and Undambi peoples of the Great Sandy Region, every patch of this 'uncharted' land and sea familiar to them. I walked the Cooloola Wilderness Trail, an established Aboriginal track and site of Mrs Fraser's rescue, which was in the process of being widened: the rainforest root system was damaged, its fragile canopy of foliage rent by bulldozers. I learned the Badtjala creation myths of the ancestral beings who shaped the land, including the story of Teewah, the rainbow serpent, who was in love with the maiden Cooroibah who was herself abducted by Cootharaba. The act enraged Teewah: in his fury he crashed into the sandy cliffs of Cooloola, creating the spectacular Coloured Sands at Rainbow Beach.[2] The irony of another abduction and rescue, that of Eliza Fraser from her Aboriginal hosts, in the same environment did not escape my notice. Although most of my travels were exhilarating, sometimes I experienced terror as I travelled along the coast. Once I wandered off by myself in a mock attempt to find a way through the paperbark swamps at Teewah landing which Mrs Fraser traversed with John Graham to her rescue point. My mood turned sombre and then I panicked upon becoming totally disoriented within an enveloping wilderness so like that captured by Sidney Nolan in his evocative Mrs Fraser series of paintings from the 1956–7 period.

The study by Buchanan and Dwyer which I read in Stromness also suggested that Mrs Fraser was 'born and reared in Ceylon', another location I would visit before completing the research. The phrase stunned me at the time – two more incongruous colonial locations for the story could not be imagined. It was then that many Mrs Frasers began to dance before my mind's eye. There was the historical figure: Eliza Anne Fraser, née Slack; mother, Elizabeth Ann Britton; age given as thirty-six at the time of the shipwreck in May 1836. No one had been able to locate a birth, baptismal or death certificate for her; her accident-prone, sea-faring husband left no will; none of her family appears in either the 1820 or 1830 census for Scotland;

details of her life after her marriage to Alexander John Greene and return to England in 1838 remain a mystery. And there was the plethora of images produced by historical commentators to supplement the considerable gaps in the archives: an indulged daughter of the Raj; a child of Derbyshire peasants displaced by industrialisation; an ardent and devoted wife; a sea-going mother who abandoned her children; a stern Presbyterian churchgoer; a devilish 'She-Captain'; a victim of shipwreck and starvation; a widow facing a 'fate worse than death' at the hands of 'cannibals and savages'; a seductive, sensual and fickle betrayer of her convict rescuer; a vengeful rape victim; a survivor; a sideshow performer; an opportunist, a fraud, a cheat and a liar.

The idea of this, perhaps the first, white female shipwreck victim facing 'the natives' in a remote and uncharted area of Australia evoked strong responses in all of Eliza Fraser's commentators. In the wake of 'first contact', the tale adapted itself to fantasies and myths of national and racial origin for white writers in a number of post-colonial settler societies – the United States, South Africa and Canada, as well as Australia. Versions appeared in 'high' and popular forms, directed at serious scholarly audiences as well as a mass public. And 150 years after the event, it still had the ability to capture an audience. 'Mrs Fraser' had been rebuked, sensationalised, sensualised, vilified, revered, mocked, and politicised in a variety of contexts and locales; imperial, colonial, neo-colonial, and now anti- and post-colonial. Clearly, the story resonated with divergent meanings across time, the effects of which I had only begun to recognise.

Although I never gave my paper in France, I was able to present an abridged version of it at a conference in Giessen just a few days before my departure back to Australia. The paper, an expanded version of which was subsequently published in *Kunapipi*, drew enthusiastic responses. Many of my listeners encouraged me to continue the project, suggesting new sources of material and avenues of investigation. They offered insights, information, and new directions to pursue. Upon my return to Australia, my relationship to the project had changed, becoming at once more subtle and enticing but also far more demanding, as my attention turned to novels and plays, paintings and installations, poetry, films and television documentaries which have come in the wake of the shipwreck of the *Stirling Castle* and Eliza Fraser's alleged 'captivity' amongst 'savages and cannibals'.

What had begun as a limited investigation of Patrick White's depiction of the Eliza Fraser story in *A Fringe of Leaves* had been transformed into a touch-stone event supporting an intensive and ongoing study of the culture of colonialism and its contemporary effects. When I shifted my interest from the woman and the shipwreck as historical subjects to the culture that her story and the event had helped to produce, I found, if not the perfect feminist heroine, an engaging, multi-faceted colonial legend requiring an extensive

post-colonial critique. Colonial writers at the time of the shipwreck represented the event in ways that attempted to establish the boundaries of
identity and difference, to secure what was then a precarious power base.
Post-colonial critique enabled me to challenge those boundaries after colonial power (but not its legacy of race, class and gender relations) had been
dismantled. I abandoned my search for 'truth' and began to trace the specific
and interconnected, unfinished and ongoing contestations of power made
possible by representations of the event.

On a number of occasions while writing the book, I sought out readers
with specific areas of expertise who provided additional information or generously made helpful critiques of various aspects of the study. They include:
Jude Adams, Mary-Ann Bin Sallik, Elaine Brown, Gordon Collier, Yolanda
Drummond, Shirley Foley, Lee Cataldi, Andrew Lattas, Frances Lindsay,
Roslyn Poignant, Margaret Plant, Sidonie Smith and Carolyn Williams. I am
also grateful to the many creative artists whose work I examine in the book
whom I visited, or corresponded with, or contacted by phone, or to whom I
sent chapters for comment. They responded with enthusiasm and helpful
critical advice. They include: Michael Alexander, André Brink, Gillian Coote,
Fiona Foley, Allan Marett, Peter Sculthorpe, Barbara Blackman Veldhoven,
and David Williamson.

Along the way I have had many helpers, the book's extended kin so to
speak, to whom I am gratefully indebted. I would like to extend my gratitude
to all who have assisted me during the last six years of the project. Special
thanks to Anna Rutherford and Gordon Collier for their early support and to
Gordon for his ongoing and rigorous intellectual and editorial assistance
along the way. Late in the day, I am grateful to the staff at Cambridge University Press, especially Janet Mackenzie, my able sub-editor, and Jane
Farago, who has kept me on track with copyright details and permissions.

I received generous help from a number of researchers, archivists and
librarians. The include: Thomas Askey, of Chatsworth House, Derbyshire;
Alison Fraser, Archivist at the Kirkwell Library, Orkney Islands; Dr
Wimalaratne, Director, Sri Lankan National Archives, and the charming Sam
Mottau, its former Director; as well as numerous helpful staff at the Fryer
and Oxley Libraries, Queensland; the British Library; the Public Record
Office, Kew; Somerset House, London; the Guildhall Library, London; the
Derbyshire Record Office, Matlock; the Stromness Museum, Orkney Islands;
the Newberry Library in Chicago; and the State Library of New South
Wales, Mitchell Library. Thanks also to Peter Lauer, former Director of the
University of Queensland Anthropological Museum, and the late Gerry
Langevad, of the Queensland Division of Aboriginal and Torres Strait Islan-
der Affairs, for guidance on anthropological aspects of the research, and to
Professor K. M. DeSilva and Dr Ian Goonetileke for their expert advice

concerning Sri Lanka's colonial history. I am also grateful to Julia Millen, Jenny McDonogh and Sharmilla Henry, my New Zealand, South African and Sri Lankan researchers respectively. A special thanks to the woman, whose name I have lost but who lives vividly in my memory, who silently sacrificed her lunch and her lunch hours to keep open the Museum at Stromness after hours, thus enabling me to read the extensive files.

I would also like to thank Ann Mather, Art Librarian, University of South Australia; Juliana Engburg, Curator, and Anna Clayburn, Assistant Curator, Heide Gallery; Jane Clark, then curator at the Queensland Art Gallery, now with Sotheby's in Melbourne; and staff at the Roslyn Oxley9 Gallery, all of whom assisted in my art research and the pursuit of paintings and illustrations included in this volume. I am immensely grateful to Sue Murray at the Geography Department at the University of Adelaide for providing the knowledge, skills and patience to enable me to produce the maps included in the book. For various forms of support, information and assistance, thanks to Janine Burke, Geoff Brown, Lanie Carroll, Kate Darian-Smith, Dorothy Driver, Barry Dwyer, Greg Greco, Sue Kossew, Alan Lawson, Michael Luke, Ian McNiven, Wendy Morgan, Lynette Russell, Ron Slack, Leon Scatterthwait, Pauline Strong, Peter Sutton, John and Sally Treloar, Michael Venning, Mike West of FIDO, and Nancy Williams.

A special thanks to Irene Christie, Secretary, Tewantin Historical Society, for her excellent guided tour of the Cooloola region and for taking the 'author's' photograph of me beside the commemorative plaque which (incorrectly) marks the site of Eliza Fraser's rescue. Similarly, to Mrs Gomeja, Banda, and the staff of the Grand Hotel, Nuria Elya, for their extraordinary generosity in providing contacts, guided tours and transport, and for making arrangements for my research in the hills district of Sri Lanka.

Closer to home, I am grateful to my research assistants Anne Barrie, Rob Foster, Helen Innes, Arien Koppe and Sarah Shepherd, who performed many odd jobs and often coped patiently with my confusion and panic in the face of various deadlines along the way. Many of the ideas in the book were first tested with Women's Studies post-graduate students, always a vital source of inspiration, in my subject 'Women and Popular Culture' at Adelaide University in 1992. I am particularly grateful to Janet Kitchner, Chryss Bryce and Margaret Smith for their research and writing, which extended my own thinking about contemporary, popular cultural formations. In addition, I made a number of wonderful friends in the course of the project. Special thanks to Elaine and Geoff Brown and Barbara and Harry Garlick in Queensland, Roslyn Poignant in London, and Anne Abeywardene in Colombo, for opening their homes and hearts to me, extending hospitality, personal and intellectual companionship, and lightening the load at the bleary end of an extended research day. Finally, to my colleagues, friends and family, especially Muriel Lenore, Jill Golden, Maureen Dyer, and my husband Robert, who lived with me through the highs and lows and never failed to assist as supporters of the project, sounding-boards and 'ideal' readers, my heartfelt gratitude.

Sections of this book have appeared elsewhere. My first article on the Eliza Fraser story contains the seeds of ideas developed over several chapters. It first appeared as 'The Eliza Fraser Story and Constructions of Gender, Race and Class in Australian Culture' in *Hecate:* Special Issue on Women/ Australia/Theory, 17, 1 (1991). An expanded version of this article was republished under the title 'Australian Mythologies: The Eliza Fraser Story and Constructions of the Feminine in Patrick White's *A Fringe of Leaves* and Sidney Nolan's Eliza Fraser Paintings', in *Them and Us: Translation, Transcription and Identity in Post-Colonial Literary Cultures*, edited by Gordon Collier, and published by Rodopi Press, Amsterdam and Atlanta, 1992. Portions of Chapters 2 and 3 have appeared in several articles. These include parts of my article entitled 'Nationalism and the American Captivity Narratives' in *Captured Lives: Australian Captivity Narratives*, co-authored with Kate Darian-Smith and Roslyn Poignant and published by the Sir Robert Menzies Centre for Australian Studies, University of London, 1993; 'Colonizing Gender in Colonial Australia: The Eliza Fraser Story', an article published in *Writing Women and Space*, edited by Gillian Rose and Alison Blunt, and published by Guilford Press, New York, 1994; and 'Trial by Media: The Case of Eliza Fraser', which appeared in *Antipodes: An American Journal of Australian Studies* (USA), 5, 2 (Winter, 1991). Parts of Chapter 10 are included in my article 'Australian Feminisms, Aboriginality and National Identity in the 1990s', which appeared in the *Journal of Cultural Studies* (UK) (1995). I am grateful to the publishers for permission to reproduce material in this book.

CHAPTER 1

Her Story/History: The Many Fates of Eliza Fraser

Colonialism remade the world. Neither Europe nor the Third World, neither colonizers nor colonized would have come into being without the history of colonialism . . . Colonialism continues to live on in ways that perhaps we have only begun to recognize.

Nicholas B. Dirks

This is a book about a legend. The legend concerns the fate of Mrs Eliza Fraser, the wife of a Scottish ship's captain whose brig, the *Stirling Castle*, was wrecked off what is now the south-east coast of Queensland in 1836. Mrs Fraser and other survivors of the wreck spent approximately thirty days at sea and a further fifty-two days on what is now called Fraser Island and the adjoining mainland in the company of Aborigines. Eventually Mrs Fraser was rescued by a government party sent out by the Commandant of the Moreton Bay Penal Settlement. She thus became known as the first white woman to encounter Aborigines in the wild, so to speak, and to tell her (less than sympathetic) tale. Her tale enters colonial discourse not as a story of survival amongst her Aboriginal hosts but as a cruel captivity amongst savages and cannibals. Her story attracted considerable interest at the time, especially in England where she received sympathy as an innocent victim of Empire before being accused as an imposter and of perpetrating fraud, but it receives scant attention in subsequent historical texts. In contemporary Australia, however, as a twentieth-century figure of legend – as a captive victim who seduced and then betrayed her convict rescuer – Mrs Fraser has taken on mythical status as a cultural figure of some note, as anyone could attest who has read Patrick White's novel, *A Fringe of Leaves* (1976), or has seen any of Sidney Nolan's paintings from his 'Mrs Fraser' series (1947–77), or has viewed the David Williamson and Tim Burstall film *Eliza Fraser* (1976).[1] This is one reason why Eliza Fraser is remarkable. She is one of a very few women – along with Caroline Chisholm, Daisy Bates, and Louisa Lawson – to have walk-on roles on the stage of an Australian mythology of nationhood.

Her story is legendary today; but the legend has little to do with the actual woman or the historical event. What is known of the woman and the event, however, is less significant than the representations and the fantasies which this minor colonial episode set into circulation, fantasies situated at the

1

borders of the Western self and its others.[2] For a brief while in the nineteenth century, the 'captivity' of Eliza Fraser amongst 'savages and barbarous natives' became a sensation in England. Her sad tale stirred the hearts of noble Britons who contributed generously to a subscription fund established for her welfare. That is, until the legal authorities cast doubt on the woman's veracity; then the sensation turned to scandal. Her story circulated in the British and American press and throughout the colonial world, feeding the academic interests of natural science as well as the prurient pleasures of the mass public. At the time of its occurrence, versions of the event were framed within and contributed to the rise of imperialism, the spread of Christianity, notions of a hierarchy of racial types within the natural sciences and gender divisions within Victorian sexual politics. Controversy surrounding the event in England also contributed to the evolution of Australia as a site of colonial adventure, a remote and dangerous outpost of Empire.

Mrs Fraser was nearly forgotten in the twentieth century, until renewed interest in the 1970s produced a multitude of materials to bolster her legend throughout the post-colonial world. New historical, artistic and mass cultural representations appeared in England as well as in Australia, Canada, and South Africa, all white settler societies with a nineteenth-century British heritage. With the advent of cultural pluralism in the 1970s, a number of contemporary adaptations placed the story within a Western modernist aesthetic. In universalistic terms, Mrs Fraser became an Everyman character, testing and transgressing the physical, spiritual and ideological boundaries between white and indigenous cultures; her avatars aided modernist writers, like Michael Ondaatje in Canada, André Brink in South Africa, and Patrick White in Australia, in attempting to come to terms with their country's racist colonial past. In nationalistic terms, the story flowed into changing ideological and political currents within Australian culture as well as that of Canada and South Africa; writers refashioned the tale into one which exposed a common humanity between colonised and colonising peoples. By the 1990s, when the story was revived again in Australia, the sureties of (male, white, Western) universal humanism had succumbed to the global challenges of post-modernism as well as local anti-colonial perspectives supported by a previously suppressed white history of Aboriginal oppression, appropriation and marginalisation. Over the 160 years or so since the event occurred, its retellings have been a locus of contested ideological representations. Circulating within both 'high' and popular culture, representations of the event have operated in diverse ways to differently place white women and men, convicts, ship's officers and crew and indigenous women and men in relation to Western history and British colonial authority. Adaptations of the story have contributed to myths of national identity (as well as challenges to those myths) for a number of new settler society nations, the effects of which can be traced within international cultural politics today.

This study examines the Eliza Fraser story not so much as an historical event but as foundational fiction aligned with the maintenance of a colonial empire and, later, with the makings and remakings of the Australian nation. The event has generated an abundance of both popular and intellectual knowledge which circulated together to produce, maintain, contest and uphold various representations of difference. Focusing on the nineteenth century, I will attend to a variety of texts which reproduce materials related to the event in a variety of colonial genres – including Mrs Fraser's first-person accounts, government documents, histories, a sensationalised captivity narrative, ballads, handbills, and newspaper reports. Turning to the twentieth century, I will detail the ways in which the story enters contemporary culture through art, drama, opera, film and television documentaries, as well as popular and literary prose accounts. The analysis aims to study the work of representation: to examine the position(s) in the narratives of Mrs Fraser and of other speakers, writers and commentators; to examine the ways in which she is constructed as a victim and/or survivor of native savagery; to ask how her story gains authority through the testimonies of the speakers, their investments in the social institutions and practices as well as the cultural attitudes and beliefs of the time; and to read the documents to examine the ways in which different forms of narrative contribute differently to colonial constructions of 'race',[3] gender and class divisions and hierarchies. The study examines how the texts have been read and received, not only at the time of the event but also by later readers – including historians, painters, novelists and film-makers, as well as their critics and commentators – as representations which uphold or resist conflicting notions of colonial or national authority in different historical contexts. It examines the ways in which Aboriginal readings of the story can subvert white notions of cultural identity, power and representation. The approach assumes that there is no guarantee of knowledge beyond the textual representations of the event. The event, through narration, becomes placed in a number of fields of meaning. For the most part, the fields in which the Eliza Fraser story has circulated have been enmeshed within Western, rationalist, imperial and nationalist discourses of history.[4] But each of these is a site of contestation; all are challenged by Aboriginal perspectives – no meaning is fixed. There is no 'real' which is accessible outside its representations.

The Eliza Fraser Story: A Reconstruction

First, a reconstruction of events related to the shipwreck of the *Stirling Castle*, is offered here. It serves to establish a ground on which it is possible to speak about and also contest the story, and to create for myself and the reader a point of reference/departure.

In 1836, Eliza Fraser, the English wife of an ailing Scottish ship's captain, James Fraser, accompanied her husband on what was to prove to be a fatal voyage to the antipodes. The couple left behind them a teenage daughter and two younger sons in the Orkney Islands off the north coast of Scotland, in the care of the Presbyterian Minister at Stromness. Their brig, the *Stirling Castle*, was a merchant ship which carried goods and emigrant passengers from England to the colonies. On this voyage, which carried goods and three emigrant families to Van Diemen's Land (now Tasmania), it had a crew of nineteen men in addition to the Captain and his wife. The crew included two of the Captain's nephews, one its second mate and the other a twelve-year-old boy, as well as two 'men of colour' – a 'negro' cook and 'mulatto' steward from South America. From the outset, the voyage was eventful. First, the brig suffered damage as a result of a collision shortly after casting off, necessitating a return to harbour and a three-day delay to the departure. This event, traditionally taken as a bad omen by sailors, coupled with the knowledge of the Captain's ill health and his prior record of having commanded a ship on a voyage to the antipodes four years earlier which had been wrecked, did nothing to instil confidence in the crew, a number of whom signed off when the vessel reached port in Sydney. This change of circumstance required that the Captain take on new crew, unfamiliar with his command, for the return voyage. Then, en route from Sydney to Singapore, the vessel went aground on shoals some 800 kilometres off the present Queensland coast and was dismasted in a violent storm. The survivors set off in two leaky lifeboats, bailing water, battling sharks and storms. They voyaged through treacherous seas for more than four weeks, surviving without food or water for much of the time. The stronger and more stroppy crew on the more reliable pinnace mutinied, heading south. The abandoned members of the longboat included a frenzied Captain Fraser, weakened by illness, and his pregnant wife; they eventually landed on what is now called (after the Captain) Fraser Island, but only after the crew threatened to 'draw lots' if the Captain, who feared native violence and cannibalism, did not pull ashore. Mrs Fraser and seven members of the crew eventually survived the ordeal.

On the island, the crew met up with several groups of indigenous peoples belonging to perhaps three clans with distinct territorial affiliations and speaking two related languages.[5] The shipwreck survivors straggled south along the beach in small groups, bartering clothes and navigational instruments for food with various small bands of 'natives'[6] for a few days, before being 'captured' and assigned to different family groups and subjected to native custom. Initially, until the local women came for her, Mrs Fraser was completely abandoned. In both physical and psychological terms, her suffering was great. Already in a weakened and sunburnt condition, she was stripped naked, separated from her husband and crew, and given a sickly, lice-infected child to nurse. In addition, she was forced with firebrands to climb trees in search of honey, taught to search swamps and lagoons for fern roots and water lilies, made to fetch water and carry wood, and only permitted to sleep outside the native shelters, even during heavy rain. Before arriving on the island she is reputed to have given birth in the brackish, knee-deep water of the longboat, four days out to sea, to a child which drowned; she had been separated from her young nephew, John, who had been pressed into service on the pinnace when it separated from the longboat and who subsequently was drowned while collecting oysters for the starving crew. While 'in captivity',[7] she witnessed the spearing and death of her husband and the miserable sufferings of several other crew members, before being rescued during a corroboree by the convict John Graham. She may have suffered sexual abuse, as well, leading to severe mental derangement, although the nature of her sexual encounters is shrouded in uncertainty.

Although Graham is the rescuer of record, he may have been assisted by another escaped convict, David Bracefell, the rescuer of legend. Graham had volunteered his services to the official government party, hoping for a pardon in return for his co-operation. Prior to 1836, he had escaped from the penal colony and had lived as a 'white blackfellow' for six years, during which time he 'married' a native woman and adapted well to tribal life, coming to know the land, language and customs, before returning to serve out what he mistakenly hoped would be the final months of his sentence. Bracefell had escaped the settlement on several occasions and was 'at large' at the time of the shipwreck. When he was returned to civilisation in 1842, after the penal colony had been disbanded, he alleged that he had rescued 'the lady', and walked her back to Moreton Bay. But, complaining of his treatment, she had betrayed him at the edge of civilisation, breaking her promise to intercede on his behalf for a pardon. The official report, however, names Graham alone, who is said to have claimed Eliza from the 'hostile natives' by representing her as the ghost of his dead wife. She had spent fifty-two days in their company.

Descriptions of Mrs Fraser at the time of her rescue reveal something of her suffering. Lieutenant Otter, who waited with clothing at a pre-arranged spot on the beach after Graham negotiated with the natives for her release, described her thus:

> You never saw such an object. Although only thirty-eight years of age, she looked like an old woman of seventy, perfectly black, and dreadfully crippled from the

(Following pages)
Map 1   The New South Wales coast, 1830s. The boxed area corresponds to the area shown in Map 2.
Map 2   Location of principal events relating to the shipwreck of the *Stirling Castle*.

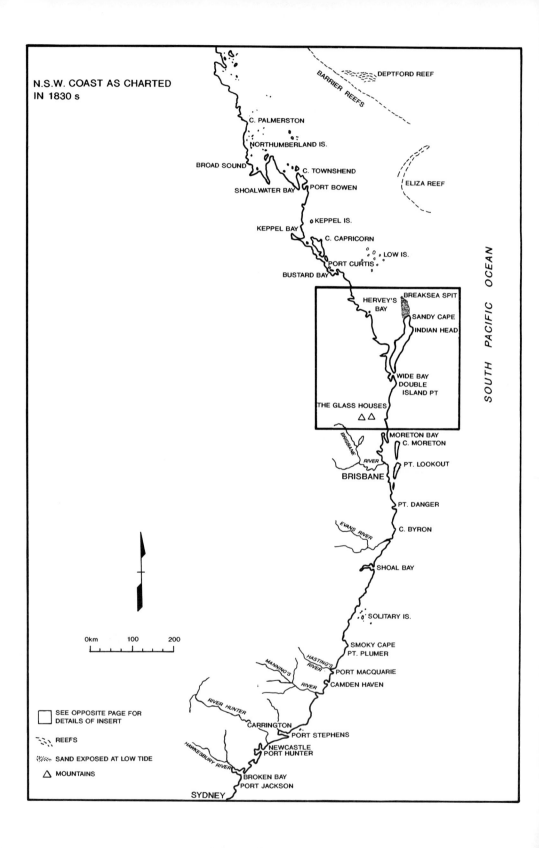

N.S.W. COAST AS CHARTED
IN 1830 s

DEPTFORD REEF

BARRIER REEFS

C. PALMERSTON

NORTHUMBERLAND IS.

BROAD SOUND

C. TOWNSHEND

ELIZA REEF

SHOALWATER BAY

PORT BOWEN

KEPPEL IS.

KEPPEL BAY

C. CAPRICORN

LOW IS.

PORT CURTIS

BUSTARD BAY

HERVEY'S
BAY

BREAKSEA SPIT

SANDY CAPE

INDIAN HEAD

WIDE BAY
DOUBLE
ISLAND PT

THE GLASS HOUSES

MORETON BAY
C. MORETON

BRISBANE

RIVER

PT. LOOKOUT

BRISBANE

PT. DANGER

EVANS RIVER

C. BYRON

SHOAL BAY

SOLITARY IS.

SMOKY CAPE
PT. PLUMER

HASTING'S RIVER

MANNING'S RIVER

PORT MACQUARIE

CAMDEN HAVEN

RIVER HUNTER

CARRINGTON

PORT STEPHENS

NEWCASTLE
PORT HUNTER

HAWKESBURY RIVER

BROKEN BAY
PORT JACKSON

SYDNEY

SOUTH PACIFIC OCEAN

0km   100   200

SEE OPPOSITE PAGE FOR
DETAILS OF INSERT

REEFS

SAND EXPOSED AT LOW TIDE

△ MOUNTAINS

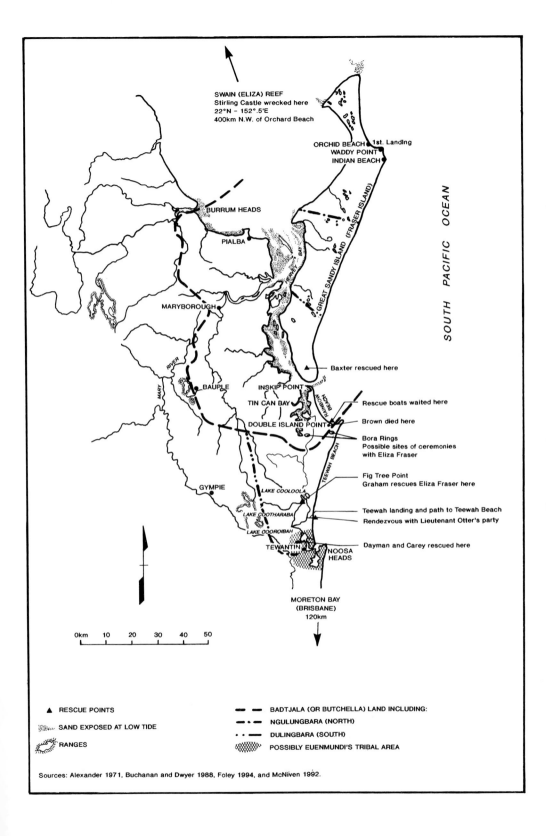

SWAIN (ELIZA) REEF
Stirling Castle wrecked here
22°N – 152°.5'E
400km N.W. of Orchard Beach

ORCHID BEACH ● 1st. Landing
WADDY POINT
INDIAN BEACH ●

SOUTH PACIFIC OCEAN

GREAT SANDY ISLAND (FRASER ISLAND)

BURRUM HEADS

PIALBA

MARYBOROUGH

MARY RIVER

BAUPLE

INSKIP POINT
TIN CAN BAY

DOUBLE ISLAND POINT

GYMPIE

LAKE COOLOOLA

LAKE COOTHARABA

LAKE COOROIBAH

TEWANTIN

NOOSA HEADS

▲ Baxter rescued here

Rescue boats waited here

Brown died here

Bora Rings
Possible sites of ceremonies
with Eliza Fraser

Fig Tree Point
Graham rescues Eliza Fraser here

Teewah landing and path to Teewah Beach
Rendezvous with Lieutenant Otter's party

Dayman and Carey rescued here

MORETON BAY
(BRISBANE)
120km

0km 10 20 30 40 50

▲ RESCUE POINTS

⬚ SAND EXPOSED AT LOW TIDE

RANGES

— — BADTJALA (OR BUTCHELLA) LAND INCLUDING:

—·— NGULUNGBARA (NORTH)

·—·— DULINGBARA (SOUTH)

POSSIBLY EUENMUNDI'S TRIBAL AREA

Sources: Alexander 1971, Buchanan and Dwyer 1988, Foley 1994, and McNiven 1992.

sufferings she had undergone. I went to meet her, and she caught my hand, burst into tears, and sunk down quite exhausted. She was a mere skeleton, the skin literally hanging upon her bones, whilst her legs were a mass of sores, where the savages had tortured her with firebrands.[8]

After the rescue, Mrs Fraser was taken back to Moreton Bay, where she excited considerable curiosity. There she and other survivors were interviewed by the Commandant who filed several statements and an official report. The local women residents nursed her back to health before she departed for Sydney. In Sydney she attracted more notice, giving several interviews to the press about her experiences before meeting Captain Alexander Greene of the *Mediterranean Packet*. Eliza married Captain Greene seven months after the death of her husband and accompanied him back to England. Greene seems to have had an ambivalent relationship to Eliza, perhaps viewing her as a winning ticket to a lucrative new life. The citizens of the new colony had donated two trunks of clothing and four hundred pounds to her welfare prior to her departure. Yet, on arrival in England, she appealed to the authorities (first in Liverpool and then in London) for funds, representing herself as 'Mrs Fraser', a poor widow woman without a farthing. She also gave further interviews to the press, some say at the contrivance of her 'Svengali' husband, which by now had taken on a wildly exaggerated air.

Soon after her arrival in England, sensational stories of her captivity began to appear in the London papers, and they were quickly taken up and circulated through the American and colonial press. A subscription fund was set up by the Lord Mayor of London; it attracted some five hundred pounds before news reached the city that her claims were somewhat inflated. She was accused of being an ingenious imposter and of perpetrating fraud. A Commission of Inquiry followed, after which the Lord Mayor, embarrassed in the midst of an election campaign, transferred the money collected by subscription to a trust fund for her three children, then under guardianship of the Minister at Stromness. Details of the inquiry were reported daily in the press and later resulted in the publication of the first 'official' history of the event, *The Shipwreck of the Stirling Castle* (1838), which was written by John Curtis, a court reporter for *The Times*. About this time, a woman representing herself as Eliza appeared as a sideshow attraction in Hyde Park, telling her tale of barbarous treatment and miraculous escape. Admission sixpence. This sideshow Eliza is the last sighting history records of the woman who was already passing into myth.

The story I have just told needs to be contested and deconstructed. It represents a culling of facts based on the rules of logic and evidence which attend the discipline of history. In relating the story as a historical event, I stand in for a supposedly neutral, objective (masculine) authority within a Eurocentric, humanistic philosophical tradition. My account attempts to outline uncontested details of the event taken from official records, extant letters and subsequent histories. It focuses on Eliza Fraser's ordeal, and purports not to speak on behalf of anyone in particular. But this is impossible. The story, like all historical narratives, is itself a fiction. It tells the story from her perspective and not that of other survivors. Still, 'her' story, itself, is authorised by colonialism; her personal testimony places her within the discourses and institutions which shaped her daily life. The retelling also utilises terms which are racially charged and historically determined (natives, captivity). It masks the divergent voices and positions of marginalised others (the indigenous people, the crew, the runaway convicts). It inevitably employs a terminology which speaks on behalf of those in authority (*whose* mutiny, *whose* captivity, *whose* savages?). It brings to life a unified subject, Eliza Fraser, who evokes the sympathy of the reader ('her sufferings were great', etc.). It suggests an immediacy and authenticity through a first-hand, eye-witness account ('You never saw such an object . . .'). It engages in speculations, motivations and intentions supplied by later historians (the frenzied Captain, the stroppy crew, her Svengali husband). And it reconstructs aspects of the event which, despite their presence in the historical accounts, are obscure (her pregnancy, the birth at sea, innuendoes of sexual abuse, conflicting stories of her rescue, and her psychological condition after the event). In terms of narrative structure, it employs a logic necessary to a progressive realist text: it has a beginning, a middle and an end; it constructs a story through principles of cause and effect; it revolves around the theme of survival; it suggests a series of links between the event and its aftermath; and it provokes reader interest with reference to the mystery of a shipwreck, a captivity, murder, sex, savagery and rescue. In addition, it provokes speculations and fantasies around an enigmatic woman/Woman and her alleged captors. All these structuring devices are already invested with significant meaning from other narratives, other genres, other discourses.

Further, any discussion of a 'first contact' event presents problems of perspective, particularly with reference to the location of the speaker/writer. The event itself is a liminal experience – one which takes place in an in-between space of cultural and psychic incomprehension, outside representation.[9] It becomes known and codified through the texts, discourses and histories in which it becomes embedded. There are always multiple histories, perspectives and contestations, including the overlapping cultural domains of the coloniser and the colonised, which involve contesting cosmologies, each with their own understandings and imaginings.[10] But textual representations within a colonial or a nationalist history reduce these multiple perspectives into a narrative of Empire and/or nation. The story becomes a sign of 'The People', one of many events told within a people's history which establishes an 'imagined community', in Benedict Anderson's terms, a cultural community of common interests and identifiable social and psychic identities.[11]

There are a number of 'takes' on the term 'first contact'. They have relevance for the ways in which the story has been represented within Australian history and the problems of that history's monologic, Eurocentric reductions. Henry Reynolds studies first-contact interactions on the frontier as a space of negotiation. In attributing agency to Aboriginal actors, he addresses the politics of frontier contact from both sides, in terms of the ways in which Aborigines engaged in acts of both accommodation and resistance to white invasion. He interprets the Aboriginal response to invasion as 'positive, creative and complex'.[12] In his reassessments of the evidence of first contact, Reynolds challenges white historians to reassess Eurocentric tellings so that they and the historical endeavour they support might deal with Aborigines on more equal terms.

If one accepts Reynolds's perspective in examining the data available in relation to the Eliza Fraser story, several problems emerge. One could say that the event when represented as a 'first-contact' story in colonial discourse is a fabrication in many senses. These shipwreck victims were not the first white people to interact with the Fraser Islanders. The indigenous peoples had gathered to watch explorers' ships pass by the island on several occasions, sightings which they had recorded in song.[13] Captain Cook records in his journal that a group of natives gathered and gestured to the *Endeavour* as it made its way up the north-east coast in 1770. In an imperial gesture of naming, he called the promontory 'Indian Head' in recognition of the sighting. There were also a number of contacts between whites and Aborigines in the Fraser Island area between 1823 and 1836. These included a number of shipwreck victims and absconded convicts who encountered Aborigines in the area. From all extant reports they were treated with 'uniform kindness'.[14] After the penal settlement was established at Moreton Bay in 1824, a number of convicts escaped to the bush, found refuge in Kabi territory and were integrated into Aboriginal life as 'white blackfellows'. At least one of them, John Graham, had returned to the penal settlement and was pressed into service as a key player in the rescue of the *Stirling Castle* survivors. In addition, there had been a number of minor skirmishes between the colonial administrators and the indigenous peoples in the decade preceding the wreck of the *Stirling Castle*. British troops had encountered the local people during hunting parties and in attempts to recapture the bush convicts. Although murders are not recorded, several 'unfortunate' encounters are alluded to in the colonial records.[15] The *Stirling Castle* was not the first shipwreck in the area, nor the first time these indigenous peoples had encountered shipwreck victims. It was, however, the first reported instance of white 'captivity' amongst 'savages and cannibals'. Even in regard to the *Stirling Castle* incident, in opposition to Mrs Fraser's claims that the survivors had been treated with 'the greatest cruelty', several crew members expressed admiration and gratitude towards 'the natives' whose behaviours aided their survival and were far less hostile than actions which occurred between some members of the destitute crew.[16] However, none of the popular accounts of the event attempts to view the indigenous people as equal subjects in an intercultural exchange, or to consider the 'captivity' as a 'salvation'. Yet data to support these historical aspects have been available to researchers of the event and are emerging with more visibility and force at present as the White Man's Story becomes increasingly vulnerable to post-colonial decentrings. Mrs Fraser's tale is represented, not as one of survival amongst her Aboriginal hosts, but of captivity amongst barbarous savages.

Although this contradictory evidence exists, it was Mrs Fraser's story which became the reference point for official historical and popular accounts. Her story was important to the colonial imagination because it was the first time that a white woman had encountered traditional Aboriginal society – a kind of primal and sexually charged story of colonial beginnings. If her 'captivity' fuelled fantasies of first contact, her descriptions of 'native' life and customs lent themselves to the political imposition of imperial control of a superior over an inferior race, of civilised culture over a brutalised state of nature.

Still, even within this limited domain of colonial history, this particular event has continued to spur the interest of historians, ethnographers and biographers for a variety of reasons. There is an absence of Aboriginal perspectives (which might be rectified, but would raise its own set of problems).[17] Moreover, there are also many gaps in the records, gaps which future commentators endeavour to supplement with their own speculations and desires. The questions raised by the story and probed in later reconstructions are many. What were the origins of this unfortunate woman? Was Eliza a gentlewoman bred on the Orkney Islands of Scotland, or the poor daughter of tenant farmers in English midlands around Derbyshire; or was she born and reared in Ceylon, and thus an early daughter of the British Raj, as some historians suggest? Did her husband, Captain James Fraser, have a reputation as a competent or hopeless ship's captain? Was he culpably negligent, as accused in the *Bombay Courier*, for failing to investigate a shipwreck and rescue survivors off the coast of India in 1834? How many of his ships, besides the *Stirling Castle* and the *Comet* (lost in the Torres Strait in 1830), were involved in accidents at sea? Did the original crew 'jump ship' in Sydney? Did the ongoing crew intentionally mutiny after the shipwreck and, if so, did they have just cause? What were the cultural backgrounds of the two crew members listed as 'men of colour' (the cook and steward) taken on at Sydney? Why did the steward, who became Mrs Fraser's faithful manservant, remain loyal to her throughout the ordeal? And why was the Captain so afraid to go ashore for fear of native cannibalism? What did he know of 'savages and cannibals'?

How were the survivors treated on the island? Were they deliberately tortured and burnt at the stake as Mrs Fraser claimed? Did Baxter, the second mate, witness infanticide and cannibalism as he later told the London reporters? What alternative explanations and understandings might be forthcoming if the event were told from Aboriginal perspectives? What were the customs and beliefs of the local indigenous peoples? How did they incorporate the shipwreck survivors into their community? Were they cruel or kind to the survivors? Did they practise cannibalism as the Captain feared, and, if so, in what contexts? Did they intend to kill the Captain and the first mate? Why did Eliza's story of native behaviours contradict that of the runaway crew survivors?

Why did Eliza decide to accompany her husband on this voyage? Had she been to sea before? Was she a devoted or indifferent mother? Did she abandon her children? Did she give birth at sea or was this a story concocted in Britain after the event to evoke further sympathy for her cause? Was she sexually abused? And if so, where, when and by whom? Was she deranged by the events of 1836 or a cunning manipulator of people's gullibility? How and by whom was she rescued? Did some of the crew survive by eating their mates? What rumours to this effect reached Sydney and why were they suppressed in public accounts? Did David Bracefell claim to be her rescuer when he was returned to Moreton Bay in 1842? Or is this story, recorded nearly fifty years later in the memoirs of Henry Stewart Russell, itself a fabrication? Was Bracefell betrayed by Mrs Fraser as he claimed? Did he rape her on the edge of civilisation?

Was her second husband, Captain Greene, a co-conspirator in fraud, a raconteur or a psychologically abusive man? What happened to her, and her family, after the wreck? Why is it that although historians refer to her death in 1858 (either in Melbourne as a result of a horse-drawn tram accident or in New Zealand in an asylum) no evidence of a coronial inquest, no newspaper reports and no death certificate have yet been located? If you are a historian, what do you do when your subject, who has no recorded past, emerges briefly, and then completely disappears from history? How much speculation is acceptable and who decides?

These are questions subsequent commentators have raised, often but not always to contest the dominant history on behalf of its others – the woman, the working-class crew, the runaway convicts, the Aborigines. Even on the supposedly disinterested level of 'a good story', given the richness of the tale, who wouldn't want to know? There is much to attract the would-be biographer or historian: the lack of evidence, contradictory reports of the major players, undocumented suppositions of later historians, and prurient and not-so-prurient public interests around issues of race and sexuality, to name a few. At present extensive research is being carried out by two women, one for a master's thesis on the history of Fraser Island and the Cooloola region of Queensland and the other for a definitive biography of Eliza Fraser, including her New Zealand connection.[18] I am in touch with both researchers and vitally interested in the results of their research. Indeed, have even done some fairly extensive snooping into the archives myself, travelling on several occasions to London, the Midlands, Edinburgh, the Orkneys, and Sri Lanka, as well as to Fraser Island and libraries in Brisbane, Sydney and Melbourne. I have walked the so-called Eliza Fraser Trail (or the Cooloola Wilderness Trail, in fact a pathway cut by the Kabi-Kabi long before Eliza Fraser's arrival) which was established by the National Parks and Wildlife Service in 1986 to commemorate the 150th anniversary of the event. I have stood on the sands of Orchid Beach where the longboat came ashore, and followed John Graham's rescue route as far as speculations from the records would allow. I have talked with local historians, archivists, curators, anthropologists and environmentalists as well as descendants of white settlers in the area and Fraser Island Aborigines to gather their views on the event. While in London, I interviewed the historian Michael Alexander, author of *Mrs Fraser and the Fatal Shore* (1971), to ask about his sources of information and, in particular, his claim that Eliza Fraser (née Slack) was reared in Ceylon (now Sri Lanka).[19] He reported that the assertion was based on the slenderest clue, provided in a letter from a New Zealand descendant of Mrs Fraser, the source of which he had forgotten. And I spent weeks that turned into months tracing down that tantalising clue through available archival records. After months of fruitless archival searching at the end of a four-month study leave research trip, I finally found an Eliza Fraser in Ceylon – born there in 1832. For a brief time I speculated that she could have been the niece of 'our' Eliza – her father the brother of Captain James Fraser. At intervals over a six-year period, I have immersed myself in this quest for 'truth', frequently spinning my own webs of fabulation, enjoying the highs and lows of search and retrieval, for the most part happy to be frustrated by so many tangential paths in this twisted tale of colonial encounter.

To enter the guise of the empirical historian, several suppositions need to be taken on. They include the belief that if only all the facts were in and all the evidence reviewed dispassionately, it would be possible to know what *really* happened, and that, somewhat paradoxically, the 'real' Eliza Fraser could be known and brought to life through an analysis of the information available about her. This belief, in turn, depends on the assumption that 'reality' (or what really happened) is of an order of knowledge and being outside and beyond the knower. The historian, writing about the reality, positions him/herself as a knower observing documents to determine 'what really happened' through reason and rational analysis. What is becoming increasingly apparent to a range of social, feminist, anti-colonial and post-colonial historians, however, is that the relationship between 'the real' and historical constructions of reality requires a philosophical imposition of dominance: history on Eurocentric terms, within Western understandings, tied to imperialism and colonialism, and within a rationalist discourse. The will to truth – to know origins, to construct a coherent narrative – is accompanied by powerful feelings and emotions which motivate and drive the historian/biographer, who is not a dispassionate observer at all. The quest for knowledge situates the quester inside other sets of narratives. These emerge within a range of academic disciplines and circulate through the modalities of popular culture, producing a multitude of fantasies, anxieties and desires. Finally, even the most diligent historian will conclude that the woman, the real Eliza Fraser, is not there to be found behind, beyond or at the bottom of the detritus of documentation – she has been constructed in, by and through the various narratives of the event. She has no knowable life beyond them.

This is not to say that there never lived a woman called Eliza Fraser. Not at all. But we can only posit the meaning of her life through discourses and texts which themselves reconstruct her life history, create ideological and histori-cal contexts for her life, and position readers to regard her story in specific but significant ways. The belief that she somehow stands behind it all and can be rescued by the historian or biographer may be a belief necessary to the task, but it is an illusion.

My Search for Eliza

Although I knew this when I took on the project and the dilemmas of empirical research, I couldn't help but be curious about her origins. I asked: Could she really have been reared in Ceylon as Michael Alexander stated in his history, or, better still, 'born and raised' there, as recent historians assert?[20] By what extraordinary coincidence could this rare creature in the history of Empire have been involved in the earliest British presence in Ceylon (taken over by the British only in 1798, with a skeleton administra-tion and no civil service until 1802, and with few British families residing there until after the establishment of coffee plantations in the 1830s) and also the first white woman to encounter Aborigines in north-eastern Australia? How might her upbringing in Ceylon, a European colony with an ancient indigenous culture and tradition, have affected her understanding of her experience in the antipodes in the early years of colonisation? I wanted to find her behind the textual representations; to speculate on her person-ality, motivations and beliefs, which were (could only be) my projections on to her and the event.

Another concern was that nearly all the commentators on the event have been white men who characterised Eliza Fraser negatively in class-based and gendered terms of difference. They represent her as a bad mother, a bossy and dominating lady, a seductress and betrayer of men. Further, these reconstructions were the work of men writing within post-colonial global contexts underwritten by a legacy of colonial and neo-colonial dominance.[21] The colonial condition demanded that a boundary be established between 'civilisation' and 'savagery'. Through Mrs Fraser's tale, the 'natives' of the Great Sandy Region could be represented as primitive savages who posed a menace to Empire and a threat to the colonial settlement in Australia. She becomes a 'conduit' of both the white race and of Empire.[22] These nineteenth-century constructions have been challenged in the twentieth-century accounts; but each white, Western version of the Eliza Fraser story has its others. In the twentieth century, in Australia, her story remains a classic narrative of 'first contact' between white and Aboriginal peoples. As a narrative of nation, the story revolves around questions of national identity. Identity requires difference. In the Australian myths of nationhood the boundaries and categories of difference are multiple and interconnected. They include: women (in relation to white men), Britons (in relation to native-born white Australians), the middle class (in relation to the working-class Irish), and Aborigines (in relation to white culture). Through the Eliza Fraser stories one can trace the ambivalent constructions of gender, class, and race as they intersect with the demands of 'nation' as an imagined community. Although recent narratives no longer rely on genetic or biologically determined theories of 'natural' superiority to justify an imperialist cause, they nonetheless produce new hierarchies of difference enlisted in the cause of nationhood. The nation has no fixed identity; it reinvents itself regularly. The dilemmas of 'nation' resulted in massive changes to Australian cultural life posited in the 1970s after the coming to power of the Whitlam Labor government, and these dilemmas seem to be mirrored in the various ways in which the Eliza Fraser story has been reconstructed. The story resonates with mythic possibilities when read as a foundational fiction of nation.

The greatest spur to my interest in the story, however, was the emotional impact produced when I accidentally encountered the first painting in Sidney Nolan's 'Mrs Fraser' series (Figure 1). It depicts a naked woman in a dog-like pose, framed from behind and blending with the natural scrub, inscribed within the oval shape of a spy-glass or gun-barrel. My first surprised view of this painting, which I remember seeing, big and bold, on the cover of a book of art criticism – the masculine possessiveness of the gaze and the extreme vulnerability of this debased, feminine creature – struck me like a blow to the chest, evoking feelings of both anger and vulnerability. I felt anger that any woman, and especially one so victimised by history, could be portrayed in such a fashion; vulnerable because I felt myself to be implicated by and subjected to the debasement. The sensation I experienced as a 'blow to the chest', followed by powerful feelings of anger and vulnerability, locked me into this story, this history. My first view of Nolan's 'Mrs Fraser' linked my disturbing experience of my own subjectivity – split between my

Figure 1   'Mrs Fraser', by Sidney Nolan, from the 1947–8 series.
By permission of Lady Mary Nolan.

social and psychic 'selves', or my social agency and imaginary (but socially
constituted) lack – to the linguistic and visual practices through which
women have (and have not) been culturally constituted as both self and
other.[23]

So, why was I keen to follow Eliza's legendary trail? Retrospectively, I
might suppose that, caught in these multiple traps of self and other, I wanted
to master my own feelings of vulnerability as a woman by taking on the
masculine authority of the academic. I wanted to tell her story from a feminist perspective in a way which also challenged the racism embedded in the
accounts and reconstructions. And I wanted to get my own back on the
highly esteemed men who had represented her with such hostility. Well, not
really. I knew that these were impossible desires, and that what I was
encountering in the texts and paintings was not a woman at all but a series of
speculations and fantasies which revealed more about masculinity than
about femininity; more about Eurocentric projections, fears and fantasies of
racial otherness than about Aboriginality; more about the split subjectivity of
white men than of women or of Aborigines. Nonetheless, I was acutely aware
of the intersections of processes – historical and cultural, linguistic and visual
– through which the lives and subjectivities of women and Aborigines are
subjected to such representations. As a white woman, I was trapped inside
the multiple constructions of my social and psychic, modernist and post-
modern, selves.

What convinced me finally to forgo my quest for origins occurred during a trip to Sri Lanka. While visiting the Hill Club, established in the late nine-teenth century for the exclusive use of colonial administrators, planters and plantation managers, I met a woman from Perth, Western Australia, who was in search of her roots. Her father had been the manager of a remote plantation in the hills of Ceylon. Her mother, a nurse who had met him and nursed him back to health in England before being seduced by his stories of a privileged colonial life, married him and accompanied him back to Ceylon. My friend was born in England in 1938 but raised in Ceylon, where she lived until after the war in 1948 when as Sri Lanka it gained independence from the British. What happened to her on this journey of discovery is her story and not my place to tell. Suffice it to say that the remembered Ceylon of her childhood bore little resemblance to the Sri Lanka she encountered in 1993. The bricks and mortar of dusty, crowded towns and impoverished rural areas could not match what was stored in the recesses of her memory and imagination. But what stood out for me, and what no doubt was painful for her, was how in terms of the records, she did not exist. Although she knew her father had been a member of the Hill Club, he seems not to have been a member of the Executive; therefore, his name was either not recorded, or if recorded, in documents that had since been destroyed or lost. She went to a school which remained in existence and discovered that one of her former teachers was still residing there. The school kept attendance records for the pupils. But she did not appear on the rolls, although she could locate her class records and was familiar with a number of names they contained. She was a blank, a cipher. Her history was only forty-five years old.

So, my failure to locate documentation which would place Eliza Fraser in Ceylon (or Stromness or Derbyshire) may have had as much to do with the nature of the records as with whether or not she was actually raised there. Even if I had located a reference which could fix her with certainty in Ceylon in the early years of British colonisation (or in the small, spartan fishing village of Stromness at the modest beginnings of the herring industry, or in Derbyshire at the start of the industrial revolution when towns disappeared and desperate tenants were driven from their lands by the aesthete sixth Duke of Devon), the discovery would lead only to more stories, more specu-lations to support the illusive truth of her presence, her being. A mark on a record does not constitute a life. At best, it supplements an absence. An endless chain of marks, the historian's empirical evidence, can only defer knowledge that the quest for truth is an impossible quest, the 'truth' a mirage, however alluring: like the mirror image of the national self.

The impact of the powerful desire to know origins is evidenced by the fact that the suggestion that Eliza Fraser was raised in Ceylon could lead me and others to carry out research trips around the world, through countless museums and archives, and into an array of historical texts, only to dream up a score of possible pasts for this mysterious woman. The search for me was compounded by the fact that I knew from the outset that each clue led not to truth but to further representations which called for more interpretations. Documentation might have satisfied my desire for certitude and added another dimension, another context, to be explored and interpreted. But it would have brought me no closer to the 'real' Eliza Fraser. As Foucault reminds us, what we find at the centre of things is dispersal, not a place of origin but rather of loss.[24]

A major problem for the modern reader is the various ways in which Eliza Fraser has been interpreted by journalists, historians, balladeers, novelists, painters and other commentators over nearly 160 years – that is, as an innocent victim, a model of Christian virtue, a bossy and domineering lady, a 'Captain's Lady', a fraud, an imposter, a vixen She-Captain, a seducer and betrayer of men, and a bad mother who deserved her fate. A number of positions can be taken up which resist the dominant (and masculinist) read-ings. Biographies might tell the story from 'her' side and see her in heroic terms. Histories might attempt to reconstruct events from her perspective or from the perspectives of the crew, the runaway convicts, the Aborigines. But those contestations, too, carry risks similar to those embodied in dominant perspectives. They too construct self-and-other categories, them-and-us positions on which to build a coherent narrative. They construct a coherent narrative by imposing thematic continuities on a discontinuous series of events and historical contexts. They challenge bias or prejudice of past accounts in regard to race, *or* class, *or* gender, but the particular standpoint adopted within a contesting account precludes it from registering the range of ambivalences and contradictions in every text, every speaker, every reader of the event.

A feminist can challenge the masculine presumptions of mainstream his-torians; Australians can challenge the perspectives of the English; perspec-tives sympathetic to the interests of the convicts and/or the working-class crew can challenge that of the colonial authorities; local Queenslanders can uphold their version against the official records in the New South Wales archives; Aborigines can contest their representation within white history. In each case, those who have been marked as other within self–other repre-sentations call into question the authority of the dominant voice, challenging it on the grounds of partiality, bias, prejudice and vested interests – and substitute opposing truth claims. The contested narratives can be set against the dominant ones. The problem is that they also partake of the mechanics of dominance, depending on where the writer of the narrative positions her/himself. Each version would do it differently, but all would do it. This is because realist narratives, and the textual strategies they employ, *themselves establish authority*. They might reconstitute an alternative history but they still maintain self–other relations of dominance, even though those relations of dominance might challenge power hierarchies of the past.

Each of the characters in this story (as in life) is contradictorily and ambivalently positioned within it. Eliza Fraser could well be seen as a good *and* bad wife/mother/member of the rescue boat, her husband a competent *and* flawed ship's captain, the crew justified *and* culpable for their actions, depending on the context of and the perspectives through which the story is told. All characters in the drama, as well as their commentators over time, were caught inescapably in ideologies and modes of representation specific to their times. In 1836 these included the dominant structures of British imperialism and emergent forms of bourgeois capitalism, aligned with patriarchal, colonial and Christian ideologies of power. These, in turn, translated differently within an Australian context due to Australia's identity as a penal colony and emerging colonial settler society. Still, the story of the shipwreck tells only the European version of the story, although from time to time the texts give evidence of Aboriginal resistance to narrative containment. Within dominant accounts, the positions of the Captain, Eliza, the crew and the Aborigines are marked by shifting power relations as they intersect with Eurocentric understandings of gender, class and race. These characters become specifically placed within the different narratives of history, biography, and the more popular forms of film and fiction (history and biography also being forms of fiction, ones marked differently by their various truth effects). As constructed in the various texts, they can at best be read as occupying unstable subject positions within a network of power relations. Still, there is much reconstructive work to be done by the historian or biographer. Much has been hidden from history. Once one abandons hope of producing the definitive, authoritative text, of representing others in terms of the self, it becomes possible to re-engage in a writing of histories which present multiple and contradictory perspectives, including ones in which white women can examine their own role in the colonising process and white historians can engage in dialogic accounts which accept Aboriginal knowledge claims to 'history' on more equal terms.

This text too tells a story. My approach, however, is not premised on a search for truth but rather on a process of tracing the Eliza Fraser stories through their imperial, colonial and national adaptations as loci for ideological representations and contestations of difference. My aim is not to review the past, but to understand how past constructions and understandings of difference impinge on the politics of the present. Recent post-colonial critics maintain that the basis for a contemporary politics of both global and national power can be found in the complex web of nineteenth-century relations embedded in the discourses of colonialism. Feminist writers suggest, further, that through an analysis of colonial discourse it is possible to trace the dynamics of contemporary Western knowledge by attending to its categories and assumptions which marginalise women, ethnic minorities, the working class and indigenous peoples. As Balibar insists, a 'nation' or a 'people' are historical constructs, 'by means of which *current* institutions and antagonisms can be *projected into the past* to confer a relative stability on the communities on which the sense of individual "identity" depends [emphasis his]'.[25] Contemporary feminist and anti-colonial research in Australia has begun to uncover not only how Western discourse brings its 'others' into being but also how the legacy of nineteenth-century colonial understandings continues to underwrite gender and race relations today. Caught between a colonial past and a not yet post-colonial future, Australians find their 'identity' increasingly enigmatic. The pressures are particularly intense around issues of race. As Ann Curthoys cogently argues,

> for the descendants of the indigenous peoples . . . the rest of the population, European and non-European alike, are invaders, conquerors, oppressors, colonisers and illegitimate occupiers, interlopers still. The process of colonial dispossession belongs to an ongoing present, not to a distant past. A post-colonial *political* situation could be said to exist only when Aboriginal peoples achieve security, recognition, sovereignty, compensation, and political autonomy.[26]

In regard to rewriting the nation's history and facing up to the repressions and silences of the past, more is needed. For Aboriginal and non-Aboriginal people to engage in equal dialogue in the present political contexts of reconciliation, both must figure as subjects whose different but equally viable knowledges need to stand in relation to each other. As Debbie Bird Rose reminds us, 'There are many ways of concealing history, and one is to deny its survivors a legitimate voice.'[27] Western history objectifies; it appropriates others; it exaggerates difference. New forms of intercultural communication are emerging, however, which recognise a reciprocal relationship between different peoples from within different cultural contexts and knowledges.[28] These political and social dimensions of contemporary Australian cultural life provide a basis for why 'my' story counts today. The various adaptations of the Eliza Fraser story have served a long, if discontinuous, history of white Western dominance. Although the focus has always been on the woman, the narrative has also been about 'something else'. That 'something else' takes many forms: fears of an insecure colonial or national power base, class struggles, authoritarianism and lawlessness, homosexuality and feminism, but above all, racial difference. It is my hope that this study might contribute to more complex understandings of the interests and disavowals which attend the nationalist enterprise, as well as cultural constructions of racial and gender differences and their ongoing political effects.

The Contexts of Empire and Nationalism

In terms of Empire, representations of the Eliza Fraser story helped to define what it meant to be British (or rather English) in the 1830s. One hundred and fifty years later it would be reinvested with the markings of Australian nationalism. In Benedict Anderson's influential book which examines the formation of the modern nation-state, he argues that nationalism (for our purposes, read 'white, male, Anglo-centric Australian nationalism') depends upon the idea of the nation as an imagined community. By this he means that nations are *imagined*, 'because the members of even the smallest nation will never know most of their fellow-members, meet them or even hear of them, yet in the minds of each lives the image of their communion'.[29] He understands the nation as *community* because, 'regardless of the actual inequality and exploitation that may prevail in each, the nation is always conceived as a deep, horizontal comradeship'.[30] Although he does not mention issues of gender or sexuality in his account, a recent anthology entitled *Nationalisms and Sexualities* extends his thesis by calling attention to the libidinal economies which attend this 'deep, horizontal comradeship'.[31] For Anderson, nationalism is understood as being more akin to the affiliations of kinship or religion than to ideologies of liberalism or fascism. And like religious or familial affiliations, ambivalent desires and anxieties underlie the illusions of a unified community. Those anxieties revolve around multiple threats of difference – the main ones being sexual, racial, ethnic or class differences. Those differences are vital to the formation of national identity ('they' are what 'we' are not). But 'they' must be dealt with: either assimilated, eradicated, bounded within or segregated from what is imagined as 'the body politic'. This masking of the threat of otherness is accomplished by a variety of means, not the least of which is the work of textual representation. As the editors of *Nationalisms and Sexualities* note, one of the most common and erotically charged modes of representation is to imagine the homeland as the body of a woman whose 'honour' must be defended at all costs. (In our case, this becomes the fantasy of an actual woman violated by 'savages' on the borders of homeland as Empire.) This makes obvious the nature of the imagined community as a community of men, a fraternity requiring an identity through homosociality. Social bonding is achieved through the ownership, exchange and protection of women, both actual and imagined, literal and metaphorical.

Anderson argues that nationalism is a product of texts as they represent historical events. He stresses the importance of novels and newspapers in promulgating bourgeois values in the early nineteenth century; they were the accessible public tools of an emerging middle class.[32] Mary Louise Pratt extends Anderson's insights by examining the ways in which the languages of science and sentiment (two distinct forms of narrative) aided the construction of (masculine) bourgeois subjectivity.[33] The newspaper accounts of Mrs Fraser's story of captivity engage readers in both scientific and sentimental (or sensational and sexually charged) discourses of difference in a form which is available and accessible to all literate bourgeois readers. The bourgeoisie produces itself as an entity through the processes of othering. The middle-class male becomes the marker of culture. Women, the working classes (at home) and the 'savages' (abroad) occupy the shifting but peripheral spaces of otherness which are traceable in and sustained by the textual accounts – a significant site for the production of new knowledges.[34] These forms of representation produce a homologous entity, the modern nation-state, as an imagined community marked by continuity, unity and transcendence in which Man finds his identity. In terms of race, newspapers and popular fictionalised accounts become key sites for the construction of the relationship between Britain and the colonies where Western principles of innate and inherited racial superiority underwrite the colonial regimes. In terms of gender, these popular forms promulgate manners and morals, as well the division between public and private spheres in which Woman/women are both idealised within and excluded from the dominant culture. In terms of the work of representation, both groups are excluded from the body politic. Women are bounded within the domestic sphere, while persons of colour are segregated and afforded 'special' treatment by the State. Neither has rights of citizenship.

During the decade of the 1830s significant shifts in power relations occurred. As a result, something called 'the English middle class' effectively challenged the aristocracy; domestic ideologies of femininity emerged to strengthen the division between public and private spheres and between working-class and middle-class manners and mores; and, although the English Empire was in the ascendant, one of its constituting institutions, slavery, was abolished in the colonies.[35] Slavery was abolished in 1832 after more than a decade of public and political missionary activity by both men and women. This activity successfully challenged the conservative attitudes to slavery and the nature of black peoples. According to Catherine Hall:

> By the early 1830s an emancipationist position was effectively an orthodoxy within respectable middle-class society in England – only the paid lackeys of the planters would publicly defend slavery. The famous anti-slavery slogans, 'Am I not a man and a brother? Am I not a woman and sister?', and the icon of the kneeling slave seeking British help, represented the belief in the civilisational equality of the negro, the potential of the negro to be raised from the state of savagery, through childhood to manhood, which characterized the cultural racism of the anti-slavery movement.[36]

Both the high-minded Tory press and the sensational stories of the chapbooks, ballads and fly-sheets represented Eliza Fraser's story as a captivity narrative in which she was subjected to torture and bondage at the hands of savage barbarians. These representations ran counter to the dominant emancipatory rhetoric and political positions of the government of the day with regard to colonised peoples. But the multiple perspectives on 'race' circulated together, formulating popular knowledge in a series of acts of production, reception and consumption. Her story interrupts the humanitarian rhetoric associated with the abolitionist narratives, at least in Britain if not in the United States. In Britain and the colonies its circulation pandered to fears which lay beneath the civilising discourses. These stressed the rights to freedom and equality under law, as well as moral improvement for peoples represented as being on a lower, but no less worthy, scale of human society. The story of her ordeal serves to reinforce older, pro-slavery beliefs in racial inferiority within a more rigidly defined social order. These biologically determined racist beliefs would gain favour again in the violent decades of the 1860s and 70s in Britain and its colonies. During that decade of rapid expansion of pastoral interests throughout the colonial world, liberal and progressive views gave way to more overtly racist beliefs, supported by Social Darwinism and buttressed by religion, which held that black people were a different species of men, born to be mastered by their superiors or to die out in the white man's inevitable march of progress.[37] The Eliza Fraser story presages these developments.

   At the same time, eruptions of difference flared across the social terrain of Great Britain as marginalised others attempted to contest definitions of middle-class Englishness. During the year of the shipwreck there was massive social protest in England. Some protests were brought about by the visit of the 'Irish agitator' Daniel O'Connell to London and by the resistance of the Catholic Irish at home against religious persecution and the tithe system; others occurred over taxation and under-representation of the Scots and Welsh; still others were mounted by working-class and middle-class women pressing for social improvements through church-related reform societies; and there were strikes in the collieries which united the working-class English, Scots and Welsh against their middle-class bosses associated with the emerging factory system. The middle-class men who purported to speak on behalf of Britain did so by suppressing the voices of those who identified with the aristocracy or the working class, as well as the Welsh, Scottish and Irish men. Male reformers across class lines worked both with and against the interests of women of all classes and ethnicities within the United Kingdom. The categories of gender, class and race were then (as they are now) contested, fluid and shifting. Middle-class power was produced and sustained by the production of difference within different sets of articulations; these sometimes worked in consort with, and at other times in contradiction to, each other. The boundaries of self and other which constituted what it meant to be English were negotiated within complex networks of power, and these were articulated within discourses, politics, subjectivities and through the experiences of everyday life.

Interest in the Eliza Fraser story follows a slightly different trajectory in Australia, where the story, as a liminal narrative of first contact between white and Aboriginal peoples, fed the fears of an insecure settler population. The first 'local' account appears in the first children's book to be published in the colony, *A Mother's Offering to her Children* (1841), written by Charlotte Barton, 'a Lady Long Resident in New South Wales'. It takes the form of a mannered conversation between a mother and her four children, an 'entertaining' tale of shipwreck which she relates to them as one of her 'amusements of the evening'.[38] The mother details the atrocities which befell Mrs Fraser and the crew during their 'captivity' with the savages. The tone and ideological flavour of the narrative can be inferred in the response of one of the children, Clara, to her mother's tale: 'Such wanton barbarities fill one with horror and indignation; and a wish to exterminate the perpetrators of such dreadful cruelties.'[39] The account turns the story into a local moral tale of an innocent white woman taken victim by savages. Its 'lesson' is one of Christian endurance in the face of calamity. The 'mother' who authorises this text constructs categories of race, gender and subjectivity appropriate to the imperial desires of the new colony. There is no doubt of the superiority of the white population, a belief which entitles the new settlers to the land. It may even confer rights of extermination. This onerous suggestion, coming in a children's moral tale from 'the mouths of babes', links a child's naive voice to the mother's rhetoric of imperial domination and Christian righteousness, all of which furthered the justification of white expansion. W. H. Traill repeats this 'mother's offering' in his celebratory account of Queensland's colonial past, *A Queenly Colony* (1901), published in the year of Federation when the decline and dispersal of Fraser Island Aborigines, through neglect, abuse, frontier violence, disease and dislocation, had virtually reached its peak.[40]

The final rescue in 1842 of the escaped convict David Bracefell also revived local Queensland historical interest. Although he was recaptured in 1837, the year after Mrs Fraser's rescue, he escaped again to the bush. In 1842 he reluctantly returned to Moreton Bay but only after a party of explorers, intent on land settlement, persuaded him that Moreton Bay was no longer a penal settlement and he no longer 'faced the lash'.[41] His reported version of the rescue of Eliza Fraser is included in Henry Stuart Russell's memoirs, *The Genesis of Queensland,* published to commemorate the centenary of Queensland in 1888. Here, Bracefell's final qualifying phrase as to why the lady would complain of him (because of his abuse of her) is conveniently left out of the celebratory nationalist account.[42] Fifty years after the event, Russell places Eliza Fraser's rescue within an emerging Australian colonial context. By erasing from history the possibility that the 'heroic' Bracefell may have raped Eliza at the end of her ordeal, just hours before her final rescue, Russell dispels any residue of sympathy for Mrs Fraser. He also masks any recognition of her sexual vulnerability and the fragility of Victorian morality in the liminal environments of Australian colonialism. Russell's celebratory Queensland version of the rescue is still rumoured to be the 'true' account by some locals and tourist operators today. In it Eliza becomes a foil to Bracefell, her British duplicity standing against his convict heroism. According to one popular source: 'If indeed Bracefell spoke truthfully [as Russell maintains], then Mrs Fraser's suffering among savages had made her inhuman – a monster of ingratitude.'[43]

The centrality of Bracefell's place in the narrative would be displaced in 1937 with the publication of a book by Robert Gibbings, *John Graham, Convict, 1824*. The historical biography, written to commemorate the sesquicentenary of Australia, tells of Graham's heroic past, his impoverished background in Ireland, his transportation to New South Wales for a petty felony of stealing six pounds of hemp to support his widowed mother, and the harshness of the British penal system on the Irish. Constructed from Graham's log as well as other historical documentation, it details his daring rescue of crew members Carey and Dayman at Lake Fyans; the second mate, Baxter, at McClays Islands; and, finally, Mrs Fraser on the mainland prior to a corroboree in the midst of 'seven hundred cannibals and savages'. Richard White comments that these celebratory accounts of nation, occasioned by Federation and anniversaries of the founding of the colonies, provided an effective focus for the emergence of national myths in which the nation manifested itself. He writes:

> what had previously been an idea became, on the national day, a political entity; the anniversary of that date enters the calendar and becomes an annual celebration of nationhood ... [In each heroic retelling of the glorious past] a pre-existing heroic conception of the nation is fulfilled by a political act.[44]

In this case, Gibbings's narrative lends itself to the idealisation of the Irish against the British in national myths of nation, and further fuels the controversy surrounding this 'first contact' story. These accounts transform a very adaptable 'Eliza' into the contexts of Empire and nationalism.

Overview

In the first half of this study I examine Eliza Fraser's personal testimonies about her ordeal, the narratives written and published on her behalf, and other nineteenth-century accounts. I consider them in the contexts of conflicting relations of power and the appeal of captivity stories in aiding the expansion of Empire through its intersecting political and ideological formulations. Chapter 2 considers three versions of the story attributed to Mrs Fraser, their historical contexts and their transformations in the popular press, including the publication and reception of the story as an American Indian captivity narrative. Chapter 3 turns to the first history of the event,

The Shipwreck of the Stirling Castle (1838), by John Curtis, his defence of Mrs Fraser against charges of fraud, and the contradictory effects of the story within the contexts of Empire. Chapters 4 and 5 narrow the focus, examining the nineteenth-century materials and the rhetorical, ideological and institutional constructions of the categories 'woman' and 'native' within British imperial and Australian colonial narratives.

The nineteenth-century historical materials form a background to twentieth-century constructions of Eliza Fraser in Australia, Canada and South Africa, which are taken up in the second half of the book. Chapter 6 opens with a discussion of a new history of the event prepared by Michael Alexander (1971) before examining Sidney Nolan's 'Mrs Fraser' series of paintings and the ways in which the story and the theme of betrayal preoccupied the painter for over forty years. Chapter 7 focuses on Patrick White's transformation in his internationally acclaimed novel, *A Fringe of Leaves* (1976). This leads to a discussion of several adaptations of the legend of Eliza Fraser, both in Australia and overseas, spurred by Nolan's first international exhibition in London in 1956. His paintings, and the catalogue essay from his first international exhibition, form the basis for Gabriel Josipovici's play *Dreams of Mrs Fraser* (first performed in London in 1972), André Brink's South African novel, *An Instant in the Wind* (1976) and Canadian-based Sri Lankan author Michael Ondaatje's long poem, *The Man With Seven Toes* (1976). Ondaatje's account provoked further Canadian interest in the tale, resulting in a commission for Australian artists Peter Sculthorpe and Barbara Blackman to produce a piece of music theatre. These adaptations are examined within the universal, humanist and psychological frameworks to which the story lent itself for both Australian and overseas artists and their audiences. After examining these versions in Chapter 8, I turn to the popular film *Eliza Fraser*, and examine the controversy surrounding it as well as the Australian film industry and its place within debates about national identity in the 1970s in Chapter 9. The final chapter considers the latest revisions in the 1990s – a Japanese Noh play directed by Allan Marett and performed in Sydney and Toyko by music students at the University of Sydney; and a television documentary, 'Island of Lies', directed by feminist and political activist, Gillian Coote. Finally, the book considers a very different, anti–colonial rendering of the Eliza Fraser story in a series of art works and installations by the Aboriginal artist, Fiona Foley.

In the main, the 1970s adaptations turn the tale into a romance, with a David Bracefell type as the woman's rescuer and lover, whom she eventually betrays. The shift of emphasis to a transgressive love affair might be read as a sign of how in the 1970s artists in Australia, Canada and South Africa struggled with their identities within post-colonial nations, nations which, nonetheless, in their imagined relation with indigenous peoples, remained tied to their colonial past. The politics of racial difference in these adaptations can at best be typified as assimilationist; the representations are further acts of (mainly) white cultural domination, although ones mediated by the rise of multicultural perspectives within the framework of a universalist liberal humanism. Taken together, these twentieth-century recuperations of the story illustrate the questionable nature of the term 'post-colonial'. In each of the instances, as later chapters will demonstrate, texts reveal how the politics of nationalism within de-colonised countries remains embedded within prior discourses of neo-colonialism and its various forms of domination. Although these various representations will be taken up in relation to their specific historical contexts and the contested politics of production and reception, there remain limitations to my critique. In the main, my analysis remains within a Western epistemology. This study might be seen as a precondition to a more equal dialogue between players – Aboriginal and non-Aboriginal, male and female – in a nationalist arena, a partial displacement of the 'authority' of Western discourse and its representations.

In some senses the 1970s were not unlike the 1830s – both decades were marked by dynamic shifts of power relations throughout the world. The 1970s adaptations occur in Australia in the wake of the Whitlam era of Labor Party dominance when Aboriginal politics, class-based and multicultural concerns and the Women's Liberation Movement were exerting considerable force. As in the 1830s, many voices struggled to contest dominant power relations. Both decades were ones of crisis, transition and rapid social change. What is at stake in these reconstructions are questions not of historical truth but of the efficacy of a universal humanism juxtaposed against assertions of imperialism and national identity within fluid cultural contexts.[45] Feminists, unionists, Aboriginal people, Australians from non-English-speaking backgrounds, social historians and cultural critics challenged unified notions of national identity. Debates flowed out of the academy, into the streets and the press and on to the screen, as is evidenced by the controversy surrounding the popular film, *Eliza Fraser* (1976).

Since the 1970s there has been a great deal of critical attention to historical constructions of the other.[46] Some of that work has focused on representations of difference with regard to either race, slavery, ethnicity, women, and/or the working class; some of it locates the problem within a particular domain of struggle, that is, within political life, the home, the workplace, the academy or everyday life; some of it considers the hybridisation of voices and positions within the colonising moment that makes colonial practices, at best, ambivalent. Since the 1970s readers have been inclined to read against the grain of history, to trace fissures in the social fabric sustained by representations of difference, and to register the inseparable connections between various discursive and non-discursive domains. The Eliza Fraser texts and the debates they set in train within popular culture as well as in academic circles reveal contradictions and tensions which resist structures of

Eurocentric bourgeois authority. In addition, there are now (as there were at the time of the event) critiques which take up different positions with regard to woman, the working class, the convicts and Aborigines in Australia's colonial past. Most recently, these include anti-colonial Aboriginal and white perspectives which challenge Eurocentric history, describing it as a monologue with itself. The early 1990s adaptations of the Eliza Fraser story by Allan Marett, Gillian Coote and Fiona Foley challenge the imagined unity of earlier academic and populist accounts. Foley's art practice does more. It opens up the possibility of a new dialogic space in which cultural difference might be relocated. These counter-hegemonic texts are emerging now in a different social order from that of the 1970s as 'the West' faces its crisis of authority both at home and in relation to the rest of the world.

The recent feminist and Aboriginal, post-modern, post-colonial and/or anti-colonial critiques introduce different questions and different strategies of analysis. They focus not on the truth of history but on how the concept of history is produced; not on its coherence but on the limits of a text's historical field; not on truth but on ambivalent knowledges and desires; not on the production of fixed identities but on their dispersal. The present period is a time of new calls and new departures: calls not to find a place in history for its apparent victims, but for an end to facile attempts at assimilation; departures not within white history to retrace or oppose white domination, but to begin from different cultural contexts which might enable and support specific and contested knowledges. The aim is not inclusion, but a reciprocal intercultural dialogue between Aboriginal and non-Aboriginal Australians.[47] Only some of these complications will be unravelled in the discussion which follows, a discussion which draws attention to the politics of representation, the contexts of positioning and the textual strategies of political control.

CHAPTER 2

Eliza Fraser's Story:
Texts and Contexts

During the decade of the 1830s scores of shipwreck and castaway stories filled the colonial press, supplying imaginative reconstructions to excite a popular interest in the horrors to be found elsewhere. News of each event sparked renewed interest in the dangers of the colonial adventure. The shipwreck of the *Stirling Castle* was a minor event, its story one of many which gave substance to the colonial endeavour. But it generated a plethora of materials: official reports, a government inquiry, newspaper accounts, historical reconstructions, ballads, captivity narratives, and other sensational stories which circulated throughout the colonial world. They contributed to an expanding discursive network, supporting new knowledges and sustaining the imperialist impulse of the West. The story of the shipwreck, captivity and rescue of Mrs Fraser challenged, but also upheld, hierarchies of race, class and gender in both England and the colonial world.

There are two issues at stake here. One concerns the appropriation of indigenous cultures and peoples into Western modes of representation. The other concerns the ways in which the story helped to mould a British Victorian identity and model an emerging bourgeois consciousness. In relation to the first point, Carolyn Porter, amongst others, has studied the ways in which Western discourse brings 'others' into being. History itself is a process whereby 'the marginal becomes a cultural product of a dominant discourse'.[1] In the Eliza Fraser story, the indigenous people of Fraser Island became objectified through their Eurocentric textual representation; their pre-contact existence was denied as they were represented within Western history. This is not to say that Western representation negates the prior and continuing existence of Aboriginal traditions, customs and cultures; it does, however, work to supplant that pre-contact existence in ways that affect both European and indigenous cultures and beliefs in post-contact times. In this regard, Aboriginal commentator Marcia Langton remarks that white

Australians do not relate to Aboriginal people but to stories about them told by former colonists.[2] The Eliza Fraser story is a case in point. The discursive representations of 'the natives' in the Eliza Fraser stories mark the entrance into Western history of the indigenous people of Fraser Island and their culture as objects for 'study, discipline, correction and transformation' by the West.[3] Representations produce stereotypes of the primitive other in the popular imagination which fuel white fears and promote exploitation. These discursive strategies accomplish an appropriation and an effacement of indigenous cultures which were not in fact subordinated or colonised at the time. The texts produce a colonial ideology which justifies the desire for political control of indigenous peoples and their land. At the same time, the suppression of other voices, other histories, other perspectives, produces multiple points of instability in the texts – points which can be interrogated by later readers and commentators.

The second issue concerns the work of representation within a British framework. The Eliza Fraser story emerged at a time in history when contested knowledges concerning women and the working class, as well as colonised peoples, were evolving within contexts of difference which gave meaning to what it meant to be British. This decade witnessed the rise of a British presence (or rather an English presence which represented itself as British) throughout the world. What were the dominant and resistant ideologies of class, gender and race prevalent at the time of the shipwreck? In relation to the formation of the boundaries of class, E. P. Thompson maintains that a firm sense of working-class consciousness was already present in the 1830s. This consciousness was mediated by diverse resistances to English middle-class ideologies of nationalism mounted by Irish, Welsh and Scots workers and patriots. Catherine Hall reports that from the 1830s to the 1850s the popular press and women's magazines concretised the gendered ideologies of private and public spheres through definitions of masculine and feminine identity. In regard to racial differences, Hall suggests that in the 1830s, as Empire and the emancipatory rhetoric which resulted in the abolition of slavery in the colonies were reaching their zenith, the English took on the role of liberator of the slaves in Africa and the Caribbean.[4]

These claims take on substance when considered in relation to the lead stories and news events reported in *The Times* during the three-month period between Mrs Fraser's arrival back in England on July 1837, and the conclusion of judgements against her as a result of the Lord Mayor's Commission of Inquiry, reported to the press on 30 September. In May 1837 a youthful Queen Victoria had ascended the throne, succeeding King William IV. Mrs Fraser entered history at the dawn of the Victorian era. During the period between July and September 1837, news of the general elections filled the press. In these elections the Conservatives suffered heavy losses to the Whigs. Agitation in Ireland over Protestant control and Irish resistance to the

English tithe system sent the 'Irish agitator' Daniel O'Connell to London for a series of fiery speeches resulting in 'terror in the streets'. As might be expected, he and his campaign drew repeated and universally scathing attacks in *The Times*. At the same time, Welsh colliers prepared to strike against intolerable factory conditions, which included a sixteen-hour day for women and children. Scottish workers met to rally against the middle class, which had not voted in accord with the workers' economic interests as had been expected. Reports of these activities in *The Times* invariably pitted the readers against the emotional mob, called for a return to reason and drew readers' attention to the essential need for law and order in a civil society. Bankruptcies dominated the announcements section of the paper. There were 400 in the three months between July and September 1837, along with suicides (64), murders (46), and shipwrecks (7). The press contained notices concerning hundreds of police actions for murder, rape, assault, robbery, forgery and fraud (including the Fraser inquiry). One year later, when John Curtis's history *The Shipwreck of the Stirling Castle* was published, the same issues continued to dominate *The Times*, along with extensive coverage of the Poor Law report and the end of the slave trade in the Caribbean.[5] Mrs Fraser entered history, then, in a period when bourgeois relations in the United Kingdom were in formation, at a time when contested knowledges vied for control of what it meant to be English, middle class, male and white – that is, what it meant to be 'British'. In this context, Mrs Fraser's story takes on added significance, far beyond the localised contexts of shipwreck in the antipodes. This chapter will examine the texts and contexts relating to Mrs Fraser's testimony about the shipwreck and 'captivity', the accounts which appeared in the popular daily press in Sydney and London, and the transition of the story into a classic American captivity narrative, including its wide circulation and publication in the colonial press of Empire.

The various accounts of the shipwreck, captivity and rescue appeared and spread their influence in two different but complementary directions. On the one hand, official government reports, news items, testimonies from the Lord Mayor's Commission of Inquiry and the first-hand histories of the event helped to regulate knowledge under the guises of reason and 'truth'. On the other hand, the sensational, melodramatic stories of the popular press provided fantasies of horror about 'otherness' which propelled anxiety and desire. The different narratives and their generic wrappings circulated in different fields of knowledge – providing not only 'knowledge' but pleasure as well. Over time, the more academic accounts were largely buried. The more sensationalised, populist materials supplanted them and influenced later generations. The source and origin of the story became linked to the two major spokespersons for the event: Mrs Fraser herself, and John Curtis, her apologist. Mrs Fraser gave an official report to government officials and numerous interviews to Sydney journalists before putting her name to the sensational accounts of her adventures published by the British, American and colonial press. Her name on a document registers the autobiographical quality of the narrative, positioning readers to accept it as an engaged, authentic and truthful, although subjective, account of personal experience. The name 'John Curtis' has a different reading effect. A journalist for *The Times*, Curtis reported on the inquiry and subsequently published the first historical account of the event, *The Shipwreck of the Stirling Castle*, in 1838. His is a polyvocal text, blending interview journalism, biography, history, ethnography and natural science. He presents himself as a disinterested, scientific and objective observer. Relevant here is Mary Louise Pratt's argument that science and sentiment were the two clashing but complementary languages of the imperial frontier, languages which contributed to the evolution of bourgeois subjectivity.

Mrs Fraser's reports passed quickly into the domain of popular culture, where her story emerged in the form of ballads and broadsheets, magazine accounts and a captivity narrative, all complemented by an array of illustrations, woodcuts and cartoons which kept alive the popular colonial themes of sex and savagery. Curtis's history blends many narrative modes, which in the course of the nineteenth century would be divided into distinct disciplines within the academy. These disciplines contributed to the imperial expansion of European economic and political control. Both speakers claimed discursive authority, although the nature of that authority relied upon markedly different realms of meaning. Mrs Fraser derived her authority from the authenticity of a first-person account in the realm of privatised experience. John Curtis derived his authority from the objectivity of a detached observer in the realm of public knowledge. But these guises of subjective, and objective, private and public, feminine and masculine speaking positions are not essential characteristics of the speakers themselves. Rather, they are textually constructed. Further, one position (Eliza Fraser's) underwrites the authority of the other (John Curtis's) and provides the feminine (debased) context for his masculine (elevated) standpoint. In addition, although the intellectualised narratives of Curtis, the courts and *The Times* give rise to ideological forms of social control, the sensationalised accounts attributed to Mrs Fraser give rise to multiple pleasures of a working-class audience, pleasures which subvert the former guises of social control. The two operate in a complementary fashion, a mutual engagement of science and sentiment; knowledge and desire; reason, imagination and pleasure. The textual strategies employed by the various authors position readers differently. That positioning, an act in the formation of bourgeois consciousness, contributes to the rise of the middle class, to the division of British society into public and private spheres, to an understanding of the colonial world into domains of colonisers and colonised peoples, and to an asymmetric relation between masculine and feminine modes of understanding and experience, reason and sentiment.

Mrs Fraser's First Version: The Official Report

The narrative of the shipwreck of the *Stirling Castle* is a model of broader contestations of power emerging in England at the time of the wreck. It provides materials relating to the everyday behaviour of Mrs Fraser, the Captain, the officers and seamen, as well as the indigenous people at the time of the shipwreck, captivity and rescue. These materials give evidence of a challenge to and defiance of English, white, male and middle-class (and upper-class) authority, which the narratives and modes of social control struggled to manage and regulate, to suppress and disguise. After the rescue, all members of the known surviving crew were interviewed and official reports taken at Moreton Bay. The crew presented contradictory perspectives in regard to 'native' hostility. Initial sympathy for the crew soon dissipated as stories of their mutinous behaviour and rumours of white cannibalism amongst survivors emerged.[6] Official and media attention quickly devolved to Mrs Fraser alone. While in Moreton Bay, the survivors Darge, Dayman and Carey, whom Mrs Fraser accused of mutiny, were subjected to close official surveillance, discharged from their quarters and put on ration number five, in other words a starvation diet, deemed by the Commandant to be 'much more than their past conduct merits'.[7]

The event enters the realm of public knowledge through a series of government reports, which, although documented, were not available to the public until 1936, and popular accounts, which were released to the media. Through the popular accounts, Mrs Fraser attracts sympathy; in giving herself over to journalists, she becomes what might be called a 'conduit of race and Empire'.[8] Her sacrifice, the white woman's burden, was valorised by the defenders of colonialism, even as it came under attack by her suspicious detractors. To what degree, then, can we attribute agency to Mrs Fraser in relation to her own testimony of the event? On the one hand, it might be said that she tells her own story. She 'speaks' through personal testimony. But that testimony, far from being the authentic or unmediated expression of her own experience, is an authorised recitation of a life story – a placement of herself within the discourses and institutions which shape her daily life. That is, she is both the subject who speaks and also one who is subjected to the discourses and practices in which her story becomes embedded. One cannot assume that there is a unified voice, or presence, behind the narratives attributed to Mrs Fraser, although local audiences at the time of the event may have read the texts with this understanding and keenly desired it to be so. Mrs Fraser 'speaks' through the authority of her husband, her class status, her maternity, her identification with Empire, and she is spoken for in other texts through available constructions of femininity, race and nationhood.

As a white woman, however, she has the (contextually limited) power to speak on behalf of others, particularly Aboriginal others. In Eliza Fraser's

nineteenth-century accounts, the 'natives' of Great Sandy Island are represented as primitive savages who pose a menace to Empire and a threat to
the colonial enterprise in Australia. The nineteenth-century texts produced
by the event include her personal testimony, as well as the emergent sensationalist narratives of her 'captivity' in ballads, stories and flysheets, and
the ethnographic, scientific and legal interest her story generated in the press
and in academic texts. Those texts reframed the event according to previously established imperial and colonial relations of power. In them, the
white woman figures as an innocent victim of barbarous savages. Her story is
represented through a racially and sexually charged myth of Empire which
resonates through the discourses and fuels the masculine imaginary of
Western colonialism.

Mrs Fraser's first testimony, to the Commandant at the Moreton Bay
penal settlement, upholds the authority of her husband and his naval command. This first official report is a document of some 1500 words. It is
concise, accusatory and direct, best described as an exercise in power, a
narrative performance of authority. It can be read in several contradictory
ways. On the one hand, to a naive reader or one who equates the status of an
official statement with 'truth', it is a remarkable document for a woman of
the period, demonstrating her ability to represent herself and her husband
against a middle-class code of women's silence, particularly in the public
sphere, in which women were expected to be represented by other dominant
men. On the other hand, the demands of the form mould her experiences
according to the requirements of an official statement. Official statements
subject their authors to the demands of the governing body, in this case the
military authorities whose interests lay in maintaining law and order. Still,
she can be understood as having limited agency, a product of her position
within the ideological frameworks which authorise her right to speak on
behalf of others. The official statement needs to be considered with these
confounding issues in mind.

Two-thirds of Mrs Fraser's statement to the Commandant details the shipwreck and the behaviour of the Captain and crew, while the final third
summarises events which occurred on the island and describes her treatment by the natives. The summary of her experience with the natives is
some six lines long. Her hardships are recounted, hardships which would be
considerably embellished over time:

> During the whole of my detention among the natives I was treated with the
> greatest cruelty, being obliged to fetch wood and water for them and constantly
> beaten when incapable of carrying the heavy loads they put upon me; exposed
> during the night to the inclemency of the weather, being hardly ever allowed to
> enter their huts even during the heaviest rain.[9]

This brief summary is the extent of the information about her fifty-two days
of 'captivity' on Fraser Island provided in the original account.

In the main, the document attends to the shipwreck and mutiny of the crew. It details particularly the Captain's orders and the crew's repeated resistance. Five times, in five parallel sentence constructions, it reiterates how the Captain gave orders which were refused, until the crew became 'very mutinous':

[h]e *gave orders* [not to leave the wreck] . . . *the men* however *insisted* . . . some of them said if he would not come they would leave him behind, *he then consented* . . . *He now ordered* beef and bread and water be brought up . . . some of the crew said that if he wanted it he might fetch it himself. [Later,] *the Captain requested* the men not to insist on going anymore on shore . . . [The crew] became very mutinous . . . [Once on shore] *the Captain and the two mates* now *employed themselves* in repairing the Boat in the best manner they were able, the *seamen refusing* to lend a hand . . . *He then requested* they even assist in launching her, but *they refused* to do it [emphasis mine].

The report gives evidence of a serious breach in command. The crew openly defied the Captain's authority. This aspect of the event prompted government interest, both in the colony and in England. Corroborative evidence from Mrs Fraser and the first mate, Brown, as well as contested reports of other surviving crew members, tells of high drama at sea from the start. Lacking water and provisions, subject to violent storms followed by a drought at sea, chased by sharks, bailing water from the two leaky lifeboats and under the command of an incapacitated Captain who had wrecked another boat just four years earlier in adjacent waters, the crew took command of the perilous situation. At first the men threatened to leave the Captain behind if he would not launch the rescue boats; then they would not rescue provisions from the brig; and finally they threatened to throw him overboard if he would not pull ashore. About ten days out, the pinnace – with the majority of the crew and Mrs Fraser's twelve-year-old nephew on board – parted company from the longboat which held Mrs Fraser and the Captain, the steward, the first and second mates and several seamen. The Captain would consider it a mutiny. A different account is given by a crewman, the recalcitrant Youlden, who remained on the longboat after the wreck but parted company with the Captain's party upon reaching the island. Some years later he published an article in *The Knickerbocker*, a North American magazine, in which he presented his version of the wreck. He contended that, once ashore, he had contacted one of the surviving pinnace crew, who indicated that the pinnace had pulled away to search for oysters off the reefs for the entire party and was lost at sea. But neither this story nor Youlden's article, which came to light only in the twentieth-century histories of the event, play a part in the official accounts at the time.

After nearly four weeks at sea, the longboat landed on Fraser Island (or Great Sandy Island, as it was known on the navigational charts of the day), despite the Captain's endeavours to dissuade the crew with warnings that they would be murdered if they went ashore. Once on land, according to Mrs Fraser, the remaining crew refused a request from the Captain to assist in the repair of the longboat. Instead, they took possession of provisions, weapons and ammunition, heading out on foot for Moreton Bay, leaving the Captain, the first and second mate, and Eliza 'totally defenceless'. The Captain's pretence of authority broke down as the contesting authority of the crew exerted itself in this liminal environment of desperate survival.

In Mrs Fraser's official report there is no mention of the Captain's irrational fear of cannibalism, his frenzied ravings, nor his debilitated condition. These appear in the reports of other crew members. Absent as well is any mention of Eliza's pregnancy, birth at sea and the drowning of the infant which appears in the later London accounts. Nor does her official report mention the fidelity of the mulatto steward, Corallis, who rescued two trunks of provisions for the couple and set off promising to find help for them when the Captain became too weak to move. It does, however, specifically single out one member of the defiant crew by name, the above-mentioned Henry Youlden, who 'curses' Eliza and takes a precious cup of rainwater from her which she had collected for her ailing husband. His words are the only ones to appear in direct quotation: 'Damn you, you She-Captain, if you say much more I'll drown you.' It is somewhat ironic that the inclusion of this incident in the report and reference to Youlden's words by direct quotation serves to cast a shadow on Mrs Fraser's reputation in later accounts, as well as that of Youlden at the time of the rescue. Mrs Fraser would thereafter be referred to by some twentieth-century historians as the 'She-Captain'. Youlden, who seems to have evaded the authorities at Moreton Bay, would be marked as the ringleader of the mutineers on the island. His description of Mrs Fraser, included in the *Knickerbocker* article, further erodes sympathy for her character. He wrote:

> The wife of the captain was on board, and on her account eight of the men had deserted. She was very vixen; but as I do not feel she is worth the ink, to say nothing of time and paper, I shall only add, she was a terrible liar, and the most profane, artful, wicked woman that ever lived; indeed, coming very near my idea of the Devil.[10]

The first report to the Commandant struggles to redress the improper balance of power which occurred between the Captain, the ship's officers, Eliza and the rest of the crew. Their defiance resulted in the loss of her own (borrowed) status and authority. Her report led to the crew being ostracised and put on meagre rations at Moreton Bay. Later all survivors with the exception of Mrs Fraser, including her nephew, the second mate, Baxter, would be denied funds raised on their behalf in Sydney. By all reports, Corallis was faithful to his employers, resilient in the face of danger and a reliable defender of their position of authority. But he disappears from history, rendered invisible by his inferior race and class position. Youlden's side of the story would emerge a decade later, in *The Knickerbocker*, ostensibly written to warn would-be gold prospectors of the dangers of a voyage to Australia, but also no doubt to vindicate himself from the charges brought against him.[11] It appears to have been unknown to parties involved in the episode. Curtis, in his history (1838), reports that Youlden succumbed to heart failure several years after the wreck. In the light of Mrs Fraser's testimony, one can understand his desire for invisibility. Mrs Fraser's report of the shipwreck to the Commandant is clearly addressed to an official audience. She speaks not only for herself but also for her dead husband. Her report attempts to relieve the Captain of responsibility for mismanagement or wrongdoing and to restore a respectable identity to her own person. The crew could claim no such authority and had no such official access through which they might restore their own reputations in the light of Mrs Fraser's testimony.

The last portion of Mrs Fraser's narrative concerns events on the island. It details how the party was stripped 'perfectly naked', divided between several 'tribes of natives' and made to forage for food. It reports that the Captain was speared in the shoulder; that Brown, the first mate, suffered burns to his legs and back; and that Baxter, the second mate, was abandoned after each of the men became too weak to carry out work required of them. The Captain and Brown subsequently died from their injuries. Although popular accounts would subsequently suggest that the Captain was deliberately murdered by the natives, Mrs Fraser recounted in London that she did not believe that it was ever their intention to kill him. In this first official narrative, although 'the natives' are accused of treating the party 'with the greatest cruelty', there is no accusation of deliberate murder. There is no suggestion of savagery, barbarism or cannibalism, and none of the horror, sentiment and melodrama which creep into subsequent accounts attributed to Mrs Fraser.

How does this first official account, attributed to Mrs Fraser, variously position her within contesting relations of power and resistance? Her speaking position within the specific locations of power is complex. The report is addressed to an official and limited audience. In it she stands on the authority of her husband. Thus, she takes up both masculine and feminine, middle-class and imperialist positions in the narrative. She is complicit with the politics of domination, situated within the discourses of power – patriarchy, imperialism, Christianity and capitalism – but in contradictory ways.

Testimony by Mrs Fraser and other crew members concerning what happened on the boat at the time of the shipwreck gives evidence of further contestations of the woman's power, status and authority. She had accompanied her husband on the voyage as his helpmate. Since he suffered from ulcers, she had prepared special foods which she packed away in two trunks to last him the whole of the expected fourteen-month journey, not an insignificant undertaking for a woman in 1836. As his wife, nurse and help-mate she had demanded that the trunks be rescued at the time of the wreck, a task which Corallis undertook to perform for his employers, despite the objections of the crew. (The importance of the trunks to Mrs Fraser can be registered in her lament to John Curtis later that the Indian trunk which contained her china purchased only two mullets when traded to the natives for food.[12]) In addition, on board the longboat, she took the Captain's turn bailing water and on the island she came to his aid at the time of his death.

It is necessary to look beyond her personal position in regard to the first official narrative and to her place within a maritime context. She was the Captain's wife, travelling on a trading ship which also took emigrant families from Britain to colonial Australia. But there were no emigrants on board at the time of the wreck, no passengers who could have helped her uphold the Captain's authority and position. Given the authority vested in ships' cap-tains in the nineteenth century, and given the condition of her particular husband, her insistence on his authority in her first account is not surprising. During the wreck and its aftermath, Captain Fraser was ill and possibly mentally unbalanced. His weakness strengthened the resolve of the crew. Neither Mrs Fraser's attempts to enforce his authority nor her wifely responsibilities to nurture him in his weakened condition would be respected. In the shipwreck situation, the couple were beyond the bounds of reason, order and civility, the social controls necessary to the maintenance of Empire when its citizens were far from home.

Once on the island, her race took on significance, represented as a civilised white woman amongst the savages. But she was no conqueror. Placed with a small group of women and children, without the company or protection of her husband or any of the crew, without language or knowledge of the indigenous culture, she was quickly subjected to local customs. In this situ-ation, her race (a white woman amongst indigenous peoples); her class status (one of assumed middle-class authority amidst a working-class crew); her patriarchal position (wife of an ailing captain and aunt to the ship's second mate); and her imperial cultural disguise (a Christian, civilised Briton amongst heathen primitives) were to no avail. But race, class and gender hierarchies were restored to her in her official report and subsequent his-torical constructions of the event. Indeed, her identity was constituted in and through the ways in which the official discourse enabled her to position herself within the relations of power in which she, the crew and the Fraser Islanders were differentially embedded. In addition, her assertions of West-ern cultural superiority depended upon the successful negotiation of these relations of power, both at home and abroad.

One can read the narrative accounts to search not for 'truth' but for evidence of a complex and contested network of power relations in which each of the various actors was embedded, and through which it was possible for him or her to understand and give meaning to the experience of the shipwreck and its aftermath.

Spatial Delineations of Power

These distinctions have relevance when considering the spatial dynamics of power which structured the everyday life experience of the event as well. An emigrant ship was a microcosm of class and power relations in England.[13] Its space was assumed to be a unitary social space, promoted as a community but divided, policed and regulated along the boundaries of power. The Captain, regardless of his class background at home, was by rank the supreme authority on board his vessel. Vested with the judicial powers of arrest and punishment, he also possessed religious and secular power to baptise, marry and bury while at sea. His authority was mapped out in the spatial arrangements on board – in the distance between the captain, ship's officers, first-class and second-class passengers, and the crew. These spatial arrangements conferred power on the captain, but that power had to be constantly policed and enforced by the social practices of daily life at sea. The captain's quarters occupied the poop deck, at the apex and at the rear of the ship, mirroring his position at the apex of its command structure, his gaze directed out and down upon his empire. The crew, on the other hand, were billeted in the worst accommodation, in the forecastle before the mast, and denied access to space allocated (albeit differentially) to the passengers. According to Hassam,

> the division of space on board an emigrant ship work[ed] primarily on the basis of exclusion, of excluding different groups from certain areas of the ship, and this in turn [led] to contestations of space which provided the focus for the bringing into being of the captain's power and a focus for the affirmation and maintenance of social identity.[14]

Even though incapacitated by ill health, Captain Fraser, backed by his officers, apparently maintained his control, status and class position while the ship was at sea prior to the wreck, despite the absence of passengers whose place might have further enhanced his authority. But the wreck brought a disintegration of the social order and a breakdown of boundaries, both physical and ideological. Try as she might, Eliza could not step into his shoes. Her reputed physical stamina, forceful personality and desire to command the vessel on behalf of the Captain were no substitute for masculinity. She was no match for a mutinous crew.

If one reads the shipwreck survivors' accounts to examine shifting relations of power, it becomes clear that the Captain's authority broke down with the division of crew into the two lifeboats.[15] The longboat, into which the Captain was put with his wife, was larger but less seaworthy. The survivors' evidence records that the Captain placed the first mate in charge of the longboat and the second mate (his nephew) in charge of the pinnace. This might be understood as an attempt (somewhat feeble, as it turns out) to reinforce his command. His ability to control the space was a measure of his naval command. His personal authority broke down, however. The second mate became ill and was transferred to the longboat. His twelve-year-old nephew was pressed into the service of the pinnace crew, and the pinnace subsequently abandoned (or drifted away from) the party.

On another level, Mrs Fraser attempted to demand respect for her own and the Captain's status by demanding that her/their possessions be brought on board. The crew refused, but Corallis rescued them for her from the brig. She thus extended the space occupied by the couple through the presence of two large trunks in the longboat. This act also established a domestic woman's space on board the longboat: the trunks were all that she had to represent 'home', although they were mightily resented by the crew.

She reported to John Curtis that she was afforded no privileges, however, as she was expected to bail water for both herself and her ailing husband. This is the time and space in which she is said to have given birth, knee-deep in water, attended by Brown, the first mate, who wrapped the drowned child in his shirt and commended it to the deep. But first mention of the birth in the records of the time occurs in an addendum, appended to Eliza's third, and most sensational account, written by an unknown hand and prepared for publication upon her arrival in England. There is no mention of it in documents written by commentators who purport to have had access to the examining physician's report from Moreton Bay, nor in surviving letters written to relatives in England by residents at Moreton Bay. Mrs Fraser's nephew, John Baxter, recalls the details in his testimony to the Lord Mayor's Inquiry in London. But his evidence contains a number of inconsistencies with that of other survivors. The 'extra detail' (the birth) may have been included as an addendum to the narrative to elicit more sympathy (and public funds) for her plight. Conversely, it could have been omitted from prior reports to preserve the 'lady's' privacy. The childbirth episode remains shrouded in mystery. The location of the first mention of Mrs Fraser's pregnancy and birth in the exaggerated Liverpool account casts doubt on the authenticity of this dimension of the story, although it was not denied by surviving members of the crew. If, indeed, she did give birth in these circumstances, her post-partum condition may help to explain why she was assigned to a small party of debilitated females and young children once on the island. The bizarre and tragic nature of the childbirth scene guarantees its inclusion in virtually every legendary retelling.

On the island, another configuration of spatial relations evolved. It included Eliza, her husband and the ship's officers in a group identity with the other crew members against the Fraser Islanders. To the survivors, the island was a wholly alien space. It was roughly mapped only as coastline on navigational charts and never before inhabited (or known to be inhabited) by white Europeans. Here the shipwreck victims stayed together, interacting tentatively with several groups of indigenous peoples, bartering clothing for food. They knew themselves and their identity as Britons primarily through their group identity, their proximity to one another. After a conflict at Orchid Beach, on the island's northern coast, the longboat party separated into two groups. Mrs Fraser's party clung to the shoreline, making their way south, until surrounded by local people and divided amongst several small groups. Mrs Fraser was left alone until taken up by a party of women. This is a new social space, totally outside the boundaries of European knowledge. If it can be said that Mrs Fraser was 'in captivity', it is more because of the alterity of this space than because of the physical controls and constraints placed upon her. Within Western realms of knowledge, she was 'nowhere'; that spatial positioning robbed her of an identity. Mrs Fraser's subjection was effected through her location and absorption in the imagined, unknown and threatening space of otherness.

But not completely. When she was found, her rescuer John Graham reported that she was wearing an old sou'wester on her head, the waistband from a pair of sailor's trousers and a tangle of vines around her waist which 'her dead and most lamented husband had put on'. In this tangle she hid her wedding ring and earrings.[16] This tangle of vines becomes the inspiration for the title of Patrick White's novel, A Fringe of Leaves. Thus, readers of subsequent texts are reminded at the point of her rescue of the symbolic presence of her husband through the fringe of leaves which inscribes her body within patriarchy and calls attention to her status as female. This fringe protects herself and her femininity from total dissolution. It represents a border in a number of senses. It maps the space of her body and indicates the ways in which the body can be read as a symbolic space, marking the border between white civilisation and native barbarism, between culture and nature, as well as between the indigenous and white women. Both border and body are policed by the symbolic meanings which underwrite Western culture, and known further through the everyday experience of sexual difference within patriarchy. The presence of the fringe of leaves in the Eliza Fraser story produces a borderline, a marker of her difference from the other women, through which a production of knowledge occurs. It ties her irrevocably to the West. So these events which attend the shipwreck, captivity and rescue, as well as the various narratives which give form to the story, all evince a complex array of forms of power and resistance which both contest and sustain class and gender hierarchies, negotiate racial divisions and concretise the authority of the colonial presence in Australia.

Mrs Fraser's Second Version: Sydney and the Public Accounts

The wreck occurred on 21 May 1836. All survivors were rescued and returned to white settlements by late August. Early reports reached Sydney at the same time and began to appear in the press. Filtering in from several sources, some items mention hardship and torture endured by the crew. During September and October, news items in the *Sydney Gazette* frequently portrayed Mrs Fraser and the seven male survivors as hapless victims at the hands of brutal savages. As suspicions mounted about the behaviour of the crew during the time of the shipwreck and captivity, the crew received less sympathy and were placed under close surveillance.

At a religious service at St James Church in Sydney, which Mrs Fraser did not attend, a subscription fund for all the survivors was announced. During the service four of the crew were made to sit in the aisle without their jackets, presumably, suggests one historical commentator, 'to recreate something of the "spirit of shipwreck" and excite generosity for their welfare'.[17] Only Mrs Fraser, however, who had already been given a trunk of clothes and a purse of money by the residents of Moreton Bay, would benefit. Baxter, the Captain's nephew and the ship's second officer, was given a fresh suit of clothes and granted a free passage back to England, but only after considerable delays and the intervention of the Governor. He refused the offer with considerable chagrin, so that he could work during his passage and earn money to support his aged grandmother. According to Youlden (the seaman Eliza complained about in her official report), the other surviving crew members were told that, since they could not be trusted with money, their shares would be paid out to them at the time of sailing. They received five pounds each, paid out in clothes and sea stores, 'at extravagant prices'. Undaunted to the end, Youlden concludes his narrative thus: 'Where the rest of the money went I will not say; but if it will help his conscience at all who has it, I freely make over to him my share of it.'[18] The distribution of funds reveals another mode of public regulation of the structures of power. Mrs Fraser, represented as an innocent female victim, gained public support, sympathy and considerable financial reward. Her gain came at the expense of all members of the surviving crew. The ship's officers and stroppy seamen were all lumped together as unworthy deviants. The Church, like the colonial establishment at Moreton Bay, played its part in this regulation of power and authority.

In Sydney Mrs Fraser gave several reports of her ordeal to local journalists.

These accounts were slightly more sensational than her official statement. They focused on Eliza's encounters with the 'natives' on the island, and not on the shipwreck or her fractious involvements with the crew (who were, after all, at hand and could tell their side of the story if only they could find an audience willing to listen). Her newspaper account detailed how Mrs Fraser was taken by a group of older women and a few children with whom she spent about three weeks in the bush before encountering her husband in a debilitated condition. She reported that while she was away performing tasks, he was speared in the back of the shoulder and subsequently died. The 'cannibals' then tortured and killed the first mate, Brown, and caused numerous privations, including fatigue and starvation – but not torture – to Eliza and Baxter prior to their rescue. For the first time a clear delineation of us-and-them categories emerges in relation to Mrs Fraser's testimony about her ordeal and her captors. She employs the terms 'cannibals' and 'savages' to describe the Fraser Islanders, and she represents herself as an innocent victim, miraculously rescued from her plight. The press reports emphasise her vulnerability as a female, and her 'present destitute state – her husband having been murdered by the savages, and herself thrown upon the world without the present means of subsistence', eliciting further sympathy on her behalf. Thus, in Sydney, aided by the newspaper production of the historical event and the bishop's subscription campaign, 'the people' rallied to support Mrs Fraser; she became a *cause célèbre*, an innocent white woman ravaged by brutal savages. The subscription campaign allowed the middle class to stand with her against the unruly others threatening their authority and privilege – the incursions of a recalcitrant crew close at hand, and the barbarous natives in the unknown and uncharted landscape beyond.

The Third Version: The Construction of a Media Event

Eliza Fraser gave at least three different accounts of her ordeal, each one becoming more and more exaggerated, more and more sensational, as it reached a wider, less discriminating, and more eager public. Her third account was dated Liverpool, 2 July 1837, fourteen days before the actual date of her arrival. It was published in the London *Times* and the *Courier* on 19 August 1837, a month after her arrival in England with her new husband, Captain Greene. This version of the event reached the widest public. Within days of publication in London, it appeared in provincial and colonial papers; within a month, it took on a variety of popular forms. Woodcut illustrations and cartoons appeared, depicting her perilous ordeal. Broadsheets and hand-bills summarised the most lurid details. A sideshow performance was organised in Hyde Park. The account was adapted into a chapbook version in England and transformed into a classic captivity narrative in the United States. Mrs Fraser became a 'media' event.

Something happened to the story between Mrs Fraser's departure from Sydney on 16 February 1837 and her arrival in Liverpool on 16 July which would make the lady (in)famous. We cannot know, but Yolanda Drummond, her New Zealand biographer, surmises that that something came in the form of Captain Alexander John Greene, a man with knowledge of the power of the press, skills of manipulation, and an understanding of female vulnerability.[19] Greene was not only the captain of a whaling ship newly arrived from New Zealand; he also regularly contributed articles concerning shipwrecks and captivities to the local press. He had accumulated a repertoire of stories before meeting Eliza Fraser upon his arrival in Sydney on 29 November 1836.

Drummond hypothesises that a few years earlier, while in Sydney, Greene had learned of the fate of one Betty Guard. She had been taken captive by the Maori off Cloudy Bay after the wreck of the *Harriet* in 1834. Her husband, Captain Jacky Guard, an ex-convict from New South Wales, was one of the pioneers of the emerging New Zealand whaling industry. After the wreck, twelve of the *Harriet* crewmen were killed by Maori in retaliation for the murder of several natives by whalers and seamen's abuse of the native women. Guard proceeded to Sydney, where he enlisted the help of the New South Wales government in rescuing his wife. The colonial government despatched two well-armed vessels, each with more than sixty soldiers on board. They mounted a military offensive against the Maori and, after rescuing Mrs Guard and her three-year-old son, engaged them in a battle. This resulted in the deliberate murder of several chiefs and a slaughter so widespread as to provoke an official inquiry. Upon the arrival of Betty Guard in Sydney, in 1835, a subscription campaign was launched to raise funds on her behalf.

In the next year reports appeared in the Sydney papers of another shipwreck, that of the *Charles Eaton*.[20] This shipwreck account, in many ways more gory and sensational than Eliza Fraser's tale, included reports and evidence of decapitation and other savage rituals by natives in the Torres Strait area.

These were among the many sensational tales which filled the press in the year preceding the wreck of the *Stirling Castle*. But Eliza Fraser's somewhat less sensational ordeal attracted more widespread attention in the colonial press and for a longer period of time than did the other stories. Her gender may have relevance here. Davidson suggests that:

> Eliza Fraser not only represented the values that customarily placed women on pedestals as creatures of unblemished virtue; in her person Christian civilisation had been most exposed to savagery. Hers was the soft underbelly of imperialism, most vulnerable to spiteful attack from natives too ignorant to realise that they must give way to a new order.[21]

The press played an important role in promoting these connections between femininity and imperialism. Newspapers provided the necessary forum for colonial ideologies of power and bourgeois morality. They fanned the fires of sensationalism in this politics of representation. Captain Alexander John Greene, mariner, writer and adventurer, may have been the clever catalyst in ensuring the popularity of Eliza's tale. Whether or not the evidence supports this particular construction of the mythical Greene, it is clear that the popular press sought out such adventurers and fed an insatiable public on the sensational tales of such colonial types. Greene, 'a connoisseur of such adventures' according to Drummond, had supplied first-hand accounts of his difficult dealings in the South Seas to the Sydney papers. Immediately before arriving in Sydney in November 1836, he had been embroiled in battle with both a mutinous crew and hostile Maori in the Queen Charlotte Sound area of New Zealand. He reported that his crew had deserted ship in Cloudy Bay, and plundered the vessel. Then he learned of a scheme to seize his ship and kill him in retaliation for the death of one of the chiefs. He escaped only after an informant from another tribe warned him of the scheme.[22] He reported news of these adventures to the *Sydney Morning Herald* soon after his arrival at Port Jackson. This evidence leads Drummond to conclude that Greene was an opportunist who knew well how to excite the popular imagination with lurid tales of savagery and cannibalism. From the Betty Guard experience, he was also well aware of the lucrative nature of a subscription campaign, especially if the victim was a woman and a mother. In Sydney he met and married Eliza, barely seven months after the death of her husband. In February 1837, having collected two trunks of clothes and over four hundred pounds from the generous citizens of Sydney, she accompanied him back to England on his ship, the *Mediterranean Packet*. There was no Married Woman's Property Act at the time, no legal mechanism to protect Eliza from further exploitation and financial abuse by a possibly exploitative husband.

In England the story continues thus: upon arrival in Liverpool in July, Mrs Fraser, presenting herself as a destitute widow, visited the Commissioner of Police and, later, the Mayor, to solicit funds for her welfare and that of her three surviving children, left in the Orkney Islands. She had with her a new narrative of the shipwreck and her captivity, signed in her hand and dated Liverpool, 2 July 1837, even though she had not arrived in Liverpool on board the *Mediterranean Packet* until 16 July. This is the famous third narrative, full of new and inventive details of her 'bondage' amongst cannibals. As we have seen, this version was circulated to the colonial press around the world in a matter of weeks.

The popularity of this wildly exaggerated variant of the *Stirling Castle* experience deserves some attention. Barely two months would pass between the time of her arrival in Liverpool and the opening of the Lord Mayor's

Inquiry in London into her veracity concerning stories of her shipwreck, captivity and rescue. During that time, sensational accounts were fed to the local and international press. It is this third version of the story which was summarised in 'mournful verses' on the first handbill to appear on the streets of London, accompanied by a shocking woodcut illustration under the title: 'horrib treatment of the crew by savages' (Figure 2).[23] It depicts the strange scene of Mrs Fraser, babe in arms, being chased by savages dressed in American Indian skirts. The savages are represented with stereotypical African lips, earrings and bones through the nose. They wield daggers and whips. In the foreground of this chaotic and violent scene lie the beheaded bodies and remains of several other men, women and children. In the background Polynesian or Maori war canoes and a tri-masted schooner float in a bay surrounded by volcanic hills. A seven-verse ballad accompanies the woodcut. It tells of Mrs Fraser's pregnancy and childbirth; the Captain's murder by a native spear that pierced his heart; her courage as she removed the spear from his body at the point of his death; the beheading of the chief mate, Brown; and the beheading and burning at the stake of John Major, a crew member from the pinnace. The final four stanzas, which have been reproduced in or have formed the basis for several twentieth-century accounts, read as follows:

> And when they reached THE FATAL SHORE,
>   It's [sic] name is call'd Wide Bay,
> The savages soon them espied,
>   Rush'd down and seiz'd their prey,
> And bore the victims in the boat,
>   Into their savage den,
> To describe the feelings of these poor souls
>   Is past the art of man.
>
> This female still was doom'd to see,
>   A deed more dark and drear,
> Her husband pierc'd was to the heart,
>   By a savage with his spear.
> She flew unto his dying frame,
>   And the spear she did pull out,
> And like a frantic maniac,
>   Distracted flew about.
>
> The chief mate too they did despatch,
>   By cutting off his head,
> And plac'd on one of their canoes
>   All for a figure head.
> Also, a fine young man they bound,
>   And burnt without dread,
> With a slow fire at his feet at first
>   So up unto his head.

WRECK OF THE STIRLING CASTLE

Horrib Treatment of The Crew by Savages

A COPY OF MOURNFUL VERSES

Ye mariners and landsmen all,
Pray list while I relate,
The wreck of the Stirling Castle
And the crew's sad dismal fate.
In an open boat upon the waves,
Where billows loud did roar,
And the savage treatment they
  receiv'd
When drove on a foreign shore.

The Stirling Castle on May 16th
From Sydney she set sail,
The crew consisting of twenty,
With a sweet and pleasant gale.
Likewise Captain Fraser of the
  ship,
On board he had his wife,
And now, how dreadful for to tell,
The sacrifice of human life.

Figure 2   Broadsheet ballad, 'Wreck of the Stirling Castle: Horrib Treatment of the Crew by Savages', 1837.
By courtesy Mitchell Library, State Library of New South Wales.

When you read the tortures I went thro'
  'Twill grieve your hearts full sore,
But now, thank HEAVEN, I am returned
  Unto my native shore.
I always shall remember,
  and my prayers will ever be,
For the safety of both age and sex,
  Who sail the raging sea.[24]

The ballad represents the indigenous peoples in ways which locate them beyond the bounds of civility. They appear heartless, brutal, violent, wily, deceitful, treacherous and animal-like in their behaviours. This form of ballad had mass cultural appeal in the early decades of the nineteenth century. James Catnach, the main ballad printer of Seven Dials, produced a multitude of similar illustrated ballads and chapbooks throughout the 1820s and 1830s which attests to the vitality of this form of plebeian popular literature.[25] The texts aroused working-class interest, particularly around issues of middle-class morality and political scandal. The popular forms fed the working-class love of melodrama and farce, spectacle and pageantry.

The longer versions of the tale also refer to similar scenes of 'horrible barbarity' and contain sensational illustrations. They claim to be 'faithful narratives . . . of the captain's widow, whose unparalleled sufferings are stated by herself, and corroborated by the other survivors'. A preface to the piece, which appeared in *Alexander's East India Magazine,* draws the readers' attention to:

> the deplorable case of Mrs. Fraser and others, who have miraculously survived an awful shipwreck, and the cruelties practiced on them by the savages of New South Wales, amongst whom they were thrown, and by whom the majority of the ship's crew have been enslaved in lowest bondage, and in short tortured to death, by means at which the old Inquisition of Spain might blush.[26]

The new version of events contains tales of warfare between two clans of indigenous people, and refers to their savagery and cannibalism in ways that had not been reported to the official government administrators in Moreton Bay or journalists in Sydney and were not reported by other crew members at the time. It utilises a mythic structure of a shipwreck, enslavement, bondage and torture before a miraculous rescue from 'a fate worse than death'. And it refers to the Spanish Inquisition, an already mythologised barbarous event, here employed in a British narrative to cast aspersions on their foreign, Catholic rivals in the colonial enterprise. In a series of fantastic descriptions, this popularised version tells of grotesque, blue-haired natives who pluck the hair from Mrs Fraser's body and tattoo her all over. It contains a gruesome tale of the torture and beheading of John Major; his body was said to have been burnt and eaten by natives and his head preserved for use as figure bust for one of their canoes.[27] This version also appeared in the *Army and Navy Chronicle* (Washington, DC) in October 1837, followed by publication in the monthly magazine *Tales of Travellers* (London, 1837) and was later reproduced in an editorial article in the *Sydney Gazette* (January 1838). In the words of a recent historian, 'this one article set black/white relations in the Wide Bay area [of Queensland] back at least a hundred years'.[28]

Nationalism and the American Captivity Narrative

Within months of the London account, the Americans had published a local version of the captivity narrative, entitled *The Narrative of the Capture, Sufferings, and Miraculous Escape of Mrs. Eliza Fraser*, complete with tepees, squaws, Indian chiefs, tomahawks, bows and arrows and crude illustrations. This final section of the chapter will study the transformation into the genre of the captivity narrative within an American context

The captivity narrative as a genre has a particular history, audience and function in the United States. Richard Slotkin in his major study, *Regeneration through Violence: Mythology of the American Frontier, 1600–1860*, maintains that the captivity narrative is the first coherent and most enduring myth-literature developed in America.[29] North American feminist historian Carroll Smith-Rosenberg concurs, arguing that 'the American Indian captivity narrative more than any other genre asserts the Euro-Americans' American and civil identity, denying both to the American Indian.'[30] Mrs Mary Rowlandson's narrative of 1682 was the first and most popular book devoted to one captivity, in print for nearly 150 years and widely distributed in England and the colonies. In America between 1682 and 1800 some seven hundred captivity narratives were published. By the late eighteenth century 'fake' captivities appeared in England, complete with the stylistic melodramatic embellishments of the sentimental novel, which in turn were incorporated into the North American versions. By the time Mrs Fraser's narrative appeared, the 'truth'-effects of the genre were so challenged by melodramatic embellishments, exaggerations and improbabilities, as well as frequent plagiarism, rhetorical and illustrated borrowings from one event to another, that disbelief was the likely result of publication.[31]

My interest here is in the transformations of the captivity narrative, a narrative in which the figure of Woman mediates the space between civilisation and the wilderness, between Empire or Nation and its Others. According to Slotkin, the basic structure of the captivity narrative involves a man (*sic*, although he later maintains that the female captive is the archetypal figure) in a happy state of innocence or complacency, who is plunged into a perilous ordeal and ultimately saved.[32] The captivity narratives, when read through the structuring discourses of 'Nation', pit civilisation against the wilderness, white against dark-skinned peoples, coloniser against colonised, and Man against his physical, psychic and symbolic others, although the meanings of those terms shift considerably over time. Always, God is on 'our' side. In each journey, the narrator negotiates a passage from old world to new, imagining in and through the act of writing a (white, masculine) community of affiliation. This act, as Homi Bhabha reminds us, also at the same time 'contains moments of disavowal, displacement, exclusion and cultural contestation'.[33] Women, ethnic minorities, slaves, and the diverse population of indigenous peoples commonly lumped into the unified category of 'Indian' and/or 'Aborigine' all have experienced the exclusionary effect of these performative acts of nation. In the discourses of Empire, white women can be included with men as actors who advanced the cause of civilisation, and also can be marked as other, socially and discursively, by their sexual difference. Aboriginal subjects, both men and women, are objectified – they become the alien, racially codified, other through which European personal and national identity is measured. White women 'in captivity' mark the boundary between civilised and savage life: their vulnerability, as females, and their imagined submission to savage life, as captives, present a compelling pretext, in political and symbolic terms, for a rescue mission.

In the early Puritan narratives, the wilderness was inhabited by Indians and French Papists; it was the domain of sin which tested the faith of its God-fearing victims. The early accounts highlighted Indian outrages which solicited strong anti-Indian sentiment. As settlement continued, the wilderness and its inhabitants succumbed to White Man's Ways; the brutal and barbarous Indians of the nation's imaginary gave way to a dying race of Noble Savage types. The later narratives incorporated melodramatic effects to evoke pity and terror for the innocent captive. Like the gothic novel, popular at the time, they also elicited horror in the imagination of a growing band of readers, and encouraged commercial sales. Still, the captivity narratives functioned to create and maintain the boundaries between the evolving imagined community of the American nation and its Others who threatened the illusion of national unity and coherence. Given shifting networks of power, any group could be imagined as other (not only the Indians and French Papists but also the English, the unruly lower classes and, later, the slaves). In time, it could be admitted that even white, female victims of captivity could adapt to native ways and learn to 'love the enemy'.[34] The captivity narratives as a genre had power to articulate in mythical terms the fear of miscegenation; the fear was not so much that women could be violated but that they could be *seduced* by their captors. This articulation remained an enduring characteristic of the genre. And, in the few examples where captives professed their love or admiration for their captors, later commentators on their narratives would label this love a perversion, or a sign of degeneration which could only happen within the lower ranks of white settler society. In the end, suggests Slotkin and Fiedler before him, what is at stake is a battle between pale- and dark-skinned men.[35] The Woman who figures in the text is never more than a marker of exchange. She provides the context through which a rescue operation can take place. What is being rescued is not a woman, but an idea of nation, 'the people'. This idea both includes and excludes her as a subject/object of possession, while it simultaneously displaces and calls into being the 'Indian' as a category of meaning within white culture.

Further, the woman acts as a cultural sign in the captivity narrative in a way that allows the reading public to identify her rescue with a celebration of humanitarianism over brutal savagery, valorising the feminine principle within (masculine) culture. Andrew Lattas suggests that the literature of captivity contributed to the coding of certain cultural principles as feminine, particularly those which deal with the body as a site of feeling and empathy. The rescue of the woman not only restores law and order; it also grounds an ethics of civilisation in an ordered, divine state of nature (the white body) as opposed to the disordered, unfeeling state of nature embodied in black bodies.[36] The literature of captivity, then, can be more closely associated with the cult of sensibility and feeling through which bourgeois culture valorised feminine virtue. Here, the Western self's pride in its sensitivity as the basis of its civility is outraged by the coarse brutality and savage spectacles of the barbarian other. As Europe, and later America, abolished slavery, the brutal violence and spectacles of torture which had been the marks of Western colonial violence were projected on to the indigenous people. These attributes became the defining marks of colonised black peoples. The white woman and her white, male, redeeming rescuer brought into play foundational fictions of racial and gender divisions, Christian civility, ownership and power which underwrite bourgeois culture for the modern nation-state.[37] Further, as certain sets of meaning became codified within myth (or the genre of captivity narrative), social differences became naturalised, taking on the guise of 'truth' within the 'natural' order of things. Myth plays a significant role in the construction of the category of the indigenous other. As Roland Barthes reminds us, however, myths provide a vehicle through which cultural concepts and values can be transmitted, disrupted, and transformed.[38]

Robert Berkhofer, in his study *The White Man's Indian*, surveys the captivity genre and concludes that an array of discursive traits marks the Indian through time. Indians can be both good and bad. The worst sins of the bad Indian include cannibalism and human sacrifice, followed by cruelty to captives, brutal warfare, indolence, superstition, slavery of the native women and laziness of the men, nakedness, lechery, passion, vanity and promiscuity. The good Indian is a free man of the plains who exists in a utopian state of primitive harmony with nature. He is loyal, honest, wise in Indian lore and above all a helper of the white destiny in America.[39] The identified traits fit easily into Terry Goldie's analysis of the commodities within a semiotic economy through which colonial white discourse constructs the indigene. He names those commodities which function as textual strategies of control as: sex, violence, orality, mysticism and a prehistoric temporality.[40] Within the North American tradition the Indian becomes the reverse or negative image of the white man through which white civilisation attempts to construct a stable identity, here in the conquest of good over evil. In JanMohamed's terms, what is being played out is a Manichean allegory of putative superiority of the colonial American over the supposed inferiority of the native, a duplicity which is capable of reversal.[41]

With the North American context in mind, I want to focus specifically on the captivity narrative of Eliza Fraser, in its North American, English and Australian variants. The shipwreck of the *Stirling Castle* and the fate of its crew is not a captivity in the classic American sense – no one was captured nor coerced to live against their will. The white party fell upon the island after floundering at sea for nearly four weeks. Upon arrival, they were met by the island's native inhabitants, who faced the dilemma of how to deal with the ghostly strangers. The members of the party were separated and grouped among small bands of Fraser Islanders as they made their way south on the island and then across to the mainland. There is no evidence of 'capture' or coercion until the point of rescue, which is said to have occurred just before a corroboree in which Mrs Fraser was dressed for display before a gathering of neighbouring groups. At that time, but only at that time, she had been placed under guard, necessitating careful negotiation for her release. In addition, Mrs Fraser's accounts of her ordeal take various forms, largely in response to the demands or expectations of her audience. The event itself, occurring in a liminal environment where meanings were indeterminate, was without plot or structure. The captivity narrative, as a genre, gives the tale a structure and purpose, placing it in a field of previously determined meanings. As a narrative performance, it translates the diffuse nature of her experience into a coherent colonial myth which justifies the white settlers' continued presence in a new land.

Although the shipwreck took place in the antipodes and concerned the fates of an English party, the publication in New York in 1837 is one of the first coherent narratives of the event. It is a hybrid, hodge-podge variation of the North American captivity narrative. Published well after the height of interest in the genre and influenced by virtually all its predecessors, it is a bit of a curiosity. Its discursive elements include intertextual reference to the Puritan tale of religious deliverance and the secular propaganda tract of good white hero versus the treacherous Indian. Like other narratives produced at the time, it contains a number of 'fake' English embellishments, as well as elements of the sentimental novel and the psychological thriller. Before examining the narrative as text, I will focus on the two illustrations and the preface which introduces it. The first, full-page, illustration depicts the death of Captain Fraser (Figure 3). The second drawing occupies half a page under a tantalising preface, and carries the caption: 'An Indian Chief in the act of forcibly conveying Mrs. Fraser to his hut or wigwam'. These same illustrations would be used again to preface the *History of the Captivity and Providential Release therefrom of Mrs. Caroline Harris*, printed by New York publishers Perry and Cooke in 1838 (Figure 4). Mrs Harris, along with her friend Mrs Clarissa Plummer, was said to have been taken captive by 'Camanche' Indians during the emigration of their families from New York to Texas in 1835. The Indians reputedly held the prisoners 'in bondage' for nearly two years, during which time they witnessed the deaths of their husbands before being 'providently redeemed by two of their countrymen'.[42] In both cases, I suspect that readers are to imagine a relationship between the two events (the death of the husband and the conveyance of the wife to the Chief's hut) depicted in the illustrations. Both are stock narratives in which the woman is depicted as a 'frail flower' in need of protection, whose plight arouses both horror and sympathy.[43]

The illustrations are a telling example of how the colonial discourses imagined indigenous peoples as a universal type. In the Eliza Fraser captivity narrative, the 'natives' wear full togas or skirts, ankle-high moccasins and feathered head-dresses; they stand in stoical postures of a static time. They fight their rivals with tomahawks, brutalise their captives, and have designs on the fully clothed, delicate white heroine of the sentimental novel as she laments the passing of her fully clothed, handsome young Captain. In Berkhofer's terms, these are 'Bad Indians', exhibiting the worst traits of human sacrifice, cruelty to captives, brutal warfare, indolence and lechery.

The text, entitled *Narrative of the Capture, Sufferings, and Miraculous Escape of Mrs. Eliza Fraser* is prefaced by the following abstract of events. After the wreck, the crew

> were driven to and thrown on an unknown island, inhabited by Savages, by whom Captain Fraser and his first mate were barbarously murdered, and Mrs. Fraser . . . [was] for several weeks held in bondage, and after having been compelled to take up her abode in a wigwam and to become the adopted wife of one of the Chiefs, Mrs. F. was providently rescued from her perilous situation.[44]

From the outset this text, addressed to the reader in the form of a first-person autobiographical account, is stamped in the mould of the American captivity narrative. Here the crew, which is quickly reduced to a woman, is plunged into a perilous ordeal, from which it (but textually only she) is miraculously rescued. The text, like that of other captivity narratives of the time, proceeds to establish Mrs Fraser's credentials as a reluctant narrator, unprepared for her performance, having had an 'indifferent education' and deprived of the aid of her husband. But she promises a 'plain, unvarnished tale; exaggerating nothing, but recording truly and faithfully the particulars'

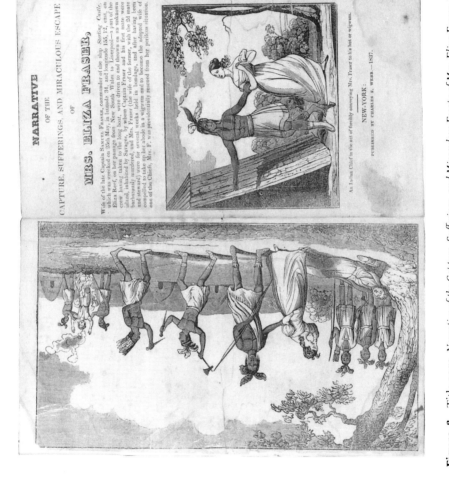

Figure 3 Title page, *Narrative of the Capture, Sufferings, and Miraculous Escape of Mrs. Eliza Fraser*, 1837. By courtesy Newberry Library.

Figure 4 The pictures shown in Figure 3 form a composite plate (left) to illustrate the *History of the Captivity and Providential Release therefrom of Mrs. Caroline Harris*, 1838. By courtesy Newberry Library.

of her ordeal; an ordeal in which she moves from 'a state of content and enviable happiness, to that of inconceivable wretchedness' before being 'miraculously rescued' from her 'bondage'. True to Goldie's semiotic categories, the natives are marked by their violence, their physicality and their orality. The husbands are 'lazy' or 'naturally very indolent'; the squaws are 'savage monsters' who nonetheless perform 'the most laborious duties . . . cheerfully . . . without complaint or murmur'. Eliza is placed in the abusive care of a 'squaw-mistress . . . a savage monster who, in her fits of rage, would, beast-like, gnash her teeth, and sometimes seize [Mrs Fraser] by the throat until [she] nearly strangled'. All natives yell, whoop and howl. That is, they portray the qualities which mark them as closer to animals in a debased state of nature: they have no language, they act violently, without restraint, according to their instincts. And the women are worse than the men. In short, they were everything readers in a civil society wished themselves not to be.[45]

This narrative, like that of Mrs Harris, revolves around the death of the husband (or his 'savage/brutal murder' at the hands of 'remorseless demons,' to be true to the text). This moment of the Captain's death produces a climax in the text which plunges Eliza, the heroine, into chaos. Threats of sexual violation follow, signalling a melodramatic crisis of narrative address: 'Alas, it is impossible to reflect on what I endured . . . to imagine the shock of horrors to come . . . The reader cannot have any idea of the horrors I suffered . . . and still greater torments' . . . until, finally, Eliza is rescued 'not from the devouring jaws of a ravenous lion,[46] but from the hands of a savage ruffian, far more to be dreaded!' And the readers can stop biting their nails.

In terms of narrative structure, illustrations, format themes, techniques, and rhetorical devices, this retelling maintains attributes added to the genre of the captivity narrative in the early nineteenth century. These attributes confound any attempts to consider the story as either an authentic account or one which allows any reliable access to ethnographic knowledge. The repetitious devices include a typification of the Indians as demonic others, the Captive as a vulnerable and subservient female, her Captor as a threatening, dark-skinned male, and the Redeemer as a valiant, heroic white male.[47] The Squaws, typically 'filthy and ugly', play an important, if subsidiary, role within the genre. They act as 'insolent mistresses', abusing captives 'at their pleasure a thousand inexpressible ways', repetitive descriptions which link the feminine with the instincts, duplicity and disorder, and can be traced back at least to the salvation tracts of Cotton Mather. In addition, as the representation of captivity becomes more abstract over time in America, females become more vulnerable, particularly to sexual seduction and violation after the death of their husband and loss of his paternal protection. The rescuer, standing in for the absent husband, takes on the

mantle of paternal authority. In the Eliza Fraser captivity narrative the rescuer is a an official government party, a collective entity, referred to in the
text as 'thirteen resolute young men under the command of Lieut Otter'.

What place(s) can we assign to this instance of a worn-out genre within the
North American tradition? By the end of the eighteenth century, the popularity of captivity narratives as a genre was in decline. But in the decade
1830–40 they experienced a revival in the United States. In the 1820s Samuel
Drake of Boston began a series of anthologies which reprinted earlier
accounts and continued to be published until the 1860s. Generally these
anthologies collected up the more popular narratives from earlier times,
although a few sensational accounts, like that of Mrs Fraser, began to appear
as well. After a lapse of nearly a decade, six separate, new captivity narratives
were published in 1838. Their re-emergence and popularity might best be
understood within the context of US slavery and land expansion. In 1832 the
anthology *Indian Biography* was published, followed by *The Old Indian Chronicle*
(1836), *Indian Captivities* (1839) and *Tragedies of the Wilderness* (1846). Prefaces
typically stressed the historical accuracy of the accounts, which were said,
perhaps somewhat facetiously, to feed the ethnographic interest of scientists
and historians. This is the age of natural science, heralded by Darwin's
voyage of the *Beagle* which took place from 1831 to 1836. The 'Indian' was
falling prey to the gaze of the naturalist as an object of scientific inquiry. In
addition, the accounts filled the need for cheap and readily available copy in
the increasingly popular literary forms of magazines, novels and newspapers.
The captivity narrative satisfied the reader's desire for both information and
amusement. In its original, popular form published in the press, the captivity
narrative can best be described as a form of sensational literature directed to
the pleasures of a mass culture. But in the republication of a series of captivity
narratives in anthologies, another audience was addressed. The narratives
were repackaged as quasi-ethnographies addressed to a new audience of
curious, scientifically-oriented scholars. In the prefatory words of one
'scholar': 'the philosopher who speaks with delight, of the original simplicity,
and primitive interest of mankind, may here learn, that man uncivilised and
barbarous, is even worse than the most ferocious wolf or panther of the
forest'.[48] Here one can detect the ambivalence between philosophic perspectives which categorised indigenous peoples in romantic terms as Noble
Savages, examples of man's arrested humanity, as opposed to those which
classified them as savage barbarians, more animal than human. The rational
man of science is enjoined to consider the case again. And besides the scientific interest, the politics of progress demanded a renewed production of the
myth of the treacherous Indian and/or the rebellious slave – the enemy to be
fought.

In the period between 1831 and 1857, the best legal minds of America
debated the legal status of indigenous peoples and slaves: in other words, the

definition of what it meant to be an American. Arguments surrounding two Supreme Court decisions – Cherokee Nation vs Georgia (1831) and Scott vs Stanford (Dred Scott, 1857) – reveal the symbolic processes of identity formation at work at the time. The debates effectively legislated subjectivity in and for the emerging nation.[49] The resultant decisions defined indigenous peoples and slaves as non-citizens, beyond the boundaries of the political entity constituted by the phrase 'We the People'. A number of recent historians have studied the legislation around 'the Indian Question' and the ways in which it marked for America a 'self' and its others. Michael Rogin argues in psychoanalytic terms that white colonial discourse constructed the emblematic character of the 'savage Indian' as a figure of both threat and attraction, projecting fears of white aggression on to the Indian. 'Indian threats to the self-defense of expanding white America suggest that early time when a secure self has not emerged, when it is threatened with retaliatory extermination for its own aggressive rage.'[50] 'The Indian Question' deflected a young nation's fears and insecurities onto its others, thus positing their alterity as a means of buttressing national unity. The Cherokee Nation and Dred Scott decisions, taken together, excluded 'non-whites' from the imagined community of nationhood, an exclusion which in time would extend to the Chinese and other ethnicities. As Priscilla Wald comments, 'White America could see its own alterity, or alienation, reflected in the fate (and often quite literally in the face) of the racialized other.'[51] Thus, although the days of Indian captivities of white settlers had long passed, the genre which best symbolised 'Indian treachery' continued to provide a potent weapon in the battle for nationhood.

The North American version of the Eliza Fraser captivity differs only in minor details from those published in England and in the colonial magazines. Commentators in the United States have suggested, in regards to a specific and pragmatic political context, that its interest may have been motivated by white settlement patterns leading to the outbreak of the Seminole Wars between the colonists and the indigenous peoples of Florida. The story and the broader interest in captivity narratives in the 1830s would also have had the effect of mediating pro-abolitionist sentiments in the United States. Although Mrs Fraser is said to have been captured by 'Indians' in the antipodes, the overt racist and sexual overtones of the tale could evoke in readers a fear of the barbarity and titillating interest in the sexual prowess of the black slave as well as the Amer-Indian. The year 1831 saw the Nat Turner insurrection in Virginia. The slave revolt resulted in the murder of seventy-five slaves. It also set off a new wave of oppressive legislation which prohibited the education, movement or assembly of slaves in the South. The Nat Turner revolt, coupled with anti-slavery legislation in England, refocused the nation's energies on its 'peculiar institution'. Anti-slavery societies evolved in the North, and abolition supporters were increasingly condemned and persecuted there during the decade, leading to the murder by a mob of abolitionist editor Elija P. Lovejoy in Alton, Illinois, in 1837.

In addition, giant railroad systems were established in the 1830s in America, and in the 1840s 2800 miles of track were set down – heading south and west into the interior, into Indian territory. Beyond the local interest, there was the American myth of Manifest Destiny. It was imagined to include not only the geographic territory of what is now the continental United States, but territories beyond. Two contemporary historians who have compiled a recent anthology of captivity narratives, including the Eliza Fraser story, comment on the appropriation of tales from the antipodes into the North American genre in terms of Manifest Destiny. They write that 'inevitably, these patterns [of appropriation] included the notion that the Pacific was yet another American frontier'.[52]

Eliza Fraser's tale is one of many discursive moments through which the physical, psychic, sexual and symbolic boundaries of the ever expanding nation and colonial territories were being sustained and extended. The political questions and national obsessions with difference may have been different in America from those of Empire, but the Eliza Fraser story functioned to extend patterns of Western colonial dominance in both contexts. Mrs Fraser became a figure of display for an imperial/colonial audience. Her story became a myth by which the popular imagination understood the civilised world by means of its difference from the savage others at its margins. In terms of the construction of social space, Mrs Fraser's captivity narrative helped to provide the justification for control by the West over the rest of the world.

The narrative, with slight variations, appeared in *Tales of Travellers* and *Alexander's East India Magazine* as a colonial text of Empire. These colonial publications contained endless first-person accounts of shipwrecks, castaways, runaways, mutinies, abandonments and captivities. As Pratt points out, popular survival literature depended on the growth of mass print culture. Mass print culture, in turn, provided readerships 'primed on sentimental dramatisations of the contact zone'.[53] In addition, publication of shipwreck stories afforded survivors the financial wherewithal to start again, a fact not likely to have been lost on the likes of Captain Greene. These adventure narratives had wide appeal and worked on their audiences in diverse ways. They were celebrations of Empire, which positioned the reader with the narrator in a guise of superiority of the civilised West over the barbarism of the rest of the world. They provided a superior standpoint from which to judge the captivity experience within an ethnographic framework. And they afforded a mass popular audience with voyeuristic pleasures in regard to sex and savagery, more of which will be discussed in Chapters 4 and 5. They were modes of constituting knowledge and subjectivity for a range of readers identifying not only as national but also as colonial subjects. At the

same time, the dominant voices were also heterogeneous voices in struggle
with each other – the English versus the colonial administrators, the Whigs
versus the Tories, the ship's officers versus the mutinous crew, *The Times*
versus the popular press, Mrs Fraser versus those who would speak on her
behalf. The various accounts of Mrs Fraser's ordeal can be read not only as
promulgating dominant ideologies but also as sites for contestation and
disruptions within the complex, social fabric of English colonial, and early
American national, life.

Women's Texts and Questions of Agency

Carroll Smith-Rosenberg argues that white women played an important role
in constituting political subjectivity for themselves, and in so doing denied
subjectivity to women of colour, through the genre of the captivity narrative.
She writes:

> British-American women helped construct white Americans as true Americans and
> native Americans as savages in three distinct moves: by assuming the role of
> innocent victims of barbarous savagery, by assuming the role of authoritative
> writers, and by authorizing themselves as an alternative white icon for America. In
> appropriating the right to write and to represent a white America, Euro-American
> women assumed the dominant male discourses of imperialism and social
> order.[54]

Although a feminist historian might want to argue that women did appropriate these rights of representation in relation to early narratives of captivity, the argument would be difficult to sustain over time as the woman's
voice and place within the genre become more stereotyped and less authoritative. In the case of Mrs Fraser's narrative, it would appear that the
woman herself had little control over the narrative which bears her name.
Further, if one reads the captivity narrative attributed to Mrs Fraser against
some of her reputed testimony recorded in John Curtis's text *The Shipwreck of
the Stirling Castle*, several significant differences can be detected. In the sensationalised versions, as in the Rowlandson captivity narrative which Smith-
Rosenberg studies, the enunciative position attributed to Mrs Fraser allows
no sympathy to devolve to her captors. It could be said that 'she', like
Rowlandson, 'refuses [her captors] those most basic forms of human subjectivity, agency and will'.[55] But in the Curtis text, on at least three (albeit
rare and textually muted) occasions, Mrs Fraser's testimony does extend
sympathy and attribute agency and will to the Fraser Islanders. In relation to
her own hunger, her testimony acknowledges that she lived on the island
during a particularly harsh season when the entire group lived without
adequate food, a condition which motivated the move to the mainland in
search of a better diet. Her account describes how she was taught to search

for honey ants and to stalk a snake. Later, it relates that her 'sable mistress', whom she called 'Robina', befriended her, treated her wounds, and never failed to intercede on her behalf. At another time, the narrator observes that the native women displayed an inordinate love and affection toward their children. If one wants to consider Mrs Fraser as a historical agent, it could be said in reference to these incidences that Mrs Fraser exhibited some limited sympathy for her captors and acknowledges their human needs, emotions and kindnesses to her person. These allusions, however, are totally absent from the sensationalised captivity narrative which bears her name. In addition, in the Curtis text, they are discounted by the author's disparaging commentary. Even if one sets aside the proposition, which has been enter-tained in my study, that *texts* produce the authority of their speakers, it remains the case that these discursive strategies, which are employed in both the sensational accounts and in Curtis's text, make it difficult to maintain that Mrs Fraser herself had control over her testimony or its transformation in either popular or academic settings. The nature of those transformations, which serve to regulate the borders between civilisation and savagery, will be further examined in Chapters 4 and 5.

At the same time, it is still the case, as Smith-Rosenberg observes, that when the woman writes (or signs her name to) captivity narratives which circulate throughout the colonial world and engender sympathy for the white woman as a victim of Empire, she comes to be read as an agent in the colonial enterprise. But her agency can be read in a variety of ways. Smith-Rosenberg argues that the woman as victim 'reverses the traditional engen-dering of the British imperial body, making that body female ... her victimization legitimating his ruthless penetration.'[56] She suggests that women's captivity stories justified the extension of frontier violence against the natives. As was remarked earlier, the woman can also be enlisted to signify quite the opposite – the humanitarian, feminine virtues of a civil society. Her virtue, and the sentiment her story evoked for the audience, could be read as markers of Western feeling and sensitivity against the unfeeling and barbarous state of the natives. This reading allows for humani-tarian reformers to suggest that the natives can be reclaimed for civilisation. Ambivalent readings then signal shifting political and ideological allegiances within the body politic through time. Contrary to Smith-Rosenberg, I would argue that woman's agency in the captivity narrative is limited in at least three ways: through modes of narrative address, formal structures of the genre, and the discursive codes of nationalism, Empire, civility and bourgeois propriety through which 'the feminine' is variously signified.

Although narratives told by women were relatively rare, their texts were marked in sexually specific ways which invited identification by an audience of Western readers. The textual construction of the female narrator singled out in the genre of the captivity narrative (that is, Eliza's ordeal presented as a plain unvarnished tale, told by a reluctant narrator with an indifferent education and without the assistance of her husband) was a typical marker of the sensational, feminised text.[57] In the case of the Eliza Fraser story, the significance of the narrative turns on a key structuring event, the Captain's death. This event more than any other act plunges the white woman and, symbolically, the entire white community of survivors into chaos. Within the larger social order, this transgression of the 'natural' law produces a crisis for imperialism. Mrs Fraser's sexual vulnerability after the death of her husband set up the context for another rescue operation, this time not in a battle for the American West as Nation but within the farther-flung fields of Empire.

The importance of the Captain's death to colonial variants of the tale can be registered through its repetitious depiction in the illustrations which accompany the various narratives as well as through an analysis of their narrative codes of address. The English colonial magazine *Tales of Travellers,* for example, featured a line drawing of 'The murder of the Captain' (Figure 5). This time it occurs at the hands of two naked, dark-skinned natives; Eliza,

WRECK OF THE STIRLING CASTLE.

[THE MURDER OF THE CAPTAIN.]

Figure 5 'The murder of the Captain.' In *Tales of Travellers,* 1837. By permission of The British Library.

pale-skinned, semi-naked, and wearing a head-dress, attempts to intervene as the couple stands before a suggestively threatening fire. Mrs Fraser's official biographer, John Curtis, also included a drawing of the Captain's death in *The Shipwreck of the Stirling Castle* (Figure 6). These iconographic representations allow for at least two different readings of the Captain's death. Although both instances are cited as 'murder' (despite Mrs Fraser's assertions that she did not believe that the natives intended to kill her husband), in one illustration the death results from a direct attack. In the other the Captain is speared in the back as he attempts to flee – a cowardly attack. Differences in the stories and illustrations as to the nature of the Captain's death were picked up in the news reports and later cited as contradictory accounts by Mrs Fraser herself.

Captain Fraser's dying words, 'Eliza, I am gone', may have reflected the passing of one of Empire's more inept patrons, but his death would be refigured productively into diverse networks of colonial power. Imperialism had many centres, many overlapping and even conflicting spheres of influence. As this analysis has demonstrated, the plethora of Eliza Fraser stories which arise within the colonial discourses of Britain, the United States and colonial Australia, contribute to and are the effects of shifting centres of power and multiple forms of gender, race and class domination within differing contexts of nation.

The idea of nation, as I argued in *Women and the Bush*, emerges out of social and cultural constructions which posit identity through difference.[58] If the

Figure 6 'The spearing of Captain Fraser.' In John Curtis, *The Shipwreck of the Stirling Castle*, 1838.
By courtesy Fryer Library, University of Queensland.

nation is an imagined community, as Anderson maintains,[59] the maintenance of a coherent identity relies on narratives which posit and secure its
continuance. As this chapter has attempted to demonstrate, dominant
understandings of national identity are never secure; 'sureties' require constant textual attention and productive buttressing. In the case of Australia, a
dominant coding for national identity is figured with reference to the white,
native-born, Australian and his (sic) battle with the land/Aborigines/others,
framed against the English parent culture. Although women are said to be
absent from the annals of Australian history, the feminine figures metaphorically as a category of difference from the masculine, in a play of
masculine sameness and of feminine otherness. The white Australian native
son battles against a hostile feminine environment, an 'enemy to be fought'.
Sometimes actual women are the enemy; at other times they position themselves with men as the builders of Empire. More often the category of
otherness is filled in by fire and flood and drought, and by the presence of
Aborigines, the Chinese and other migrants. Discursively, at least, man posits
his identity as 'Australian' in opposition to his others – that which 'he' is not.

Although it is generally assumed that Australian national identity emerged
in the 1890s, it could be argued that decade fused elements already nascent
in the underlying imaginings of the colonial state. This analysis of the Eliza
Fraser story and 'Eliza Fraser' as a marker within shifting structures of power
leads in this direction. As a character in a nineteenth-century drama of
Empire, she is sometimes figured as a (masculine) colonial subject and given
status and authority as a heroic, imperial survivor in a colonial conflict, and
sometimes figured as an innocent feminine victim of captivity whose ordeal
helps to define the finer sensibilities of Western peoples. Her story can be
invoked as proof of native savagery or British civility. It can be enlisted in
campaigns for humanitarian reform as well as violent retaliation. In late-
twentieth-century Australian versions of the story, she is consistently located
as an 'other' within an Australian imaginary with respect to the British parent
culture. She betrays the local hero, her underdog, convict rescuer. In both the
nineteenth- and twentieth-century accounts, however, whether directed
towards mass culture or a high-minded academic audience, 'Eliza Fraser'
marks the territory of a superior white civilisation. Her story polices the
borders of difference within colonial, neo-colonial and post-colonial frameworks of meaning. The tale, within an Australian context, passes eventually
beyond its colonial variants and into a national mythology.

Twentieth-century Interventions

There are aspects of the classic captivity narrative which do not translate well
into the Australian setting. The Eliza Fraser story demands other frames of
reference within an Australian tradition, frames which result in several alter-

ations to the genre. The captivity narrative makes no sense in Australia. New inhabitants were not taken captive. Convicts escaped *to* rather than *from* the bush. For them the bush was not a howling, alien wilderness but a retreat from the brutalities of convict life. For the settlers, conquest over the land was a necessary mark of their identity. The battle for the land/identity was fought in ideological terms both against the British parent culture with its imperialistic practices and against the Aboriginal population. In terms of national identity, several shifts take place. On the one hand, the historical Eliza is aligned with her inept husband to an affiliation with a despised British culture. But on the other hand, as in the North American versions, she takes on the mantle of nationhood whose ordeal secures a symbolic and civil identity for white women and men, displacing the interests and identities of the indigenous population. Within the texts, she signifies both (masculine) British Empire and (feminine) sexual vulnerability. In both cultures, however, the place of the native inhabitant, whether Amer-Indian or Australian Aboriginal, is displaced and disavowed on a white man's mythical landscape of progressive survival. What marks the story as a foundational fiction in Australia in the twentieth century is the convict hero as nation-builder.

In the late twentieth century, the ex-convict's status as the Australian native son and the coherent plot of mastery and survival of a white male Australian cultural tradition are undermined as other stories are told from feminist, Aboriginal and post-colonial perspectives. These recent interventions call attention to the constructed and exclusionary nature of nationalism. In Bhabha's terms, they can be seen to disseminate notions of progress, time, narrative, and the margins of the modern nation-state. These issues will be taken up in more detail later in the book. Contemporary interventions lead away from the notion of the nation-as-one. They open up other possibilities of other narratives of 'the people' and their differences, of people no longer contained nor willing to be constrained by national discourses nor the 'teleology of progress'.[60]

CHAPTER 3

John Curtis and the Politics of Empire

The Lord Mayor's Commission of Inquiry created a new venue for the Eliza Fraser story, and another dimension of the event for future commentators to feed upon. In the nineteenth century the inquiry moved the episode out of the realm of the sensational and into an investigative political arena. It provided the press, the police, the political system and the public with a localised performance concerning the nature of colonialism and the nature of women – two burning questions for early-nineteenth-century British society. If the inquiry was the main performance, Curtis's text, *The Shipwreck of the Stirling Castle*, provided another site for its staging and a lasting script. More than an apologia for Mrs Fraser, that script is a text of Empire. The book, in its complex web of defences and contradictions, particularly along the axes of gender, race and class divisions within England and the colonies, illuminates the diverse aspects of a fluid colonial condition for modern readers. The text is concerned not so much with the nature of woman, but with what it meant or should have meant to be white and British. Within the context of the 1830s, Curtis's text seems to suggest that this meant belonging to and upholding a society which, despite its extreme tensions, was believed to be rational, ordered, moral and civil. Furthermore, the text respects the division of men and women into separate spheres, the public world of men and the domestic world of women, and of distinctions between social classes – although the readers encompassed by Curtis's 'We' to whom he addresses his defence are decidedly middle-class and conservative. Curtis, in his defence of Mrs Fraser, as well as in his digression into the fields of navigation, ethnography, the penal system and the like, stands as a spokesman for Empire. His text might be read as a cauldron of shifting social, political, moral and ethical interests out of which the Victorian middle class was forged.

In its structure the text loosely re-creates the drama of the courtroom, placing Mrs Fraser in the position of the accused. She stands against charges of being an imposter and attempting to defraud the public, charges which were brought about by the public outcry over accusations made by the Liverpool Police Commissioner. Prime witnesses for the accused include John Baxter, the second mate and the Captain's nephew, and Robert Darge, one of the mutinous seamen. Their testimony establishes fact of the shipwreck and Mrs Fraser's veracity in regard to her story of captivity. Captain Alexander John Greene, her new husband, remains a minor player in the drama. His is a notable absence, given his role in the popular and widespread reconstructions of the event and his preparation of the petitions presented to the Lord Mayor representing Eliza as a poor widow woman without a farthing.

Thoughout the Lord Mayor's Inquiry and in its textual reconstructions, evidence evoking sympathy for Mrs Fraser as an innocent victim of a barbarous fate continually overwhelms questions of fraud. John Curtis, the court reporter, vacillates in his history between two positions. He takes the place of counsel assisting the inquiry, supplying contextual (mis)information on native life and customs, as well as the nature of women; and he also acts the part of the judge, instructing his readers as to how to interpret the mass of conflicting evidence. Throughout, he acts as the arbiter not only of Mrs Fraser's behaviour but also that of the natives and convicts and crew. The readers, like the public at the time of the inquiry, observe the event and read the evidence (disguised as impartial but actually embedded in dominant perspectives and power relations of the day) as a *de facto* and by no means disinterested jury.

Although the Lord Mayor's Inquiry is ostensibly about Mrs Fraser's actions in Liverpool and London, it operates primarily as a site for the production of knowledge, fantasies and representations about Colonial Man and his Others: women, convicts, natives and the colonial enterprise. Mrs Fraser's position shifts from being an imposter and a fraudulent individual to being an innocent victim of barbarism and, finally, one of Empire's heroes. She is rescued from her position in the civil wilderness back into the body politic of Colonial Man. Another barbarous captivity; another heroic rescue. This occurs through the strategic textual management of her ambiguous status into that of a morally upright woman. Discursive constructions of her position in the drama slide between allowing her some degree of masculine authority, idealising her feminine sanctity, and challenging her deviance from middle-class norms of feminine propriety. She becomes a cipher, an object of meaning, which is utilised to regulate the borders between civilisation and barbarism, masculine sameness and feminine difference, self and other that are produced and sustained through hierarchies of gender, class and race. Her trial becomes a site for the staging of the cultural superiority of white civilisation, upheld by the dictates of Christianity, natural science, and early Victorian bourgeois life.

It is necessary to look closely at the role which journalism played in the nineteenth-century constructions of the event, and the way in which newspapers attempted to represent 'the truth' (whether through accounts represented as factual or sensational fabulations) to a nineteenth-century audience. It becomes obvious that the newspapers engaged in a manipulation of knowledge, exercised through strategies of power, the residue of which continues to affect the neo-colonial Western world today.

The trial became necessary as a result of events which occurred after Mrs Fraser returned to England in July 1837. Although the press accounts elicited considerable sympathy for Eliza Fraser after her arrival in Liverpool, the local police were not taken in by her pleas for public charity. They investigated her story further and learned of her marriage to Captain Greene and a rather more secure financial situation than she had reported. The Liverpool authorities were unconvinced by her now wildly exaggerated story and unsympathetic to her plight. Indeed, it may be the case that the sensationalism of the story which appeared under her name in the local and colonial press mitigated against a belief in the authenticity of her tale. She continued to London where, again with the help and at the likely instigation of Greene, she repeated her supplications with further embellishments of her trials and tribulations, and with more success. The Tory Lord Mayor, himself in the midst of a close re-election campaign, received a petition on Eliza's behalf from Greene and promised a public subscription. A month after the subscription was announced, a 'leaked' letter appeared in the *Morning Advertiser*, the populist rival to the Tory *Times*. Addressed to the Lord Mayor and signed by the Liverpool Police Commissioner, it accused Mrs Fraser (Greene) of being an imposter and of perpetrating fraud. The letter, and the public outcry which followed it, prompted the Lord Mayor to call for a Commission of Inquiry.

At this point John Curtis entered the story, and technology joined fabulation and ideology in effecting further twists to the tale. Curtis was a reporter for *The Times,* called in to report the testimony given at the inquiry. He had attended Mrs Fraser's initial appearance and appeal before the Lord Mayor on 18 August when she was accompanied by Captain Greene (not recorded as her husband at this time) and a lady with whom she was allegedly staying. Curtis is believed to have reconstructed an account of Mrs Fraser's interview with the Lord Mayor from what *The Times,* in a disclaimer which leads into its news report the next day, described as 'a statement necessarily confused and incoherent'.[1] His news story of her account contains excerpts taken verbatim from the exaggerated and fictionalised version of the shipwreck, captivity and rescue, with its unsubstantiated tales of savagery and cannibalism, which had been published in both *The Times* and the *Courier* under her name and dated 'Liverpool 2 July, 1837'. Other London, provincial, and colonial papers soon followed Curtis's lead and published his

Times account as a true record of her testimony. Ironically, history records that Curtis's reporting skills allowed him to publish the news and the colonial press to pick up and distribute the story almost at once, since he was the inventor of a method of shorthand, published under the title *Stenography Simplified or Shorthand Made Simple* in 1835.[2] But this was not the case. His 'verbatim newspaper report' is a fictional invention, plagiarised from the sensational account prepared for public consumption before Mrs Fraser's arrival in London. Further, although it is by no means certain, it appears likely that Curtis was not the inventor of courtroom stenography, as has been claimed. The National Union Catalogue lists the author of *Stenography Simplified* as 'the Reverend John Curtis, Shorthand writer' in an entry separate from that for John Curtis, author of *The Shipwreck of the Stirling Castle*. On the basis of this conflicting evidence, bibliographic librarians at the British Museum are of the opinion that the two John Curtises may be different men.[3] This is an example of historical inference which has led to even further confusions within the historical reconstructions.

Curtis's press report of 19 August 1837 concludes with a statement from Captain Greene attesting to the fact that Mrs Fraser was 'not mistress of a farthing' and a comment from the Lord Mayor, stating, 'I shall most willingly receive contributions for her benefit, and I am sure that the call will be soon answered. I never heard of anything so truly dreadful in all my experience.' His comments have an even greater (albeit ironic) resonance for contemporary readers, given the hindsight of history and the benefit of further research. At the time, however, neither his veracity nor his reputation was called into question. By the time the leaked letter from the Liverpool Police Commissioner was published in the *Morning Advertiser* a month later, the Lord Mayor of London had collected a sizeable sum of money and was risking political embarrassment. Perhaps to rescue himself from the potentially damaging situation, he cleverly placed the bulk of monies collected (some five hundred and fifty pounds) into a trust for the three Fraser children left in the care of the Minister at Stromness. Curtis continued to report the event for *The Times* and later summarised the whole series of events in *The Shipwreck of the Stirling Castle*. This pseudo-history/defence justifies Eliza against charges of immorality, misrepresentation and fraud. It even suggests that the citizens of Sydney were to blame for her premature marriage to Captain Greene, due to their lack of sympathy for her cause.

This charge drew an angry response from the editor of the *Sydney Gazette*, who responded in an editorial dated 25 January 1838. There he reminded readers of 'the brutal tortures of bloodthirsty savages to the north of NSW', accused Eliza of 'inexcusable ingratitude in concealing the kindness she met with in Sydney', and labelled Greene a liar. He ended by claiming that the unfortunate situation was 'injurious to the national character', by which he presumably meant the character of his readers, the transported Britons now settled in New South Wales.[4] There were aspects of Mrs Fraser's time in Sydney and later in Liverpool and London which would cause a rift in alliances between the emerging middle-class citizenry in Sydney and in London. The rift supplied the colonial residents of Sydney with an identity separate from their brethren at home. When their generosity was unfairly challenged by criticism in the London press, colonists could find reasons to fault this 'innocent victim'. Her 'premature' marriage to Greene would be seen as a breach in public morality (marrying after less than a year of widowhood) and cast doubt on her character. Mrs Fraser's status as a woman could have a variety of consequences.

This final phase of the Sydney story is interesting in the light of Benedict Anderson's analysis of the role of newspapers in the production of national identity and the rise of bourgeois life. Among the bourgeois colonial population of Sydney, Mrs Fraser's reputation was in ruins. In press reports, editors denounced the ungrateful woman. She had overstepped the bounds of feminine respectability, broken the middle-class conventions of manners and morality and, in not reporting the kindness and hospitality of the locals, had cast aspersions on the national character. Michael Alexander details these events in a chapter of his history entitled 'Publicly Exposed'.

I want to suggest that what needed to be exposed was not the reputation of Eliza Fraser, but the motivations which maintained public and political interest in her story. Even at the time of its occurrence, little of this narrative was about Eliza Fraser Greene. Rather it was about regulating relations of race, class and gender; maintaining the dominant ideologies of colonialism, Christianity and Victorian morality; and extending the debates between Tories, Whigs and Radicals concerning gender and racial divisions and hierarchies. In addition, it aided in the evolution of a sense of an identity separate from England for the emerging colony of New South Wales.

The Shipwreck of the Stirling Castle

Curtis's book becomes the official account of the event and a reference point for future commentators. It contains what is reputed to be the authentic testimony of all known survivors, including that of Mrs Fraser, John Baxter, Robert Darge, Robert Hodge and Joseph Corallis. The book is ostensibly written as an apology for Eliza Fraser (and a defence of the Tory Lord Mayor). Eliza Fraser, as a character in the drama, comes to occupy her position within an emerging cult of true womanhood. Through Curtis's constructions of her character and the contexts of her life, one can trace larger debates about human nature which contributed to the emergence of the Victorian middle class.

At the time of the publication of Curtis's text, the press was full of Chartist debates about how to improve the 'worthiness' of working-class men, so that the vote might be secured on their behalf, and the duty of middle-class wives to maintain 'civility' in the home. Middle-class reformers stressed women's purity and their 'finer' qualities of sentiment. As the voices of middle-class women and both male and female members of the working class began to be heard in the public sphere in the 1830s in relation to emancipist and economic debates, women came to be associated with emotion and sentiment. A number of scholars have studied the 'cult of sensibility' and its relation to shifts in the way gendered subjectivity evolved in the nineteenth century.[5] They argue that throughout the eighteenth century these qualities of sensibility were said to mark the civility of the 'man of feeling' who had served as a model of moral virtue. In the shift from the romantic to the Victorian era, the idea that Man was essentially benevolent and sympathetic gave way to Man defined by logic and reason, a definition which eventually eroded the sentimental image and the 'man of feeling' as a type. As 'civilisation' expanded to encompass the working class at home and the 'savages' abroad, new fears about social and moral control emerged. Within these changing historical contexts, the 'man of sentiment' gave way to the 'man of reason'; optimism yielded to uneasiness; and the benevolence which had been extended to the Noble Savage contracted into fear and distrust of the savage barbarian, his violence and passion pitted against the measure of British civility. Sensibility, passion and excess gradually became equated with women and, by extension, with the body, the lower orders and the savages. The bourgeois man of reason gradually distanced himself from the interior, domestic, private space of women, at the same time as the middle class delineated its distance from the rabble of the working class. Within bourgeois thought there occurred dissociation between public reason, properly exercised by men, and private emotion, properly exercised by women. At the same time, bourgeois civilisation continued to pride itself on its sensitivity – the basis for its humanitarianism, its ethics and morality, in other words, its sense of being 'civilised'. So, the signification for woman, or the feminine aspects of bourgeois culture, slid between associations with the 'higher self' – with civility, sensibility and humanitarianism – and the 'lower self' – with the body, excessive passion, deviance and brutality. The place of sentiment was negotiated within larger movements for social change. Reason, the superior quality of mind, was called upon to rein in the feminine emotions and finer sentiments of the heart, which could be overcome by passion (and linked to the 'lower orders'). Middle-class men were called upon to protect women – 'courageously' – against the vices to which they might so easily fall prey.

Curtis's defence of Eliza Fraser positions the woman on the border between public and private spheres, reason and sentiment, middle-class morality and working-class decadence, civilisation and barbarity. In a construction similar to Rousseau's Enlightenment view of the nature of women,

Mrs Fraser is represented as morally and sexually weak but capable of inspiring men toward moral advancement. Her ordeal in 'captivity' serves as a lesson concerning the barbarities to which Man is capable of descending. The 'captivity' allows bourgeois culture to celebrate its own humanitarianism over a debased life of savagery; Mrs Fraser's body becomes a site which provokes feeling and empathy, emotions which ground an ethics of social control. Her story demonstrates how Man (a category which includes woman, but always with a difference) who exists in a pre-ordained, divine state of nature can overcome the disordered, unfeeling, brutalised state of nature embodied in black (and also working-class) bodies.[6] The codes of gender and race here provide the West with an ongoing sense of its own cultural identity against the rest of the world.

In his introduction to the book, Curtis reports that he is sorry to have to detail the sufferings and hardships of a woman known to be 'the fairest, the most sensitive, and the kindest . . . the best gift God bestowed on man'. His idealisation refers to Woman in general and Eliza in particular. This was the woman, we remember, whom the mutinous seaman Youlden described in his later article for an American journal as 'the most profane, artful, wicked woman that ever lived; indeed coming very near my idea of the Devil'.[7] Curtis has specific objectives in mind in describing her thus. They are not ostensibly related to larger social movements of the time, but are implicated within them all the same. He maintains that his purpose is 'to convey a moral lesson and useful instruction' in which he will confirm and corroborate the facts already before the public concerning Eliza's innocence. He intends as well to detail the 'chivalrous conduct of a British officer, and the brave men under his command who . . . volunteered their services to rescue a suffering lady from a horrible captivity, as well as her companions in misfortune'. He concludes that his aims are sixfold: to convey a moral tale and useful instruction; to justify Mrs Fraser's cause; to tell the story of the wreck, captivity, and rescue; to encourage missionary work among the natives; to promote emigration; and to enhance ethnographic knowledge. He says nothing of the need to save the Lord Mayor from political embarrassment. To his suggestion that the text might serve as a stimulus for missionary work among the natives, 'the sons and daughters of ignorance and cruelty',[8] one might respond: 'Aye, there's the rub'.

Curtis's book is a wildly polyphonic text, embedded in the discourses of imperialism, Christianity and colonialism. Throughout the text, Curtis engages the reader in a spirited defence of Eliza Fraser. His defence serves to mask the wider social, political and ideological implications of this first contact between the innocent, saintly, white female victim and a savage otherness at the margins of Empire. In addition, in going against the Liberal tide of public opinion in regard to racial attitudes, the text opens up a space of conflict which will be exploited in the decades to come by those less sympathetic to the interests of indigenous peoples. Curtis's position in regard to the natives is ambivalent. On the one hand, he refers to them as part of God's family which might be redeemed through the humanitarian impulses of the missions; on the other, he places them in the zero order of the Great Chain of Being and warns of the need for their surveillance and social control. His defence promotes both humanitarian theories of equality and the natural science theories of inferior and superior racial types. The main text attempts to reconstruct events which occurred on the island by telling Eliza's story, corroborated by selected testimony of other witnesses. Throughout the text Curtis assumes the role of a privileged narrator, the colonising subject entitled to speak on behalf of others (women and natives), although he can hardly be said to be 'in control' of this dense, polysemic text. He speaks on Mrs Fraser's behalf as a representative of the universal imperial British family. His narrative position and the textual devices he employs help to establish for the reader the sincerity of Eliza Fraser, a belief in the authenticity of her recollected experiences, and an overall credibility for her tale. Textual strategies include the presentation of a series of allegedly verbatim accounts from witnesses, references to official reports, and reproductions of newspaper accounts. In addition, the main text contains a sprinkling of religious aphorisms, hymns, prayers, poems and ballads which provide some Regency melodrama, some Victorian sentiment, and a firm Christian and ethical stance for the reader. At the same time, extensive footnotes create a subtext of rationality, through which Curtis addresses the fields of navigation, emigration and the legal system, as well as presenting a wealth of anthropological, geological and scientific data. Between these two textual spaces there is a negotiation between doubt and certainty, between Eliza's apparently fabulous story of captivity and the verities of scientific truth. The text utilises a number of narrative modes, including those of testimony and evidence, debate, description, exhortation, the scientific treatise, the diary, the epistolary and the gothic novel.

The narrative proceeds in fits and starts. It also succumbs to a series of narrative crises. The promise of new disclosures and proofs concerning Mrs Fraser's veracity and innocence of wrongdoing is constantly subverted by tangential textual delays which occur in the footnotes and all but take over the page. These diversions occur particularly before the disclosure of possible evidence of rape or cannibalism, hinted at but never quite proven and said to have been perpetrated by the natives who exist within the 'zero order of civilisation'. An irony here is that the scientific verities are wildly inaccurate. Curtis's description of Fraser Island Aborigines, for example, which he includes in a lengthy appendix, appears to have been lifted from an 1827 ethnography of the Eora peoples located around Port Jackson; his descriptions and illustrations of ritual cannibalism and other burial practices are derived from sailors' tales of the South Pacific, possibly brought back by

Captain Greene, Eliza's new husband. The second half of the book contains a narrative of another wreck, the *Charles Eaton*, including the illustration of the forty-five skulls, mentioned previously, displayed around a totem by the natives of Cape York Peninsula in the far north of the continent.

The Shipwreck of the Stirling Castle serves primarily as a defence of the Lord Mayor's actions in relation to the subscription campaign on behalf of Eliza Fraser Greene. This function alerts us to the subtle relationship between the quest for narrative order and the representation of political order. After surveying all the evidence, Curtis turns finally to the woman's character and his judgements concerning her actions. He concludes that the woman's weakness led her to conceal certain facts about her premature marriage and the kindness she had received in Sydney prior to her departure. He relates that 'she is fully aware that she has sinned against strict etiquette, and been guilty of an indiscrete secrecy'. But, he concludes, no matter what her behaviour, even if 'volatile and gay . . . evincing the most unblushing and barefaced depravity', still, she is a mother, with responsibility for her destitute children.[9] He praises the Mayor's wisdom in agreeing to let the appeal proceed on the condition that the monies raised be transferred to the Minister of Stromness in trust to the Fraser children. Mrs Fraser Greene received only enough to enable her return to the Orkney Islands. The final section, entitled 'British Benevolence: the Fraser Fund', reproduces details of monies received and dispersed by the Lord Mayor – some £553, of which £50 was dispensed to Mrs Fraser. In Curtis's final words: 'Our history exhibits not only a detail of the barbarity of the heathen, but also the benevolence of the Christian.'[10] The text closes with an affirmation of the benevolent nature of the English people existing within an ordered, sane and just moral universe.

Curtis and Empire

The text is connected to Empire in diverse ways. It was published in 1838, a year after the founding of the British and Foreign Aboriginal Protection Society and the same year as the Sydney-based Aboriginal Protection Society came into existence. The latter established the term by which indigenous peoples would be uniformly categorised as 'Aborigines' and through which their affairs would be managed.[11] These societies arose as a result of the emancipatory humanitarian rhetoric and widespread political activities of the 1830s. They were to provide a forum through which Christian intellectuals and civic leaders would act as teachers and improvers of their fellow men and women. In time, this humanitarian rhetoric of the Enlightenment, which called for humane treatment of indigenous, colonised peoples, would give way to the dominance of a scientifically supported ideology of biological determinism. The conservative calls which Curtis makes in 1838 to the builders of Empire would be heeded in succeeding decades, in part in Mrs Fraser's name.

In Australia, the first official expedition to Fraser Island and surrounding coastal areas was mounted in 1842, officially to explore the land and its resources and to bring back the runaway convicts whom Mrs Fraser had encountered. It resulted in the first official survey of the land for white settlement, the European naming of landmarks (including 'Fraser Island') and the demarcation of possible sites for capital expansion of the pastoral and timber industries. What followed brought about the Queensland settlement wars of the 1850s, white colonisation, mission reserves from the 1870s, illness, death and the widespread dispersal of remaining indigenous peoples in the area as well as knowledge of their pre-contact language and culture.

Although these events are not directly connected to the shipwreck of the *Stirling Castle*, nor to Curtis's account, the dynamics of power and the powers of representation evident in the *Stirling Castle* phenomena would be evoked again. The settlement wars of the 1850s in Queensland, for example, brought the indigenous peoples and the invading population of settlers into closer contact and provoked more overt violence and savagery (on the part of whites) than the mythic captivity stories could ever countenance (on the part of Aborigines). Although details of this conflict have been suppressed for a over a century, recent histories like those of Henry Reynolds, Kay Saunders and Ray Evans indicate that the 1850s were a decade of forceful, violent, and for a time highly successful, black resistance to the encroaching land usage of the white settlers in the Wide Bay and Cooloola area. European colonisation, aided by the Native Police, poison, horses, savage dogs and the gun, secured control for the white settlers, despite strong, if sporadic, Aboriginal resistance and the inconsistent humanitarian convictions of government authorities and Christian missionaries. It was estimated that for every instance of native violence, the settlers retaliated tenfold. Violence culminated in the fearsome massacre of Aborigines by white settlers on 27 October 1857, after an Aboriginal attack which resulted in the murder of nine members of a family named Fraser (*sic,* a wry coincidence) at an inland station. According to Raymond Evans:

> This flash point for massive retaliation was not usually ignited simply by Aborigines killing a disparate number of white individuals, such as shepherds [despoiling their waterholes and dispersing their flocks over native lands]. Rather, it was induced after they had struck down members of that social unit which was virtually identified with the coming of civilisation into the wilds: the European family unit. The themes invoked here of ravished femininity and outraged innocence acted upon the settlers as a goad for revenge which would be pursued with a passion that even transcended their passion for land.[12]

Amidst the passion for revenge and the passion for land, ravaged femininity serves as a reason for a massive, irrational orgy of slaughter. That orgy displaces the domestic ideologies of feminine innocence and disguises the depths of the settlers' capacity for violence prompted by their un-pre-possessing lust for land.

Later, Christianity would supply another reason. The mission movement, so favoured by Curtis, found little financial backing in the Wide Bay area of Queensland until the 1870s, and no conversion success at any time. The first churchman to show interest was John Dunmore Lang, a Presbyterian minister and a sincere, if inconsistent, advocate of both colonial agricultural expansion and Aboriginal protection. (Coincidentally, Lang had sponsored the emigration of sixty families brought to Australia in an earlier sailing of Captain Fraser's *Stirling Castle* in 1832.) In 1838 Lang sent an advance party of twenty missionaries to Moreton Bay, but there was insufficient financial backing for his proposed mission and little interest in his agricultural scheme.[13] It was not until the 1870s, with the advent of the timber industry on Fraser Island and frequent outbreaks of 'violence and savagery' on the part of both the settlers and the native people, that a mission settlement was established, largely through the humanitarian efforts of the religious missionary societies. The mission movement would prove hard to defend, however, since it lacked the material or human resources to sustain itself. In time, Aboriginal numbers dwindled significantly due to illness, disease, alcohol, poison, and frontier violence. There was not enough altruistic sentiment for their plight nor money in the public coffers to turn the tide of benign neglect. The movement faltered not to be revived again until 1897. Then the Protector of the Aborigines, with the backing of the government and assistance of the local police, used his powers to 'muster' up the last, debilitated, opium-crazed and venereal-diseased natives from the streets of Maryborough and moved them to a mission reserve on Fraser Island. Two years later he would make the mission 'the one great central permanent aboriginal home for all South Queensland . . . [thus solving] "that Aboriginal problem which has baffled Australian Governments and private philanthropists from the earliest period to the present time" '.[14] Within four years, this effort too would be abandoned. In 1904 the remaining 218 Aborigines were sent to mainland reserves and penal colonies. Only two families were left on the island, thought to be all that remained of the estimated 2000 to 3000 natives who were living in the Fraser Island and Cooloola region at the time of the *Stirling Castle* wreck.

An array of contradictory and ambivalent motives and impulses governed colonial interventions into native life. A humanitarian concern to respect traditional Aboriginal customs could be coupled with a desire to Christianise the natives; greed for land acquisition with the desire to compensate them for the loss of their land; sponsorship of the missions with the impulse to punish natives for their incursions into settlers' properties; outrage at white violence with a fear of native retaliation; a desire for access to the native women with the fear of contagion. Eventually, but by no means inevitably,[15] the conservative ideologies emerging in Britain after the Indian Mutiny of 1859 and the punitive impulses coupled with the increasing strength of the settlers in Queensland came to govern the actions of colonial authorities and replaced the more altruistic, humanitarian or Christianising motives of the early mission movement. These subsequent events, however, have little to do specifically with the shipwreck of the *Stirling Castle*, although recent historians and a documentary film-maker (whose approaches will be discussed later in the book) have linked them together in a developmental sequence of events leading to the decline and dispersal of Fraser Island Aborigines. The recent reconstructions which take account of a racist Queensland history and the dispersal of the declining Aboriginal population cite Eliza Fraser and the shipwreck as the point of origin for the later events. The Eliza Fraser story serves as an easy reference point of origin for contemporary historians sympathetic to Aboriginal perspectives on Australian history and the nineteenth- and twentieth-century history of frontier violence. But each of these subsequent developments has its own specific historical context, its own local contestations and shifting networks of power.

The Eliza Fraser story continued to surface from time to time throughout the nineteenth century in both England and Australia. In the 1850s in England a salacious ballad, 'Eliza and her Black Man', circulated in the popular press.[16] It tells of the lustful obsession of Eliza for a black man, ugley (*sic*) as the devil's brother, and her insatiable love for 'his diddle um de'. In this ballad Eliza returns with her black man to Australia after a trial by the local Mayor. Her allegedly opportunistic desire for financial gain is transformed into insatiable lust for a black man at the expense of the working class. The ballad depicts the opportunistic black man as deriving social and economic privileges in excess of what he 'deserves' in relation to the labouring poor; this sentiment is not totally absent from white racial prejudices in some quarters of Australian society today.

> O he gets lots of tin they say
> sometimes 11s a day
> Four times as much as an englishman's pay
> is given away to the black man
> They can have both women & wine
> while a poor mechanic remains behind
> For he may beg till he is blind
> and not get as much as the black man
> She could not be reclaimed of course,
> he feeds her on steak and oyster sauce
> To leave his meet [*sic*] she'd feel the loss,
> for Eliza loved her black man.

The ballad revels in an easy slippage between libidinal and political categories of desire, in which both the woman and her 'captor' are harnessed into
class-based projections of otherness. Although the references to Eliza Fraser
are oblique and indirect, the ballad is a rare nineteenth-century instance of a
specific implication of a sexual relationship between Mrs Fraser and her
black captors. It excites working-class sympathies against Mrs Fraser by
detailing her sexual debasement as a result of her contact with primitive
cultures. She becomes lustful, brutish, wily – like 'them'. This type of ballad,
which traces the debasement of a middle-class woman from respectability
into working-class stereotypes of animality and physicality, was one of the
most popular forms of mass cultural pleasure in the early nineteenth century. Not only does it give the working class an entrance into the discourse
and a way of negotiating power relations: it also offers unbounded pleasures
of titillation and salaciousness at the expense of the middle class (but also of
women and 'natives' in general).[17] This rendition of the story, through por-
nographic ballad, allows the popular memory to express what is repressed in
other accounts, creating a space within popular culture for voices and desires
otherwise absent from dominant ideological accounts.

Foundational Fictions

In the nineteenth century the Eliza Fraser story emerged as a liminal narrative, that is, a narrative arising from first contact between Europeans and
the indigenous people, Europeans and the foreign land. These liminal stories
of first contact, which in Australia would include shipwreck, captivity and
convict escape, could be said to have several important, although discontinuous, effects on the Empire, England and Australia. In the first place, they
occurred on a previously unexplored boundary which, at the time of the
event, had no 'meaning', no prior fix within a Western discourse. Secondly,
they took shape not only within situated narratives which attempted to
understand and interpret the event for a colonial audience but also, and
perhaps more significantly, as performing acts of Empire and nation.

The phenomenological investigations of Paul Carter call for a rethinking of
the possible meanings which can be ascribed to liminal, 'first-contact'
events.[18] Carter attempts to imagine such events as embodied performances
of reciprocity and mutual incomprehension which presented a plurality of
meanings to the actors involved. Although he works primarily with
explorers' journals and narrative accounts, his speculations remind readers
that there are irreducible dimensions inherent in all first-contact experiences
which cannot be contained within the representations of history, text or
story. Western narratives obscure the multiple realities inherent in the event
itself. They reduce it to textual and visible cues, which are then given meaning within a Western (and monologic) episteme. The experiential subject-

to-subject relationship of actors in a mutual exchange becomes transformed into one of subject to object. This objectification is an inevitable outcome of narratives represented as 'captivity' or those experienced within and then written from a colonising frame of mind, where any notion of inter-subjective reciprocity between white and Aboriginal actors cannot be coun-tenanced. Through newspaper articles, oral histories and local legends these sensationalised stories bring the other into being, incite the popular imagin-ation and provide initial accounts which contribute to constructions of difference which emerged within the colony.

'First-contact' events in the colonies frequently generated greater popular, political and scientific interest in England, where they helped to define the whiteness of Empire, than in their actual locations, where they could strike terror into the hearts and minds of a small band of insecure settlers. Through re-creation in popular forms and historical accounts, the narratives contrib-uted to constructions of bourgeois consciousness, of civility and order, of popular and high culture, of public and private life and the divisions between them which helped Britain to provide a model of social life for the colonial world. The 'first-contact' event, transformed into text, helped to underwrite the imperial and colonial creation of new knowledges, locations and peoples defined in the multiple interests of Empire.

In the colonies, these liminal stories of first contact could have more direct, pragmatic consequences. In relation to the Eliza Fraser story, the early news-paper accounts in the colony, as in England, marked the beginnings of epistemic dominance of the West over the indigenous peoples of Fraser Island. This dominance muted Aboriginal subjectivity and denied Aboriginal knowledges, and its effects continue to influence race relations and relations of power within national life today. At the time, these stories also provided readers with a site of terror which threatened to expose the fragility of col-onial control. 'Captivity' narratives, however, had further political conse-quences.[19] Through rescue expeditions, they made possible the first mappings of the land, producing a new Western geography, a social pro-duction of mastery over the threatening environment. Official governmental and academic interest followed in the wake of these historical events and narrative reconstructions. The governmental interest concerned colonial policies and practices. Knowledge of the shipwreck and captivity led to further geographic expeditions, observations of Aboriginal life, missionary work, penal surveillance and punishments, as well as the institution of social, ethical and moral values. These all furthered the illusion of mastery for the white settlers, and changed the character of colonial life. These more academic activities were of interest in England where new knowledges prompted other academic, historical and ethnographic interest, and fed information into broader Western academic classification systems and tax-onomies (natural history, philology, ethnography, cartography). In both locations, the stories stemmed the fears and insecurities of British identity and control through textual and political measures of dominance. They set in place the mechanisms of surveillance for the indigenous population, the appropriation of local skills, the repression of white violence. The layers of textual repression, what is unspoken in the texts, allow writers to transfer their own violent habits, their propensity for drinking and illicit sex, for murderous impulses and unspeakable acts of violence, on to the 'natives'. Taken together, the effects of these crisis events created, maintained and reinforced hierarchies of race, class and gender within English and local contexts, but they also challenged them. Although contested both 'at home' and abroad, these events also served to legitimise the 'natural superiority' of Western rule *and* provided the structures, ideologies and institutions of power utilised to constitute new nation-states.

With regard to the Eliza Fraser story, the various versions of captivity in the English and colonial press aided contestations within England and Australia in relation to human nature and the nature of women, the control of deviance within the 'lower orders' as well as colonial constructions of race. As an object of representation, the woman slid between idealised and debased representations within the category of the feminine; actions of the convicts and resistant crew became instances of the irrational degradations of the lower classes to which a white middle-class society was thought to be susceptible; while the indigenous people were taken up and constructed in the space between Enlightenment philosophies, Christian humanitarianism and biologically determined forms of racist discourse. In the period between 1836 and 1838, Mrs Fraser's story had more relevance and resonated more effectively within an English context than in the Australian colonies as it became enmeshed in the political conflict between the ascendant Whigs and less than secure Tories. In England, through the press reports and the Lord Mayor's Inquiry, her story helped to extend principles of Victorian middle-class morality as it defined proper femininity; it regulated differences within the unruly categories of deviance with respect to the lower classes, mutineer and convict behaviours; and it aided the Conservative planter and settler interests, furthering the imperialist politics of control over colonised peoples.

The discourses around the event worked primarily as propagations of knowledge and productions of power. News reports constructed knowledge as truth. They also attempted to position readers to receive the accounts in certain ways and in accord with previously established, although discontinuous and contradictory, networks of power. There were connections and contradictions between the historical accounts, 'authentic' first-person narratives, media reconstructions and differing responses to Mrs Fraser's narratives both in the colony and in England. They are all rendered through the politics of representation and take on new possibilities for meaning when referenced within the first history of the event, *The Shipwreck of the Stirling Castle*.

CHAPTER 4

Policing the Borders of Civilisation:
Colonial Man and His Others

Mrs Fraser's testimony to the Commission of Inquiry, reported in *The Times*, as well as her interviews with John Curtis, reported in *The Shipwreck of the Stirling Castle*, become forums for her defence. They, in turn, are dependent on and regulated by notions of British civility and feminine propriety. To this end John Curtis's text employs a number of textual devices which, in effect, police the borders of civilisation. Those devices, and the ways in which the symbolic Woman functions to uphold dominant systems of representation which constitute the British Self against notions of the primitive Other, will be the focus of this chapter.[1] Through them the colonial writer endeavours to construct a set of coherent representations out of the confused and incoherent circumstances which presaged Mrs Fraser's entrance on to this particular stage of history. They provide a way in which the West comes to know (and not know) itself.

Textual Constructions

In *The Shipwreck of the Stirling Castle* these devices are both visual and linguistic. In preparation for the publication, Curtis commissioned a series of nine illustrations specifically prepared for the volume. They include portraits of Mrs Fraser, significantly wearing a widow's cap (Figure 7), and John Baxter, views of Hobart Town and a map of the central coast of New South Wales, and lush line drawings of several key events. The line drawings depict Mrs Fraser perched precariously on a rocky cliff face in search of water for her husband; Mrs Fraser witnessing the the spearing of Captain Fraser in the back (Figure 6); and Mrs Fraser's rescue by a naked native and a semi-clothed white man from a scene of devilish revelry (Figure 8). The scenes depict a narrative of woman's devotion to her husband, his murder by duplicitous savages, and her miraculous rescue from a fate worse than death.

MRS FRASER,

Widow of Capt. Fraser.

Figure 7 'Mrs. Fraser.' In John Curtis, *The Shipwreck of the Stirling Castle*, 1838. By courtesy Fryer Library, University of Queensland.

Figure 8   'Mrs. Fraser's escape from the savages.' In John Curtis, *The Shipwreck of the Stirling Castle*, 1838.
By courtesy Fryer Library, University of Queensland.

The rhetorical strategies the text employs extend these themes, particularly in regard to constructions of Mrs Fraser. They include an emphasis on woman's character as frail, emotional, sensitive and in need of protection; the use of indirect witness to remove this particular woman, Mrs Fraser, from scenes of excess; and poetic allusions to maternal sanctity; as well as a number of devices which establish differences between native and white women, convict and military rescuers, proper and improper marriages. These, in turn, call upon notions of civility and barbarism, normative behaviour and deviance, reason and the instincts, sanity and madness. The effect is to produce a category – 'We the People', or, more specifically, the British race – within which the reader can identify: a 'monolithic, unified and powerful "us"'.[2] The 'we' might be fragmented in terms of its political affiliations, ethnic, class and gender divisions, or the location of different speakers within different sites of Empire. But the modes of address employed in Curtis's text assume an audience united in the assurance that they formed a part of a superior race against the illusion of a lower order of primitive people. The ways in which Curtis's text constructs the category 'we' centres on its regard for Mrs Fraser, a woman in need of rescuing from the category of deviance to one of civility within the dominant bourgeois norms of British society in the 1830s.

The presenting problem that Eliza Fraser represents to the reporter and the public in 1837–8 is one of her veracity. The public eagerly consumed

press reports of her ordeal which moved them to contribute a handsome sum
to her welfare . . . until they were challenged with their own gullibility. Were
they taken in by an imposter? The doubt produced a political situation which
resulted in an inquiry. Mrs Fraser was put on trial. Her stories met with
suspicion; her self-representation was cast into doubt. Her 'premature' marriage to Alexander John Greene became a matter of public scrutiny; her
private life, a matter for public debate. This turn of events becomes an
occasion for the regulation of sex, race and class within institutional networks of colonial power: the courts and the press. Against charges that she
was a liar, an imposter, an immoral woman and possibly mad (all forms of
feminine excess beyond the bounds of propriety), Curtis's defence struggles
to construct her as truthful, sincere, moral and sane. Her ordeal is transformed into a performance of femininity; her sexuality comes under surveillance. The courts and the press engage not in a repression but a
production of sexuality, a textual construction of Woman. Discourse establishes the category of the middle-class female through its constructions of
difference. In this case, these constructions include her gender difference
from her husband, her class difference from the mutinous crew, her racial
difference from the 'natives', and her gender and racial difference from the
indigenous women. In each category there are certain prescribed behaviours
and prohibitions which define her as a proper female and a worthy citizen of
Empire, when measured against the Others who stand in opposition to her.

The Swoon of Forgetfulness

Curtis's text gives evidence of an array of textual strategies. These include
occasional swoons of forgetfulness and indirect witness on the part of Mrs
Fraser, and frequent reminders to readers of her maternal devotion.
His defence is a defence of her proper femininity, her wifely fidelity, her
maternal sacrifice against charges of her deception, immorality and maternal
neglect. Although she had been married to Alexander John Greene for seven
months prior to the inquiry and perhaps another year prior to the publication of the book, Curtis unfailingly refers to her as 'Mrs Fraser', even when
he considers her culpability for her 'premature marriage' and her duplicity in
representing herself as a 'poor widow woman without a farthing'. The text
performs a double operation of both alluding to and removing Mrs Fraser
from scenes of excess (including a widow's excess). In relation to her time on
Fraser Island, it makes reference to her sexual experiences and scenes of
witnessed savagery; but it carefully distances the woman from these events
by alluding to the fact that in each (suspicious) circumstance she fell into a
'swoon of insensibility'. The following, which accompanies Curtis's descrip-

tion of the death of Captain Fraser in a footnote to the text, is typical: '[Mrs Fraser] felt her brain swim, and a sound in her head like the ringing of bells. . . . [She] fell to the ground completely petrified and bereft of sense' (148). Descriptions such as these occur at the time of the reported birth and drowning of her child in the longboat, the death by spearing of the Captain, the torture and burning at the stake of Brown and another shipwreck victim, and the beheading and eating of the body of John Major. These events are featured in the sensational accounts which feed the public craving for proof of native depravity, which, in turn, supplement the conviction of Western superiority. They are also events which no 'lady' should witness. These instances in the text of the 'swoon of insensibility' work in contradictory directions: they juxtapose the sensibilities of a frail and delicate white female against the tortures of a primitive and unfeeling race; they supply fantasies of possible depravity amongst the 'lower orders' which titillates the reader's imagination; and they fuel the reader's desire to know 'what really happened'.

Indirect Witness

Reconstructions of Mrs Fraser's story which circulated in London prior to the Lord Mayor's Inquiry contained allusions to white cannibalism and to the near assault on the white woman by native (or convict) men. Both of these extraordinary, excessive events are carefully regulated in Curtis's text. One strategy employed by Curtis is to mute these aspects of the story by alluding to them indirectly, not through Eliza's direct account but through the voices of other, credible male witnesses. So, it is Baxter, the second mate and Mrs Fraser's nephew, who testified at the inquiry that the crew threatened to 'draw lots' if the Captain did not pull ashore. Curtis avoids entirely the mention of tales which circulated in Sydney of cannibalism amongst the surviving mutinous crew members, although he alludes to instances of such practices amongst survivors of other shipwrecks in the footnotes.[3] What is made clear in his text, however, is that in a choice between eating their mates and starving to death, the crew would choose cannibalism, but this crisis is averted – the threat of cannibalism (rather than the practice in this instance) is invoked as a strategy of power over the irrational Captain. An altogether different moral choice is prescribed for Mrs Fraser when confronted by the possibility of a sexual encounter with 'the Chief'. This is a 'fate worse than death', which cannot be countenanced. The text can flirt with the threat of miscegenation, but the actual act must never occur. In *The Shipwreck of the Stirling Castle*, Baxter and later Lieutenant Otter, rather than Mrs Fraser, allude to Mrs Fraser's bodily (not 'sexual') sufferings, the details of which are suppressed. Her scars, those bodily inscriptions of 'barbarous cruelty' which 'she will forever bear on her person', are referred to on three occasions by Curtis and indirectly through Lieut. Otter's letter to his cousin, describing his first sight of her at the time of rescue, quoted in Chapter 1. These allusions, like those promoted in the sensationalised captivity narrative, strike pity and terror into the heart of the reader, evoke sympathy for the innocent victim, and uphold the belief in the superiority of the white race.

Mrs Fraser's vulnerability as a woman and her expectation of protection from her husband are made clear in several sections of Curtis's text. In his presentation of her narrative, constructed out of several interviews in London and plagiarised from the Liverpool account, there are few direct quotations. They signal moments of crisis in the text, crises of identity for Mrs Fraser. The first occurs at the time of Mrs Fraser's reunion with her husband, perhaps ten days after she was separated from the male survivors. Upon sighting the Captain, who appeared in an exhausted state from his exertions and sought her help in carting wood, Mrs Fraser implores, 'Why did you leave me on the beach?' The query, which can be read as a sign of her vulnerability at having been left alone and also as a peevish reprimand to her husband from whom she would expect protection, signals for her a crisis of identity. How could she survive without the physical protection of her husband? The conversation presages the Captain's death, after which time punishments of her are said to increase. In Curtis's text, as in every other contemporary account, Mrs Fraser exclaims: 'Jesus of Nazareth, can I stand this?' (147), variants of which include the assertions 'I can bear/endure this no longer!' in the US captivity narrative and the *Tales of Travellers* account. The direct quotation, presented as a refrain in Western versions, locates her outside civil protection but not beyond the protections of Divine law. The symbolic relation of husband and wife was respected not only in Western society, but in Aboriginal society as well. Within Aboriginal society the symbolic relationship between Mrs Fraser and her husband would have afforded her status and protection. After his death, she had only religion for solace. Curtis reports that after the demise of the Captain, the 'heartless brutes' preyed upon her 'like bloodhounds', treating her with 'derision and mirth', laughing at her 'writhings and alarm'.[4] The text makes repeated but oblique references to Mrs Fraser's vulnerability to sexual assault at this time, references which explicitly detail native savagery but give evidence of a productive silence in relation to (white) female sexuality. They are further disguised in Curtis's narrative reconstruction:

> The unfortunate lady attempted to cast a veil over part of her sufferings, which in truth were the most revolting of all, and which were explained to us by Baxter, who was a frequent eye witness of them: but the same delicacy which restrained her tongue restrains our pen from describing them. The mere conception of pangs she must have endured, both bodily and mentally, strikes us with amazement that human nature could exist under them, and almost freezes our blood.[5]

The momentary lapse into sentiment metonymically links the Curtis narrative to the sensational accounts. It also links the sensibilities which Curtis and his readers must feel upon hearing the stories ('amazement . . . which almost freezes the blood') to those of Mrs Fraser herself (who it will be remembered was said to have been 'petrified and bereft of sense'). Curtis's rendition of this scene also incites further interest in the (imagined) details, suggesting miscegenation but not her possible rape by Bracefell, the mention of which remains a productive absence in his text. To reinforce Mrs Fraser's feminine respectability, Curtis quotes from a letter received by the relatives of Lieutenant Otter in which Otter refers to 'the unfortunate lady'. Otter reports that she 'was treated with as much cruelty as the rest. The savages having no regard for the *beau sexe*' (183). What this coy reference to feminine delicacy fails to disclose is that the others did not report their treatment as unnecessarily cruel or excessive. In fact, at least two survivors amongst the crew, Darge and Youlden, reported that they fell easily into local customs, did not offer resistance during a series of mimed interactions with the islanders, and were treated well. The Captain, first mate Brown and Mrs Fraser, on the other hand, who appear to have insisted on their superior status and resisted falling in with the customs and requests of the indigenous people, were more severely punished. An additional suggestion is that the seamen would have been accustomed to a rough life and thus were more adept at coping with the shipwreck situation, whereas Mrs Fraser and the officers of the ship were not. Within Victorian culture, sexual assaults on Mrs Fraser would have been the most heinous of all punishments in captivity, sufficient to cause mental imbalance, even madness. Lieutenant Otter's letter, like Curtis's history, disguises these dimensions, treating them with the delicacy demanded of the times, in keeping with the presumed greater sensitivity of the British race. Nonetheless, Otter's letter registers Mrs Fraser's unique situation as a woman, 'the *beau sexe*'. This oblique detail in the letter prompts Curtis to remark that Otter, 'her gallant deliverer', gives 'succinct details of her sufferings; and, as far as delicacy would permit, the insults she had undergone' (185). Feminine 'delicacy' surfaces as a cover and subterfuge for revelations of possible sexual assault no fewer than four times in Curtis's apologia.

Maternal Sanctity

Another rhetorical strategy employed in the text in the service of Empire is to construct Mrs Fraser within the realm of the Maternal. This requires that the text ignore the sensational accounts, accentuate her feminine behaviours, and place the events within a Christian framework, as tests to be overcome. This is accomplished with reference to Mrs Fraser's pregnancy and childbirth at sea, an event which features in Curtis's account with extensive authorial and tangential textual support. Her maternity and wifely devotion become the main props in a defence of her against charges of fraud, dishonesty and immorality. No reader could fail to sympathise with this grieving mother who had suffered such public indignities and personal grief.

As has been said, the first report of the birth at sea emerges in a postscript in an unknown hand appended to Mrs Fraser's third, sensational and exaggerated account, which she delivered to the police and the press upon her arrival in England with Captain Greene. In Curtis's text, Mrs Fraser's 'faithful narrative' repeats the circumspect evidence of the postscript childbirth verbatim, recording it as a first-hand account of what she had experienced.[6] This (dubious) confession of what should be a private and domestic event is accompanied with excessive materials, the supports of Victorian sentimentality, which supplement Curtis's construction of Mrs Fraser within the realm of the Maternal. First the narrator comments that Mrs Fraser 'can not account for the extraordinary vigour she was able to bear up under the severe calamity she was doomed to be exposed to' (130). He then relates how she fell into 'temporary insensibility', from which she recovered some time later, to find that the child had been drowned. Supplementary materials to this extraordinary event include a footnote which contains a copy of the poem 'On Captain Fraser's Child Born in a Boat', which had first appeared in the *Soldier's and Sailor's Magazine*, a hymn of deliverance, and a scriptural reference to Divine Providence. In addition, there is authorial praise for Mrs Fraser's 'extraordinary vigour' (a masculine attribute) explained with reference to her wifely duties and responsibilities: 'Perhaps the infirmities of her husband gave impetus to her exertions . . . [and her] hardships . . . divested her of the timidity and scrupulousness which are ever the characteristics of well-educated and delicate females'(132). This supposition is supplemented by another lengthy footnote; it contains stories of heroic wives caring for older invalided husbands, a further 'tribute of respect' for Mrs Fraser, and a poem, 'The Kindness of Women', by Thomas Haynes Bailey, an 'eloquent and gallant champion' whom 'no doubt the fair sex will shortly canonize' (133). Overdone? Without doubt. These wild and extensive digressions supplement a gap, an absence, a doubt in the form of woman who is thus rescued by her maternal femininity into an order of complementary sameness with men. A number of twentieth-century commentators on the event will refer to and further embellish details of Mrs Fraser's maternity, although not always with the reverence of John Curtis's text.

Policing Other Borders

Curtis's defence engages in a range of narrative operations to supplement the unsettled aspects of this historical event. These occur with reference to Mrs Fraser's sexuality, but also delineate difference across race, class and gender lines. In particular, the text distinguishes differences between 'native' women and white women (race and gender), convict rescuers and military officer rescuers (class), proper and improper marriages (Victorian morality), and English and Australian allegiances (national identity). The Eliza Fraser story, as taken up by the Lord Mayor's Inquiry, the press and Curtis's history, provides the opportunity for a further policing of these complex boundaries within a specific colonial context. In this regard, it is important to consider Mrs Fraser's story as a foundational fiction for Australia. It became a sensation within the colonial world because through it she was represented as the first white woman to encounter indigenous peoples in Australia and to tell her tale. That telling, in its diverse contexts, provided then, and continues to provide, a rather singular opportunity for the extension of colonial networks of power, the promulgation of knowledges and the inscriptions of desire.

Native and White Women

All aspects of the event in its textual, as well as social, manifestations posit an immense gap between colonisers and colonised peoples, between British and indigenous women, but also between free and convict women on the basis of both race and class. As we have seen, when females are invoked within categories of otherness they generally signify even greater deviations and excesses in the realm of barbarism or deviance. This was apparent in relation to representations of Indian squaws in the American version of the captivity narrative and its colonial magazine variants, in which the 'squaws' were deemed to be more cruel, more ugly and more debased than their 'masters'. It can also be demonstrated with reference to convict women, who were valued differently, subjected to greater surveillance and treated with far more suspicion than convict men in the convict system of New South Wales.[7] Within this historically determined set of racial and gender codes, 'native' women are assumed to be inferior to 'native' men, whom they served as their 'masters'; convict women more deviant and potentially disruptive than convict men. Yet, *all* women, white and native, were treated badly, in physical, sexual and psychological terms, by *some* men from both races and all social classes. At the same time, Curtis relates through Otter's testimony that, 'the native women . . . are utterly devoid of those tender sensibilities, which shed a halo around European females' (239). Here feminine delicacy is idealised as a way of celebrating Western superiority over the inferior orders by distancing Mrs Fraser's behaviours from those of the unfeeling native women.

The sensational accounts make a further distinction between the races, based on gender. In the American captivity narrative, as well as those published in *Tales of Travellers* and *Alexander's East India Magazine*, Mrs Fraser, just prior to being taken by the 'Chief', implores the brother of her cruel (squaw) mistress – whom she refers to as 'Robina' – to save her from the importunate desires of the Chief. The brother is about to oblige when her white rescuer, Redeemer, appears. This aspect of her ordeal is not reported to the inquiry, nor does it appear in Curtis's text. In fact, details taken from Mrs Fraser in London and reported by Curtis in *The Shipwreck* detail quite another relationship between Mrs Fraser and her companion 'Robina', as mentioned in Chapter 2. In the section entitled 'Mrs. Fraser's Narrative' in John Curtis's book, the woman relates her gratitude to 'Robina', who applied leaves to her skin to dress her wounds and never failed to intercede on Mrs Fraser's behalf (145). The sensational accounts, however, suggest that the white woman was afforded only some degree of paternal protection while 'in captivity'. The native women, on the other hand, were not. According to Curtis, who could only take his cues from captivity narrative versions of the Eliza Fraser story and the highly-charged perceptions of the survivors, the native women were more cruel to those in their power than the native men. With a complete lack of knowledge or understanding of native custom, he explains that this cruelty is 'engendered by the cruel manner in which they are treated by their sable and imperious lords; since living in a state of promiscuous concubinage, they have no one to whom they can fly for protection in the hour of insult and coercion' (239). This authorial gloss allows the reader to identify with the finer feelings and 'tender sensibilities . . . of European females', while it places indigenous peoples on a lower scale of degradation with reference to sexual licence (Victorian morality) and gender relations (patriarchy). In addition, it suggests that Mrs Fraser, as a white woman, had an entitlement to deferential treatment *which was or should have been respected by her captors.* Further, it discounts the gratitude expressed by Mrs Fraser towards the 'native' woman. But Curtis's version, like that of the sensational accounts, suggests enmity between Mrs Fraser and all the 'native' women and sets in place a demand for the proper respect for femininity by 'native' and British 'gentlemen' alike – a universal category in the making.

Convict and Military Rescuers

Specific reference is also made to the differences between the convict and official military rescuers. Both the press accounts and Curtis's text heap praise on Lieutenant Otter, her 'gallant deliverer', and not 'the brave though guilty Graham' (119). In the Curtis account, Otter is the hero of the hour. Curtis assigns to Otter both the reason and sentiment of the ideal, civilised Englishman. Not only did he safely escort Eliza to the ship which took the party back to Moreton Bay, he also 'for a time, divested himself of the bold daring of the knight-errant, and became the watching, anxious, and administrating nurse' (169). Graham, the hero of note who vies with Bracefell for fame in the twentieth-century Australian accounts, was, after all, Irish, and, in addition, a convict, serving his term as a convict at Moreton Bay, and thus not a fit hero for the times (*The Times*). Precisely at the time of the Lord Mayor's Inquiry and throughout the period of Curtis's preparation of *The Shipwreck of the Stirling Castle*, the Irish were said to be causing terror in the streets of London as a result of O'Connell's fiery speeches. In a series of scathing attacks in *The Times*, the well-attended evening performances were reported as having introduced 'rabble and discontent' within the civil and ordered society.[8] It would have been impolitic for the paper to boast of a heroic Irish convict rescuer for Eliza. Curtis refrains from directly attacking Graham, whose efforts were generously acknowledged by Mrs Fraser in the Sydney accounts. Instead, he polices the border of ethnicity by placing Graham within the deviant category of the criminal.

Convicts, as Curtis informs the reader in another of his many authoritative if tangential footnotes to his text, were despicable characters who deserved the harsh penalties meted out by the military, including flagellation, hard labour, reduced provisions and being placed in irons (fn, 170–3). This curious footnote has a number of contradictory effects in its reference to British military sadism. It highlights the relationship between convicts and officers in the colony in a way that might also provide further titillation for some readers. It effects a means of distinguishing the colonial and military authorities from the convicts through the imposition of brutalising, authoritarian practices. The account also may have served to provide, through terror, a means of controlling working-class crime in Britain. At the same time it details tortures performed by Englishmen on Englishmen far in excess of those ascribed to the Fraser Islanders in their treatment of Mrs Fraser and the other surviving members of the crew. It is one of those excessive textual moments when contradictions concerning British propriety erupt in the text.

Curtis allows no sympathy or praise to devolve to the Irish convict rescuer, John Graham, who had been promised a reward and a pardon for his part in the rescue but had to wait four months for it to be granted, and then only by the fiat of the Home Secretary. The reward, determined by the colonial government, was thirty guineas (£31 10s). This was hardly an adequate recompense for his central role in the negotiations that led to Mrs Fraser's release as well as that of three other survivors, which involved what Lieutenant Otter claimed were 'indefatigable exertions . . . exposing him to very imminent risk'.[9] Curtis is coy about John Graham's part in the rescue. He reveals, for instance, that he could, but will not, divulge Graham's crimes which led to his transportation to New South Wales. One might assume that they were serious. In fact, Graham was transported for seven years for a minor felony. He had served seven months in prison prior to deportation, which were not counted as part of the penalty. His term was due to expire in May 1837, nine months after he effected the rescue of Mrs Fraser and three other survivors.[10] He was finally granted his ticket of leave on 2 January 1837, only four months before his seven-year sentence would have been completed. Although Curtis's account spares no sympathy for the (doubly deviant) Irish convict Graham, Graham's history was recuperated and his heroism lauded by Robert Gibbings a century later in his anti-English biography, *John Graham, Convict, 1824.*

A final detail concerning convict behaviour emerges in Curtis's account. It calls attention to behaviours which might have occurred, but did not. This is followed by an admission of behaviours which should not have happened, but did. It concerns the social dynamics of Mrs Fraser's rescue. Readers might wonder how she was treated by these 'despicable characters', the fourteen convicts acting as crew on board the rescue boat, during the time it took to return to Moreton Bay, given that 'convicts' as a class have been marked discursively as instinctual beings in need of control of their animal appetites. Curtis assures his audience that the convicts who accompanied the military officers during the rescue of Eliza acted in a 'fitting manner' during the rescue operations and the 36-hour sail back to Moreton Bay. He also specifically mentions that, at the time of the rescue, Graham was the only white man to see her in her nearly naked state, since she hid in the sand dunes and clothed herself in the petticoat that Lieutenant Otter had brought for her use, before being turned over to the official government party. He relates, however, that neither the convicts on the rescue boat nor the British soldiers could control their laughter at her 'grotesque' appearance as she entered their midst for the first time, 'coloured and her head bedizened with feathers and other ornaments, after the manner of the natives' (165–6). The first admission of safe conduct allows the reader a projective fantasy of sexual licence, a discursive mark of class difference. This is followed by explicit mention of her nakedness (which was witnessed only by Graham), thus constructing a fleeting illicit suggestion of her femininity and sexual difference for the reader. The final detail of Mrs Fraser's appearance, which provided comic relief for the rescue party, allows the reader to discharge the earlier fantasies. But it does so through a Victorian and colonial signification of difference – for Woman and the Aboriginal Others.

In addition, Curtis's high-minded concern for Mrs Fraser's treatment on the rescue boat, which at the same time allows the readers their illicit fantasies, contrasts sharply with the absence of detail concerning her actual sexual experiences during her ordeal. Victorian morality dictated a certain reticence: 'The unfortunate lady attempted to cast a veil over part of her sufferings, which in truth were the most revolting of all . . .'. The silence itself constitutes a production of sexuality, a site of anxiety and desire. The effect of this absence, however, is to mute Mrs Fraser's claim to the Commandant at Moreton Bay that the white men she met treated her more harshly than the blacks. This comment, as well as Bracefell's story of his part in the rescue and his sexual liaison with Mrs Fraser (told, without the admission of rape, years later to the Russell rescue party and expedition), escape the ever surveillant gaze of the objective historian. This lapse in Curtis's text makes doubly ironic Michael Alexander's twentieth-century complaint: 'It is clear that she had some unpleasant experiences, but her inconsistency and natural reticence in encountering them has led to a lack of credible information on the subject.'[11] Curtis reports that she cast a veil over her experiences. But there are many ways to cast a veil, and not all of the veils are cast by the lady herself. Many unpleasant aspects of this extraordinary event are in need of camouflage in the construction of subjectivity for an emerging bourgeois English audience.

Proper and Improper Marriages

It will be recalled that one of the most serious claims against Mrs Fraser's veracity was that she was not, as she claimed, Mrs Fraser, a widow woman with no visible means of support, but Mrs Greene, a newly remarried bride with a considerable 'dowry'. It may be hard for present-day readers to imagine the seriousness with which Victorian society treated the dictum that a widow wait at least a year after the death of her husband before contemplating the change of station. In Eliza Fraser's time the prohibition was real enough to cause public sympathy to turn against her. Curtis defers battle with this most controversial aspect of the affair until the very end of his narrative, after his textual constructions of her saintly character and her perilous ordeal have run their course. It may also be the case that Curtis himself was unaware of Mrs Fraser's remarriage until late in the reconstruction of the events he reports in the text; he, too, may have been gulled by his subject. At the end of the text he argues that Mrs Fraser had only her children in mind when she appealed for support. He continues to represent her as a 'poor, forlorn, debilitated female' at the time of her remarriage (she may have been forlorn and debilitated, but she was not destitute by any means), thus excusing Greene of duplicity. Besides, he reminds the reader, focusing once again on her maternal responsibilities, 'the change in her condition of life did not alter the destitute position in which her fatherless children stood' (210–11). When directly discussing Mrs Fraser Greene's hasty marriage, Curtis is far less sympathetic to the woman herself than he had been earlier in the text. He reserves his sympathies for the fatherless children in her charge. The remarriage is represented as her 'indiscretion in so speedily throwing off the weeds of widowhood' (213), and again as a '*provident*, although according to the general notion of the world, a *premature* and ill-timed alliance' (215, emphases his). However, Curtis, in another indirect allusion to the sexual licence of the 'lower orders' common in the bourgeois rhetoric of the times, reminds his readers that the passage back to England took five months, a time in which her *virtue* could have been preserved but her *reputation* might not have survived the journey (215, emphases mine). He concludes that her only sin was a venial one, a sin against 'strict etiquette', her guilt one of 'indiscreet secrecy' (215). Thus, her indiscretion is judged to be only marginally outside the bounds of social convention and Christian morality. This attribution of guilt has bearing later when questions of Mrs Fraser's sanity arise.

Mrs Fraser's welfare as the wife of Captain Greene is another area suppressed in the discourses which surround the event and is open to further speculation. According to the Liverpool Police Commissioner, she represented herself as a destitute widow because she professed a need of funds to enable her to escape Greene with whom she was having 'matrimonial jars'. Curtis alludes to this complaint, which was reiterated to him by Eliza during his preparations for publication of the book. But her claims were not investigated, despite considerable evidence of Greene's lying to authorities, his skills at manipulation and his apparent opportunism. Then as now, 'matrimonial jars' were deemed a private domestic concern, best left to the parties involved to sort out. All players (with the possible exception of Eliza) apparently were content to uphold the emerging bourgeois notion of the division between public and private spheres – a woman's privatised domestic space contained within (but regulated by) the public world of men. Indeed, within nineteenth-century constructions of women's place, it was deemed improper for a woman to speak publicly on her own behalf, despite considerable disrespect for this 'custom' in some (particularly working-class and Chartist) quarters. Laws and social custom considered it proper that women be represented in public and spoken for by men, their guardians.[12] They had no rights to property.

Mrs Fraser's situation was not unlike that of Mrs Weedon-Stock, which has been examined recently by the feminist historian Catherine Hall. Mrs Stock suffered an abusive marriage and separated from her husband in 1822, thus losing all rights to her children and her property. She complained bitterly to the newspaper:

> When man injures woman how can she defend herself? Her frame is weaker, her spirit timid; and if she be a wife, there is scarce a man any where to be found who will use the slightest exertion in her defence; and her own sex cannot, having no powers. She has no hope from law, for man, woman's enemy, exercises, as well as makes those laws. She cannot have a jury of her peers or equals, for men, every where prejudiced against the sex, are her jurors; man is her judge.[13]

Like Mrs Stock, Eliza Fraser's public authority extended only to the degree that her performance sustained divisions between the public and private spheres.

A Question of Madness

The last dark frontier on the horizon of otherness is madness. For Mrs Fraser to be a credible, authoritative witness of her own experience, she must be sane. For her testimony to stand in for the authority of her husband, the ruling class and Empire, she must be reasonable. Yet, at every point of the 'plot', disturbing suggestions arise. Reports of her behaviour at the time of the rescue by Lieutenant Otter; during her recovery at Moreton Bay by the physician, Dr Robertson; in Brisbane by her host, Stephen Owen; and in London by witnesses at the inquiry, all give evidence of mental derangement. Curtis himself gently hints that 'we think we have seen a tendency that way ourselves' (188), but only in a casual aside at the end of a chapter ironically entitled 'Recovery'.

There is a problem of how to establish credibility for Mrs Fraser, and the social order the text upholds through her construction, within the discourses of reason given the evidence of her mental instability. At the same time, Mrs Fraser's condition further serves to illustrate the greater sensitivity of Englishwomen, and through them the British race, when compared to the unfeeling nature of her tormentors. Her condition evokes further sympathy, aligning feminine feelings and empathy with the civilised aspects of British society. The official history, even though itself a polysemic montage of inter-textuality, nonetheless presents her case in the guise of a reasoned argument. Curtis, in effect, performs the duties required of a gentleman. Through his text he constructs Mrs Fraser within the limits of feminine propriety. He distances her from the the excesses of native savagery, seamen's treachery, convict depravity and the sexual licence of the 'lower orders', all of which are highlighted in the politically charged narrative. Ultimately, these invasive signs of otherness cannot be fully controlled, although Curtis tries valiantly in his text of many voices. In terms of Mrs Fraser's culpability, he suggests that her sanity as a rational subject is not in question; she is guilty of only a temporary lapse of will, a 'slight trespass' of the conventions of morality, which led to an error in judgement. As a credible proponent of Empire, she stands for truth, even though her vulnerability as a woman might produce 'symptoms of aberration of mind' which lead her into error and irrespon-sibility. The text and its 'impartial' author engage the reader in an act of Christian charity, of benevolence, an opportunity to offer proof of their humanitarian spirit. Mrs Fraser's actions are to be regretted, but forgiven. In a final throwaway line which reveals more about the substance of the case than all that has come before, Curtis reminds the reader that 'It would be unEnglish to discredit her.' What it might mean to be 'English' within a system of social and symbolic differences – this is what has organised the rhetoric and positioned the reader of *The Shipwreck of the Stirling Castle* from the start.

Reading the Natives: 'The Zero Order of Civilisation'

Throughout the civilised world, wherever indigenous peoples came under the control of the colonial West, they were commonly referred to as 'primitives' and 'savages'. Once placed in a category of exclusion, their role as Others became manageable in scientific, religious, political, moral and aesthetic terms. The terms *primitive* and *savage* do not refer to actual people but to a category of discourse, an object of knowledge. The terms designate people on a lower scale of human evolution from those who name them. *Primitive*, as a term within scientific discourse, indicates a stage in development, a marker of the past, although the term also has moral, aesthetic and political implications. Primitives were both childlike and bestial. They were located within the human community but at an earlier stage of human development, and yet at the same time they were represented as being outside the human community, on the very border between animals and man. For Curtis and other colonial writers, the 'aboriginal' Other lived in a primitive past, a time not coeval with that of Western observers and commentators. Time, as Johannes Fabian has ably convinced us, is used within Western scientific discourse to both create an object as Other and to distance it from the observer.[14] Time, in addition to categories of difference, gives form to relations of power and inequality.

Part of the policing function of the rhetoric of Empire was to establish a genealogy of classifications of life-forms – a hierarchy of value. Where a group of people was placed on the scale of human development depended on both philosophical understandings and scientific observations. Enlightenment philosophies delineated the stages of social progress from hunting and gathering societies, to pastoralism, agriculture and finally commerce. Natural science observed the behaviour of native peoples and described the physical signs of their animality. These observations served as a basis of rating 'them' (in relation to 'us') as base characters with primitive instincts and no sentiment. Even before racial designations began to be scientifically assigned in the 1850s, natural science placed the natives of Tierra del Fuego and Aboriginal Australians together at the 'zero order of civilisation'.[15] The more 'advanced' the primitive culture, when judged against this scale, the closer it was to being classified as fully human and, more importantly, the more entitled it was to claim ownership to the land. Scientists carefully delineated the 'races' (which they were bringing into existence) on the scale of human perfectibility from the zero level of civilisation to its apex.

Although Australian Aborigines, as Curtis continually reminds us, were placed within the zero order, followed by African, American Indian, Chinese and Indian peoples, the Australian Aboriginal, African and Indian types could be easily transposed. In the various representations of the Eliza Fraser story, the first English woodcut illustrations depicted the natives as African;

subsequent illustrations, following the American captivity narrative, depicted them as Amer-Indians. As printers developed woodcuts and engravings, these images would be commonly reused to reproduce representations of primitive life. Illustrations and descriptions of their dress, habits, customs and behaviours follow the traits which Berkhofer delineated in the construction of the White Man's Indian within the genre of the captivity narrative and Goldie explored in relation to his study of nineteenth-century colonial literature of America, Australia and New Zealand, discussed in Chapter 2. Those traits were: cannibalism and human sacrifice, cruelty to captives, brutal warfare, indolence, superstition, slavery of the native women and laziness of the men, nakedness, lechery, passion, vanity and promiscuity. Although Berkhofer referred specifically to the colonial American construction of the Indian, these traits also characterise colonial writings about Australian Aborigines. The primitive Other was a universal category within colonial discourse, although the category itself allowed for distinctions between different orders of otherness. The Australian native seemed to occupy the lowest level of humankind, below the American Indian, and of another order again from the ex-slave of an emancipatory discourse. The behaviours and semiotic descriptors for the indigene detailed by Berkhofer and Goldie can be found in various versions of the Eliza Fraser story, parcelled into the definitive package of Curtis's history. In addition, as Curtis's text indicates, stories from one 'tribe' on Fraser Island could be explained with reference to a description of another in Port Jackson or Cape York, New Holland or even New Zealand. Although the West prided itself on its reasoned ability to make fine distinctions, when it came to setting up categories of inclusion and exclusion, the Western imagination gave free rein to the loose but excessive category of the Other.

One of the political effects of this universalising tendency is that diverse peoples are imagined as one, without distinction. Those placed within the universal category of aboriginality are also denied individual rights. The actions and reputed crimes of one individual or group of people can be substituted for those of another, or attributed to another. Thus, minor infractions into settler society by an individual or small band of indigenous people often met with the indiscriminate punishment of large groups of others. This totalising logic of radical otherness, although it ran counter to Western notions of a reasoned, discriminating civil society, well served the political objectives of colonialism.

Curtis refers to natives of Fraser Island as being not at the lowest *level* of civilisation but in the zero *orders*. Locating a group of people on the 'zero order of civilisation' requires classification in at least two contradictory directions. Not only must the discourse struggle with a scale of human attributes from lowest to highest, but it must also negotiate the border between human and non-human orders of being, between Man and Nature. Hulme observes wryly that 'human beings who eat other human beings have always been placed on the very borders of humanity'.[16] This was especially true if they were black. In Western fantasies, 'they' present the most terrifying spectacle of what 'we' might become (and did). The nineteenth-century ethnographers were fascinated by Australian Aborigines because 'they seemed to symbolise a primordial human origin, a problematic point where humanity began to differentiate itself from nature'.[17] For Curtis, following the emerging ethnographic debates of his day, those borders were clarified by the distinction between reason and the instincts. But those distinctions also reveal projections of what the white race feared of its own regressive self.

Although Mrs Fraser is constructed as a rational, sentient being, instinctual, animalistic behaviour accounts for the easy lifestyle of the savage. The appearance of the 'natives', especially that of the older women, whom Curtis described as 'absolute frights, and appear only to want an additional member to render them analogous with the long-haired fraternity' (115), reminds the reader of their links to the lower orders. Curtis's narrative participates in Western constructions of primitive peoples through marked reference to their nakedness, indolence, sexual promiscuity and lack of shame, which also designates them as irrational, immoral and close to their animal origins. Curtis leaves it to Mrs Fraser to make the most striking comparison. In a sentence surprising for its rhetorical polish, taken 'verbatim' from a woman otherwise demonstrating signs of mental derangement, Mrs Fraser is quoted as saying, 'To me it appears, that as to decency of conduct, and sensibility of mind, there is no difference between them and the beasts of the forest, or if there be, it consists in the latter being less ingenious in their cruelty.'(158). This rhetorically constructed statement, attributed directly to Mrs Fraser, lends the authenticity of a first-person account to Curtis's 'scientific' observations. At least three times in the text Curtis refers to the animal instincts of 'the natives' and compares them explicitly with 'beasts of the forest'. The last reference emerges in direct opposition to a comment attributed to Mrs Fraser concerning the devotion she had witnessed on the part of the women towards the well-being of their children. He clarifies her sympathetic observation with the authorial statement that 'the lioness and leopardess do the same' (239). These instances strengthen the conviction that Mrs Fraser herself may have played a very minor role in the construction of 'her' story, although the illusion of her presence was essential to the verisimilitude of the account.

Although both 'native' men and women are said to exist on the 'lowest order of civilisation', Curtis attributes traits of extreme cruelty to the women, due to their baser instincts. Curtis suggests that the cruelty suffered by Mrs Fraser in the company of the women may possibly have been due to the women's jealousy of her because of the attentions she received, attentions 'of a diabolical nature' (158) from the men of the 'tribe'. He also reasons that the women may have been more cruel as a result of 'the way they are treated by their sable and imperious lords' (239). This sentence is as close as the Curtis text comes to referring, albeit obliquely, to the nature of Mrs Fraser's sexual encounters while on Fraser Island. It appears, however, during a discussion of native *women's* cruelty and jealousy. Further, the asumed lack of human sentiments on the part of the women is attributed to both instinctual and environmental factors. These factors influence the men as well, although with different results. The men are said to engage in perpetual wars, concubinage and child-murder. These actions may be deemed more savage, but they are explained with reference to environmental demands – they have the positive scientific result of maintaining a small population. Thus, in the Western discourses on Aboriginality, base behaviours are explained as responses to environmental conditions as well as to biologically determined racial inferiority, although the women are deemed to be more instinctual than men. Sexual divisions mark another border between reason and the instincts, culture and nature, masculine and feminine realms of being, with women/the feminine signifying a further level of inferiority.

At the same time, Curtis notes that the natives occasionally demonstrate that they possess the 'higher faculties'. They act as able guides; they exhibit the ability to reason, and can be taught to read and write. In another of his many footnotes, Curtis poses a problem for the 'Christian, the politician, and the philanthropist to ponder': if they are intelligent, that is, 'above debasement', then 'why do they live on the zero order of civilisation?' (114). And, even more troubling, why do the runaway convicts choose to live with the natives, even professing to be happy in their state? His position shifts throughout the narrative, sometimes aligned with 'Christian benevolence' and at other times with the political force of law and order. He suggests that the natives are debased human beings, capable of intellectual and moral improvement, although their 'natural inclination' is to live in a savage state of nature. They live at the 'dawn of civilisation', representing where 'we' have come from and what 'we' might become if we were to lapse back into nature (114, 240). In other words, if 'they' are to supersede their animal state, 'they' need reason, which it is 'our' responsibility to provide. Curtis's ambivalent position between a pose of Christian benevolence and an insistence on the rule of law can be detected in these summary remarks:

> They appear to be under the arbitrary control of animal instinct; and it may be said of them, (and we mention it more out of commiseration at their degraded condition, than of contempt of the moral and intellectual debasement of our species,) – they are 'earthy, sensual, devilish' [239].

The final phrases leap up from the page, evoking that terrible spectacle of what 'we' might become if the instincts are not channelled by the forces of reason. This rhetoric also locates Curtis's text within a biologically determined discourse of racial inferiority, rather than the more popular liberal emancipist rhetoric of freedom which had been associated with the anti-slavery campaigns. It mirrors Carlyle's view of Negroes as 'an ignorant, uncivilized, and grossly superstitious people . . . creatures of impulse and imitation, easily misled, very excitable . . . full of evil passions [and] . . . little removed in many respects from absolute savages'. This, Catherine Hall maintains, became the orthodox view of racial inferiority, and was to influence the campaign against the Emancipist Society in England in the 1840s.[18]

These remarks reiterate typical attributes of Aboriginality within a colonial Australian context.[19] In an article which discusses the category 'Aboriginal' in colonial Australia, Andrew Lattas argues that the term functioned as a signifier of power and dominance within a white political, moral and ideological universe. Far from describing actual human beings, commentaries employ the category 'Aboriginal' to construct a point of origin for human existence within conflicting discourses of Christianity and scientific evolutionism. On the one hand, the category functioned to place man between God and nature within a Christian cosmology. On the other, it organised evolutionist concerns about the division between human and animal realms. In addition, it functioned as a conceptual weapon in the regulation of colonial class relationships. Lattas comments that

> the primordialness of Aborigines consisted in their being part of that material realm where human feeling assumed a naturally violent form because they had not been subject to guidance. Aborigines were part of material reality, approaching the undiscriminating, non-rational, non-moral level of inert nature.[20]

Power and the Other

The question of how white society should effect a transformation of the natives from a state of savagery to one of civilisation is a question of Western power expressed as a universal moral dilemma: what is to be done? This moves the debate into a broader arena as to what forms of power should be employed by a scientific, rational society to quell the threatening, irrational forces transposed on to the other but also threatening to erupt from within. The question of how to transform the natives from a zero order of civilisation to one closer to that of their white colonisers disguises the colonial imperative of how to effect control of a foreign land and its inhabitants. The humanitarian impulses of the Christian commentator disguise a need to justify the greed for land and the desire to exploit the natives, their bodies and their labour. Curtis's text appears at a time of epistemological shift from classical to Enlightenment philosophies. The classical position took the natives of colonised lands to be slaves and possessions on a less than human scale; the newer views stressed the common humanity of all men on which the abolition of slavery was based. His narrative vacillates between the two positions, viewing the natives as both lesser than human and also capable of reform and advancement; both radically different and potentially the same. Possibilities for the transformation of natives on the scale of human perfectibility are explored in the text: they range from philanthropic projects to employ the missions in educational and religious instruction to the more punitive impulse towards incarceration, violence and even extinction. Which course of action is advocated in the text and the larger social order depended on a variety of religious, educational, philosophical and political contexts and on the speaker's position as to whether or not 'primitive' peoples were capable of reform. As settlement progressed, these issues increasingly hinged upon the practical and pragmatic concerns as to how close the indigenous people were to white settlements and settlers' properties.

Curtis takes up a number of these positions at different times in the text. Knowing nothing of the conditions at Moreton Bay, he reasons that change might come about naturally, as a result of 'more frequent coalition' between the natives and white settlers. He reminds readers that the natives living closer to Moreton Bay, encountered by crew members Darge and Corallis, exhibited a different, more humane, behaviour from those who attended Mrs Fraser (198). It never occurs to him that the behaviour of the survivors, whether resisting or accepting of indigenous ways, may have contributed to their own fate, nor that the white invaders may have owed their survival on the island to the ministrations and skills of their hosts. Indigenous peoples stand outside time, outside human history; thus they can have no agency in colonial accounts. Later, Curtis lapses into a more 'scientific' explanation for the 'natural' differences between the two 'tribes' encountered by Mrs Fraser and the other crew members, maintaining that the 'zero of civilization is at the northern point of Australia, and . . . southward, the tribes of natives become gradually less sanguinary' (222). This would suggest that nature, not culture, is responsible for determining their behaviours. In the last instance, Curtis's text supports Divine intervention, in the form of missionary activity, to teach the natives civilised ways, moving them from a state of 'heathen barbarity' to one of Christian civilisation. But, he cautions, darkly, that more overt and direct political force may be necessary. The means matter less than the end result.

Going Native

Why white men would choose to live with the natives presents a more puzzling problem for Curtis, and one which gave him occasion to ponder more

drastic measures of social control. Curtis's narrative makes mention of two
runaway convicts, Tursi and Tallboy, both named in seaman Darge's story of
the shipwreck of the *Stirling Castle*. Darge's testimony before the inquiry is
appended to the Eliza Fraser narrative near the end of the book. Darge
maintained, contrary to the testimony of Mrs Fraser and Baxter, that he and
Corallis had been treated humanely by the natives and that the runaway
convicts who lived with them existed in a state of content. He reported that
the two convicts lived an 'indolent' existence in the bush where they would
be content to live and die rather than face the harsh brutalities of the penal
system (228). He even suggested that the experiences of hair plucking and
painting the body with gum and red ochre, reported as excruciating
instances of native savagery by Mrs Fraser, were not forms of punishment
but rather 'influenced by etiquette or fashion . . . they were so intent upon
the toilet, and securing the beauty of their persons' (226). Darge's testimony,
based on his experience and his interaction with the runaway convicts,
stands in stark contrast to many of Mrs Fraser's reputed explanations of
native behaviour. It credits the indigenous people with compassion, intelligence and superior skills in coping with the environment. Curtis's only
defence is to comment that Darge and the runaway convicts 'had become
naturalized – demi-barbarized(?)' (240). He then engages in a critique of *all*
deviants in the colony, degenerate runaways and natives alike. Commenting
on the progress of the colony of New South Wales, Curtis concludes: 'It
matters but little, we conceive, by what means the savage nature of men is
subdued, and civilisation extended; whether from the effect of fear, or from
sordid policy, so that the important point be achieved'(198). In other words,
for the advancement of mankind, when reason and moral persuasion fail, it is
totally appropriate to resort to the force of law.

Escaping convicts were a constant problem for the authorities at Moreton
Bay. Research into the frequency of escape led one later anthropologist, who
researched, collected and published narratives of the runaways, to remark,
perhaps somewhat flippantly, that they were 'the original Public Service –
gone before Christmas and back by the end of January'.[21] At the time, however, judgements were more severe. Lattas reports that mission tracts
regularly railed against the runaways, whose moral condition was deemed to
be far more perilous than that of the natives: that 'of tenfold darkness; for
unlike the benighted Heathen, they have sinned against light and knowledge,
and amid the blaze of gospel day . . . [have wilfully] chosen darkness above
the light'.[22] The convicts who chose to live with Aborigines were classed as
more evil and degenerate than the natives because, through their own free
will, they sinned against reason. The mission tracts utilised Western notions
of degeneracy (attributed to both Aborigines and convicts) to assimilate the
lower orders into the moral universe of bourgeois society, demonstrating

that early class relations in the colony were predicated not only on a class division between colonial authority and the convicts, but also on racism.

These rhetorical gestures underline the multiple threats posed by the natives, convicts and crew within colonial society. Reading from the margins, the constructions of difference also point to signs of resistance to colonial authority, fissures in the social fabric which challenged the structures of power. Just as the mutinous crew resisted the authority vested in the Captain at the time of the shipwreck, convicts and indigenes resisted the imposition of penal codes and the formation of settler society. White runaway convicts engaged in a range of reciprocal relationships with the Aborigines. Together they learned survival skills of mutual benefit. In the south-east of Queensland, until the 1830s, the indigenous people accepted runaways into their society as the returned ghosts of departed relatives. They also offered protection to the convicts away from the penal settlement. The runaways taught their companions a range of retaliatory tactics in dealing with the white invaders, including how to steal sheep and produce, to avoid gunfire and to ambush white hunting parties. Runaways, if accepted, became a part of Aboriginal society and took on prescribed kinship roles in relation to wives and children and other members of the group. Together with the indigenous men, they resisted the incursions of constables and soldiers into the camps in search of women to be (ab)used as concubines. At times the Fraser Islanders turned the convicts in to the authorities for a government reward. The Native Police, working far from their own territories and under the control of the local white constabulary, colluded with white authorities against the interests of the indigenous population. These actions attest to the fluid nature of social interactions and the instability of evolving networks of power.

In time, philanthropic measures prompted by the religious tracts proved too weak a weapon against the actions of either the runaway convicts or the native population. Increasingly, these measures of control were replaced by the force of law. The various acts of dominance in Australia's early colonial history, whether imposed textually or located in the practices of everyday life, led to the formation of bourgeois relations within the modern nation-state. The silences in Curtis's history and the countless colonial and neo-colonial texts of white commentators had their effect. Through their various constructions of the other, they masked unspeakable acts of white cannibalism and savagery against Aboriginal people and male violence against women, which until very recently have been hidden from history. The hidden histories, only traceable at the point of suppression or narrative tension in the earlier texts, have emerged gradually, for the most part since the 1970s.[23] Henry Reynolds estimates that throughout the nineteenth century there were ten white runaways living with natives for every native who chose willingly to cross over into the 'safe harbour' of mission settlement. There were ten white acts of violence against Aborigines for every Aboriginal act against whites. Tales of 'savagery', like those associated with the Eliza Fraser story, inflamed the popular imagination and supplied data which was transformed into scientific 'truths' to uphold the superiority of British civilisation. They justified the sadistic tortures devised by the penal authorities against the convicts, and white settlers against the Aborigines. Shortly after the wreck of the *Stirling Castle*, between 1839 and 1842, the penal colony at Moreton Bay was dismantled. But the fears of white settlers living in sparse populations on the Queensland frontier, coupled with the lessons learned of surveillance, regulation, incarceration and violent punishment, would further extend colonial power, resulting by the end of the century in the forceful control and wide dispersal of the indigenous population.

Over time, Mrs Fraser, the shipwreck and its various retellings began to constitute a field of meaning filled with a historically specific content. But it is a field of meaning dependent on representations of her voice, her presence, her veracity constructed as a point of origin, or those of others who would speak on her behalf. Social institutions employ her story, told and reshaped after the event, as a mode of policing the borders between civilisation and barbarity, culture and nature, ship's officers and crew, colonisers and colonised peoples, convicts and officers, ruling class and labouring class, white women and native women, masculine authority and feminine nurturing, strength and vulnerability. Textual narratives, in the guise of 'truth', engage the reader in anxious fantasies of desire. Desire to locate the other in a domain separate from the self also produces fantasies within the self which maintain the fictions of difference.

As we have seen, in the mix of everyday experience and its various representations, the borders of national, class, racial and sexual difference are both regulated and transgressed. If anything, the Eliza Fraser story as event demonstrates the instability of the social order, the fragmentation of the self. Different speakers invoke different sets of inclusions and exclusions to justify their cause. Different groups contest and resist power. Multiple mediations are possible. On the one hand, discourses, social institutions and practices utilise the story as a site of power to produce and promulgate knowledge about race, class and gender hierarchies within a national and colonial context. On the other, every site of production is also a site of resistance to power. Anxieties about the unity and coherence of the self underlie every discursive formation, threatening to erupt (in the text and for the reader) at any time. In the end (in 1838 which is not the end at all), domination through knowledge and the force of law settled the specifics of the matter. The Lord Mayor established a trust fund for the Fraser children under the guardianship of the Minister of Stromness. The Colonial Secretary granted a pardon to John Graham by executive fiat. In countless other stories, other sites for the promulgation of power and production of knowledge, those unspeakable practices of cannibalism, sadism, irrational violence and sexual excess were repeatedly invoked to constitute the domain of the Other. They were at the time, and will continue to be, read otherwise, in an endless but not inconsequential play of contradiction and recuperation.

CHAPTER 5

Cannibals: Western Imaginings of the Aboriginal Other

When John Baxter took the stand to testify at the London Lord Mayor's Commission of Inquiry, he was asked to verify Mrs Fraser's account of her sufferings. To the Lord Mayor's question: 'You have read Mrs. Fraser's account in the newspapers? This is not worse than was the fact?', Baxter replied: 'No description could come up to it all. None of us knew the minute we were to be staked and consumed over a slow fire. It was horrid beyond anything that ever happened.'[1] What Baxter indicates here tells us not so much about the quality of actual sufferings but rather about the power of imagined ones, which are inexpressible. As we have seen, this inability to express the inexpressible was reiterated in the first popular account of the shipwreck, the broadsheet which announced the 'horrib treatment of the crew by savages' accompanied by a lurid woodcut illustration of murder and decapitation along with the 'mournful verses' which read in part: 'To describe the feeling of these poor souls / is past the art of man'.[2] In both instances the horror which was evoked for the reader involves the capital sin of otherness: cannibalism. Baxter's reputed testimony specifically refers to burning at the stake and being consumed (by fire, but readers can imagine that ingestion might follow). The broadsheet announces 'horrib' treatment; the word 'horrib', which could be read as a simple misprint, also has the power to suggest a metonymic link to 'Carib', as in Carib peoples, the original perpetrators of these grave deeds, at least in a nineteenth-century Western imaginary.

Reading the Evidence

Traditionally, these descriptions require explanations based on empirical evidence. Historians, ethnographers, and journalists, as well as writers of popular fictionalised versions of the story, have continued to raise the questions: Were Australian Aborigines cannibals? Was Mrs Fraser treated in a barbaric manner? A number of studies have attempted to address these questions, although in less than definitive terms.[3] Aboriginal customs prior to white occupation are not recoverable within a historical framework. Nineteenth-century reports of first contact can be culled from diaries, journals and testimonies like that of Mrs Fraser; they were framed not only by the historical contexts and limited understandings of the Western people involved but also by notions of civility and propriety, primitivism and barbarity already available to them through prior discourses of difference. The irrational fear of cannibalism, bordering on paranoia, which can be detected in these texts has aroused the interest of a number of present-day readers.[4] One commentator, whose analysis will be taken up in more detail in the course of this chapter, has recently proposed that the irrational fear of cannibalism arose not out of actual events but out of the circulation of a dark fantasy of otherness, shared by seamen, explorers, castaways and indigenous peoples alike, beyond the limits of reason. Evidence of cannibalism in first-contact experiences and second-hand accounts is slim and inconclusive; in addition, Western historians and ethnographers interpret it from their assumed stance on race, class and gender relations, their fantasies of fear and desire. All of these possibilities are further compromised by the subject positions and psychological projections of the people who experienced the events, the authors who wrote about them, and readers of the texts.

Post-colonial studies of first contact which have appeared in the past decade tend to displace the empirical interest in 'what really happened'. They suggest that there is little to be gained by questioning whether or not indigenous peoples of colonised territories actually practised cannibalism. Whatever customs might have been practised or observed at the time were placed inside available Eurocentric understanding and given meaning within it. The indigenous survivors were never given a voice; the understandings, perspectives and imaginings which they brought to first-contact events have been lost to history.[5] 'Our' ethnocentrism produces 'their' barbarism. In addition, what shipwreck survivors imagined might be their fate produced in them a terror which bred uncertainty; that uncertainty spiralled into irrational fears which produced still more terror.[6] As has been mentioned, after the shipwreck of the *Stirling Castle*, long before the crew landed on Great Sandy Island, Captain Fraser became obsessed with fears of native cannibalism. Survivors interviewed by John Curtis describe the events thus. After the wreck the crew drifted for fourteen days, existing without food or water for the last seven. 'Despair and dismay sat upon every countenance' (35).[7] The Captain, filled with instinctive dread, bit his tongue in a hysterical frenzy. He agreed to beach the longboat only after some members of the crew proposed that they draw lots for the sacrifice of one member to supply food for the others. Once on the island, the Captain assumed that the crew of the pinnace (which had deserted the Captain's party on the long-boat) had already been taken prisoner and 'in all probability eaten'(33). He urged his party to prepare for escape during a 'corrobery' when the natives would be 'dancing in a circle around a favourite friend . . . [or] a miserable captive, whose flesh they would presently greedily devour'(41). Given that Fraser Island Aborigines were not known to act in this way and that the historical records cannot explain this morbid and irrational fear, how might the Captain's behaviour be understood from a post-colonial perspective? In other words: what did Captain Fraser (as an imaginary subject) know about cannibalism (as a historical construction)?

What did Captain Fraser Know about Cannibalism?

A fear of cannibalism has fascinated bourgeois colonials since the time of the publication of *Robinson Crusoe* (1719). Michel de Certeau comments on Crusoe's fear as the fear of the conquering bourgeois hero in his *Practice of Everyday Life* (1984). His remarks might strike the present-day reader as somewhat exaggerated. They do, however, closely parallel descriptions of Captain Fraser's behaviour as represented in the reports of the shipwreck:

> The conquering bourgeois is transformed into a man 'beside himself', made wild himself by the (wild) clue that reveals nothing. He is almost driven out of his mind. He dreams, and has nightmares. He loses his confidence in a world governed by the Great Clockmaker. His arguments abandon him. Driven out of the productive asceticism that took the place of meaning for him, he lives through diabolical day after day, obsessed by the cannibalistic desire to devour the unknown intruder or by the fear of being devoured himself.[8]

A number of critics have commented on the obsessive nature of this white fascination with cannibalism, a fascination bordering on terror. They inter-pret it in several ways. Within a colonial mentality, cannibalism represented the ultimate denial of a common humanity, the ultimate sign of depravity, the ultimate mark of savagery and, above all, a guarantee of European superiority. Cannibalism represented to the bourgeois colonial subject an intolerable menace to be mastered, as well as a psychological threat to the integrity of the self. Michael Taussig comments in his study of colonial encounters with the Andean Indians of South America that the European has always been complicit with this fear, seeing behind the mask of the cannibal the face of the coloniser. He argues that, paradoxically, this major trope of colonialism produces at its heart a fear of what colonialism itself is: an over-whelming force that devours the body politic of the indigenous peoples.[9] In her study of cannibalistic practices, Maggie Kilgour concurs, suggesting that Eurocentric readers sublimated their own fears and desires by a displace-ment of cannibalistic fantasies on to the natives. With Stallybrass and White, she concludes that sublimation was a strategy of cultural domination, 'the main mechanism whereby a group or a class or an individual bids for symbolic superiority over others'. In addition, this particular instance of sublimation had an advantage over cannibalism in that it could claim 'to subsume the other for the other's own good'.[10] In terms of both the colonial mentality and the fantasy it feeds, cannibalism presents an instance of tabooed practices and the fear and desire they evoke on the part of the colonisers which they transpose onto the colonised peoples. But 'cannibalism' in the European narratives is designed to distance readers from this awareness.

Throughout the late eighteenth and early nineteenth centuries, stories of cannibalism circulated freely amongst seamen and travellers, adding a certain tension to their expectations and providing a context for understanding their experiences. Consider this tale, recorded in the journal of Johann Reinhold Forster, one of the crew who accompanied Captain Cook on his second voyage of discovery:

> There circulates on board a Story, made up I believe on purpose, that the Natives told, that a Ship arrived on the Coast of the Northern Isle in a great storm, & was there broke to pieces. The Men in her were safed [sic] on shore, & had an Engagement with the Natives, wherein they killed many Natives, but not being able to keep up a Fire, the Natives came up & killed & devoured them all.[11]

It is interesting that Forster claims that the story was made up and told by the natives, suggesting that they possessed a more complex understanding of their situation (not to mention the imperial psyche) than is generally allowed. Apocryphal stories similar to these may have fuelled Captain Fraser's morbid fear. They may have also aided Captain Greene in his ability to embellish his tales of the South Seas, embellishments which were added to the Eliza Fraser story.

It should also be recalled that Captain Fraser had experienced shipwreck before in the South Pacific. His brig, the *Comet*, had made its final journey six years earlier when it was wrecked in the Torres Strait. The only evidence from that wreck is a poem the Captain sent to his wife, in which he laments the loss of two lambs, a cat and a parrot, 'for which [he] had great regard'.[12] The *Charles Eaton* also came to grief in the area in 1835, the wreck which John Curtis discussed at the end of his narrative concerning the wreck of the *Stirling Castle*. As we have seen, survivors of the *Charles Eaton* drifted to the Cape York Peninsula, where it was reported that the Captain, his wife, and one of their two children had been murdered and their heads taken. A rescue boat sailed from Sydney, returning with two boys, the younger son of the ship's captain and the ship's boy, the only survivors. The boys, whom Mrs Fraser met during her time of recuperation in Sydney, brought back stories of cannibalistic head-hunters. While at Cape York the crew found some forty-five skulls which they confiscated and returned to Sydney, where they were forensically examined to determine their origin before being buried in the Bunnerong Cemetery. It was reported that seventeen of the forty-five heads were European. The skulls had been publicly displayed at Cape York around a totem (an illustration of which appeared in the local and colonial press and was reproduced in John Curtis's history).[13] The boys' stories, coupled with the ethnographic evidence, were cited in the colonial press as proofs of native savagery and cannibalism.

The indigenous inhabitants of the islands in the Torres Strait between Papua New Guinea and the northern coast of Australia had a reputation for 'savage rituals', including cannibalism, ritual warfare, and the proud display of jawbones and skulls. The present-day Murray Islanders (recipients of the Mabo High Court decision which overturned the doctrine of *terra nullius*) admit to this reputation in their past but repudiate it today.[14] But the Torres Strait is some 1700 kilometres north of Fraser Island. Although both locales are within the tropical environment of the South Pacific, the assumption that indigenous peoples living in both areas would have the same customs, engage in the same habits and produce the same reactions to European first-contact invaders, is an example of the Western propensity to collapse all indigenous peoples into the common category of 'savages and cannibals'. What Captain Fraser experienced as a result of his previous shipwreck is unknown. It is likely that the circulation of stories of cannibalism contributed more than his memory of past events to his fears and expectations after the *Stirling Castle* wreck. Perhaps we can best understand his hysteria as an effect of a white imperialist mentality which categorised as 'the same' peoples from widely disparate areas and made them all 'our' barbarous and troubling others.

The Dark Bond of Cannibalism

European seamen, travellers, explorers and settlers all brought with them both a selective 'knowledge' of primitive life and a morbid fear of cannibalism. How did these ideas come to life? What fed and perpetrated them? In a recent study of the voyages of Captain Cook, Gananath Obeyesekere suggests that the British had a preoccupation with cannibalism, a preoccupation which he labels a 'cannibalistic complex' and treats as such.[15] This obsession can be traced in explorers' journals, an oral tradition of sea stories, travellers' diaries, settlers' tales, records of ethnographic expeditions, and the sensational accounts in the press. He explains it on three levels:

1 the British reading public wanted to hear accounts of cannibalism;
2 cannibalism was what voyagers most expected to find; and
3 it was what they most feared.[16]

Further, he puts forward an argument in favour of universal psychic structures for all peoples – one which finds some support amongst other post-colonial theorists of 'first contact' events.[17] He suggests that the historical preoccupation with the horrors of cannibalism is based on a primal fantasy within the psychic structure of *both* British and indigenous peoples. He theorises that anxiety from childhood concerning the loss of the integrity of the self leads to adult fantasies and inferences which, at the time of first contact between Europeans and indigenous peoples, were reinforced by both parties. Not all commentators subscribe to Obeyesekere's theory of universal primal fantasies as the origin for the obsession. They agree, however, that, for whatever reason, the British assumed that the natives were cannibals. They took this 'knowledge' with them on their voyages of discovery. They found cannibalism everywhere, even in locations where it was not known to exist. Obeyesekere argues, on the basis of his research concerning the voyages of Captain Cook, that British assumptions that natives in the South Seas were all cannibals were as much a product of British behaviours and fantasies as of any historical evidence. Furthermore, as Arens and others suggest, indigenous peoples also told stories that their neighbours and/or enemies were cannibals. This is the case in regard to some traditional Aboriginal narratives as well. The term crosses cultures as a useful ploy for identifying the ultimate mark of otherness.

Oppositional Strategies: Reading Otherwise

Obeyesekere presents a skilful anti-colonial reading of historical documents from the imagined position of the native Hawaiians on first contact with Captain Cook. He suggests that the Hawaiians, who did not practise cannibalism, thought the British were cannibals. This was a reasonable supposition, given that the British arrived in an emaciated condition, were prepared to fight the Hawaiians as their enemies, and mimed cannibalistic behaviours when asking if the Hawaiians, like other indigenous peoples, ate their enemies. The terrified Hawaiians, muses Obeyesekere, fearing and also witnessing British atrocities, suspected cannibalism must be a habit of the British. The Hawaiians had witnessed the killing and decapitation of their own people and the display of their heads on board the British ship. They also received requests from the seamen for artefacts and 'curiosities' (skulls and bones and such like) which the British could take back to England and put on display in museums as 'proof' of cannibalistic practices. And they (like the Maori, who, he claims, were cannibals) used British fear as a weapon against British power and the unequal force of guns. When the British mimed cannibalistic behaviours in the form of a question about native practices, the natives mimed it back, perhaps in a response calculated to terrorise the British. Obeyesekere calls it 'one form of terror against another'.[18]

There are a number of elements in Obeyesekere's critique which overlap with the Eliza Fraser story and could be applied to it. In both cases, the voyagers came with an expectation of cannibalism. In both cases, what they experienced confirmed their beliefs. Further, reports and evidence of cannibalism were eagerly sought by the press and public, whether based on speculation or reported experience. Like their counterparts in Hawaii, the *Stirling Castle* survivors actively searched for clues. Mrs Fraser reported that during their first days on the island the crew found the remains of a child's bonnet and several pieces of European clothing. They took this evidence, coupled with native gestures simulating violence, to be a sign that other ships had been wrecked off these shores and that the survivors had been murdered. Murder, at least to the Captain, implied that cannibalism would follow. Murder of a family, that sacred unit of bourgeois life, implied that no one, including Mrs Fraser, was safe. The sighting of the clothing increased the fears of the crew and heightened the Captain's resistance to native demands, a reaction which may have placed his life in further jeopardy. A few days after landing on the island, the crew attempted to escape down the beach. Baxter reported that the natives cajoled them to stay by gesturing that they should remain in place and miming the brutal behaviour that the other groups on the island would bestow upon them should they escape. These miming behaviours would be cited in the London newspapers reporting on the Lord Mayor's Inquiry, and in the Curtis and Alexander histories, as further proofs of native savagery.

Incidents around the deaths (reported as murders) of Captain Fraser and the first mate Brown also seem to have been products of a fertile imagination, this 'dark bond of cannibalism'.[19] The Captain, in an already weakened state, succumbed to death after a series of spear wounds. His death is variously referred to in the literature as a 'death by spearing' or the 'murder of the Captain', both references which imply intended acts of native violence. It will be remembered that the illustrations in the Curtis text depicted the scene as one of spearing in the back as the Captain was attempting to escape (Figure 6). But at the inquiry and in subsequent interviews, Eliza Fraser is reported to have said, 'I don't think it was their intention to kill my husband.'[20] This suggestion of an accidental death, or of one brought about as a result of the Captain's increasing belligerence, or necessitated by his weakened condition, never enters the popular accounts. It is not what a reading public would want to hear.

The unknown fate of the Captain's remains presented further cause for speculation. It appears that only Eliza was present at his death by spearing and she fell into a 'swoon of insensibility'. Harry Youlden, the mutinous seaman who published his account of the shipwreck in an American magazine fifteen years later, reported a different story. He said that 'when found, the captain and chief-mate were dead. Both had perished of starvation.'[21] But he was not present at the time. Baxter reported to the Lord Mayor's Inquiry that he saw the Captain's body carried away, and he believed that it was buried as he saw a fresh mound a few days later, like that of a grave in a country churchyard. Curtis comments in his history that this was *a highly unlikely story* (emphasis his, 73), told presumably to put Mrs Fraser at ease. One can infer from the anxious italics that the body was eaten. Years later a government party set out to explore the Cooloola area for possible settlement and to recapture the runaway convicts still at large. They inquired after and searched extensively for the remains of both the Captain and Brown, but neither bones nor signs of burial were ever found.

Exaggerated tales of native savagery filled the press reports at the time of the Lord Mayor's Inquiry. They were contradicted at the time by the testimony of Robert Darge, the surviving seaman associated with the mutinous party of survivors, who came forward late in the day and was interviewed by the Lord Mayor. When asked about the cannibalistic practices of the natives, Darge, who claimed to have been initiated into his 'tribe', replied: 'I do not believe that any of the tribes I was amongst ate human flesh. I never saw anything of the kind.'[22] Baxter, especially, seemed prone to supply sensational accounts of savagery which enjoyed full coverage in the press, although similar stories had not previously been reported by the other survivors. At the London inquiry he inflated the number of natives encountered to seven hundred (other estimates suggested that from two to four hundred indigenous peoples from the island and adjoining coastal areas might have gathered together for the corroboree). He also testified to the spearing of seven and murder of four crew members, who were 'put to death in the most horrid and barbarous manner'. He then supplied what was reputed to be an authentic first-hand account of Brown's death by burning at the stake:

[A]fter going about a mile horror-struck was I to find him [Brown] tied to a tree hand and foot, and a slow fire made at his feet, but much more so to see one of the men on the stake close by and writhing in the greatest agony, their last words being to let their mothers know of their untimely end.[23]

The final melodramatic detail surely quickened the pulse of every English mother's breast, fostering public sentiment and support for the extension of colonial control over indigenous peoples.

Baxter is the only survivor to report the deliberate murder of any crew member and he reports these crimes only in London. In regard to Brown's death, by Baxter's own admission and that of other survivors, he was not present at the scene. Mrs Fraser, who was present on the island in the same location as Brown, reported that he had been burned about the legs (anthropologists suggest that firebrands may have been applied to his legs as a cure for ulcers) and later left to die in his debilitated state. But she reported to John Curtis that she fell into 'a violent stupor' and could not say 'whether his body was partially or wholly consumed' (155). The second man who was reputedly burned at the stake in Baxter's account, and who is called 'John Major' in the sensational stories fed to the press, might refer to tales which circulated concerning the victim of another shipwreck in the South Seas, not connected with the *Stirling Castle* at all.[24] His is the body fetishised in the lurid *Tales of Travellers* account, where he is said to have been beheaded by the natives with sharpened shells, after which parts of the body were eaten and the head preserved and affixed as a figurehead to one of their canoes.[25] What prompted Baxter's testimony at the inquiry? Michael Alexander, who does not question the veracity of this dimension of Baxter's testimony, speculates that the natives may have simulated an instance of burning at the stake as a warning to Baxter to comply with their demands. Alternately, it could have been a story concocted by Captain Greene, who could have coached Baxter prior to his testimony in London. Alexander's interpretations, as well as other reports of intimidating behaviours on the part of the islanders employed to coerce the shipwreck survivors to behave in consort with their wishes, correspond to the speculations of Obeyesekere concerning the natives' use of British fear as a weapon against British power. It is likely to have been a psychological weapon skilfully employed against their own local opponents as well.[26]

The final mention of cannibalism in Curtis's first published history of the event occurs in a curious chapter called 'Interlude', inserted between chapters which record Baxter's testimony and that of Mrs Fraser. Curtis maintains the purpose of this interlude is 'to pave the way for the subsequent, and perhaps, although of a melancholy description, the most interesting part of the history'.[27] The textual delay builds suspense for the reader. It signals a narrative tension, a site of anxiety. In this interlude Curtis provides a rambling, unreferenced pseudo-ethnography of native physique, tool use, hunting customs, superstitions, and the like, indiscriminately gathered and supposedly containing knowledge of tribal groups and practices in New South Wales, New Holland, New Zealand and the South Pacific (the last, possibly, from the imagination of Captain Greene). Curtis's account includes a lengthy, overdrawn narrative of tribal cannibalism. It maintains that the natives practised cannibalism 'in a manner most revolting'. They would eat members of other tribes, Europeans and even children, engaging freely in blood-letting and 'devouring greedily' in times of extreme hunger. He maintains (but supplies no direct testimony) that Baxter witnessed an instance of a father 'compelling' his wife to kill new-born twins whose bones, 'say Mr. Baxter and Mrs. Fraser', were carefully preserved 'after feeding' (107–8). This is not to suggest that the survivors could not have witnessed instances of anthropophagy. In times of extreme hunger, or in particularly dry seasons, Aborigines were known to practise infanticide, especially after the birth of twins. This was necessary to protect both the health of the mother and the survival of the group as a whole. The *Stirling Castle* was wrecked during such a bad season. Baxter's story could relate to an event he witnessed. But, even if this were the case, his understanding of its significance, the context which Curtis supplies for his report, and the sensational accounts which surround it, give it a Western meaning beyond the event itself. Curtis's incorporation of other stories from other places on the basis of other second or third-hand accounts, like explanations of 'real' events based on primal fantasies, is a regular feature of colonial discourse. These discursive devices maintain the circulation of horror.

The Collector's Impulse and the Promotion of Violence

As with the British subjects of Obeyesekere's research, British subjects connected to the *Stirling Castle* episode were interested in collecting artefacts for their personal possession or public display. Obeyesekere reports that during Captain Cook's stay in New Zealand, the crew collected cannibal stories and paid the Maori for heads. Their curiosity led them to cut open skulls of murdered natives and present them to the Maori to eat, thus provoking atavistic behaviours, unnecessary murders and the continuance of tribal wars. They also kept 'collections' on board their ships, primarily dried scalps, heads and bones; these made their way into scientific collections, which were later mounted in university anthropological displays and museums.[28] This practice led the New Zealand government to issue a regulation prohibiting the traffic in human remains, a regulation discussed in some detail in Alexander's history (130–1).

Several persons connected to the *Stirling Castle* episode were collectors. Captain Greene, Eliza's second husband, collected a parcel of Maori fishing hooks and bones which he presented to the Orkney Museum upon his return to Scotland with Eliza. In 1837 the skulls of the *Charles Eaton* wreck which occurred in the Torres Strait, illustrated in John Curtis's history, were displayed in Sydney. Later, when Andrew Petrie and Henry Stuart Russell searched on Fraser Island for the burial remains of Captain Fraser and the first mate Brown, they were shown a dilly containing bones. At the time, Walter Wrottesley, a visiting British member of their party, bought a dilly in exchange for a fishhook. Later, Andrew Petrie's son Tom happened upon a group of Aboriginal people in mourning on Fraser Island. Yabba, the grieving mother, displayed for him a dilly containing the skin of her son with head and hands, hair, fingers and nails intact. He reported the event to his father who offered 'flour, tea, sugar, tobacco, a tomahawk, anything for the skin'. The women kept it but later an old blackfellow presented Tom with four pieces of the skin from 'Yabba's son', an event which marked Tom's initiation into the tribe as 'turwan', or great man.[29] Petrie, although eager for 'curiosities', also showed great respect for Aboriginal rituals and burial customs. Such was not the case with a majority of other collectors.[30]

White Cannibalism

And what of white cannibalism? Obeyesekere relates that there was a British tradition of white cannibalism typically associated with shipwrecks.[31] So familiar and expected was the behaviour that it became legitimised, convention-bound, normal and normative. He delineates a code of practice derived from studies of shipwreck survivors. It typically involved the drawing of lots and the drinking of the victim's blood. Obeyesekere relates, however, that the lots were manipulated so that the member of the group who could be marked as 'other' became the first victim. That is, if one of the survivors was ethnically or racially foreign to the group, he would be chosen first. (Obeyesekere does not detail the fate of female survivors in such circumstances.) Thus white cannibalism involved overt racism inflected with fantasies of the libidinal potency of dark peoples. If there were no 'others' among the crew, then a boy or unmarried youth would be chosen. Only after these choices were closed off would one's own comrades be selected, with strict adherence to conventions of the lottery. Obeyesekere reports that, although cannibalism was forbidden by law, survivors were seldom brought to trial.

In the case of the shipwreck of the *Stirling Castle*, both Mrs Fraser and seaman Hodge reported that, before reaching land, the starving and emaciated crew threatened to 'draw lots' if the Captain did not pull ashore. There also was talk in Sydney that the mutinous crew, which included Hodge, may have practised cannibalism to survive. Speculations on this score centre around the remains of the aforementioned John Major – the seaman referred to in the sensational accounts as having been burned at the stake by blue-haired natives who decapitated him before making a meal of his remains. Michael Alexander, who had a fascination with cannibalism, examines the various descriptions of Major's demise in his twentieth-century populist history, and speculates that the excessive accounts may possibly disguise cannibalistic practices not of the natives, but of Hodge's party.

Robert Hodge was the only survivor of the pinnace party which had pulled away from the longboat shortly after the wreck. He arrived at Port Macquarie, having been rescued by the captain of the schooner *Nancy*, on 10 August, a day before the official rescue boats departed from Moreton Bay in search of Mrs Fraser. In a brief account, unusually short on detail, he claimed that all members of his party – including the Captain's twelve-year-old nephew, John, another ship's boy, several seamen, the Negro cook, and John Major – had succumbed to disastrous ends. The two boys were said to have drowned; two of the crew had been speared and left to die because they would not relinquish their waistcoats to the natives; the black cook had died of exhaustion; and John Major had been burned and eaten (presumably by natives). Hodge was the sole survivor of the mutinous pinnace crew. No one was at hand to refute his story. However, Baxter later claimed to have seen the remains of the body of Major. His account to John Curtis lends itself to speculations about other possible motives for Major's death. In *The Shipwreck of the Stirling Castle,* Curtis reports that the cutter which took the Moreton Bay survivors back to Sydney pulled in at the site of Hodge's rescue; there the crew found the grisly remains of Major, whose burnt and decapitated body had been devoured by kangaroo dogs. The crew were able to identify the remains due to the fact that:

> from some cause or other, the sanguinary brutes who put him to death, had either from forgetfulness, or that their rapacity was blunted by a deed of bloodshed, failed to denude him of a well-known waistcoat, the colour and remaining buttons of which were recognised by Baxter and his companions [Curtis, quoted in Alexander, 103–4].

The detail of the waistcoat comes as a surprise, since every survivor reported that bartering clothing for food had been the first act of exchange between the islanders and the crew. By Hodge's own admission, two of his party had been speared and left to die because they refused to relinquish their waistcoats. This detail prompts Michael Alexander to speculate that it is more likely that the white party resorted to cannibalism to survive. Further, he suggests, in relation to John Major, that Hodge 'murdered and partially ate the victim' – or that he had 'met with an accident while sleeping in a deserted shelter, which caught fire during the night' (104). Alexander recounts that the suggestion that the survivors resorted to cannibalism was heard in both Sydney and London, although details were suppressed each time a whisper of suspicion arose. There are no reports that the suspected practice brought about an investigation, however. This, possibly the most sinister dimension of the story, is further explored in the comic farce film *Eliza Fraser* (1976), wherein the dark, sadistic behaviours of the mutinous survivors are juxtaposed against the comic plot.

There is an Australian case of white cannibalism which did attract public notice and a trial just a few years before the wreck of the *Stirling Castle.* This involved two escaped convicts in Van Diemen's Land, Alexander Pearce and Thomas Cox. Dying of starvation in the wilderness, Pearce killed and ate Cox, whose head was later displayed in the Museum of Man at the University of Pennsylvania.[32] Pearce was brought to trial and hanged for his misdeeds. Marcus Clarke, in the convict novel *His Natural Life*, fictionalises the episode and includes a footnote which relates that while the proofs went through the press he had been accused of 'exaggerating the facts to create "sensation" '. In his defence he states that he based the episode on the actual confession of Pearce. As if this were not enough, he goes on to relate another 'white cannibal' anecdote, one told by the locals and referred to by 'Mr. James Bonwick

in his "Bushrangers" '. He concludes: 'I would not have introduced so repul-
sive an incident as this cannibalism of escaping convicts, were not such
incidents hideously frequent among absconders; and no writer, professing to
give a truthful picture of the results of the old convict system, can afford to
ignore them'.[33] His text suggests a more widespread practice than is generally acknowledged, although histories of the period, even the most recent,
fail to deal with these incidents.[34] That repression is part of our legacy of
imperialism.[35]

   The difference in the treatment of white cannibalism amongst shipwreck
survivors, as opposed to escaped convicts, may have more to do with the
status of the perpetrators than the taboos associated with the actual act of
cannibalism. Convicts, even in the wilds of Van Diemen's Land, were never
outside the bounds of British law. They were brought to trial and punished as
a public demonstration of their depravity. Shipwreck survivors existed in
liminal environments where aberrant behaviour was more acceptable. And
besides, public notice of cannibalism amongst otherwise 'innocent' white
British citizens might rend the fragile social fabric of colonialism. If and when
the behaviour occurred, it generally passed without public notice, investigation or criminal proceedings. Moral judgements differed, as well. In
survival conditions amongst shipwreck victims, the practice was deemed to
be regrettable but forgivable. Ritual cannibalism, however, which may have
been practised by indigenous peoples to incorporate the spiritual essence,
special characteristics, or power of the deceased into the living members of
the group, was judged by the West to be the ultimate mark of inhumanity.

Accretions of the Tale

Cannibalism and Human Sacrifice in Queensland

It is difficult to find even one reference to native cannibalism in the local
Australian press in the early days of colonisation. This remained the case
until the late 1820s when the *Sydney Gazette* began to publish letters from
settlers attesting to scenes of native cannibalism. The letters coincide with
the expedition of Wentworth, Lawson and Blaxland over the Blue Mountains, which made possible further colonial expansion and brought the
settlers in closer contact with Aborigines in the central west of New South
Wales. Stories of native savagery, including cannibalism, began to appear in
the *Sydney Gazette* from this time forward. They helped to justify colonial
practices of extermination. Two decades later, the early explorers and
potential settlers of what now is Queensland began to speculate about practices of human sacrifice and cannibalism in conjunction with the early years
of colonial settlement north of Moreton Bay. John Dunmore Lang, the Presbyterian minister who later became a Member of Parliament and who was

intent on Christianising the natives, wrote a letter to the Governor, Sir George Gray, in 1837, petitioning for funds to support an Aboriginal mission at Moreton Bay. In the petition he detailed the wreck of the *Stirling Castle* in which he claimed erroneously that 'the captain and first officer, and several of the crew, [were] barbarously murdered'.[36] Funds for the proposed mission were not forthcoming, but native savagery was duly noted. When Henry Stuart Russell wrote his memoirs, published in 1888, he recalled (although he was not in Queensland at the time and most of his 'recall' is hearsay) that the Captain and Brown were 'killed and eaten', the Captain first, and Brown 'reserved for later deviltry'.[37] Russell seems to have delighted in his memories of the terror of cannibalism. He was one of the explorers who formed the government party to track down the remains of Captain Fraser's body and to bring runaway convicts back to Moreton Bay in 1842.

The report of that expedition, which failed in its mission to locate the grave site of Captain Fraser, led to the naming of Fraser Island in the Captain's honour (and many other local sites in honour of the rescue party). Russell records that the name of the island was conferred on 10 May 1842. Other native place names were recorded during the trip, names which give the lie to ethnographic accounts which held that the natives were ignorant savages without the ability to reason or discriminate. Russell relates the following:

> By the assistance of Bracefelt [*sic*] we took down the native names of the mountains seen in the interior; Mandan, Carura, Coollimew, Coura, Yure-yaro, Eirange and Boppol are the most remarkable. The natives are so observant of everything in nature connected with their own peculiar run, that they have a name not only for every tree, shrub, grass, flower, bird, beast or insect, although every tribe differs in language but they know every piece of ground in the same district by its own peculiar name, every mile of river bears its own appellation from the source to the mouth, and the mouth itself has always a name of its own. These are the streets and roads through the bush, by which they can direct each other almost to within a hundred yards of the intended rendezvous.[38]

This detailed description reveals something of the nature of the assistance rendered to the early explorers by the native guides. Far from being passive, childlike or savage, these guides provided the knowledge and skills which made exploration possible. Further, the passage demonstrates the islanders' facility for language acquisition and their social dominance in regard to providing sources of information to the invaders. Their skills were essential to the white enterprise, although these skills have been deliberately repressed in the national memory.[39] A number of place names have been replaced with Anglicised names, like Mount Herman and Scrubbers Creek; the trails are now bitumen highways or designated bushwalks like the 'Eliza Fraser Nature Trail'; and the territories which once delineated the affiliations of the

Ngulungbara, Badtjala and Dulingbara peoples to their country are now mapped, divided and named according to Western notions of space, and their traditional owners dispersed. These facts all attest to Taussig's assertion that whites' fears of cannibalism reflected a repressed knowledge that their own behaviour constituted an overwhelming force that could (and would) devour the body politic of the indigenous peoples.

Although oblivious to these dimensions of his own narrative, Russell often returns to his cannibal theme. Russell was newly arrived from England when he joined the party sent to Fraser Island to obtain information on the burial site of Captain Fraser and to return the runaway convicts. When recalling the party's approach to the island, while crossing dangerous water around a sandy spit, he quips that 'the consciousness that the blacks were only waiting to make a meal of us, if capsized, did not add zest to the appetites which but a few minutes before we affirmed to be ravenous'. This comment comes from one of a party which had hired a local guide to accompany them and made it their first priority to procure (by force, if necessary, aided by the threatened use of firearms) an island guide. In this they failed, the natives being shy and particularly frightened by 'Mr. Wrottesley's red shirt'.[40] Although the tone of the narrative suggests that the natives' behaviour was curiously childlike in this regard, perhaps it can be better understood if one considers that red shirts were the mark of the colonial administrators whose hunting parties frequently resulted in violent and sometimes fatal confrontations with the indigenous people.

The stories of native cannibalism became more bizarre in time and with further white settlement. John Dunmore Lang's son George, who resided in the Wide Bay area of Queensland for some years, recorded other commonly rumoured practices which excited the settlers' imagination. In a pamphlet entitled *Queensland* (1864), he reported that for the triennial feast in the Bon-yi Mountains 'young girls [were] marked out for sacrifice months before the event by the old men of the tribe', slain and 'subjected to the horrid rite of cannibalism to satisfy their cravings' . . . for more than bunya nuts. This is not to say that the Aborigines in the area never engaged in the eating of human flesh; rather, that Eurocentric reports of reputed cannibalistic behaviour have more to do with fantasies of the Aboriginal as (savage) other than with actual events or their possible meaning for members of the group. Responding to this outrageous but widely held view of the Bon-yi ceremonies, years later, Tom Petrie, who attempted to understand Aboriginal practices from an Aboriginal perspective, refuted the story as being 'totally untrue'; he cited the recollections of his father, Andrew:

> There was no such thing as sacrifice among the Queensland aborigines, neither did they ever kill anyone for the purpose of eating them. They were most certainly cannibals, however, as they never failed to eat anyone killed in a fight, and always

ate a man noted for his fighting qualities, or a 'turwan' (great man), no matter how old he was, or even if he died from consumption! It was very peculiar, but they said they did it out of pity and consideration for the body – they knew where he was then – 'he won't stink'. The old, tough gins had the best of it; no one troubled to eat them; their bodies weren't of any importance, and had no pity or consideration shown them.[41]

His final comment reminds us that it is likely that indigenous men also regulated power relations between men and women within their groupings in relation to their symbolic rituals and actual behaviours.[42]

Before and After First Contact

What this suggests is that, whatever cannibalism may have meant before the arrival of the British, it meant something quite different, in practice as well as in discourse, after their arrival had had its effect. On the basis of the accretion of evidence of native cannibalism in Hawaiian and New Zealand societies, Obeyesekere maintains that it can only be understood in the context of 'domination and terror'. He reports that evidence from early voyages to New Zealand suggests that the Maori, although they engaged in ritual warfare and religious rites involving the consumption of human flesh, did not eat Europeans. (Nor did the indigenous people of north-eastern Australia.) Best evidence from the accounts of early ethnographies of New Zealand suggests that the Maori practised sacrificial and ritualistic cannibalism within strict tribal codes and customs. For example, according to Marshall Sahlins's review of the evidence, a common practice was for a Maori chief to accept and eat the eye of his enemy after battle. But the Europeans were not traditional enemies. They would not have been looked upon as suitable material for ritual. Not until the coming of the British did the Maori alter their behaviours, and the British understanding of those behaviours described them as aberrant within white colonial discourses.

One can make close comparisons with the situation in Australia. Although there were fatalities on both sides in the frontier experience of colonial New South Wales (which included Queensland until 1859), and later Queensland, there is no evidence of Aboriginal people consuming the bodies of their European victims.[43] This lack of evidence, of course, does not prevent the discursive production of the myth. In Queensland, rumours have been active since the Palmer River gold rush of the 1870s that, although Aborigines ate the flesh of Europeans, they had a particular predilection for the Chinese. Historical anniversaries seem to be the most favoured times for the generation of these horror stories. Lack and Cilento, for example, in their centenary history of Queensland, report that thousands of Chinese were killed and eaten on the Palmer River in Northern Queensland. As late as 1989 a journalist for the Brisbane *Sunday Mail,* Ron Saw, transformed these unfounded historical assumptions into a humorous column, 'Black menus put Chinese on the Boil' which was published by Brisbane, Adelaide and Perth newspapers. Despite forceful and persistent protests to the Press Council and the Australian Journalists Association by a journalist academic and a Catholic priest that the article was both inaccurate and racist, no action was taken by the professional associations nor the paper to report the complaints, to reproach the writer nor to refute the evidence.

David Bowman, in a recent article on the controversy, argues that stories about cannibalism have different effects at different historical periods.[44] As a general explanation of the propaganda supporting the colonial condition, Bowman quotes the classical scholar Gilbert Murray:

> Unnatural affection, child-murder, father murder, incest and the violation of the sanctity of dead bodies – when one reads such a list of charges against any tribe or nation, either in ancient or modern times, one can hardly help concluding that somebody wanted to annex their land.[45]

More specifically, in terms of Australian history at the time of the Queensland gold rush in the 1870s, rumours of cannibalism would discourage the Chinese from venturing to the Palmer River, thus reducing competition for the Europeans. It would deflect attention away from European violence and sexual licence as well. In the twentieth century the recirculation of the stories, whether represented as historical fact or tabloid humour, maintains the perpetration of racism. The possible effects of these stories cannot be underestimated in the 1990s when Aboriginal land rights, claims to native title, and quotas on ethnic migration are all on the national political agenda.

Bowman reports that during the sixteen months that Richard Buckhorn, the Catholic priest, unsuccessfully pursued avenues of redress, a spate of other articles and letters to the editor appeared attesting to sensational stories of savagery and cannibalism. In addition, a new history by Michael Cannon was published stating that cannibalism was a normal practice amongst some Aboriginal tribes in the nineteenth century, and a television documentary, 'Cape of Dreams', was broadcast which featured an old-time resident recounting the Aboriginal recipe for 'Palmer River chop suey. (Laughter).' His story would be familiar to many Queenslanders as a part of the local folklore. At the same time the protests were effective in other venues of public regulation. The Minister for Aboriginal Affairs and the Royal Commission into Aboriginal Deaths in Custody spoke out against biased and inaccurate news reporting, calling for a code of practice for presenting Aboriginal issues, which has been developed at least by the ABC and SBS. What Bowman does not comment on and is, perhaps, more relevant when searching for explanations, is that 'the truth' is not the major issue. It is not merely a matter of correcting the inaccuracies of the press or making perpetrators of racist falsehoods accountable. Whether or not Ronald Saw truly believed that Aborigines ate the Chinese, the story attracted (white) readers' interest because it provoked their anxieties and their desires: anxieties about their own dark fantasies and desires to distance these unspeakable practices from the self while transposing them onto others. Neither reason nor moral outrage can be effective weapons against the irrational forces evoked by the sensational stories which continue to feed the appetites of a contemporary audience.

The Ludic and the Serious

Cook's arrival in New Zealand, like the Frasers' arrival on Great Sandy Island, was an experience of first contact. Although no European victims had ever been known to be subjected to native cannibalism, nonetheless journals kept by crew members from Cook's voyage report that the Maori mimed, emphasised and exaggerated the eating of flesh for the Europeans with relish. Obeyesekere interprets this behaviour as a blend of the ludic and the serious, speculating that the Maori probably enjoyed the British reaction of disgust and fascination. The combination of ludic and serious motivations and behaviours which Obeyesekere attributes to the Maori in his dialogic reading could also be applied to the *Stirling Castle* episode. Throughout his text, Curtis takes delight in reporting and commenting on the sadistic pleasures which engaged the islanders at the expense of Mrs Fraser and the crew. They took the survivors fishing in a canoe and unceremoniously dumped them overboard, laughing at their clumsy attempts to escape drowning.[46] They laughed at the appearance of the crew members, plucked their hairs and applied firebrands and sand to sensitive, sunburnt skin.[47] And they passed the party from one native group to another, watching the survivors make their way south in hopes of reaching Moreton Bay not knowing that they were on an island, while the islanders mimed gestures of brutality and human sacrifice to the survivors along the way. For Curtis, these behaviours reveal both a childlike innocence and sadistic depravity, utterly devoid of human sentiments, behaviours which place the natives at the 'zero order of civilisation'. With no understanding of the totemic worship of animals, he marvels with Baxter that the islanders seemed to have no respect for human life, no way of discriminating between the value of human and animal lives. He relates with apparent incredulity that they would worship the dugong but throw the white survivors overboard from their canoes. But other nineteenth-century commentators and contemporary historians posit that the natives engaged in a range of behaviours, not with intended or deliberate cruelty, but in order to teach the newly arrived white ghosts survival skills and behaviours in keeping with their customs. It was the unexpectedly inept European response which brought them pleasure. Like parents to children, they enjoyed witnessing the cultural incompetence of the newcomers at fishing, swimming, grooming, hunting, protecting themselves from the sun and generally finding their way around. Often Aboriginal behaviours demonstrated a fear of the spectre of difference presented by the white strangers. (How could they be kin returned from the spirit world and yet be so ignorant of Badtjala ways?) At other times, perhaps, they were playing games, using the survivors for sport and enjoying the pleasures.[48] Misunderstandings along the border between the ludic and the serious could provide problems and pleasures for all parties.

Historians of early contact between white settlers and Aborigines of the Cooloola region comment on the wry sense of humour demonstrated by the Aborigines in their dealings with the new white settlers. Their actions and jokes were typically labelled 'childlike' by Eurocentric commentators. At the same time, these recollections can be read in dialogic terms as ways in which Aborigines actively challenged and subverted the European postures of mastery through mimicry and parody. The behaviours also attest to the fact that the white explorers, castaways and settlers were all subjected to intense scrutiny by the local people. Tom Petrie's *Reminiscences* are full of stories of Aboriginal pranks, jokes and mimes designed to 'take the mickey' out of the Europeans, especially in regard to impractical habits of Western dress and presentation. Of particular amusement were European beards, body hair and the ridiculous costumes worn by the soldiers and colonial administrators. The *Stirling Castle* survivors reported that the islanders paraded about the bush with breeches tied around their necks, prompting Curtis to remark that they were 'exquisite mimes of their superiors' (67). Two similar stories reveal that they quickly picked up English words, phrases and idioms, understood European class divisions, and parodied differential power relations. One is told in Curtis's history. In one of his innumerable footnotes he relates a 'cute' story about a native guide who cooked a brace of birds for a trekking party. He roasted the 'geppleman's' bird on the spit while he placed that of his servant in the embers, in a mock display of class divisions (111). Another similar example is an Aboriginal joke from the 1860s about what defines a 'gentleman', retold by Ebenezer Thorne in *Queen of the Colonies*. The story goes that there were the three types of genuine 'gentlemen' in Queensland, that is 'fellows' who do no work:

> Whitefellow yacker (whitefellow work), bullock yacker (bullock work), yarraman yacker (horse work), baal (not) gentlemen; blackfellow no yacker, walk about, kangaroo walk about, pig-pig walk about, *that* fellow gentleman. [49]

In translation this means that whites, bullocks and horses work, therefore they are not gentlemen; on the contrary, blacks, kangaroos and pigs do not work, they just walk around, therefore they are gentlemen. The play of the ludic and the serious on the part of the indigenous peoples seems to have been a part of all early contact stories. Frontier experiences were never one-sided occurrences. Rather, they initiated a time when two cultures came together and engaged in reciprocal relations which simultaneously shaped the event. The difference was, as Debbie Bird Rose suggests, that

> indigenous people were establishing a balanced intersubjectivity, effectively seek-
> ing to bridge the distance between the two groups and bring the others into their
> own sociality. It seems certain that they expected the others to reciprocate. Euro-
> peans, on the other hand, sought to exaggerate the distance between the two
> groups, and to construct a hierarchy of subjectivities with themselves at the apex
> dominating the others who they took to be reflections of themselves.[50]

Curtis records that Mrs Fraser began her testimony at the Lord Mayor's Commission of Inquiry with the words: 'the stories we have read in our childhood and the representations we have seen in theatres of savage life are mere trifles compared with real facts. . . . All that the mind of man can conceive falls short of what I have witnessed.' On a similar note, Baxter's testimony ends with the following words: 'I can safely swear that our sufferings are not to be imagined let alone to be described.' We might conclude, then, with Obeyesekere, that Aboriginal behaviours were constructed 'out of an extremely complex dialogue between Europeans and [indigenous peoples], a dialogue that makes sense in relation to the history of contact and unequal power relations and the cultural values, fantasies, and the common dark humanity they both share'.[51]

In colonial Queensland by the 1860s both George Lang, who had earlier spread the stories of the consumption of young girls at the Bon-yi feast, and Tom Petrie, who befriended many Aborigines and sympathised with their plight, were convinced (privately) that if the indigenous peoples were to survive the colonial encounter they would need to take up guns against the settlers in their uneven war against the onslaught of civilisation.[52] Some were, in fact, given guns (the Native Police), but only so that they could be enlisted into the colonial cause, to boost the strength of the colonisers' resistance against other Aboriginal groups. But the public response to the colonial encounter generally displayed less sympathy for their plight. After the settlement wars of the 1850s new settlers in the area north of Brisbane had little sympathy for the Aboriginal cause. They overwhelmingly rejected humanitarian claims concerning the justice of Aboriginal retaliation against the massacre of their own people, as can be seen in this newspaper account:

We are placed in this predicament; we must either retire from the place and leave the smiling country in the hands of a few cannibals, or we must protect our lives in such a manner as to convince the savage that he is powerless to cope with the white men's arms, and teach him that his only hope of safety lies in submission.

'Rusticus', 1861[53]

The rest, as they say, is history.

CHAPTER 6

Modern Reconstructions:
Michael Alexander's History and
Sidney Nolan's Paintings

The Eliza Fraser story has had several revivals in the twentieth century, particularly in the 1970s and 1990s. In the 1970s Eliza Fraser became a legend in Australia and her story a model for several artists working not only in Australia but also within other post-colonial societies. The legend served new, celebratory renditions of nationalism. New versions which appeared at the time included: Michael Alexander's populist history, *Mrs Fraser on the Fatal Shore* (1971, reissued in paperback in 1976); Sidney Nolan's 'Mrs. Fraser' series of paintings (4 series: 1947–8, 1956–7, 1962–4, 1971–7); Patrick White's novel, *A Fringe of Leaves* (1976); and André Brink's South African novel, *An Instant in the Wind* (1976). Other significant adaptations of the tale, which have been less widely available to an international audience, include: Canadian Michael Ondaatje's long poem, *The Man with Seven Toes* (1969); London-based playwright Gabriel Josipovici's play, *Dreams of Mrs. Fraser* (first performed in London in 1972); a collaboration between Barbara Blackman and Peter Sculthorpe for the musical composition with libretto, 'Eliza Fraser Sings' (first performed in Australia in 1978); and David Williamson's and Tim Burstall's screenplay and film, *Eliza Fraser* (Hexagon Films, 1976), reconstructed as a popular novel by Kenneth Cook (1976). In the 1990s the story provides a backdrop for a number of adaptations critical of white presumptions of national identity. These include: Allan Marett's reworking of the legend into a Japanese Noh play, *Eliza*, performed in Sydney and Tokyo (1989–90); and Gillian Coote's documentary film, 'Island of Lies' (first screened on ABC television in 1991). The legend has also been subjected to interrogation by Badtjala artist, Fiona Foley, working from an anti-colonial stance, in a series of Eliza Fraser paintings and installations (first exhibited in 1991).

The three novels, film and Nolan paintings (several of which were used as book-cover illustrations) all came to prominence in 1976, at the height of a renaissance of cultural nationalism in the arts in Australia under the Whitlam Labor government. Mrs Fraser's story, modified by Australia's most prominent creative artists, took on new meanings within an Australian nationalist framework. In these masculine reconstructions, whether marketed for a mass audience or intended for a more elite readership associated with 'high' art and culture, three common elements prevail:

1 Aboriginal life is pushed into the background. The story is refashioned as a romance between Mrs Fraser and her convict rescuer, whom she betrays.
2 Eliza Fraser becomes the focus for the story and not the other seven (male) survivors of the wreck.
3 There remains an abiding interest in her sexuality, particularly in what did happen or might have happened in the brief time between her husband's death and her rescue.

The combination of elements varies and, as might be expected, the materials are handled differently depending on the genre, the artist, the audience, and the cultural positioning of the critics. The cumulative effect, however, is to mute, even to the point of disavowal, the political anxieties inherent in the event which continue to reverberate through Australia's national mythologies. I am thinking of the underlying anxieties concerning the relationship between British power, colonial authority and national identity; the tenuous hold which colonial administrators had on the convicts and which both they and new settlers had on the land; the continued exploitation of indigenous peoples; ignorance of local customs; a forgetting of frontier history; enduring fears of difference and the like. The Australian adaptations of the story in the 1970s retain the nineteenth-century preoccupation with the captivity and rescue of a white woman in an alien environment amongst members of an alien race. In the twentieth-century versions, however, her life is threatened more by sexual peril than by 'native' savagery and cannibalism. The more recent Australian adaptations diverge from nineteenth-century narratives in that they take up a specific interest in her rescue by the runaway convict David Bracefell. The focus on his reputed rescue of her from 'a fate worse than death', the consequent romance between the 'lady' and the convict, and her final betrayal of his trust, are all elements of a larger narrative inscribed within Australian nationalism. The retellings of the story in the 1970s establish a Western (and specifically Australian, masculine) authority for the narrative, one in which political and racial dimensions of the event are displaced through the figure of the woman caught within a romantic fantasy, woman as spectacle.

Although their work in relation to Eliza Fraser is less well known, three women, two white and one Aboriginal, have taken up the story. Each of their approaches demonstrates marked differences from those of their male counterparts. That difference is inflected by national, political and racial affiliations as well as gender. The first white female creative artist to take up the story was Barbara Blackman, who wrote the poetic libretto 'Eliza Surviver' for Peter Sculthorpe's musical score 'Eliza Fraser Sings' (first performed in 1978). The second was Gillian Coote, who made a television documentary, 'Island of Lies' (1991). In the film, Coote revisits Fraser Island, metaphorically positioning herself as the ghost of Mrs Fraser, accompanied by a female descendant of the island's Badtjala people and the grandson of an early white settler. Together they examine the 'lies' which underwrite a white history of settlement. The latest artist to take up the story is Fiona Foley, a Sydney-based Badtjala artist who traces her heritage back to Fraser Island. The legend of Eliza Fraser is of particular interest for her in that it signals a disruption of her pre-contact culture. For her, the Eliza Fraser stories represent a white cultural forgetting of the devastating effects of invasion and a celebratory narrative which serves white nationalist interests. Foley recasts the story in the light of her lost Badtjala heritage in several exhibitions and, most specifically, in ten of the paintings and an installation piece shown in 'By Land and Sea I Leave Ephemeral Spirit' (Figure 15).

There are clear differences in the representations of Eliza Fraser, Australian nationalism, myth and history when one examines the work of male and female, mainstream and marginalised, Aboriginal and white Australian artists from the 1970s to the present. My interest is not to trace the changes in character or narrative, nor the evolving historical representations of the event. Rather, the analysis concerns various textual, visual and ideological strategies adapted by artists and critics, as understood by different readers and audiences in different historical and ideological contexts. These concerns include the ways in which the various artists position themselves in relation to their texts; how they address their audiences; what strategies they employ to manage the racial, sexual and political anxieties inherent in the story; and how their work has been received and interpreted both in Australia and overseas over time. As will be demonstrated in the following discussion, the adaptations by white male artists, while muting signs of racism and British authority within an Australian cultural context, do not so much ignore these troublesome aspects as disguise them behind the sexually and erotically charged figure of Eliza Fraser. At the same time, each twentieth-century version contains its own set of contradictions. Each gives evidence that its author both engages in critique and also reproduces ideologies of nationalism and dominant constructions of race, class and/or gender; each has been read in ways that both uphold and contest dominant cultural constructions.

This chapter, after locating Eliza Fraser as the subject of Michael Alexander's twentieth-century historical study, will consider the Australian representations of Eliza Fraser known principally through Sidney Nolan's powerfully evocative paintings. The analysis focuses specifically on the renewed interest in the Eliza Fraser story in the 1970s. It traces aspects of the story and its reception through Nolan with regard to the artist's personal and cultural imaginary and within the wider cultural contexts of modernism, Australian nationalism, and neo-colonial politics. It attends specifically to the ways in which Nolan, his commentators and his critics have dealt with fantasies of romance and woman's betrayal. Subsequent chapters will deal with other transformations of the Eliza Fraser story, both within Australia and overseas, which sometimes reinforce, and at other times challenge, the prevalent Australian versions of the tale.

Michael Alexander's History

Michael Alexander's populist history, *Mrs Fraser on the Fatal Shore* (1971, 1976),[1] signals a renewed interest in the event within a modern, Western context. Although a popular rather than a scholarly history, the text functions to place the event within a historical field, becoming a point of reference concerning questions of historical truth for future writers, critics and commentators. Alexander's interest in the Eliza Fraser story was spurred by a number of personal and professional preoccupations, the precipitating factor being his work on captivities and reports of cannibalism within earlier colonial contexts. In the late 1960s and early 1970s Alexander edited a volume of colonial manuscripts entitled *Discovering the New World*, which were based on the works of Theodore de Bry. He became particularly interested in captivity narratives and reports of cannibalism whilst reading de Bry's material on 'Hans Staden and the Cannibals of Brazil', one of the chapters in the book.[2] During this time Alexander encountered the Eliza Fraser legend with his discovery of the Thames and Hudson monograph *Sidney Nolan: Landscapes and Legends* (published in 1961), which featured the striking painting of a dehumanised 'Mrs Fraser' as a full-page colour plate (see Figure 1).[3] This monograph includes an introductory essay by Colin MacInnes depicting Australia as a bizarre, strange, eccentric place – a *jardin exotic*. It contains the following version of the Eliza Fraser story, which was to become legendary:

> Mrs Fraser was a Scottish lady who was shipwrecked on what is now Fraser Island, off the Queensland coast. She lived for 6 months among the aborigines, rapidly losing her clothes, until she was discovered by one Bracefell, a deserting convict who himself had hidden for 10 years among the primitive Australians. The lady asked the criminal to restore her to civilisation, which he agreed to do if she would promise to intercede for his free pardon from the Governor. The bargain was sealed, and the couple set off inland.
>
> At first sight of European settlement, Mrs Fraser rounded on her benefactor and threatened to deliver him up to justice if he did not immediately decamp. Bracefell

returned disillusioned to the hospitable bush, and Mrs Fraser's adventures aroused such admiring interest that on her return to Europe she was able to exhibit herself at 6d a showing in Hyde Park.

Colin MacInnes

This legendary retelling contains the motifs which lay the foundation for future versions. In it, Mrs Fraser's time on the island is stretched from six weeks to six months and she is rescued by the runaway convict Bracefell, whom she betrays. In addition, the account makes almost no mention of the indigenous people; and it draws an image of Mrs Fraser as a spectacle on exhibition in Hyde Park. The Thames and Hudson publication signalled the beginning of European attention to Australian art. A major monograph and lavish production, it was the first European publication devoted to a modern Australian artist.[4] Through it, an international public gained access to the Eliza Fraser story and some thirty-two paintings from Nolan's first two 'Mrs Fraser' series. Alexander was not the only creative artist to take his cue from this volume. Both the South African novelist, André Brink, and the Sri Lankan-born but Canadian-based prose-writer, Michael Ondaatje, maintain that this same text spurred their interest in the story and led to their respective adaptations: *An Instant in the Wind* and *The Man with Seven Toes*.

While Alexander worked on his manuscript project he was shown a copy of a draft novel by Queensland medical practitioner and amateur historian, Sir Raphael Cilento, titled *All Tempests to Endure*,[5] by his friend the film producer, Michael Luke. Luke himself had an enduring interest in the story. He contemplated making a film and had completed a filmscript, 'The Dreamtime of Mrs Fraser', in 1970. Luke admits the script bore no fidelity to history but was motivated by the MacInnes legend and the Cilento novel. While encouraging Alexander to investigate the story further, Luke developed the film project with Universal Pictures, tentatively commissioning John Huston to direct it and Donald Sutherland and Vanessa Redgrave to star as David Bracefell and Eliza Fraser. He was forced to abandon the project when it failed to win financial backing.

Before writing *Mrs Fraser on the Fatal Shore*, Alexander had published three semi-autobiographical adventure tales, including *The Privileged Nightmare*, an account of his own two-and-a-half year captivity when he was taken hostage by the Germans during World War II and imprisoned at Colditz Castle.[6] Alexander had not attempted to write a history before, which may account for the absence of historical documentation in his text (few footnotes or reference citations, no bibliography nor index, for example), an absence corrected in his subsequent historical studies. He recalls that his research was motivated by the sensational and bizarre aspects of the story of Mrs Fraser's reputed captivity. The historical text is organised like an adventure tale, with evocative chapter headings: 'Cast Away', 'Captured by Cannibals', 'The Domestication of Mrs Fraser', 'The Hunger of John Graham', 'Her Virtue in Jeopardy', 'The Irish Convict', 'In the Nick of Time', and 'Mrs Fraser's New Captain'. Nonetheless, the style and presentation of the text, which includes maps, illustrations, contemporary records, and an appendix of nineteenth-century documents relating to the event, popularises the story within a historical guise of truth.

To prepare his study Alexander, working from London, consulted John Curtis's text as well as official archival records and documents; contemporary nineteenth-century newspaper accounts, including those of the sensational tabloid press; historical reminiscences and memoirs from nineteenth-century Queenslanders; and personal letters and reminiscences of surviving members of the Fraser family in New Zealand and California. In addition, he collected various fictionalised versions of the event, briefly visited Fraser Island, and became familiar with local Queensland adaptations, including Cilento's novel, which contained illustrations which Alexander used in his text.

Alexander's interests have bearing on his writing of *Mrs Fraser on the Fatal Shore*. His narrative, although faithful to the documents and records available to him and presented in a factual guise, is necessarily speculative. It is speculative not only in the post-modern sense that history itself is a genre of writing as fictionalised as any other type of narrative, but also within the modernist sense of 'truth', given the nature of the materials available to the writer and his popular, rather than scholarly, approach. At the same time, the text presents an eminently readable and credible account which tells the story of shipwreck and survival from a Western frame of reference, attempting to understand the fear and confusion experienced by white survivors when confronted with the hostile conditions of their alien environment. Many chapters show evidence of a close reading of extensive archival materials and historical documents. The author reconciles contradictory accounts by a process of shrewd deduction, constructing an absorbing and coherent narrative. Nonetheless, the 'Mrs Fraser' that Alexander captures is closely aligned with the one of legend.

Mrs Fraser on the Fatal Shore appeared as a hardback in London in 1971. It was reprinted in a popular paperback edition in 1976, presumably to coincide with the renewed Australian interest in the story. The first edition featured Nolan's 'Mrs Fraser' painting on the front of the dust-jacket (the same painting which Alexander remembered seeing on the cover of the Thames and Hudson monograph, *Sidney Nolan*). The back inside flap of the dust-jacket presented a titillating summary of the Eliza Fraser story taken from nineteenth-century versions of the ordeal, admittedly not written by

Alexander but included with the likely intention to boost sales. It prepares the reader for a sensational tale:

> Captured by stone age aborigines of rude habits and cannibalistic tendencies Captain Fraser was speared to death . . . [while his wife] a lady of genteel upbringing, was stripped naked by her captors and made to perform exacting and humiliating tasks as slave to the tribe . . . Having lately given birth in an open boat to a baby, which was immediately drowned, she was forced to mother an aboriginal child which she described as 'one of the most deformed and ugly-looking brats my eyes ever beheld'. . . .
>   This is the true story, supported by documentary evidence, behind one of the great Australian legends.[7]

The text, although far less sensationalist than the cover might suggest, supplies readers with the seeds for future imaginative reconstructions which would not be kind to the re-historicised Eliza Fraser, nor to the Aboriginal people. For example, without providing documentary evidence, it includes claims, all of which had subsequently been challenged, that Mrs Fraser was physically indulgent, having been 'reared in Ceylon'; that she was captive to a primitive tribe of Aborigines known to be 'exceptionally cruel'; that she was physically humiliated, forced to perform disgusting tasks and pressed into 'severe labour' by the women; that she may have been physically attracted to the youthful men of the tribe; that she was about to be made the wife of the chief at the time she was rescued by either John Graham or David Bracefell, with whom she 'formed some relationship . . . including some secret shame she wished to keep concealed'; that she was hysterical, and told the doctor at Moreton Bay that she feared she might be pregnant; that she was manipulated by her new 'Svengali' husband; and that upon return to London she appeared in a tent, 'perhaps exhibiting her more available scars to a prurient public' as a sideshow exhibit in Hyde Park.

All of this makes for a good story under the guise of historical truth. But the hybrid 'history', which borrows heavily from the genre of adventure tale, relies, of necessity, on Alexander's speculations and interpretations in addition to those that had accrued through a century of retellings which gave Mrs Fraser the status of legend.[8] Alexander's text, like that of Curtis before him, allows him to take up the position of a privileged narrator. Readers are encouraged to bestow upon him the mantle of the historian through such narrative devices as the dust-jacket testimonial and textual apparatuses that this is 'a true story, supported by documentary evidence, behind one of the great Australian legends'. The semi-historical style and presentation of his populist narrative disguise the speculative nature of his 'story' as well as the author's complicity with dominant perspectives on race and gender. His text becomes another site for the construction of knowledges tied to dominant relations of power.

Readings of the Feminine

In the main, Alexander represents the historical Eliza Fraser as a dominating wife and a bad mother who deserved her fate. When referring to the historical Mrs Fraser, his tone is often condescending, even callous. He constructs class and racial categories with more than a touch of irony, drawing on a number of neo-colonial fantasies of difference. In a number of instances, he employs satire to undercut sympathy for his subject. For example, in a chapter entitled 'The Domestication of Mrs Fraser', which concerns her interactions with the Aborigines, he relates that she 'treated the Aborigines patronisingly as if they had been impoverished tinkers on an Orkney hill' (53).

> Had she arrived amongst the aborigines under different circumstances, as a missionary or a civilised lady visiting simple savages, Mrs Fraser would no doubt have been quite in her element and given selfless service to those less fortunate than she. The ladies of the tribe could have been taught needlework and hygiene and methods of cookery other than their endless broiling. . . . But in her present position her status as a superior being did not seem to be in any way appreciated [50].

After continuing in this vein for some pages in which Mrs Fraser's 'difficult domestication' is described, Alexander lists the physical sufferings she bore on her body – she was 'burned by firesticks and beaten with *waddys* . . . bitten by horseflies, sandflies and mosquitoes and covered with irritating sores'. He concludes: 'The poor woman cannot have had a moment's pleasure in her day'(52).

Alexander also suggests a sensual nature to Mrs Fraser quite early in the narrative by commenting that a contemporary sketch of the woman reveals a 'handsome dark-haired lady whose strong features and mobile mouth suggest contradiction between duty and indulgence' (18). Consider the sketch which prompts this remark (Figure 7). How strong is the contradiction between duty and indulgence for you? The supposition has its uses. It allows Alexander to speculate later in the text on her possibly sexual interest in one of her male (native) captors and on an attachment to one of them which 'might be more romantic than she admits' (64). Jill Ward, in an early article which compares Patrick White's fictional account with Alexander's history, comments that White may have been motivated by this aspect of Mrs Fraser to introduce his 'similar contradiction between sense and sensuality' in Ellen Gluyas Roxburgh.[9] But the supposition remains an interpolation by Alexander from a dubious visual cue, coupled with the information gleaned from one of the surviving relatives of Mrs Fraser living in New Zealand, that Mrs Fraser may have come from Ceylon.[10] This 'clue' provides another colonial reference point for the tale which leads Alexander, borrowing from

Western tropes of tropical life in the colonies, to speculate on the lady's sensuality and indulgence. Jill Ward, who made the further connection between Alexander's sensual Eliza and Patrick White's instinctual Ellen, is labelled by a present-day historian as Eliza Fraser's 'most feminist' commentator – presumably because she was the only female commentator in the 1970s to write of the event.[11] Alexander's suggestive reading of Mrs Fraser's 'mobile mouth' will later evolve into a face which contains 'a strange combination of purity and wantonness, virtue and lust' in the sensationalised popular text of Kenneth Cook, the novelist of the film version.[12]

The Gaps and Supplements of History

There is both a gap and a supplement in the textual constructions regarding Mrs Fraser's captivity and her rescue which provoke these remarks. The gap is created in historical terms by an absence of data or corroborated evidence as to what may have happened at the time of the event. The supplement is a story of her rescue by the convict David Bracefell and the couple's extended bush idyll together. This dimension of the legend was developed melodramatically in Cilento's novel and treated extensively in the works of Sidney Nolan, Patrick White, André Brink, Michael Ondaatje and Gabriel Josipovici. But it is a story with dubious historical foundation. The gap provided a tantalising silence for Bracefell at the time of his return to white society in 1842 as well as for subsequent writers, artists, historians and public figures, all of whom have attempted to supplement the story with additional projections on the Eliza Fraser of masculine sexual fantasies and desires.

The sexual interest prompted by Alexander's text occludes other political, class-based or racial tensions related to the event. It is taken up by a number of later (male) commentators on the tale. The writers excessively ponder the burning question: 'Did she or didn't she?' And if she did, 'Where, when and with whom? Did she provoke, desire, seduce or resist?' The question 'Was she raped?' is not seriously considered, although it no doubt would have been had the story been taken up by Anne Summers in her feminist history *Damned Whores and God's Police*.[13] Nor, as Yolanda Drummond points out, has any commentator ever given Eliza Fraser credit for forbearance in *not* complaining of Bracefell, the rescuer she is said to have betrayed, if indeed he did rape her during the rescue operations. Neither do later historians, who are convinced of the veracity of Bracefell's account, extend sympathy to Mrs Fraser for saving the convict from further punishment had she complained of him to the authorities.

'Did she or didn't she?', they ponder. Patrick White says 'She did': with her husband's brother before the shipwreck and with her convict rescuer thereafter, and both she and we (presumably) are so much the better for it.

Michael Alexander doesn't know, and is clearly bothered by this. He writes (in a statement that would be interesting to deconstruct) that

> It is clear that she had some unpleasant experiences, but her inconsistency and natural reticence in encountering them has led to a lack of credible information on the subject. Her most reliable biographer [John Curtis] . . . is aggravatingly unspecific about her sexual adventures [63].

In other words, we don't know, and furthermore, the above passage would seem to hint that it is *her fault* that we don't know. What we do know is that the popular Queensland version of her rescue and sexual liaison during a lengthy trek back to Moreton Bay with the convict David Bracefell did not occur, although historians still speculate that Bracefell may have been involved as a helpmate to her official rescuer, John Graham, and his 'contact' with Mrs Fraser may well have been sexual.[14] We don't know, but Alexander suggests, in keeping with the sensational tabloid accounts of the 1830s, that the corroboree which was reported to be in progress at the time of her official rescue by a government party may have been intended as a ceremony to consign her as wife to the 'head of the tribe'. In terms of Aboriginal custom, it is likely that the white woman would have been assigned to a male member of the group after the death of her husband in order to give her a place in the community and some degree of protection. Such women would not have been married to 'the chief' at the time of a corroboree organised for this purpose, although this is the customary suggestion in white versions of the (mainly American) classic captivity narrative. Aboriginal groups differed in their organisation, and knowledge of the pre-contact social organisation of Fraser Island groups is slim. But it is likely that they had no 'chiefs', nor were they organised into 'tribes'. These are white man's terms adapted from earlier colonial enterprises. In the case of Eliza Fraser, the corroboree version of her rescue appears in virtually every narrative reconstruction, including that of Alexander. The problem is not whether a corroboree was in progress at the time of her rescue (highly unlikely, since her rescue took place in the morning, but a celebration may have been planned for a subsequent evening) but the meaning that it is given in the accounts. When introduced in historical studies under provocative headings like 'saved in the nick of time' or 'rescued from a fate worse than death', it inserts a submerged and racially charged subtext into the narrative for the readers.

Alexander reports that, during the time of Mrs Fraser's recovery at Moreton Bay, her attending physician recorded that the distressed and disoriented woman seemed to be obsessed with the fear that she might be pregnant. No physician's records have been found, however. There is some speculation that Alexander may have retrieved this information from Sir Raphael

Cilento's draft novel of the ordeal, written in 1966.[15] Cilento, as mentioned, was a renowned Queensland medical practitioner and amateur historian who had been preoccupied with the story for some years. He was perhaps the first to retrieve archival documents from the Mitchell Library of New South Wales and attempt a modern reconstruction. In the preface to his unpublished historical novel, *All Tempests to Endure*, he states that every situation depicted in the novel was confirmed by official documents, except for the love scenes between Bracefell and Mrs Fraser and the death of the tribal elder, Euenmundi, which were complete conjecture.[16] Although there is some attempt to present a plausible reconstruction of events based on local knowledge of the geography and native customs, the love scenes in this novel, as the title suggests, belong to the popular melodramatic genre of woman's romance. Cilento locates Bracefell as a runaway convict living with the Aborigines who care for Eliza. In the novel, he and Euenmundi, an Aboriginal elder, rescue Eliza from the 'tribe'. The convict and the lady form a sexual liaison before Bracefell turns her over to the rescuer of record, John Graham. Eliza, presented as an archetypal romance heroine, enters into an active sexual liaison with the convict. The purple prose of these scenes indicates why the manuscript remains unpublished. During Mrs Fraser's first meeting with Bracefell, she chastises him for his familiarity in calling her 'Eliza' and then exclaims 'Hit me . . . I must be stupid, mean and narrow. I need a whipping for [being] a conceited scold' (102). And later, during their Edenic bush idyll, she flirts with him and coaxes him to tell his story. Soon she 'loses her will to struggle against his virility' (109) and the two become like Adam and Eve in their new-found paradise. Eliza fears she may not be attractive to her lover, however, because she's 'too old, too ugly'. But 'he takes her hungrily' (133). Ashamed by her own behaviour, she betrays him with a 'venomous' hatred at the edge of civilisation, exclaiming, 'Go back to your black trollop' (136). In regard to Mrs Fraser's physical condition at the time of her rescue, in the novel she repeatedly utters to Graham, 'How shall I ever live through the shame of it?' (141). Upon her return to Moreton Bay, she confides in melodramatic fashion to her personal attendant that she had 'escaped a fate worse than death' (158). She feared, however, that she might be pregnant (at this point the intrusive narrator explains that perhaps she was not having periods due to a loss of weight coupled with personal trauma of her captivity) and that she could have a black baby. Much of the illicit and class-determined quality, if not the melodramatic writing, which Cilento makes of this relationship was incorporated into Michael Alexander's history. Patrick White and André Brink reshape the romantic dimensions in their serious literary adaptations, *A Fringe of Leaves* and *An Instant in the Wind*.

It appears that Alexander took a few cues from Cilento's novel when constructing Eliza Fraser as a sexual adventurer. The only archival document known to make mention of the lady's sexual travails is the Commandant's official report, which is available in the New South Wales archives. It recounts that Mrs Fraser complained to John Graham, her rescuer, that 'the white men she met were worse than the blacks'. Which white men she met, where and when – all remains a mystery. These elusive slips of evidence within the official and unofficial records are all that exist to fuel the fires of speculation. None of them suggests the scenario which Cilento constructs and Alexander explores in his history – that Eliza Fraser was a willing partner in a sexual encounter. In fact, if anything it suggests, to me at least, quite the opposite. But the mystery, the enigma of the woman and her sexuality, invites myth. It has always been so. And with myth, the woman becomes the archetypal Other for man.

Sidney Nolan's Paintings

The importance of a modern reading of visual cues has been spurred throughout by Sidney Nolan's stunning paintings in his 'Mrs Fraser' series. As we have seen, Nolan took up the theme of Eliza Fraser in at least four different periods of his artistic career: 1947–8, 1956–7, 1962–4, 1971–7. The first series consists of twelve large, brightly coloured paintings, including the provocative 'Mrs Fraser' in bestial pose illustrated earlier (Figure 1). This, 'one of his most alarming, convinced and unforgettable images',[17] appeared in 1971 on the dust-jacket of Michael Alexander's history. Nolan's second series of thirty sombre and somewhat surreal paintings depicts Mrs Fraser and Bracefell as lonely lovers in a rainforest landscape, a fallen Eden. Nolan produced this series for his first major retrospective at the Whitechapel Gallery in London (1957), when it became obvious that he would not be able to retrieve his early works (which included his first Eliza Fraser and Ned Kelly paintings) which he had left in Melbourne at the artists' commune, Heide. The exhibition, although not fully a 'retrospective', introduced him (and, through him, Australian art) to a European audience. Nolan's third series of paintings returns to the theme of Adam and Eve in a richly coloured, dream-like paradise. One of the paintings from this series, 'Mrs Fraser and Convict' (Figure 9), was chosen at Nolan's instigation for the dust-jacket of the first Cape and Penguin editions of *A Fringe of Leaves*.[18] The fourth period in which Nolan took up the Eliza Fraser story occurred during the 1970s. At this time he reworked the materials in conjunction with the publication of a volume of poems, rainforest colour plates and drawings, *Paradise Garden* (1971), and two series of paintings: 'Ern Malley' (1972) and 'Baptism' (1977). These paintings recast themes from Nolan's earlier 'Mrs Fraser' and 'Ned Kelly' paintings (see Figure 10). Along with the poems, they make specific refer-ence to his unresolved relationship with Sunday Reed dating back to 1947.

Figure 9 'Mrs. Fraser and Convict', by Sidney Nolan, 1964.
By permission of Lady Mary Nolan and Barbara Mobbs.

Figure 10 'Beyond is anything', from the 'Ern Malley' series, by Sidney Nolan, 1972.
By permission of Lady Mary Nolan.

Nolan's Eliza Fraser paintings have been called 'the visible links in the chain of an invisible narrative'.[19] It was a narrative which continued to unfold for the artist until the end of his life. Although each part of the series was grounded in and interpreted by the personal, social and cultural concerns of its time, the story of Mrs Fraser, imagined as a traitor who betrayed her convict rescuer, seems to have been an enduring personal myth for the artist. This understanding of her historical role provided a descriptive gloss on the paintings for virtually every catalogue essay and work of art criticism. In 1989 Nolan made his first visit to the Orkney Islands in conjunction with an exhibition of the 'Mrs Fraser' series. At that time he read the more recent historical accounts of Eliza Fraser's life in the Orkney archives. Later, in an interview for the Australian press, he commented on the changing meaning of Eliza Fraser for him over time. The first series in which he brought together Mrs Fraser and the convict, he related, was connected to his emotional state at the time of painting. The second, more lyrical, series was an attempt to place Mrs Fraser within a national mythology of Australia imagined as a lost Eden. Over time, Mrs Fraser became for him 'a byword for endurance strangely matched with treachery'. But Nolan commented that he would have to rethink the narrative in the light of the new information about Mrs Fraser which he gleaned during his visit to the Orkneys, referring specifically to her spartan existence before the voyage, and her pregnancy and childbirth at sea which resulted in the loss of her baby. He is quoted as saying that this woman from the Orkneys was 'a more complex victim of harsh times' than he had previously known. (It is noteworthy that knowledge of the woman's suffering related to the loss of a child is what seems to most affect and alter Nolan's view of her. Whether or not the childbirth was a story concocted after the event, it has more than served its purpose.) The artist also related that he was contemplating the possibility of painting yet another series, in which he might represent Mrs Fraser within the stone-age culture of the Orkneys juxtaposed with that of Aboriginal Australia, as a woman tossed from one Stone Age to another.[20] It appears, then, that Nolan maintained a preoccupation with the Eliza Fraser story from his earliest period as an artist in the 1940s until his death in 1992. Through Nolan, Mrs Fraser enters the Australian legend.

In the first painting from the 1947–8 series (Figure 1), a vulnerable Mrs Fraser is portrayed as a naked animal blending into the alien bush, caught in the oval-shaped lens of binoculars or a gun-barrel. 'As an image of humanity at its lowest ebb', writes Jane Clark, ' "Mrs. Fraser" contrasts dramatically with the powerful figure of her convict rescuer in "Fraser Island" '.[21] There have been a number of interpretative attempts to come to terms with this disturbing image. Robert Melville, in his introduction to Sidney Nolan's *Paradise Garden,* suggests that Nolan identified with the convict Bracefell through this particularly provocative image. He continues, her plight arouses not pity but the sense of her openness to sexual assault. She is a woman liable to be taken from behind, like the women in some of the Pompeian wall paintings, with no preference and no certainty on the part of the taker as to which passage is being penetrated. She would spit and snap like a female dingo, without offering resistance.[22]

This decidedly misogynistic critique, written in 1971, twenty-four years after the painting was completed, may or may not reflect the views of the artist. Other readings are possible. Other critics have suggested that the crawling figure might be understood as a less than human, mollusc-like creature suffering humiliation in an alien environment, or as Nolan's adaptation of a Blake-like image of dehumanised man transformed to suit the Australian legend and to express Mrs Fraser's humiliation.[23] For Melville, however, she is Nolan's 'disquieting muse' who becomes, especially in Nolan's second series of paintings, an Australian Eve in a fallen garden who will eventually betray her rescuer, Bracefell. She represents a type of woman in Nolan's mythology, says Melville, who is 'necessarily evil'.[24]

In a manner typical of expressive currents within modernist criticism, Melville refers to 'Mrs Fraser' as a figure grown from Nolan's personal life and the circumstances which led to his separation from his patrons John and Sunday Reed at Heide, with whom he had lived in a *ménage à trois* for nearly a decade in the 1940s. Read in terms of the modern artist as a tortured genius, Mrs Fraser's betrayal of Bracefell parallels a betrayal in Nolan's own life. In terms of modern art and art criticism, the ways in which the artist transforms the trials and traumas of his life are of interest because they become, through his creative and liberating role, exemplary models for the rest of society: his insights become our redemption; as prophet and seer, he speaks for us. It is not my intention to subscribe to these critical premises. Post-modern critique has shattered this particular set of beliefs, revealing the politically grounded nature of its 'neutral' perspective and deconstructing its universal disguise. Biographical accounts themselves are fictions arising out of a culling of selected facts given meaning by the artist, critic or biographer and embedded in a politics of representation. In Nolan's case, the meaning of the biographical details is framed within psychoanalytic, Christian, modernist and nationalist understandings of the (masculine) individual. My interest is in the ways the work of the artist or critic becomes attached to and feeds off these other discourses, thus extending the networks of meaning through which the symbolic Woman as other enters and circulates within contemporary culture.

In this sense, the biographical materials on Nolan and the modernist approaches of his biographers and critics are not irrelevant to this study. They concern the artist's attempts (and those of critics who speak on his behalf) to come to terms with his own sense of betrayal which becomes projected on to the figure of a woman. The manner in which the artist and his critics come to terms with this theme allows us to examine the circulation of ideas about masculinity, femininity and the forces of desire which can be read within the discourses. In addition, they provide insight into the ways fantasies concerning Woman become embedded in the national psyche. The examination is not *about* Sidney Nolan, Sunday Reed or Eliza Fraser. His paintings and their critical contexts, however, offer rich materials for an analysis of how 'the feminine' can figure in both private and public negotiations between subjectivity and national identity across a network of diverse discourses.

Betrayal and Nolan's 'Mrs Fraser'

Betrayal as a central motif is mentioned repeatedly by art critics, commentators and curators in conjunction with Nolan's 'Mrs Fraser' paintings. Critics have constructed Nolan as Australia's foremost modern artist, 'the great mythmaker of Australian art'.[25] Several have interpreted his interest in and treatment of the Eliza Fraser story in terms of the great mythical themes arising out of Nolan's personal, Australia's national and mankind's universal consciousness. Their constructions of Nolan contribute to the notion of the modern artist as universal prophet for mankind. These critiques help us to understand the ways in which the symbolic Woman can circulate within the narratives of personal biography, national identity and humanist myth as an apparent source of man's alienation and betrayal, displacing fears of failure or inadequacy on the part of Nolan/ Man /the nation. The interpretations of Nolan's 'Mrs Fraser' series by modernist critics, then, provide an interesting case study for a particular construction of Woman as man's betrayer.

Nolan's Personal Mythology

The parallels said to exist between Eliza Fraser and Nolan's personal myth involve events leading up to Nolan's attempt to come to terms in 1947 with a series of difficult personal events. This year saw the end to his association with the bohemian household of Heide and his intimate friendship with John and Sunday Reed, his long-term patrons, associates and supporters. Adams, his biographer, describes Nolan's involvement at Heide in the following way:

> Nolan was now happy to be ensnared [*sic*] in a most intimate union with the Reeds and their close friends which allowed him to embrace a wide range of new experiences. The French would describe the relationship as a *ménage à trois*, although it was much less formal, having a freedom where all kinds of permissiveness were accepted as part of a total physical and intellectual experience. Outsiders regarded the Heide circle as a lively cultural and political group because most other activities were kept discreet, although several people on the periphery were aware of the true situation.[26]

Nolan's association with this transposed Bloomsbury circle, this antipodean hothouse of personal and creative pleasure and pain, was referred to by the artist as a highly charged emotional environment which 'no one has represented . . . well',[27] It ended in 1947 – known as Nolan's 'crisis year'. This, coupled with his brother's accidental death while attached to the American armed forces in northern Australia and Nolan's own desertion from the Army, which occurred in 1944 but had yet to be resolved, are said to have formed the background for his escape from Melbourne. In addition, Nolan and the Reeds felt an acute sense of betrayal by the public as a result of the Ern Malley hoax.[28] These events, as constructed in Nolan's biography *Such is Life* by Brian Adams, resulted in Nolan's feeling that he had been betrayed in love and had become an outlaw/outcast within Australian society. At this juncture he made his first trip to Fraser Island with his friend Barrie Reid in August 1947 and first heard the story of the shipwreck of the *Stirling Castle*, the captivity and rescue of Eliza Fraser, and her betrayal of the convict Bracefell.

Figure 11   'Sunday Reed', by Albert Tucker, 1984.
By permission of the artist.

It should be noted here that the only perspectives available to explain this period in Nolan's life are Nolan's own, those of his biographer, or of those sympathetic to his interests. Sunday Reed has no voice. Her part in the whole affair, like that of Eliza Fraser – and the proverbial Eve in the Garden, for that matter – is one in which she is represented by others through their frames of reference, which were quite possibly antithetical to her interests. The only piece of counter-memory I could find which suggests another version of the story is a painting by Albert Tucker entitled 'Sunday Reed' (1984; Figure 11). In it a contemplative woman, aged by stress and time, casts a 'guardian-like' gaze back across a room to a classic early Nolan 'Ned Kelly' painting, diminished in size.[29] The portrait suggests far more to the relationship between Nolan, the Reeds and the paintings than the histories provide. As Nolan claimed, no one has represented the Heide period well. One can only hope that, if and when the reconstructions are attempted, they include feminist perspectives and critique.[30]

Nolan has related in a number of interviews that his interest in Eliza Fraser was 'bound up with an emotional state [he] was in' at the time.[31] Melville writes that:

> Nolan identified himself with the convict. He depicted her [Eliza] as if he were Bracefell at the moment he first set eyes on her – as if he were, so to speak, an interested party, calculating what prospects her condition and situation might hold for him . . . Later [in the later series of paintings] Nolan, as if presenting evidence on behalf of Bracefell, painted a brilliant series of large pictures in which the days and nights spent by Bracefell and Mrs. Fraser in the bush were treated as a lyrical episode.
>   The bestiality, lyricism and treachery in their story reappear in Nolan's poems [*Paradise Garden*, 1971], but instead of Bracefell and Mrs. Fraser there is a painter and a female patron, and the scene is not the bush but studio and bedroom. The female patron is a 20th century version of the Classical Muse . . . [a] beautiful and gracious destructive force. . . . She steals his eyes and he sees more clearly. She destroys his work and the essential image remains.[32]

This is the woman/Woman/Muse to whom Melville refers in conjunction with the 'Mrs Fraser' painting as being 'necessarily evil'. That this imaginary Woman/woman haunted Nolan's life is evident in his last interview for the Australian press in 1989 when he reiterated that 'most paintings are connected in some way with women' and that this woman, Sunday Reed – 'a bewitching, daemonic, and extraordinary woman' – had a tremendous impact on his life.[33] The artist conceded, in what may have been a particularly insightful, self-reflexive moment, that he might finally be able to paint all the women in his life and their part in his paradise at the age of eighty when he 'would have finally got rid of the snake'.[34] In this he seems to suggest that the betrayal, the treachery of Woman, through which he knows the dark side of his own creative genius, may have been shaped by elements within himself, transposed on to the symbolic and imaginary 'feminine' as represented in his life and art. The public was not to know whether nor how this exorcism of his ghosts would have been possible. He died five years short of this goal.

The point here is not to psychoanalyse the artist. Nor is it to suggest that Sunday Reed, could she represent these events, would concur with Nolan's sentiments; nor that either of them could escape recourse to meanings inscribed within the psychoanalytic and Christian categories for masculine and feminine identity which emerge within a Western imaginary construction of the story of love and loss. Rather the intention is to trace the formation of the concept, 'Eliza Fraser as betrayer', within Nolan's personal imaginary as it connects with other cultural and psychoanalytic discourses, all of which locate Woman within a masculine economy of desire.

The incorporation of the 'Mrs Fraser' paintings into a personal mythology forms a part of the creation of the modern-artist-as-hero who experiences keenly a sense of isolation from the society in which he lives. In Australia, this figure is typically a working-class lad with a mother complex. Anne-Marie Willis, in her study *Illusions of Identity*, suggests that the modernist Australian artist lived in what was constructed as an unauthentic culture when juxtaposed against 'authentic' culture of Europe. He adopts the pose of an alienated searcher after truths who feels misunderstood, unacknowledged and unappreciated; suffering a dislocation from mainstream values here.[35] Nolan knew how to place himself within an Australian mythology in relation to ethnicity and class as well as gender. He consistently reminded interviewers of his Irish, working-class background as the son of a Melbourne tram driver, born into a family with 'no artistic traditions of any kind'.[36] (Seldom does he mention, however, that his father was an illegal SP bookmaker as well as a tram driver. His myth of origin must retain some semblance of middle-class respectability.) In addition, his representation of himself as a self-taught or intuitive genius eludes the fact that there *were* no artistic traditions in Australia available to him or other artists at the time. Like other artists of his generation, he studied art in a number of Melbourne studios and was well read in European traditions of art, philosophy and literature.

Nolan positioned himself within self-defined, as well as culturally defined, working-class and Irish/ethnic traditions within Australian culture. The ways in which he did this allowed him to slide easily into a mythologisation of himself as a larrikin figure, an outlaw, identifying with the heroes of his paintings: the Irish larrikin outlaw Ned Kelly, the ill-fated explorer Robert O'Hara Burke, the Gallipoli soldier, and the convict David Bracefell. These paintings have had strong resonances for his appreciative audiences both

within Australia and overseas. At times he represented his separation from
the well-educated, well-travelled and well-heeled Reeds in class terms. Late in
life, he explained that his departure arose out of his own decision to retreat
from a situation which was contrary to his 'working class ethics'.[37] Similarly,
he commented on his third marriage to Mary Boyd Perceval that she was 'a
Boyd' and he only a Nolan. At the same time, he also detailed his public
honours to the press, including a knighthood. All of this would seem to reveal
his life-long but deeply ambivalent attachment to country and class of origin
combined with a 'typically Australian' (dis)regard for authority and a larrikin's guilt/delight in crossing the boundaries of privilege. At the time of his
death he had become the most celebrated Australian, a man detached from
his roots and living out a myth of himself and his nation, who had sought and
received the highest accolades and most public marks of recognition.[38]

Nolan's National Mythology

Critics and reviewers frequently mention the betrayal theme in the 'Mrs
Fraser' paintings, although they generally locate it within the visionary artist's mythology of nation. Bryan Robertson, the director of the Whitechapel
Gallery at the time of Nolan's first European retrospective, is a typical commentator in this regard. He wrote that Nolan's travels took him to 'great
tracts of empty land . . . which no one [sic] had ever seen before . . . tracts
awaiting the arrival of a human being'.[39] Into this landscape, this Garden of
Eden, walked Mrs Fraser and Bracefell. Nolan painted the landscape through
his vision of their story in a way which Robertson represented as 'unaffected
by the muddled aesthetics of Europe' (not to mention the invisible politics of
racism). Further, the gallery director informs his English audience, 'since no
folk art existed in Australia – Nolan invented his own'.[40] This invention of an
impoverished Australian culture allows the critic to construct Nolan as *the*
emblematic artist of modernism; his role influences narratives of national
identity, as well. In the nationalist accounts of Australian art, Nolan's paintings in the 'Mrs Fraser' series become 'an emblem of a primary recognition of
our environment, our landscape which most of us did not see accurately, our
eyes somehow misted by Europe'.[41] This comment by Barrie Reid echoes
back to nationalistic themes associated with the Heidelberg School of
Australian painting of the 1890s, a school of painters who also were credited
with 'seeing Australia through Australian eyes'.

Mrs Fraser and Bracefell, as representatives of mythologised Australian
history, represent an enduring but imagined aesthetic relationship of Europe
to Australia and a colonial relationship of Australia to England. The inter-
connections between these two imagined relationships can be traced within
both a democratic nationalist, and a modernist, mythology of nation. In
both, broadly speaking, the Australian (white) native son is innocent, naive

and untainted by the 'civilised' ways and aesthetic traditions of Europe. In the former accounts, he struggles against the physical threats of an alien environment in order to wrest a separate identity from an English parent culture. In the later accounts, the battle lines remain much the same but the threat is both physical and psychic; man's battle with the land strikes within him a fear of failure, a 'terror at the basis of being'.[42] Again, the betrayal theme is paramount: England betrays her colonial offspring.

In this sense Nolan's mythology partakes of the more encompassing vision of modernist artists, critics and commentators, who by the 1950s had supplanted the democratic nationalists as caretakers of the cultural archive. This dimension of his art in relation to the 'Mrs Fraser' paintings is emphasised in the Thames and Hudson text and catalogue of paintings, *Sidney Nolan* (1961), edited by Kenneth Clark, Colin MacInnes and Bryan Robertson. The catalogue description of 'Mrs Fraser' introduces her as 'the traitress'. Her 'naked, grotesque . . . white European body is flung into the wild bush . . . to fend for herself . . . isolated and lost . . . [before spied upon by her] saviour convict'.[43] This rendition of the paintings places them within a modernist narrative of nationhood in which the convict (and by association the artist) emerges as the (white) native son who struggles against British authority on the distinctive Australian terrain of the bush. The Heidelberg painters, too, had been constructed as belonging to that generation of Australian-born-and-bred 'native sons' who embraced 'the bush'. This suggests another way in which Nolan, as their modernist heir, could be associated with Bracefell. These readings place 'Mrs Fraser' in a number of (contradictory) positions, which are taken up in the introduction to the volume by Colin MacInnes.

On the one hand, Mrs Fraser is symbolically linked to the British colonial authorities who came to Australia, upsetting the natural balance of things, but who did not make it their home. In this she stands out as an enemy to the convicts and settlers alike, who like the Aborigines ('stalwart natives' all) had to learn to adapt to its harsh environment. On the other hand, Mrs Fraser is depicted in the form of an Aboriginal rock art image of a woman in two of the paintings in the second series, 'In the Cave' and 'Woman in Mangroves' (Figure 12). MacInnes suggests that this larger-than-life, X-ray image of Mrs Fraser, 'her figure splayed across a rock . . . as the convict emerges from the cave', marks her as a remnant of a primordial past, with the convict emerging as a figure of the future. We note the use of time to mark 'Aboriginality' as belonging to a primordial past, an earlier stage of human existence to which Mrs Fraser is *reduced*. The use of the concept of the past and future time can also refer to a feature of (white) Australia's unique future, a new natural environment with which the convict/settler/saviour Bracefell is identified as standing against the ossified traditions of Europe. This rendition reverses the familiar refrain of Australia as an unauthentic culture. An irony, however (and one that contributes to the cultural cringe), is that the modernist

national myth of Australia gains its voice and authority through its representation in England in a lush volume introduced by prestigious British art
critics and historians.

These contradictory perspectives on Nolan and Australian nationalism are
echoed by other art critics and Nolan himself through the years, both in
Australia and abroad. This interpretation of the 'Mrs Fraser' paintings (like
those associated with his 'Ned Kelly' series) helps to establish Nolan as the
pre-eminent painter of the modernist movement in Australian art. His reputation in this regard was assisted by Robert Hughes's focus on the Angry
Decade in *The Art of Australia* (1966) and enhanced by Richard Haese's book,
Rebels and Precursors: The Revolutionary Years of Australian Art (1981). Haese's
text recounts the fable that modernism was born at Heide in the 1940s
(associated not only with Nolan and the Reeds but also with Noel Counihan,
Arthur Boyd, John Perceval, Joy Hester, Albert Tucker, Max Harris, and
Angry Penguins).[44] It details the development from the 1940s of a recognisably
modern Australian art, which had been and still could be represented as
provincial (and thus inferior) when measured against international stan-
dards of the metropolitan (and thus superior). Within prevailing currents of

Figure 12 'Woman in Mangroves', by Sidney Nolan, 1957.
By permission of Lady Mary Nolan.

art criticism, the lack of innovation was judged as the mark of provincial art; whereas 'originality' was the lynchpin of modernism.[45]

Until the 1970s, Australia saw itself as lacking a heritage, a tradition. Although a few modernist Australian artists achieved a modicum of fame both locally and overseas in the 1960s, and a few art critics had attempted to define the contours of a distinctively Australian art,[46] appreciation for their work, at least in Australia, was juxtaposed with the cultural cringe, or the feeling that 'good' art and culture had to be European in origin and/or acclaimed by a European audience. The Haese book, researched in the early 1970s but only published in 1981, becomes a reference text for a newly constituted search for national identity associated with the rise of the Whitlam government in the early 1970s. During this time modern art is acclaimed as an attribute of modern nationhood. The 1970s witnessed a return to national sentiment and authenticity in art (and also a critique of it), after a period in the 1960s which was dominated by the adaptation of international styles and abstract art, said to be derived primarily from suspect, American models. National identity had been premised on *lack*, on a shallow, newly emerging culture without distinction, history or tradition. In art, national identity had been located within the landscape tradition of the Heidelberg School. What distinguished Australia was its unique landscape and man's relationship to it. It is not surprising then that a reverence would be given to the pursuit of 'high' culture and the adoration of intellectuals and artists who were said to personify the mythology of nationhood and who also achieved overseas acclaim. Both Nolan and White were major figures in this regard. Yet Nolan did not so much break from the older traditions identified with nationalist art; rather, in relation to his Ned Kelly and Eliza Fraser paintings, he added to it a narrative myth of nation. Haese's text tends to lionise the artist, attributing to him a singular originality. In relation to Nolan's 'Mrs Fraser' series, Haese reiterates Nolan's conviction that he 'had found something close to the origins of authentic Australian experience' in Queensland, out of which he could found 'a workable tradition. *And this is true in the literal sense.*' (emphasis mine).[47] Haese continues, echoing earlier discursive themes, that the artists of the 1940s were seen as searching for an authentic national style, inspired by the material of their own lives and the lives of those around them. This, as the famous document on a new nationalist aesthetic, 'The Antipodean Manifesto' (1959),[48] was to claim, necessarily involved personal and creative myth-making on the part of the artist.

In the 1970s these constructed fragments of a national myth began to appropriate aspects of Aboriginal culture as well. Over time, the appropriating impulse affected Nolan and his changing vision of the 'Mrs Fraser' series. It is reported that Nolan's 'romance with Aboriginality' led him to identify with an 'Aboriginal way of thinking', which (retrospectively) could

be included in new interpretations of the significance of his artistic production.[49] The 1971 catalogue prepared with the assistance of the artist for
Nolan's Darmstadt exhibition seems to be the first evocation of this theme.[50]
In the first catalogue description of the 'Mrs Fraser' painting, she is described
as 'curiously sexless . . . a pale, naked mollusc-like creature' who is less than
animal, having lost her identity in the alien bush. This catalogue essay
engages in some anthropological speculations concerning Aborigines and
their death rituals. It explains to the European audience that Aborigines
believed that people were born white-skinned and returned to a white,
ghostly appearance after death. Thus, Mrs Fraser was accepted into the tribe
as a ghost (and *'less than human'*, emphasis mine), a belief which led to her
rescue by David Bracefell [*sic*], who posed as her husband to effect her
release. Readers are further instructed that in traditional Aboriginal culture
after the death of a member of the group the corpse was burned and flayed
with sharp shells, painted and eaten by members of the tribe.[51] Thus, the
ghostly white colour of the body in the 'Mrs Fraser' painting links her
appearance to Aboriginal customs and beliefs. In addition, Bracefell, the
convict rescuer, is represented as being in tune with Aboriginal nature. Thus,
the catalogue entry on 'Mrs Fraser and Convict' (1964; Figure 9), a painting
said to be modelled on Masaccio's 'Expulsion from Paradise', links Nolan's
art to the universalist perspectives and aesthetics of European art while, at
the same time, locating his theme within a specifically Australian tradition.
The catalogue entry suggests that the painting stands in an asymmetric
relation to the Quattrocento original: the old-world European Garden has
been replaced by a new-world Paradise. Eliza is Eve the betrayer, here being
expelled from nature, while Adam, the survivor tricked by woman's treachery,
returns to nature. (This description relates to a point about the mythological
landscape made in Chapter 2 in conjunction with captivity narratives and the
difficulty of transposing the genre from America, where captives escaped
from the wilderness, to Australia, where runaway convicts found solace and
survival in the bush.) The post-lapsarian Eve gazes down, her face indistinct,
her naked body blending into the striped torso of her convict rescuer, resistant to movement. He escorts the woman across the sand at the edge of
the sea, with his eyes, head and one wayward foot turned inland towards
the bush.

As a woman reader, I find myself both irritated and bemused by these
comments. I am irritated by the sight of the paintings, one of which reduces
woman to an animal-like pose, while others represent her as a vulnerable, yet
traitorous, post-lapsarian Eve; and also by the need of male artists and critics
to invoke the mythical Eve as the source of mankind's suffering. I am
bemused at the number of contexts male writers and artists can find in which
to reiterate their concern with their own myth of alienation, dispossession

and betrayal transposed on to Woman. Whose betrayal is this? If I were a reader with an Aboriginal heritage I suspect I would feel the same, although for different reasons. I would be irritated that a white European audience has interpreted Aboriginal culture and reappropriated Aboriginal concerns, getting them wrong once again, this time for the edification of a guilty white neo-colonial community aware of its neglect of Aboriginal culture. I would be bemused that an Aboriginal heritage can so easily be fused with the concerns of runaway convicts and white myths of nationhood, as well as universal insecurities of European men, and then merged with a Christian conception of the original fall from grace in the Garden of Eden. Betrayals all around. It is obvious that the various readings of 'Mrs Fraser', which also frame Nolan's relation to Australian nationalism, continually allow for a disavowal of the political concerns of racial, gendered and class-based differences of power. These troublesome aspects of national life are displaced by the figure of a traitorous Woman, a product of male fantasy, who is man's invention and also makes possible a narrative of his betrayal. Nicholas Rothwell, in his recent, celebratory *Weekend Australian* article on Nolan, comments that Nolan's conception of man's state in Australia as that of one fallen from the Garden makes his Australia 'a difficult Eden'. It is a statement with which, for varying reasons, many Aboriginal and non-Aboriginal Australians would concur, although they may not share Nolan's or Rothwell's apocalyptic vision.

Nolan's Universal Mythology

The theme of Adam and Eve and the fall from the Garden links the 'Mrs Fraser' series to a universal Christian myth of mankind. It also constructs Nolan as an artist of true genius, not only of Australia but of the world. These were the terms invoked in conjunction with his last exhibition of Eliza Fraser paintings, 'Nolan's Fraser', exhibited in 1989 in Queensland:

> [His] imagery transcends all classes; age barriers; it knows no time boundaries. Nolan communicates emotionally with all of us . . . [His art is our history,] playing a vital role in the development of an Australian painterly idiom – a national identity, a 'cultural consciousness'.[52]

Similar statements can be garnered in the media publicity which attended Nolan's last visit to Australia in 1989 at the time of the Queensland exhibition and in eulogies which followed his death in 1992. The cover story which appeared in the *Weekend Australian* magazine, 'The Homecoming: Nolan Finds His Paradise,' perhaps represents this myth-making tendency at its best. Here, Nolan is introduced through a two-page colour photograph in which he stands alone in a vast sandy desert, 'a country of dream'. The artist is photographed throughout the lengthy article in a number of poses as a searching figure, insignificant in the vast expanse of the Australian outback. The following text accompanies the opening colour spread:

> Sir Sidney Nolan, one of our greatest treasures, returns in his twilight years to 'paradise' in his beloved Australia. HEATHER BROWN joins him as he opens up about his life, loves and inspirations – and follows the shadows of his amazing past.[53]

In preparation for the interview, at Nolan's request, a press crew accompanied the artist on a journey to 'Lake Mungo – the first paradise', the archaeological site of discovery of bones attributed to the first Australians, some 40,000 to 50,000 years ago. This is 'a place of sacred mystery', a harsh land which, in the course of the article, Nolan visually possesses and then becomes possessed by.[54] Such was his fame that the artist was able to set up the interview and choose the remote location. The photographs of the vast landscape are reminiscent of Nolan's own evocative desert paintings. In this final photo essay, which sums up the artist's life in the most mythic of terms, he stands alone, in a scene which could be 'virtual reality', photographed as if he were a figure in a simulation of one of his own paintings. It is interesting to note that in Sidney Nolan's first extensive outback trip in 1948, one which changed his vision and his style of painting, he was accompanied by his second wife, Cynthia. Cynthia organised the journey, kept a diary of her observations, and completed a novel entitled *Outback* (not published until 1961) as a result of the trip.[55] The trip was, according to Brian Adams, Nolan's biographer, 'central to Nolan's existence as an artist'.[56] That first visionary outback journey with Cynthia altered forever Nolan's perceptions of the land and its people; this latest journey, even if obscured by his self-positioning, completes the mythical cycle. He has achieved his apotheosis. The man becomes a simulation of the myth of himself.

In the *Weekend Australian* article, Nolan also equates land, women and Aboriginal culture within his personal, national and universal mythology. His ruminations deserve our particular attention in that they make explicit the contradictory ways in which the land, women and Aborigines (as categories of otherness) come together in symbolic and imaginary realms of meaning. Here Nolan shifts between the Oedipal signification of the woman as betrayer (the phallic woman who threatens castration, impotence, lack of identity) and the pre-Oedipal imaginary mother of dyadic bliss and abjection (which can also be linked with the land and primitive culture). In the latter, imaginary, realm, women, Aborigines and the land come together to signify both a mysterious/alluring and an alienating/fearful feminine realm beyond language. In terms of the child's imaginary of the Maternal, this fantasy evokes the desire for merging of the self with the other, a transcendence beyond the cultural boundaries. In psychoanalytic terms, all humans yearn for and at the same time fear a return to the pre-social dyadic unity with the Maternal; an impossible desire, often linked with sex, death and mortality. Nolan comments to the journalist, 'Maybe the continent is really the fifth woman' in his life – after his mother, and his three wives. Sunday Reed, although mentioned at another point in the piece (as being a 'bewitching, daemonic, extraordinary woman'), is curiously absent from this list. Here Woman is imagined as the Maternal (the land, his mother and three wives). Nolan imagines himself as the infant united with 'her' in dyadic bliss. He cites his own mother as the number one woman, the 'beginning of the women in my life, the beginning of that wonderful oceanic feeling of bliss – as Freud calls it – that women cause in men'.[57] In this article, as it reconstructs Nolan's life-in-retrospect, Sunday Reed, the other/Other woman, remains in the background, as the phallic, castrating woman, but is present nonetheless in her absence.

Even the Oedipal equation of loss of potency with loss of eyesight is relevant here. Sunday Reed, the 'patron' who inspired the 'Mrs Fraser' paintings according to Melville's introduction to *Paradise Garden*, was said to have stolen the artist's eyes so that he saw more clearly. In this article she becomes fused with the hostile aspect of a phallic Mother Nature. The photo essay opens its Lake Mungo section with the following description: 'We find him hunched in the middle of a sand storm – tears welling in his eyes, his face wrinkled with pleasure. "It's easier to let your eyes fill up," he says. "Somehow it helps you to see."'[58]

The fantasy of woman/the land as alien, hostile, a traitor who is ambivalently loved and loathed, has been intimately connected with Nolan's work, with his fantasies of Mrs Fraser/ Sunday Reed/ the Australian landscape, and with the mythology of Australia within a modernist tradition. The woman/land by whom he felt betrayed gave rise not only to his myth of Eliza Fraser as betrayer, but also to an enduring mythology of the feminine/landscape within an Australian imaginary. In Nolan's paintings can be found both the most sublime and the most debased representations of Australia and the specular body of Woman.

According to this last interview with the artist, Nolan at the end of his life rediscovered a narrative of bliss underlying the fantasy of the traitorous continent/woman. In the narrative he represents the 'true' landscape, beyond its punishing features, as the lost Mother. The landscape tradition in art becomes his/Man's way of capturing and possessing the lost woman – 'our' lost heritage. This fantasy allows the artist (and the critic, as well as Australians and other readers caught in this web of meanings) both to idealise the memory of the Maternal and to debase the punishing Oedipal mother. Nolan carefully divides the two feminine Others (the symbolic and the imaginary) in his narrative, focusing on the Maternal woman alone after

years of apparently being possessed by her imaginary opposite and his nem-
esis. He also locates traditional Aboriginal culture within the imaginary of
the Maternal, in another slippage from a debased to an idealised significance,
but one which exists on another axis of power – determined by race rather
than gender. When he mythologises the land as the Eternal Feminine, he
evokes it in Bruce Chatwin's terms, with songlines leading back to primordial
culture. He identifies himself as a new-age nomad, the modern equivalent to
the primordial nomads of Aboriginal culture. The motif of modern artist as
nomad, as wanderer, is again part of a Western myth and mystique of the
artist. Within this way of seeing in relation to Aboriginal culture, however,
the primitive Other (once feared and loathed as a transposition of what is
lacking in the self) is replaced by the sacred Other. Here Nolan engages in a
new allegory of man's fall and redemption, a new dimension of his/'our'
evolving national mythology, and a new boundary which he/'we' can cross.
Here, white Australians can find redemption in a recognition of the sacredness of primitive culture and its values. In this way, Aborigines enter a
narrative about Australian identity in which they have been all but lost for
generations. Through his construction of 'them'/the other as remnants of a
sacred past, Nolan speaks on behalf of the universal soul, outside of temporality, shared by all peoples, transcendent. In his paintings from the 'Mrs
Fraser' series, the idea can perhaps be best aligned with a new reading of 'In
the Cave'.[59]

As the anthropologist Andrew Lattas points out, this myth of the Sacred
Other is yet another form of white racism. While allowing for a fantasy of
transcendence beyond self and other categories of being, it also engages
white Australians in a definition of Aborigines and their culture as precious
relics of an ancient time. This myth posits primordiality as both an otherness
and an origin, a site of what was lost and must be reclaimed. It represents
another appropriation of Aboriginal culture, with attendant problems of
locking Aboriginal peoples into a time outside politics.[60] The phenomenon
transforms Aborigines into our 'Holy Others' while also engaging in a claim
that these 'others' live in another dimension of time. In both senses,
'Aboriginality' becomes 'our' invention which makes 'our' history relevant,
and 'theirs' a time of myth. Aboriginal culture is posited here as representing
to humanity the lost beginnings of a mythic consciousness. Aborigines
become 'the evolutionary relics of our original psyches',[61] the lost tracings
of a universal soul, a unifying memory for mankind of the world before
separation (invoking the imaginary Maternal/mother again); an invention
under the auspices of a Western belief in the unconscious of all of humanity.
Narratives of this type focus on the existential suffering of man (and this
includes Western women) through an evocation of a myth of a lost Paradise/
the Dreaming. They suggest that we have killed our Aboriginal past, which is
a form of the universal unconscious, a sacred racial memory. Historical

violence inflicted on Aborigines through colonialism is disavowed and replaced by a sense of psychic and spiritual violence inflicted on ourselves. In such narratives, whites emerge as the true sufferers of history who have lost their souls and wander in an empty void, seeking redemption through the (m)other/Other. On another level this imaginary fantasy is linked to the imperial trope of incorporating the other into the self.[62] Yet, while the fantasy incorporates 'Aboriginality' into a Western framework of primordial human existence, it also shifts categories of representation in ways that make political change possible. The tendency can be read as both reactionary and progressive at the same time.

This analysis of the imaginary of Nolan, Australia, and the white man indicates the complex ways in which Nolan's personal myth of Woman/Other slides into several different narratives of nationhood. It shows how metaphors which give substance to gender categories within a (white, male) national mythology cross over and blend into those of race. Critics maintain that the various visions and revisions purport to speak on behalf of the man, the country and, finally, mankind. These speaking positions rely on white, masculine imaginary constructions of both women and Aborigines as (white) Man's others. We others are dispersed, our identities appropriated, our voices mimed through numbed bodies, like puppets in a ventriloquist's act, at the very moment in which we are invoked into being. At the same time, white women share this fantasy with white men in an imaginary union with the Maternal, or the dyadic bliss of the mother–child relationship beyond cultural boundaries and divisions. Women too fear cultural, if not physical, impotence, personal insecurity and loss of identity; that is, fears of difference within the self, which we transpose onto others.

Nolan's art, and the criticism which locates it within national and international contexts, masks cultural difference in its attempt to represent universal mankind within its ambit. This is not to suggest that Nolan or his commentators are to be blamed for this state of affairs; nor that their perspectives necessarily retarded race or gender relations. At this particular historical juncture, however, we can learn from these occluded dimensions of Nolan's art and criticism. All of us – men and women, Aboriginal and non-Aboriginal, Western and non-Western readers – can identify the complex ways by which Western man's cultural dominance (which sometimes includes women) has allowed him the illusion of identity at the expense of those cast into the role of his others. Women too can acknowledge that, to some degree, we have been complicitous with the maintenance of those illusions. Nolan's paintings and our readings of them make us conscious of the complex ways in which both men and women are drawn into, even as we resist, the anxieties and fears which give rise to his personal, the nation's mythological and universal modernist visions of his art.

CHAPTER 7

Patrick White's Novel, A Fringe of Leaves

Patrick White's fascination with the Eliza Fraser story parallels the trajectory of his relationship with Sidney Nolan. The writer allowed the tale to germinate in his imagination for almost as long a time as Nolan painted the subject. White first met Nolan in Fort Lauderdale, Florida, in 1958, at a time when Nolan was finishing his second series of 'Mrs Fraser' paintings and just after he had visited the Florida Everglades, an area he found surprisingly similar in appearance to the swamps of Fraser Island. Although White's heritage was as English and patrician as Nolan's was Irish and working-class, this first meeting of the two Australian artists in exile sparked an enduring friendship. David Marr, Patrick White's biographer, reports that during this first intense meeting Nolan told White the story of the shipwreck of the *Stirling Castle* off the coast of Fraser Island. Here is his rendition of the historical event, recounted twice in Marr's biography.

> All the survivors of the wreck were killed by the blacks, except for the captain's wife who was kept by them as a slave. She was stripped of everything, until she was reduced to wearing a vine around her waist – that 'fringe of leaves' – in which she hid her wedding ring. At a corroboree she found an escaped convict who took her back to civilisation.[1]

This legendary outline of the Eliza Fraser story still has currency today and is taken by many to be the 'proper' version. For White, the outline for his fictional reconstruction, the title and the setting for his novel, *A Fringe of Leaves*, all came together during this brief interlude with Sidney Nolan in the Everglades.

Marr reports that White cultivated the novel for sixteen years. During this time he visited the Great Barrier Reef and Fraser Island on several occasions; he read materials in the Queensland and New South Wales archives; he met

157

with the Aboriginal storyteller Wilf Reeves;[2] he discussed ethnographic details with his friend, the anthropologist David Moore; and devised a libretto which he hoped would be performed to celebrate the opening of the Sydney Opera House. Nolan was to design the sets since, according to White, 'One can no longer imagine Mrs. Fraser apart from Nolan's paintings.'[3] When attempted collaborations on the Opera House production collapsed, first in conjunction with Benjamin Britten and then with Peter Sculthorpe, White put the manuscript in the proverbial bottom drawer, where it sat for ten years. Finally in 1974 White returned to the manuscript, completing it by the end of 1975. During this time he had been awarded the Nobel Prize for Literature (1973), which was accepted in Stockholm by Sidney Nolan on his behalf. In awarding the prize, the judges claimed that Patrick White had 'introduced a new continent to literature'.[4] In 1975 White was named Australian of the Year, an honour he detested. His reputation both in Australia and abroad had peaked. He also had maintained his abiding friendship with Sidney Nolan, which, however, came to an abrupt end a few weeks after the publication of *A Fringe of Leaves* (1976) with Cynthia Nolan's death. Marr concludes that 'the patron of this friendship, from first meeting to final wreckage, was Eliza Fraser'.[5] The mythical Eliza has lived many lives.

Historical Reconstructions

Recorded events of Mrs Fraser's life and experience during her six weeks' stay amongst Aborigines are said to be recounted with some fidelity to the historical evidence in *A Fringe of Leaves*, although the interpretations and meanings given to the events in the novel, as well as the construction of Ellen Roxburgh's character, depart dramatically from the historical records.[6] White was not interested in authenticity. His sensuous and imaginative novel blends information from a variety of sources, including historical materials, themes and settings suggested by Nolan's paintings, and details from White's personal past. Like Nolan's paintings, the novel is constructed upon a modernist mythology of Australia, involving the metaphor of man in a postlapsarian garden, within a universal humanist perspective. The so-called historical details of the novel can be traced through a variety of mixed sources. These include the Curtis and Alexander histories; the Henry Stuart Russell and Tom Petrie memoirs, and Queensland popular mythology; Nolan's paintings and legendary account of the story; Sir Raphael Cilento's novel in manuscript form; and even, perhaps, the film script by British film producer Michael Luke which was circulating around Sydney at the time.[7] On the transposition of fiction from history, White commented, 'If I hadn't substituted Ellen Roxburgh for Eliza Fraser, little more than a hardbitten shrew from the Orkneys, [the novel would not] have had the psychological complexities, the sensibility, and the passion I was able to explore.'[8] White's novel, however, largely because of its accessibility and popularity, has supplanted what was known or had been devised from accounts of the originating event in the minds of modern readers.

Although the novel is not a historical reconstruction, both the canon of scholarship framing the novel and its treatment by many commentators call attention to the parallels between the historical event and its fictional representation. White himself, in *Flaws in the Glass*, comments that critics 'sense in its images and narrative the reasons why we have become what we are'.[9] His examination of the past event provides an insight into a present dilemma. The novel deals with the relationship between England and colonial Australia, the convicts and their masters, and the gap between white and Aboriginal Australia. In this treatment it offers a critique of what White perceived to be the deep malaise of social, moral and spiritual emptiness in twentieth-century Australian society, stemming from its English inheritance and the brutalities of the convict system. Ellen Roxburgh, as protagonist, bridges the gaps between nations, classes and races. Her intuitive life, or rather White's construction of her life, makes her a spokesperson for his existential vision and his cultural critique.

From a post-modern and feminist vantage point, this Ellen Roxburgh is a deeply ambivalent character. She functions as a vehicle for White's larger vision, becoming yet another voice of the author as 'The Prodigal Son'.[10] In addition, as a textual construction with her feet firmly planted in modernist soil, she must stand within the categories of Self and other and also be able to transgress these cultural categories to encompass otherness itself. At the same time, the figure of the instinctual woman, tied to nature and a pre-social primitive existence, also represents primal fantasy for man, a yearning for cosmic oneness beyond cultural divisions, often conveyed through the figure of Woman as man's access to the essential. Patrick White's treatment of Ellen Roxburgh's character is the most complex of all versions of the Eliza Fraser story. He, like Brink in *An Instant in the Wind*, attempts to allow the woman to speak for both colonisers and colonised peoples, white 'barbarians' and their civilised convicts/slaves. He locates a redemptive possibility for society as a whole through the woman's experiences and cultural transgressions. What gives her fictional existence this metaphorical power? In other words, through what narrative strategies, primal fantasies and philosophical frameworks might woman speak as an essential voice of mankind? And, if she speaks for mankind, can she also speak for white men and women, and for Aborigines?

A Fringe of Leaves

A Fringe of Leaves has been interpreted as one of many works in the White canon which presents the solitary individual in search of an ultimate insight through his or her confrontation with the terrifying metaphysical geography of the mind, soul and spirit. In the case of *A Fringe of Leaves*, that individual is the simple, sensual Cornish girl, Ellen Gluyas, who marries Austin Roxburgh, a sickly but mannered gentleman, and is seemingly transformed into a genteel lady by his efforts and those of his mother. Ellen is a curious heroine, however, inextricably caught up in the weighty trappings of a Western cultural heritage. This leads to a central problem in the text. Some commentators refer to it as Ellen Roxburgh's problem – her ultimate failure to live up to her vision – and others attribute it to White's inconsistency in structuring the novel. A majority of critics view White's construction of Ellen's character and perspective uncritically as 'her' perspective. But the 'problem' they detect in the novel may have more to do with the impossibility of presenting a woman as an Everyman character within a modernist critical perspective than with what they perceive as White's possibly flawed portrayal of Ellen Roxburgh's character.

Fundamental to the novel is the idea of Woman as enigma and mystery – which is, of course, a founding myth of Patriarchy. White moves well beyond a simple rendering of the Eternal Feminine by presenting in Ellen a complex and contradictory character who straddles two realities, 'two incompatible worlds' (335).[11] The representation of her character arises out of a number of distinctions between self and other. She belongs to both (and neither) the peasantry and the bourgeoisie, to nature and culture, to the instincts and reason, to a pagan and a Christian heritage. Unlike the more static characters in the novel, Ellen struggles with her contradictory selves, although it is in her surrender to the instincts that she is said to come close to realising her 'true' self. In her case, the binary oppositions which construct and maintain the modernist version of the unified self are both conflated and transgressed; but they are ultimately re-established.

From the outset Ellen is introduced as a woman of mystery, a palimpsest. This characterisation reverberates throughout the novel. She was 'something of a mystery' (15); 'had an instinct for mysteries' (41). 'She reminded me of a clean sheet of paper which might disclose an invisible writing', comments Miss Scrimshaw after a brief meeting with her in Sydney. 'I only had the impression that Mrs. Roxburgh could feel life has cheated her out of some ultimate experience. For which she would be prepared to suffer, if need be' (17). These ominous words frame Ellen's (our) quest in the novel. It takes her from an instinctual childhood in the mythical Cornish landscape of her youth; through a sterile marriage to Austin Roxburgh, a sickly, pompous, effete gentleman of the English middle class; to a journey with him to Van Diemen's Land to visit his brother, Garnet, an English settler with a shady past with whom she discovers her sexual awakening. Her guilty departure from Hobart is followed by a brief visit to Sydney before sailing for home (England) with her husband. The voyage results in the shipwreck, and Ellen gives birth to a stillborn infant at sea, an event from which she recovers with great fortitude. She arrives on 'the fringe of Paradise,' only to be enslaved by her Aboriginal captors on Fraser Island, who treat her with an indifference which she experiences as cruelty. The 'captivity' culminates in an act of cannibalism in which Ellen participates and which she views as sacramental, leading her back to the dark, instinctual side of her nature. It ends in the midst of a wild and frenzied dancing at a corroboree, during which time Ellen is 'carried away' by Jack Chance. He is a runaway convict who had been transported to the colony for killing his mistress and who had escaped the penal settlement, preferring a life with the natives to its sadistic regime. He escorts her back to Moreton Bay, during which time the couple share a transformative, passionate sojourn in which they were 'equally exalted and equally condemned' (279). Although she had promised fidelity to him, she leaves him on the edge of the settlement, crawling back to civilisation with 'a knowledge of life beyond words' but troubled by self-disgust, fear and guilt at the greed, passion and sensuality found within the depths of her being. At the end of the novel Ellen meets a London merchant, Mr Jervons, whom she is likely to marry and with whom she will ultimately return to 'an ordered universe' (366).

Critical Views

The novel has received widespread critical acclaim by critics in Australia and abroad. When it first appeared, critics invariably cited its historical ante-cedent and addressed questions concerning its historical accuracy, with Alexander's history as the point of reference for its historical truth. Over time, critics and readers shifted their concerns. They began to focus on the quest motif of the novel, explicating its themes and structure as a moral fable within the romance genre. Genre considerations led to questions of Ellen's suitability for the part of questing heroine: what was the nature of her quest; what lessons did she learn; was the quest ultimately successful? Should Ellen's return to civilisation at the end of the novel as the wife of a petty bourgeois merchant be taken as a courageous acceptance of life's limitations, or as the ultimate defeat of her understanding of the essential self? In the 1980s post-colonial critics began to address the problem of White's Abor-igines and the function of cannibalism in the novel. Although the novel appeared in the year following International Women's Year, when feminist political and critical scholarly activity was on the rise, it attracted no interest by feminist critics for nearly a decade.

In the main the novel has been received favourably by those sympathetic to White and his modernist canon. Critics interpret it as a significant work of art with an exemplary meaning which explores the tension between artifice and naturalness and reveals something of the essential life.[12] But they remain divided about the ending. If Ellen's transgression of culture's boundaries is what seems to give the novel its strength, her regression to a middle-class marriage seems to be its weakness.[13] That the problem, which is central for a majority of the critics, might be a core problem not only for the novel but also for its underlying epistemology, is a perspective seldom touched upon by its critics. Diana Brydon takes up this issue in her attempt to read the novel with feminist, post-modern and post-colonial questions in mind. She argues that White succeeds in pushing beyond the limits of cultural dichotomies, endemic not only to Australia but to Western society, towards a realisation of what the French feminists might call a feminine cultural multiplicity. In this, he 'give[s] voice to the silent, secret female centre'. She suggests that the novel has revolutionary potential in 'its shifting emphasis from a male focus to a female – more diffuse – focus . . . from a single privileged voice, from a single language to a complex interplay of competing languages, away from "either/or" towards "both/and" '.[14] For her, the novel is not about the dissolution of a civilised person in the wilderness; rather, it is about the dissolution of Western concepts of individuality in general. She argues that both women and Aborigines, marginalised by Patriarchy and colonialism, are transformed from being objects to becoming subjects; in addition, the notion of being a subject is called into question. Ellen becomes a post-modern subject. She 'understands' life beyond words. In her sharing of cultural rituals (cannibalism) with the Aborigines, she reveals herself open to multiplicity. Her testing ground, the bush, is both ' "home ground [and] foreign territory", the frightening place that nonetheless reveals society to be the true nightmare'.[15] This reading turns the novel into a post-modernist parable. And, indeed, it can be read in this way (if the post-modern can be said to accommodate parables). At the same time, White's insistence on Ellen's vision of the 'true' self beyond the artificiality of cultural roles locks the novel into a modernist project. Brydon obscures this dimension in her discussion. Yet this dimension is what imparts a universal humanist vision for mankind in the readings of other critics. This seeming dilemma will be further explored below.

An Australian Quest?

White's telling of the tale pits nature against civilisation; the instinctual self against the social self; Ellen, her Aboriginal captors and her convict rescuer against a stultifying colonial white society; the bush against the city. In this he reiterates a common theme in his writing, a critique of the Great Australian Emptiness, the immense physical, psychic, and cultural void which was his experience of Australia and Australians. For White, what constitutes the individual is not so much the regulatory moral or ethical mechanisms imposed by society, but the universal, pre-social and individual aspects of the existential self. This belief can be traced through his autobiographical writings as well as his fiction.[16] The essay 'The Prodigal Son', in which White reflects on his feelings in 1959 after his return to Australia from Europe, reflects something of this. Even the textual fluctuation between self-recognition and denial can be read as a strategy to protect White's artistic persona from the predations of his social world, and beyond them, his unspeakable fears – what Bhabha calls in relation to (neo-)colonial writing, the 'otherness of the self'. White writes:

> Returning sentimentally to a country I had left in my youth, what had I really found? Was there anything to prevent me packing my bag and leaving . . . like so many other artists? Bitterly I had to admit, no. In all directions stretched the Great Australian Emptiness, in which the mind is the least of possessions, in which the rich man is the important man, in which the schoolmaster and the journalist rule what intellectual roost there is, in which beautiful youths and girls stare at life though blind blue eyes, in which human teeth fall like autumn leaves, the buttocks of cars grow hourly glassier, food means steak and cake, muscles prevail, and the march of material ugliness does not raise a quiver from the average nerves. It was the exaltation of the 'average' that made me panic most, and in this frame of mind, in spite of myself, I began to conceive another novel.[17]

White wrote only two novels with historical antecedents, *Voss* and *A Fringe of Leaves*. Both have been read as complex, psychological studies of the individual struggling against the constraints of a colonial Australian past which also reveal, for White, something of the present social, moral and spiritual malaise. *A Fringe of Leaves* focuses a critical gaze on nineteenth-century English authority, morals and manners as they might be seen to reflect the present imperfect Australian human community. Like Nolan, White imagines Australia as a fallen garden, with Ellen Roxburgh and Jack Chance taking up their respective roles in the Adam and Eve myth as sinners seeking redemption. Within these terms, Ellen can be fashioned as an Australian heroine. She also can slide into a persona for the mythical Patrick White, self-constructed but also imagined by others as Australia's Prodigal Son: or, as the outcast from an artificial society who leaves, is transformed by his experience and returns exalted as a prophet with a new vision. In the novel, Ellen, the outcast by circumstance, with Jack, the outcast by necessity, form a bond through their romance. Like Jack Chance, Ellen suffers intense privations in a harsh landscape through which she achieves some ultimate truth. As a 'slave' to the Aborigines and later in her relationship with the convict, her 'saviour-lover', she confronts a hostile land of 'bleached grass and scorched earth' (8) and 'loathsome savages' (20). Her enslavement on the 'fringes of Paradise itself' (208) becomes a private Gethsemane. She suffers an 'agony in the garden' of the bush, 'the beginning of her martyrdom' (217). Her suffering leads her through degradation to an experience of ecstasy (238), when the 'spirit of the place . . . took possession of her' (246) and she experiences 'a kind of communion' (329) with the natives and the land.

This novel, like Nolan's paintings, also explores the theme of betrayal. Ellen is said to undergo a series of trials in the novel which result in a number of betrayals, of both herself and others. (On the theme of betrayal in terms of self-constructions: White maintains that his mother was the source of the 'fundamental betrayal' of his life. Her crime was that she banished him from his childhood paradise to the stultifying environment of a boarding-school in Cheltenham, England, at the age of thirteen. In *A Fringe of Leaves* he reserves that same Cheltenham as the home of the Roxburgh family. In 'The Prodigal Son' he credits his exile (initially imposed, later chosen) as that which made possible the evolution of his artistic vision. In retrospect, he can interpret his exile as both repressive and liberating; but he never forgives his mother).[18] Ellen's betrayals occur within the context of her love affairs, first with Garnet Roxburgh and later with Jack Chance. They open her to an awareness of the sensual delights of the body but lead to a legacy of remorse. Upon her return to civilisation, 'she sat re-living the betrayal of her earthly loves' (353). In the first instance of adultery, she betrays the marriage vows made to her husband; in the second, she betrays the bond forged with Jack Chance (J.C. – her saviour) in the wilderness. When she returns to civilisation, after she has witnessed and participated in a sacred act of cannibalism, she submits herself to a scene of personal humiliation before the convicts 'as punishment for her omissions and shortcomings' (335), knowing that she might never be acceptable in either of her two incompatible worlds, those of civilisation and the bush. Typically harsh and unforgiving, the landscape offers little solace.

Ellen's trials take place within two distinct, symbolic environments in the novel: one lush, the other barren.[19] Her passionate awakenings occur in the fertile pastures of Van Diemen's Land and within the foreboding but lush rainforests of Fraser Island. Her confrontation with the islanders, through which she encounters her own 'depraved' self, takes place in the more barren, threatening and absorbing Australian bush. Until her meeting with Jack Chance, the bush is variously described as 'a harsh land, unprepossessing, barren, stony, forbidding, empty, and hostile'.[20] During the height of the love affair, the couple inhabit a luxuriant and sensuous garden. These two environments, both 'dream worlds' of an Australian imaginary, represent her two places of trial and testing. The trials take her beyond the social and moral constraints of a self moulded by social conventions. In this 'beyond', she encounters a 'true' instinctual, essential self which she also betrays upon her return to civilisation. But where is this 'beyond' to be found? Can it be registered, as Brydon would have it, as a post-modern feminine space of cultural multiplicity, of alterity beyond the impasse of difference; or does it inevitably rely upon an idealist conception of the harmony of the individual with the universe, within a Western masculinist romantic construction of 'a world elsewhere'?[21]

White's Universalism and Critique of Class

For White, few can achieve harmony in this world, which 'tolerates humanity but grudgingly'.[22] The most suitable seekers after life's experience beyond this spiritually and sensually impoverished environment are the loners, the 'burnt ones' – free of the stultifying constraints of city life and genteel pretensions. In part, Ellen qualifies, although she is not an Australian. What distinguishes her as a protagonist is that she is not of English stock but of peasant origins, and thus closer to nature. White makes this point quite early in the novel, locating her with 'the dark people' of Cornwall (12), 'a country to which [she] *belonged* (more than [she] did to parents and family)' (emphasis in original, 92). At the end of the novel, he reiterates her distance from the English middle class in a scene at Moreton Bay during her meeting with the Reverend Cottle, who came to the colony from Somerset: ' "Oh", she replied, and with a sad look which doubted his credentials, "there's a river between us. You are from England." She laughed, not unkindly, but to dispel any illusions he might have about their consanguinity. "I was born to poor country." ' (347). Her character in this respect is constructed as being Cornish, not English; she is thus an outcast amongst the transplanted English bourgeoisie, in direct contradiction to the English middle-class status of her husband.

> Mr. Roxburgh was fully exposed. In advancing towards this land's end [as is Cornwall in England], he felt the trappings of wealth and station, the pride in ethical and intellectual aspirations, stripped from him with a ruthlessness reserved for those who accept their importance or who have remained unaware of their pretentiousness. [185]

In *A Fringe of Leaves*, Cornwall is metonymically linked to the south-east of England as the Australian bush is to the city, nature to culture, a deep mythical past to a shallow secular present.

White's novels address the middle class in Australia. Ellen Roxburgh serves as a foil against which middle-class Australian society is to be measured. Within White's literary canon, the English class system produces specimens like the vapid Austin Roxburgh, who attaches himself to a complex but spiritually empty set of social structures. In general, White's middle-class characters are shown to exercise only a tenuous control over civilised pockets of Australia, maintained through cruelty and exploitation. With the exception of Ellen, whose class status is adopted uncomfortably through her marriage, the middle-class characters in the novel, like those found in White's other works, are presented, in the words of one White critic, as 'uncongenial predators, confused, vulnerable aliens, pathetic and sinister'.[23] Other (middle-class) women and men are drawn as static, stereotypical creatures tied to social norms, who serve as exemplars for White's critique of class. Of the women, only Mrs Lovell, the wife of the Commandant at Moreton Bay who nurses Ellen back to health with compassion and understanding, is endowed with any spirit or talent. The rest exist as two-dimensional exemplars in White's existential and psychological study. Patricia Morley is one critic who takes White to task for his portrayal of women, whom she judges to be 'petty, peevish, like vultures, non-adventurous, unable to make important decisions, and vapid'.[24]

The middle-class male characters in the novel fare no better under White's critical gaze. They are shallow, lifeless bureaucrats, without soul. From beginning to end, they view Ellen as dangerous. Mr Merivale at the outset appears to be distanced and objective. But he is lured by the story of Ellen even before she appears, at the same time as his wife and Miss Scrimshaw deride her through their own jealousy and spite. She has power to bewitch men, to lure them into 'dark and strange' places of danger and desire. At the novel's end, Lieutenant Cunningham, Chaplain Cottle and Commandant Lovell all appear to be frightened by Ellen and her 'instinctive primitiveness', which they must reject to save themselves.[25]

It is with the convict and outcast Jack Chance that Ellen (almost) finds her 'true self'. And Jack Chance offers the most concise critique of class in the novel. He tells Ellen there are only two divisions of people in colonial Australia: the moral classes and the convicts. He has no faith in the moral classes, the civilised men of the colony. When she suggests that he will be pardoned if he returns her to civilisation, he demurs, concluding: 'Men is unnatural and unjust.' (253). Through Ellen's love relationship with him she transgresses the boundaries of class. Chance, the outlaw/outcast, is Ellen's (our) last chance; he offers redemption through love. This theme is reiterated in the novel's epigraph: 'Love is your last chance. There is really nothing else on earth to keep you there.'

Ellen is drawn to Jack through her instincts, her sensuality, her common bond with the land and its inhabitants; that is, through White's rendering of the essential, elemental Woman. With him she feels in harmony with the land:

> There was an occasion when she fell down, scattering skywards a cloud of ashen parrots. She would have continued lying on the ground and perhaps become her true self: once the flesh melts, and the skeleton inside it is blessed with its final articulate white, amongst the stones, beneath the hard sky, in this country to which it can at last belong. [281]

But the closer Ellen comes to civilisation, the more troubled she becomes. As her betrayal of Jack Chance nears, she attempts to restore something of her former (borrowed middle-class) 'authority and dignity'. This is the point at which, through lack of will and moral courage, she renounces the 'essential self', and betrays Jack in her mind:

> Her greatest strengths were perhaps her cunning and her stubbornness, one of which was possibly provoked by the man's presence, the other also dependent on him: although she had the will to survive, doubtless she would have succumbed had the convict not dragged her along. Of course he had strength, the physical strength, until at this late stage in their journey he seemed to be making demands on her for that moral strength she had rashly promised in the beginning.
>
> Now while she stood in the grey morning, chafing her arms and shoulders, it was not the convict she despised; it was her wobbling, moral self, upon which he so much depended. Alarm mingled with exhilaration to cause the shivers, as she contemplated the landscape and the power given to an individual soul to exercise over another. [295]

As the landscape has betrayed the Australian native son, and man his divine redeemer, so Ellen Gluyas Roxburgh will betray her saviour-rescuer. Although she entreats the colonial authorities to pardon him, she will renounce her lover, leaving him to wander as an exile in the wilderness. The middle class has been presented, in relation to Ellen, as a class of pathetic, sexually repressed, transposed Britons bound to the colony by its shallow social structures; but it is to the middle class that the outcast Ellen must return, abandoning her primal vision to the contingencies of a woman's life within an imperfect human society.

White's judgements concerning the woman as betrayer may be less harsh than those of Nolan, but White, like Nolan before him, constructs the story in terms of an ultimate human experience of the fall and man's need for redemption. In addition, previously constructed understandings of the nature of women, in particular their passivity and their links with nature and the instincts, make possible White's rendering of the tale. There are two contradictory and irreconcilable impulses in the text, and Ellen marks the boundary between them. On the one hand, White struggles with man's desire to overcome social distinctions and self–other categories of existence and also with the necessity to maintain them. Critics may be right to suggest that White attempts through Ellen's characterisation to achieve a breakthrough for the multiple self beyond difference. But it is also the case that to the degree that her character signifies a masculine construction of feminine difference – her ties with nature, the lower classes and the instincts – the novel, of necessity, compromises her position as a protagonist who is also a heroine. It obliterates that which it seeks to praise. The construction of Ellen Gluyas Roxburgh as the tie to man's sacred and primordial past is a mythic representation of Woman which remains embedded within the White Man's Story. In Australia, as well as for an international audience, that Story arises out of a number of interconnected and mutually supportive discourses:

modernist Western metaphysics and attendant romantic myths of Patriarchy (Tristan and Isolde, Pygmalion, Tintagel), Christianity (Adam and
Eve), existential humanist philosophy (Jung and Buber), and Australian
national identity (man against the land/woman/Aborigines). At the same
time, these discourses present irreconcilable contradictions. These contradictions in the novel raise questions about the degree to which the individual
can be separated from his or her social environment and whether or not the
novel can be cut adrift from its social and cultural foundations: the legacy of
colonialism, the relationship between the imperial centre and the colonial
periphery, the self and its others. Edward Said, in his study *Culture and
Imperialism*, suggests that this dimension of modernism is, at least in part, 'a
response to external pressures on culture' from what he calls the *imperium*.
He explains, in a way that has relevance for White and his readers, that
Europe knows itself to be no longer invulnerable to the troubling 'other'
inside the self. The modernist writer, he concludes, takes a more ironic than
oppositional stance. There is a desperate but impossible attempt to syn-
thesise cultural oppositions, to come to a new vision of universal humanity –
through art and history rather than geography and politics.[26]

Representations of Aboriginality

Within this universalising ambit, Aborigines serve two functions. They are
undefined background presences, a part of the hostile landscape; and at the
same time they are the source of insight which enables a reawakening from
the deadening influences of bourgeois culture. As individuals they are anonymous in the novel, a grovelling crowd of savages, imagined largely through
White's constructions of Ellen's consciousness. First introduced through
their voices, 'a curious noise, of animal gibbering, or human chatter', they
then come into view: 'one, three, half-a-dozen savages, not entirely naked . . .
[and] armed besides . . . only their dark skins had the glint of ominous metal'
(210). They are variously described as animalistic, violent and physical. They
utter 'horrid shrieks . . . their gibberish accompanied by overtly hostile gestures' (213), until they approach and surround the party, 'all sinew and
stench and exultant in their mastery' (216). The Aborigines remain a shad-
owy enigma throughout the novel. Through the day they subject Ellen to
multiple humiliations: punching and prodding her body, pummelling her
breasts, poking her with sticks and firebrands, smearing her body with charcoal. Wailing at dusk, the women couple indiscriminately by night, 'taking
their turn to satisfy (or so it sounded) man's demands' (227) in their 'stink-
ing' huts. The men appear to be 'disfigured by welts from incisions deliberately inflicted'; the 'wretched females' are 'slommacky from bearing
children', the 'hags' are 'hideously ugly'. They 'grovel' in keeping with their
humble station (221). Despite this, some men have a 'noble form'. They are

even 'handsome' in appearance, and, true to her elemental self, Ellen is attracted to them.

Several critics have attempted to come to terms with these harsh depictions. One approach is to excuse White's representation of Aboriginal life because of what is seen as his ultimately humane vision. Veronica Brady, for instance, suggests that 'White's picture of the Aborigines here emphasises their savagery not out of prejudice . . . but to underline the hostility of the natural world'.[27] They are part of an inimical landscape which challenges Ellen and provides her with the ultimate experience of life. In a later article, Brady reasons that *A Fringe of Leaves,* more than any other White novel, 'challenges the basis of our racism'.[28] By overturning the cultural dichotomies of white–black, good–evil, civilised–savage, White teaches us that a different existence is possible. He defers to the authority of the other, which wins out against the dictates of the self and society and a culture of complacent containment. Laurie Hergenhan concurs; he argues that not only are the Aborigines depicted in realistic detail, as represented through the consciousness of the white woman, but they also enrich our understanding of the colonial past. Not only does the novel provide insight into Aboriginal existence, it also challenges white readers to register another dimension of colonial life – the convict suffering at the hands of vindictive colonial administrators which led many to seek an alternative life in Aboriginal society.[29] Aboriginal and non-Aboriginal readers unconvinced by the inclusive assumptions of liberal humanism may not be entirely persuaded by these arguments. They are put forward again, with a more complex rationale, in critical discussions of cannibalism in the novel, the ultimate mark of primitive savagery which becomes Ellen's sacramental moment of communion with nature and primitive life.

The Dark Bond of Cannibalism

Few contemporary novels confront white fears raised by the spectre of cannibalism produced by the colonial experience of the West. In this *A Fringe of Leaves* is memorable, even daring. It dares to speak the unspeakable. More than this, cannibalism for White is not only the ultimate mark of savage otherness; it is also an act of spiritual communion, the fullest expression of Ellen's identification with the land and its indigenous people. When the novel first appeared, critics repressed this theme in their reviews. To date, the few critics who have directly addressed the question of White's depiction of cannibalism in the novel have been non-Australians.[30] It almost seems as if this dimension of the text was the hardest for Australian readers and critics to come to terms with – perhaps an enduring effect of colonial guilt. Those non-Australian critics who do take up the theme treat the experience on White's terms: that is, as sacramental. But even in White's terms, Ellen's

reactions to cannibalism are ambivalent. In his description of the crucial
scene, Ellen, following the native women at some distance, discovers the
thigh bone of a young girl on the path. The girl had been killed by the women
in a 'jealous fury' a few days before, then mourned by both the native group
and Ellen, who had taken the occasion to grieve for the sake of her own lost
self. The girl had been ritually skinned before being consumed by the natives.
Ellen contemplates the thigh bone:

> Her stiffened body and almost audibly twangling nerves were warning her against
> what she was about to do, what she was, in fact, already doing. She had raised the
> bone, and was tearing at it with her teeth, spasmodically chewing, swallowing by
> great gulps which her throat threatened to return. But did not. She flung the bone
> away only after it was cleaned, and followed slowly in the wake of her cannibal
> mentors. She was less disgusted in retrospect by what she had done, than awed by
> the fact that she had been moved to do it. The exquisite innocence of this forest
> morning, its quiet broken by a single flute-note endlessly repeated, tempted her to
> believe that she had partaken of a sacrament. But there remained what amounted
> to an abomination of human behaviour, a headache, and the first signs of indi-
> gestion. In the light of Christian morality she must never think of the incident
> again.
> [But she cannot forget] how tasting flesh from the human thigh-bone in the
> stillness of a forest morning had nourished not only her animal body but some
> darker need of the hungry spirit. [244–5]

Terry Goldie argues that Ellen's eating of the flesh of the thigh of the dead
Aboriginal girl signifies an assimilation of Aboriginal culture into the West,
the beginnings of their (our) assimilation into a New World. He argues that if
the neo-colonial Australian man is seen as empty, decaying and facing cultural death, Ellen's ritual represents for him the possibility of rebirth through
her surrender to the land and its indigenous inhabitants.[31] He invokes both
Christian explanations of ingestion of the Eucharist as transubstantiation
and anthropological understandings of ritual cannibalism. He uses these to
suggest that Ellen and white culture will thrive on this land only through an
ingestion of the other, which, according to White, 'nourished the darker need
of the hungry spirit' (White, 245). Goldie writes, 'through the cannibalism,
Ellen not only participates in the Aboriginal life, she partakes of the Aborigine. If the theory is that the dead person's powers will also be acquired, the
young girl is a perfect choice, a symbol of youth and beauty and said to be
"inexhaustible".'[32]
    In a critique not unlike Goldie's in its overall argument and conclusions,
Hena Maes-Jelinek refers to cannibalism as a spiritual communion, a union
with alien people through which, again according to White, 'the spirit of the
place took possession of her' (White, 246). She cites cannibalism as a 'universal phenomenon,' although 'it is the least understood and least acceptable

feature of otherness in alien peoples'.[33] For her, Ellen's act is a demonstration of the 'essential relatedness of two peoples, their kinship and myths'.[34] Maes-Jelinek views Ellen's return to civilisation with alarm since, for her, it signifies a denial of the significance of her experience. Regardless of their final analysis of the novel's theme, these critics view Ellen's ritual act as transcendental, sacramental and spiritual. They focus on this time of crisis in the novel when she passes through the heart of darkness. White undercuts the mystical quality of the experience with reference to Ellen's headache and indigestion, but the critics romanticise it with reference to Joseph Conrad and neo-colonial mythology. At the same time, both Conrad and neo-colonial mythology derive their power from the ways in which they associate the feminine and sexuality with primitive cultures and the land. The problem is that these conflations have more to do with the West's crisis of identity than with Aboriginality. Western discourse on the primitive collapses the categories of self and other in its inclusive gestures of incorporation, even when attempting to imagine a new way of living beyond racial divisions in a universe of diverse populations. These 'transgressive' acts may be the ultimate acts of (neo-)colonial assimilation – the ultimate denial of cultural difference.

White prepares the reader for this scene, thus prefiguring Ellen's cannibalism, in a number of ways. He portrays the possibility of white cannibalism as acceptable, when imagined in the dreams of a starving Austin Roxburgh at the time of the shipwreck and the steward Spurgeon's death. He also acknowledges that the practice of native cannibalism was not uncommon, as revealed through Delancy's reports to the Merivales of natives killing and eating white trespassers on Aboriginal territory at the beginning of the novel. But these prefigurations are situations *in extremis*. He prepares for Ellen's experience differently: the youthful Ellen's spiritual union with nature through Celtic mythology and her immersion in the black (primitive, unconscious) waters of St Hya's Well is linked to Aboriginal identifications with nature through cannibalistic ritual practices. In Ellen's case, the Celtic and Aboriginal pasts of mankind merge into an experience of the 'real' beyond the veil of social illusion. The two worlds meld into an order of sameness: one distanced from the artifice of a white culture of rational, socialised beings. Within White's imaginary, these Celtic and Aboriginal pasts belong to 'our' primordial being but exist within another realm of knowing, severed from and buried by the newer cultural trappings of Western, middle-class culture.

Cannibalism in the novel, then, is more than an instinctual act on Ellen's part or a biological imperative on the part of starving shipwreck survivors or Aboriginal peoples. White engages in a politics of representation here, wanting to critique the shallowness of Western existence in contrast to the sacred primordiality of Aboriginal life and custom. But his conceptions are *our* conceptions, Western conceptions. As Marianna Torgovnick explains:

within traditional European systems of thought and language, to identify 'others' is to invoke a 'hierarchy'; [Europeans] exist in relations of mastery, rather than reciprocity, with other humans and with the world. In studying primitive societies or in inventing versions of them, Westerners pretend to learn about or to create alternative, less oppressive ways of knowing, all the while establishing mastery and control over those other ways of knowing. Primitive societies and systems of thought which might critique Western ones are instead processed in Western terms. [Modernist thinkers] yearn for, but lack the ground for, radical critique.[35]

That is, Aboriginal life in the novel, like the nature of Woman, is embedded in already available Western cultural understandings and hierarchies of power and difference. The Aboriginal characters presented in *A Fringe of Leaves* belong to an invented past, an evolutionary time. They refer, in the minds of contemporary, white, middle-class readers, to a primitive people existing at a lower level of life, an earlier stage of human existence. Women, according to a parallel modernist discourse of feminine otherness, can gain access to this noumenal world because they too are closer to nature and the instincts. They are suitable guides into a state of imagined being without divisions because their very bodies signify an excessiveness which blurs the boundaries between inside and outside, self and other. These categories of people (women and indigenous peoples) whose constructed selves have come into being under the auspices of patriarchal and colonial relations of dominance cannot also be rescued by those same relations. We discover in this impasse of representation another ironic juxtaposition. In the nineteenth century the Eliza Fraser story functioned to *establish* the very notions of irrevocable racial divisions, feminine propriety and middle-class subjectivity which White so harshly condemns and struggles to move beyond, even as he is caught within them, in the late twentieth century.

As was suggested in the earlier chapters, the discourse employed by John Curtis in the 1830s involved a transposition of contemporary fears on to the Other, who then served as a monstrous reminder of what 'we' might become. The notion of the Other maintained hierarchical distinctions between different racial, ethnic, class and gender orders within England and the further reaches of Empire. Within colonial Australia such views legitimated benevolent Christian activities and the more violent and punitive measures of the State. In White's fiction, as in Nolan's perceptions late in his life, the primitive Other has been replaced by the sacred Other in a new allegory of man's fall and redemption. In this new allegory, modern culture exemplifies the Fall – in its dreary, dun-coloured, materialistic, philistinism,[36] Australia becomes a culture of gratuitous, soulless materialism. The artist as prophet offers hope of redemption through love and also a recognition of the sacredness of primitive culture and its values. As in the nineteenth century, but with different effects, 'these different forms of time represent a system of differences employed to manufacture and produce the real; a system of differences employed to establish the reality(ies) of national subjects in a culture where evolutionary theory has become part of the folklore of popular culture'.[37] White's novel engages in another form of middle-class cultural elitism, a way of chastising the middle class for their spiritual emptiness, leading them to a vision of wholeness by embracing the mystical otherness of their primordial past and, by the same gesture, absorbing cultural difference into a modernist myth of universal man. His vehicle is Ellen Roxburgh.

The Role of the Modernist Artist

Patrick White has been a privileged narrator of this perspective within Australian arts and letters. As the Australian writer of international standing, he is reputed to speak to the world through his writings on behalf of the nation. Epitaphs appearing on the occasion of his funeral give some indication of the tribute paid this great Australian writer. 'A monument in the Australian cultural landscape', wrote a contemporary Australian historian.[38] 'The greatest novelist writing in English in the twentieth century,' echoed a Canadian literary critic.[39] It was rare to find a voice of demurral. But, as John Docker was to point out in a review of David Marr's biography, the problem with White is that he speaks 'the truth' so assuredly always *on behalf of* others.[40] To get to the 'secret core of feelings', he must evoke and judge the essence of person, nation and race; ethnicity, class and religion. It is also significant that his works became canonical and himself a cultural industry in the 1970s at the very time when assurances about common cultural values and beliefs were breaking down. More than this, as White's writings became part of a revered literary canon in Australia, the man himself was becoming more engaged in a radical politics of the left. White became politically active in the final two decades of his life; he spoke out in support of the Labor Party and marched on behalf of Aboriginal land rights and environmental issues, including the fight to save Fraser Island from sand-mining and logging industries. These actions disclose a complexity of character beyond the aesthetic principles and metaphysical vision of modernism which are said to structure his novels and secure his critical reputation as a first-rate international literary figure.

Contemporary society looks to modern intellectuals to replace the priests as secular individuals entrusted with saving the nation and the self from the great void, the emptiness of modern culture. Sidney Nolan and Patrick White occupy this role in their respective reshapings of the Eliza Fraser story within modernist narratives of Australian nationalism. And they are not alone. Since the 1970s a diverse number of cultural prophets have emerged on Australia's national horizon. Their chastising judgements take up multiple columns in the daily press. They include: the novelist and republican, Thomas Keneally; the late nationalist historian, Manning Clark; the late poet and journalist, Max Harris; journalist, film and cultural critic, Phillip Adams; the late adventurer, Paddy Pallin; 'Dreamtime' artist Ainslie Roberts; the late travel writer, Bruce Chatwin; and ex-American, now Aboriginal-identified bush poet, Billy Marshall-Stoneking. Social anthropologist Andrew Lattas has examined the cultural work of these spokespersons. He is critical of the process by which they posit an underlying unifying memory for Australian culture through an evocation of a primordial Aboriginal heritage. In a discussion of the acclaim attributed to the paintings of Ainslie Roberts, he makes this critique, which could apply equally to the work of Nolan and White in relation to the evocation of Aboriginality in their constructions of the Eliza Fraser story:

> This discourse transforms Aboriginal beliefs into the collective unconscious of humanity, they become the common unifying unconscious of a nation made up of many cultural heritages. This aesthetic and psychoanalytic form of nationalism popularises the healing search for universal and timeless archetypal symbols in Aboriginal culture. As the conscience of the whole of humanity, Aboriginal culture allows the white man to escape his own particularity and merge with universality. [In the creative work of artists like Roberts, but also of White and Nolan,] Aborigines are internalised into the white man's psyche: they are rendered into the spiritual aesthetic side of the western self, becoming that unconscious realm of meaning which the West represses and must regain consciousness of if it is to re-establish its wholeness. In this fusion of Jungian and nationalist discourses, the unconscious becomes the space of the sacred for the individual and the nation. Aborigines . . . become the Holy Other.[41]

Lattas maintains that modern intellectuals position themselves, and are positioned by others, as 'having the redemptive task of caring for the nation's soul, and of saving the nation from the terrible nothingness taking over the world'.[42] But for many Australians, as he is quick to point out, Australia is not a culture caught in a meaningless void; rather, it is a diverse and contradictory culture full of significant meaning. Further, the story of cultural decay, the search for a lost soul of the nation, keeps problems of national identity on the agenda – the search for *one* identity which denies internal contradictions as well as radical differences. These voices are heard at the time when women, migrants, Aborigines, the unemployed, and other of the nation's 'fringe dwellers' have challenged its assumptions and assurances of a common identity, a unified history, a myth of mankind's primordial existence. The prophets engage the populace in perpetual vigilance, searching for signs that would lend depth to the white Australian nation, built on a shallow historical experience. They locate themselves and their Australian readers as alienated beings in the void. This journalistic excess gives evidence of the enduring power of the primal fantasy of, or desire for, cosmic oneness; but it is also another form of subterfuge to forestall a long overdue recognition, by a cultural elite which is losing its power, of the dynamics of difference. And the writers themselves know this. They are caught in a rupture which is the present condition – between modernism and post-modernity, between neo-colonial and post-colonial national and global realities. So, on the one hand these spokespersons may support campaigns for Aboriginal sovereignty or (rarely) women's rights; on the other hand their rhetoric is founded on the desire for an inclusive cultural unity underwritten by an unavoidable legacy of guilt, lack and loss within (masculine) neo-colonial culture. Their stories are yet another staging of the retarding story of fall and redemption in which women and Aborigines are implicated, their concerns appropriated, their identities absorbed into a new version of an old and increasingly vulnerable white man's mythology.

CHAPTER 8

A Universal Post-colonial Myth?
Representations beyond Australia

The Eliza Fraser story had several revivals outside Australia in the period from 1969 to 1978. They include the long poem *The Man with Seven Toes*, written by Sri Lankan author Michael Ondaatje, published in Canada in 1969 after performances at the Vancouver Festival in 1968 and the Stratford Workshop in 1969; the play *Dreams of Mrs Fraser*, written by Gabriel Josipovici which premiered in London in August 1972 and was subsequently performed by various small companies throughout England, published in 1975; and the novel, *An Instant in the Wind*, by South African author André Brink. To this list should be added the libretto *Eliza Fraser Sings* or *Eliza Survivor* by Australian composer Peter Sculthorpe and poet Barbara Blackman, commissioned by a Canadian ensemble, the Lyric Arts Trio, in 1977–8, produced, performed and published within Australia during this time. Sculthorpe had been interested in developing the Eliza Fraser legend into a piece of music theatre from the time he was approached by Sidney Nolan and Patrick White in 1964 to produce a composition for the opening of the Sydney Opera House. He had attempted several frustrating collaborations with White, as well as Alan Moorehead and Roger Covell, Chris Wallace-Crabbe, Tony Morphett and then Josipovici, before his final collaboration with Blackman.[1] The Sculthorpe–Blackman piece shares some common thematic and compositional elements with the productions of Josipovici and Ondaatje while also, like the work of Nolan and White, being tempered by a neo-colonial mode of modernism. The libretto, written by Barbara Blackman, adopts a female standpoint. It is also marked by what might be called a feminine difference. The Brink novel, on the other hand, can be linked to the universalising tendencies in the work of Sidney Nolan and Patrick White, although it is also specifically inflected by its South African context.

These late-twentieth-century adaptations of the Eliza Fraser story bear little relation to their nineteenth-century variants, and have only the most tenuous links to the 1836 report of the shipwreck. They represent new transformations in radically different historical contexts. Cannibalism, both native and white, that unspoken threat of otherness submerged in the earlier texts, becomes a bizarre but relatively unremarkable dimension of these twentieth-century works. The threat posed by Aborigines within Australian society has abated; the texts take up an assimilationist stance. Mrs Fraser's sexuality, however, an unspeakable theme in relation to the earlier Victorian audience, becomes *de rigueur* in a contemporary context. The ambivalences and anxieties of a contemporary age revolve not so much around issues of race but around constructions of sexuality, difference and identity. The different historical preoccupations, however, may not be so divergent. The modern accounts centre on the shame and guilt of the Mrs Fraser figure as a result of having been subjected to sexual assault at the hands of her Aboriginal captors and in her liaison with David Bracefell, the convict rescuer. As a modernist heroine haunted by the memories of the event, the 1970s Mrs Fraser traverses the boundaries of identity/madness. The new readings rely on concepts of the self derived from modern psychology. Mrs Fraser's dilemma (which provides the drama of Josipovici's play, Ondaatje's long poem and the Sculthorpe–Blackman libretto) is how to maintain an identity after the trauma. That experience took her over the edge and beyond the familiar oppositions of nature and civilisation, culture and barbarism to an alien space of non-identity, one represented through a Western fantasy of horror resulting from one's contact with 'the primitive'. Marianna Torgovnick suggests that Western concepts of the primitive and their connections with sexuality and gender are utterly crucial. We imagine the primitive in ways that challenge the borders between the psychological and the political. In her study of the West's fascination with the exotic, but also familiar, world of the primitive, she suggests that for a modernist audience, the primitive represents 'our id selves – libidinous, irrational, violent, dangerous'. She proposes that primitivist discourse, far from maintaining hierarchies of self and other, civilised and savage, the instincts and rationality, which might be understood as an attempt to preserve the superiority of Western cultures, instead engages in a fantasy of 'yearning for the dissolution of hierarchies and of the binary categories so deeply embedded in Western thought and culture'.[2] The imagined connection between woman's sexual excesses and the base instincts of primitive culture represent man's fear of and 'flirtations with boundary dissolution; they both test and affirm man's need to maintain separation, difference, and control as attributes of masculinity'.[3] At the same time, for men, fantasies of women and their sexuality, like those of primitives and their base natures, allow access to an imagined essential self, beyond social and psychic divisions – one both feared as abjection and desired as bliss. We will trace these modernist imaginings of 'the primitive' in the works of Ondaatje, Josipovici, and Sculthorpe and Blackman.

Michael Ondaatje's Long Poem

Michael Ondaatje, like many other commentators on the Eliza Fraser story, took his inspiration from the paintings of Sidney Nolan. At the end of *The Man with Seven Toes* (1969)[4] he includes the legendary story of Mrs Fraser which Colin MacInnes had written for the catalogue from the Whitechapel Art Gallery, reprinted in the Thames and Hudson monograph *Sidney Nolan: Landscapes and Legends* (and reproduced here on pages 130–1). His poetic treatment signals a shift in modernist interest in the story towards an investigation of woman's (Mrs Fraser's) sexuality. The poem, like Gabriel Josipovici's play and the Sculthorpe–Blackman libretto, studies the conflict between the woman's conscious memory and unconscious state, the social and the natural world, the 'real' and the repressed, the political and the psychological. Although written from what might be called a woman's perspective, on another level the poem traces Man's fears of primitive otherness. *The Man with Seven Toes* explores the troubling and fearsome enigma of female sexuality, or what Kristeva has called 'the powers of horror'. No trace of the blissful unity of self and other invades this poem. All is contained within the horror of the loss of self, the meaningless not-me, the threat of which might annihilate the self beyond the boundaries of culture.

The poem is performed as a dramatic reading for three speakers – a convict, a lady and a narrator. It opens with a traumatised woman standing alone in the parched desert, having been stranded during a cross-country train journey. Accompanied only by a prairie dog, which licks its red penis 'as if some red flower in the desert' (l. 18), she enters into a mad reverie in which she re-enacts her captivity and sexual violation – first by the 'savages', then by her convict rescuer. Images of violation haunt the poem:

> Tongued me
> felt cold metal, put
> hot fingers in my mouth, pulled
> silver fillings out,
> threaded, worn them like a charm
>
> tongued me
> spat love in my ear
> bit the lobe off,
> ate it, that wedding band
> in his stomach growing there
>
> then him in me
> in my body
> like a like a
> drum a drum [ll. 45–59]

The natural world of the poem is savage, inhabited by predators of the innocent. It abounds in images of balls and cocks and sputum spilling over or cutting into flesh torn open, bellies ripped open, 'like purple cunts under ribs' (l. 95), 'blood spraying out like dynamite' (l. 98) and the animal/human self surrendered to the savages' ravenous appetites. The sky, 'raw and wounded' (l. 118), 'a wrecked black boot' (l. 234), shares her isolation; the water, 'purple as a bladder' (l. 188), echoes her pain. And bodies rot in the sun (l. 198). The 'lady', then, is both subject to the hostile forces of nature and becomes the body of abject nature herself.

Referred to, with some degree of ambivalence, only as the 'lady', the object of the poem has no name. Her rescuer is a convict named Potter, a deformed man with seven toes. He is a rough sort, with 'tattoos on his left hand / a snake with five heads / the jaws waiting / his fingernails chipped tongues; . . . and she tensed body / like a tourniquet to him' (ll. 151–4, 157–8). The two instinctual figures make their way in this desert land, drinking blood from 'the hot vein of a sleeping wolf' (l. 214), sucking eggs, 'the salt liquid spilling / drying white on our shoulders' (ll. 225–6), and catching birds whose 'nerves clogged and rotted with drug / feathers caked with red vomit' (ll. 211–12) The woman and the convict lapse into a terrifying stage of pre-social formation in which both nature and sexuality partake of elements which Kristeva identifies as the abject feminine.[5] The convict, like the natives before him, takes the anonymous 'lady' at will:

> To lock her head between knees
> splay fingers into her mouth, hold open teeth
> bend tongue down her throat
> drink her throat sweat, like coconut [ll. 256–60]

The poem pares man, nature and the woman back to reveal an instinctual sexuality, a world of predators and victims, until the woman surrenders to her rescuer and her further victimisation. Then the couple travel, 'hooked in two' (l. 270), her body 'brown as a bruise' (l. 248), with 'no witness to our pain our broken mouths and bodies'. Her violation occurs at the hands of a white man, but one who is a renegade, an outcast, whose lust resembles that of an animal (or a black man).[6] In the wilderness, in its physical, psychological, imaginary and symbolic realms, their experience cannot be plotted along a sensible trajectory. The known world is thrown into chaos: 'Things came at us and hit us / Things happened and went out like matches' (ll. 283–5).

The return of the couple to civilisation is abrupt and occurs without the familiar (and by now almost obligatory) betrayal. Back at the Royal Hotel she 'senses herself like a map' (l. 301) and 'imagine[s] the feathers (caked with red vomit) / while she had slept / falling around her / like slow rain' (ll. 308–11); both her dreams and her waking life are haunted by the shattering experience of abjection. Ondaatje juxtaposes the poem with a final lyric adapted from a traditional Scottish ballad, 'Waly, Waly': a nostalgic lullaby, it tells of love, romance, comfort and security within a civilised universe far from harm's way ('Green rivers in these people / running under ice that's calm, / God bring you all some tender stories / and keep you all from hurt and harm'). For the reader, the lullaby supplies both an ironic and soothing ending, a return from nature to culture, from the repressed to the real, from the savage to the social. But the rivers under ice will not be calmed so easily. It is not only the escape from the wilderness which motivates and reverberates through this poem. There is something else seeded in the unconscious, something excessive which will not be quelled by the lullaby, in the fantasy of woman's sexuality and man's transgression.

The poem can be read both with and against the 'lady'. Although the narrative 'speaks' as it were from 'her' position and reflects upon her fate – her plight in the wilderness – it also identifies the woman with the wild and threatening nature she stands against. The two contrary strands come together in the image of the Medusa, or one of the classic representations of Woman in the Western cultural imaginary. The convict/rescuer bears on his left hand the mark of the seven-headed snake in the garden, or Medusa's head. This is otherwise equated in psychoanalytic terms with woman's body, her duplicitous nature, her uncontrollable excess beyond the boundaries of culture – fantasised in relation to man's fears of castration.[7] The 'lady' here becomes the body of nature, the troublesome other which haunts woman's cultural inscription through the psychoanalytic enterprise. The snake with seven heads is an emblem for the imagined body of the woman whom Perseus contemplates in his mirror with fascination and horror as an impossible image of his castrated self which must be destroyed. Readers familiar with psychoanalysis will remember that Freud suggests that Medusa's head represents for man a repressed image of woman's genitals, her sexual difference, which he 'sees' as a mark of castration. The awful cut of castration reverberates through the violent images in the poem; the cut which, in the male psyche, severs woman from man and makes her his other, in the poem, severs the woman from civilisation. She represents for Man his mirror image, the terror of otherness, a repressed fear of disintegration into the undifferentiated body, the body of woman/nature.

On some level, this figure of Mrs Fraser as the monstrous Other underlies the twentieth-century readings of the tale by male artists. In this she displaces the Aboriginal native in contemporary readings. Her troublesome body has been the site of continuous but shifting desires and anxieties. Her rescue by the convict plunges her into a pre-social world of horror before she is rescued for civilisation. This modern retelling rescues man, again and again, from his fears of disintegration, his submission to the primitive other in himself; but it also registers his distance from 'himself'. This fearful fantasy of the 'woman' who invades the 'self' provides evidence of man's split subjectivity which forever challenges the illusion of a unified and secure identity.

We cannot know what happened to the 'real' Mrs Fraser between the time of her husband's death and her official rescue. But the troubling question of 'Did she or didn't she?' remains a locus of discontentment for modern critics. Troubled by what is missing, by the lack of content, the writers become full of dis-content. This dis-content becomes the material of their creative works – both literally and figuratively. The absence of narrative details, which on another level signals a lack in the fullness of history/discourse/the self, propels the writer's fantasies and desires – to penetrate, to know, to possess, to experience an impossible fullness of being.[8] This poem and Josipovici's play, like Patrick White's novel and Sidney Nolan's paintings, all anchor that impossible desire to questions of sexuality. They supply the missing details with imaginative reconstructions. In so doing they repeat a dis-content, imagining what might or might not have occurred, filling the gap through a desire to know. (To know what? – the secrets of woman/ sexuality/desire/one's own origins?) The repetitive return to this troubling problem, the problem of woman's sexuality in the modernist productions of the Eliza Fraser story, requires both psychoanalytic and symbolic readings. The sexual violation of the woman represents man's mastery of his self over the troubling and enigmatic other; at the same time, it also engages him in a primal fantasy in which his being merges with that of the primordial Woman, as (m)Other. The fear of loss of the self/identity co-exists with the desire for a merging of selves without distinctions. The trauma of the unknowable repeats a trauma of a primal scene, of castration, the Oedipal complex and sexual difference, in which, in this instance, both women and Aboriginal people are (differently) displaced.

Circus Freaks and Eliza Surviver

When Gabriel Josipovici turns to the tale he resurrects one of Mrs Fraser's roles from the nineteenth-century accounts which had been neglected by historians of the event – the 'freak-show' Eliza. It is another guise for the monstrous feminine. Readers will remember that Henry Stuart Russell reported sighting a handbill advertisement for Mrs Fraser's performance in a tent in Hyde Park in London in the 1840s after her return to England, which he recalled in his celebratory account, *Genesis of Queensland* (1888). Historians Alexander and Buchanan and Dwyer mention Russell's recollection, but tend to discount the likelihood of the event. It is almost as if, despite the report in Russell's memoirs, historians cannot quite credit his account. Or, they suggest that perhaps it was not Mrs Fraser but rather an actress, responding to the interest and publicity surrounding Mrs Fraser when she returned to England, who took on the role. It may be that the thought of a woman who has endured intense privations, then subjecting herself to a repeat performance of her sufferings, voluntarily, as a sideshow freak, defies the historian's sense of credibility, or his own need for 'propriety', achieved through control and mastery over his own fantasies of difference. And indeed, if her 'fringe of leaves' was all that anchored her to white civilisation while on Fraser Island in the nineteenth-century accounts, what emblem could preserve her for civilisation within a freak-show context in either a nineteenth- or twentieth-century historical imaginative reconstruction? As we shall see in the next chapter, Tim Burstall allows Susannah York a compelling scene in a circus sideshow in the film *Eliza Fraser*, but the carefully groomed 'widow' glows with vitality. In the film, this opportunistic Eliza is fully in control of herself and her audience, albeit under the controlling gaze of the womanising impresario Rory McBryde.

Although one cannot know if the historical Eliza ever succumbed to this level of imagined cultural and personal degradation (and she may have), we do know that, eventually, a number of Fraser Island Aborigines were submitted to a similar fate by forcible coercion. They became 'our' freak-show others, publicly displayed to excite the popular imagination and to promote the circulation of otherness at the farthest edge of what it might mean to be human. In 1883, a German circus manager captured three Aborigines, thought to have come from Fraser Island, and toured them overseas in his circus.[9] Roslyn Poignant suggests that these nineteenth-century circus performances moved Aboriginal people into a modern matrix of meaning, away from their exotic origins. The circus fused popular culture with natural science; it introduced on to a mass world stage the New Science of Man – Anthropology. The performance of Aboriginality as freak-show attraction 'colluded in the objectification, commodification, and consumption of *other*'. Poignant concludes that 'the metropolitan appetite for the exotic was insatiable'.[10] The historical Mrs Fraser may have suffered such a fate in 1838 under the direction of her new husband. But if she did so, that dimension of the episode was muted. It took nearly another 150 years for modern artists to imagine Mrs Fraser in such a public display of otherness, this time on the London stage. With Josipovici's 1970s play, a new representation of Mrs Fraser as a sideshow spectacle intersects with the cultural cross-currents of sexual liberation and feminism.

Gabriel Josipovici's Play

Gabriel Josipovici's play, *Dreams of Mrs Fraser*, was written and performed in the permissive sexual environment of London in the early 1970s. The play opens with an invitation to the audience to 'roll up, roll up . . . come and see the tattooed lady . . . Come and hear in her own words the incredible story of her amazing adventures among the man-eating natives of the Australian jungle.'[11] The opening which, through the spruiker's invitation, offers the titillation of the circus or the nineteenth-century freak show, draws the audience into a world of their own primitive imaginings.

In Josipovici's preface to the published version of the play, he credits the paintings of Sidney Nolan and the contemporary ballads and 'mournful verses' taken from Michael Alexander's history, to which he added the *bricolage* effect of passages from Levi-Strauss's *Totemism*. In the theatre itself, the producer lined the foyer and stairs with giant-sized poster replicas of the handbills from the nineteenth-century sensational accounts, which Alexander believes to have been taken from his book without acknowledgment, and which the patrons apparently believed to be factual. One critic cited these materials as historical artefacts in his review. Delineating the fantastic as opposed to what he believed to be the historically accurate dimensions of the play, he commented,

> What is real is that Mrs. Fraser, the widow of a ship's captain, and the mother of a dead baby, had been wrecked on the Great Barrier Reef. Her husband had tossed the baby, being dead, out of the lifeboat, and Mrs. Fraser, captured by the Eagle tribe, has [*sic*] been heavily tattooed on her legs, thighs and stomach.[12]

The account repeats familiar aspects of the legend with one exception – the tattoos. The grammatical error in the review ('*has* been heavily tattooed') is interesting in that this presentation of a tattooed Mrs Fraser is, indeed, the most remarkable transformation the play effects from past to present representations of the event. The naked actress appeared on stage with tattoos on her legs, thighs and stomach. The bodily inscriptions serve to remind the audience of the connections between woman, sexuality, the flesh and the body. At the same time they fuse the image of the woman with that of the primitive in the popular imagination. We are reminded again of Torgovnick's assertion of the crucial links in Western thought between women and primitive cultures, the psychological and the political.

The play ran for three weeks in London's intimate Theatre Upstairs at the Royal Court before being performed by various small companies throughout England. In the play, Mrs Fraser moves between two stage settings: a large gilded circus cage and the bedroom. In the former, she stands completely naked, displaying her scars and tattoos as she re-enacts her dreams of the wreck and her captivity by 'horrib savages'. In the latter, robed in a loose gown, she prepares herself for an interview. In her dream world Mrs Fraser mourns for her lost child, whom, in her haunting memory, the Captain threw overboard. She reiterates several versions of the savage murder of her husband and remembers with horror the cannibalistic burning and dismemberment of crew members by Aborigines. With the prompting of a male companion, she recounts the painful tattooing and scarification of her legs, thighs and stomach, and muses on her attraction towards Bracefell and her rescue by him, and the couple's intimate seventy-day romance. And she confesses her sexual transgressions as well as her ultimate betrayal of Bracefell. But (most of all) she performs her lost identity, her madness. Full of mad shrieks, beating drums and exotic jungle sounds, as well as sounds of the lash and men's screams, the play acted out for a twentieth-century audience key aspects of the exaggerated nineteenth-century accounts, and more.

Mrs Fraser's voyeuristic confidant, named Redbold, plays the role of the soldier, rescuer, companion, accuser and judge. At one point he demands a confession from Mrs Fraser concerning her sexual transgressions with Bracefell:

> Did you sleep together in the swamps, Eliza, you naked and he in his convict suit? . . . Tell me, Eliza, tell me . . . Was it frightening? Was it fun? Tell John. Tell your Johnny Redbold. What did the Captain say when he saw you again? Did he twirl his moustache and hum?[13]

This scene of confession – the demand that she confess her most intimate secrets, her most illicit desires, for the pleasure of the cruel and dominating listener – has been the hidden desire of the voyeuristic commentator and his eager public from the time of the originating event. In the late twentieth century, however:

> It is no longer a question simply of saying what was done; but of reconstructing, in and around the act, the thoughts that recapitulated it, the obsessions that accompanied it, the images, desires, modulations, and quality of the pleasure that animated it. For the first time, no doubt, a society has taken upon itself to solicit and hear the imparting of individual pleasures.[14]

They are not, however, Mrs Fraser's pleasures, but the projection on to her of masculine fantasies of sexual penetration/devourment of the female body, that tabooed object which transgresses the boundaries of nation, race and class. The Ondaatje poem elucidated some of them. There they were horrors of violation; here they are the tabooed pleasures of sinful indulgence. There woman was feared for her sexual difference; here she is punished for her transgressions. Racked by guilt, she goes insane. She takes on to her body the marks of man's horror, his fears of his own violence/castration.

A mad Mrs Fraser alternates between her naked presence in her cage (a fantasy within a dream world) and her never-to-be-recovered social role as a bourgeois lady. In the latter world, she feigns a parody of the middle-class matron reporting on her experience for polite company. At one point, towards the end of the play, she explains in a patronising voice which one critic described as 'condescending to commend the lower orders':[15] 'The natives treated me terribly well. They ate some of the others but they treated me terribly well . . . They burned my skin with red-hot sticks . . . but that's just a custom with them and they meant no harm.'[16] An interlocutor interrupts the flow of the narrative with an anthropological gloss on totemism and the relationship between the binaries of Nature and Culture, predators and their prey, social and sexual modalities, individual and collective life. The woman moves between these spaces, her guilty body carrying the inscription of differences between nation, race, gender, class and culture. Pointing to her tattooed body she asks: 'What are they for? . . . You – tell me, what are they for?' and later, 'With those patterns, who am I?'[17]

The play closed after a three-week run. Apart from one sympathetic review in the *Sunday Times*, the critics panned the play, which Josipovici believes to be one of his best.[18] With one exception, critics described it as a tasteless performance, which sensationalised history to no good effect. Without having seen a performance of the play, it is difficult to comment on the staged version. However, I have spoken to several women who saw the play at the Theatre Upstairs during its London performance and was struck by their common reaction and the details they retained in their memory some twenty years after having seen it. All they could remember was their embarrassment at being confronted by a naked actress covered with 'band-aids' (the tattoos were 'luridly painted', according to the critics at the time), their inability to suspend disbelief, their feelings of sympathy for the actress, and a vague recollection that the play was based on an actual historical event.

Josipovici asks, what are the limits of civilisation in the twentieth century? In the play he draws parallels between the torture of Mrs Fraser as a sign of native barbarity, and the death of the baby, the betrayal of Bracefell and the lash of the gaoler as signs of 'our' violence, 'our' barbarity. In this, Josipovici's play shares some of the sympathies of Montaigne's treatise 'On Cannibals', in which the philosopher muses on cannibal behaviour to highlight the barbarities of his own age.[19] In *Dreams of Mrs Fraser* the memory of Captain Fraser casually tossing the dead baby overboard, without proper regard for his wife's maternity or her suffering, is remembered by Mrs Fraser as an act of unforgivable human wickedness. This act, and her betrayal of Bracefell, according to the one critic favourable to the play, suggest that there is 'no nobility in civilised people, not even in herself'. Mrs Fraser is reduced to the level of the savage. There is no escape from evil (her own, the world's) but madness; no recuperation for the woman but to display herself endlessly from her gilded cage.

There is more at stake here, however, than the fate of a newly historicised Mrs Fraser and a new gloss on man's inhumanity to man. The character/ actor becomes another object of fascination and horror for the modern viewer. Her sexed body becomes a public spectacle. Her body bears tattoos – the inscription of a native savagery. 'What are they for?' she asks. 'With those

patterns on my skin . . . With those patterns, who am I?' The placement of
the tattoos on her stomach, thighs and legs guides the spectators' gaze to the
actress's genital area, the sign of sexual difference. Like the 'lady' in *The Man
with Seven Toes*, the actress becomes for the audience the location of 'our'
anxieties concerning identity and a sign of 'our' barbarity – or the new
markings of a masculine culture on the vulnerable body of a woman as a site
of castration. Here, woman's sexuality, disguised under the ruse of native
barbarity, is displayed as excessive. The play focuses not on what happened
to the historical Eliza Fraser, but on the sexuality of Woman as it signifies a
psychic and cultural debasement within the masculine unconscious. Her tattooed body becomes a site not only of psychical projection but of social
inscription as well. It is not native barbarism which enslaves her, but her own
culture's notions of sexed difference. If native cannibalism was the mark of
otherness for an insecure nineteenth-century audience intent on securing a
colonial identity, woman's sexuality is the sign of otherness for an anxious
twentieth-century audience intent on preserving a masculine identity. The
tattooed woman, doubly inscribed as other/Other through a masculine fantasy of difference, becomes 'our' other as the audience is invited to identify
with their own unspeakable desires. She masks the collective guilt of man
under the signs of both colonialism and patriarchy in her excessive performance of broken femininity.

Peter Sculthorpe and Barbara Blackman's Music Theatre

Once the taboo of presenting Mrs Fraser as a sideshow freak had been
broken, the idea seemed to linger. In 1977 Barbara Blackman agreed to col-
laborate with Peter Sculthorpe on a text for music theatre. Sculthorpe, too,
visualised Eliza as an exhibit in a Hyde Park tent. The piece was commissioned by the Canadian ensemble, the Lyric Arts Trio, which specialised
in contemporary music accompanied by theatrical presentation, a year after
Michael Ondaatje's long poem, *The Man with Seven Toes*, had appeared in
Canada. Sculthorpe had been interested in composing an opera on the theme
since 1964. Those plans had been abandoned when he and White, who was
to write the libretto, failed to agree on a common interpretation. Like his
counterparts, the painter and the novelist, the composer Sculthorpe continued to dwell on the story for some time, unsure of what approach to take.
Like them he took on the project at a time in his life when he was receiving
national acclaim and international honours: he received the honour of an
Order of the British Empire in 1977. And, like them, he was intent on blending personal with national themes to incorporate Australian elements into
his work, elements which would introduce Australian themes to an elite,
international arena of 'high' culture. His musical score, composed for
soprano, flute, and piano, employs some music actually composed in col-

onial times. Critics refer to this as typical of his work, which 'fosters a dichotomy between material which is a product of a spent civilisation and that which portends an antipodean individuality'.[20] These remarks locate Sculthorpe with Nolan and White in the role of the modern Australian artist/intellectual, combining the specifically Australian with universalist mythologies of Western man.

Sculthorpe felt Mrs Fraser had been wrong to return to civilisation. His intention was to show that her return caused her to go mad; 'her schizoid tendencies sprang more from the shock of her return than from the trauma of her incarceration'.[21] Thus he, like Josipovici, envisaged her as an irrevocably deranged freak-show performer. This may relate to Sculthorpe's interest in the fantasy of a white woman merging with primitive culture. It shows a modernist tendency to imagine the civilised, rather than the primitive, world as 'barbaric' – a dream of primitivism juxtaposed against evidence of Western culture's degeneracy. This may be one of the reasons why Sculthorpe found the dramatic opera so challenging and ultimately unsuccessful.

Into this ongoing creative and interpretative conflict stepped the poet Barbara Blackman, who composed a libretto for the performance. Blackman's interest in the historical Eliza and her relevance for a contemporary audience differed significantly from that of Sculthorpe or Josipovici. She was not interested so much in man's barbaric nature but in the strategies which women might adopt to protect themselves from disintegration in an alien culture and at the hands of violent and barbaric men. She had resided in Brisbane and, for a time as a young child, lived with Aboriginal people in a traditional settlement on the Queensland coast, south of Fraser Island. Her father, a surveyor, developed both fondness and respect for the Kabi people with whom he resided and whose cultural heritage and land right claims he publicly defended in the 1920s. Blackman, then, grew up with the local legend and lived within the same geographical landscape. She recalls that she was familiar with the local legend of Eliza Fraser before being approached to write the piece. She remembered from her childhood a common refrain about Eliza Fraser whispered in white quarters about untidy housewives: 'her house is like a black's camp and she looks like Mrs. Fraser'.[22] Blackman's memory suggests that the Eliza Fraser story continued to influence white women's behaviour in the private sphere well into the twentieth century. Her comment seems to address Judith Newton's question about how systems of meaning derived from historical discourses interact with the material conditions of everyday life. Newton asks:

> What bearing did public written representation with its complex dreamwork and contradictions have on the way ordinary women and men conceptualized themselves and lived their lives? How was meaning transmitted from one layer of culture to another? And what force did public discourse ultimately have?[23]

It appears that, around the Great Sandy Region of Queensland, 'Mrs Fraser' was used to regulate the everyday life of women in the home: her ordeal and her appearance at the time of her rescue were proof that slovenly behaviour might result from imagined association with 'savages'. 'The gap between the statements made by "low" culture and those made by "high" culture [is] narrower than we might intuitively expect.'[24]

Blackman's poetic evocation of Mrs Fraser's ordeal avoids these associations provoked by the popular memory of the woman as evinced in her childhood. She does not, however, altogether escape a few 'primitive' fantasies of her own, fantasies related to those of Josipovici and Ondaatje. In preparation for writing the libretto to accompany Sculthorpe's musical composition, Blackman consulted Michael Alexander's *Mrs Fraser on the Fatal Shore* and remembered his subtitle (which Alexander's book does *not* carry but which she uses as a subtitle for her own text): 'The Sorrowful Adventures of a Lady'. Blackman's piece, 'Eliza Surviver', is the only instance of a woman writing an imagined narrative for Eliza Fraser. Does her gender make a difference to the telling of the tale?

The text of the libretto was published in *Quadrant*, an Australian literary magazine. It opens with a synopsis of the Eliza Fraser story, which conveys something of the flavour of the piece and Blackman's slant on the story.[25] After detailing the shipwreck, the birth and drowning of the baby, the Captain's spearing and death, and the crude circumstances of Mrs Fraser's life with the natives, Blackman details Mrs Fraser's meeting with Bracefell in a corroboree setting. She writes:

> In a ceremony [the blacks] exhibit their rare specimen of She-Ghost and have her mated with a He-Ghost brought from some distance by the chief Eumundi. In the holocaust she discovers that he is an escaped convict . . . though seeming now to have forgotten his English ways and speech. The horror and humiliation unnerve her.
>
> She takes refuge in a dream that this man will return as a lover and lead her away into a paradisial existence in an abundance of flowers and fruits in the rainforest and cliffs of coloured sands across the water from the island, out of range of predatory blacks or recriminatory whites. Immured in this fantasy, she is able to endure her miseries. However, she is unexpectedly rescued by another convict only interested in trading her over to the military in return for his pardon.
>
> With the shattering of her dream, her sanity is shaken. She returns to England where she sets up in a showground booth in Hyde Park and shows her scars and tells her stories to all and sundry for the price of sixpence apiece.[26]

This retelling locates Mrs Fraser in her Hyde Park booth, but the woman, although shaken, is not shattered beyond recovery. Mrs Fraser survives the ordeal by escaping into a dream-like fantasy of a world elsewhere, in which an imaginary lover leads her into an abundant wilderness set apart from the hostilities of both black and white men who prey upon her. The libretto

engages the audience in a performance of feminine split subjectivity. It studies the relationship between Eliza's social and psychic selves. Blackman's Eliza
replaces the physical trauma of her captivity with a fantasy of romance.
Although Blackman utilises the popular mythical accounts, her libretto presents the ordeal in psychological terms, attempting to explore, from a
woman's perspective, Eliza's horror and humiliation, her escape into a world
of fantasy, and her ultimate survival. Blackman's Eliza exists at several places
at once: her psychic projection removes her from the scene of her humiliation, allowing her a resistance to trauma and a strategy for survival through
a splitting of the self. That splitting of the self provides a place of escape from
her immediate physical environment. It also engages in a fantasy of woman
traumatised by her own fears of 'the primitive' and rescued by an alternate
and displacing fantasy of romance. Eliza maintains control over her 'self'
through a splitting in which she, paradoxically, becomes the object of
another's desire; an objectification which also ensures her own survival.

Eliza's horror is the horror of difference, her nightmare world the world of
the Kabi. In the performance this difference is imagined through the menacing staccato rhythms and repetitious recitations of tribal names and
territories which recur throughout the drama to represent the woman's
immersion in an alien and alienating territory which is both physical and
psychological. The audience is invited to identify with Mrs Fraser. That
identification also involves the audience in a performance of identity and
difference, wherein the self is the psychological subject of modernism and
the other is modernism's projection of the other as a dark, primitive force. It
is one of those instances, discussed by Torgovnick in *Gone Primitive*, in which
the modern artist imagines 'the primitive' in order to imagine him or herself.
Torgovnick suggests, 'the West seems to need the primitive as a precondition
and a supplement to its sense of self: it always creates heightened versions of
the primitive as nightmare or pleasant dream'.[27] The Kabi represent Mrs
Fraser's (our) nightmare. According to Blackman's interpretation, women
have the resources to undergo intense privations and humiliations and still
survive their fate. Hers is a survival discourse, one in which the woman can be
subjected to an alien environment, including physical deprivations and sexual violations, and also maintain a semblance of her own subjectivity.
Nonetheless, the poetic re-creation remains tied to and depends upon Western projections of the terror of the primitive which must be mastered.

The musical production 'Eliza Fraser Sings'/ 'Eliza Surviver', is short,
tightly structured, emotionally evocative; a twenty-minute performance
piece of considerable intensity. It achieves its effects through a complex
layering of poetic and musical rhythms, a juxtaposition of harmonious and
discordant sounds, and a rendering of multiple perspectives. Blackman
wrote her text in five sections with a prologue and epilogue. The sections
include: the shipwreck and childbirth; the island; the corroboree; her dream;

and the rescue. The piece opens slowly to sounds reminiscent of wind chimes, bird calls, and the creaking of a ship's timbers, underscored by discordant melodies and a staccato musical rhythm. A show-ground spruiker announces the presence of Mrs Fraser in her Hyde Park booth in a slow, rough, measured voice:

> ELIZA SURVIV-ER
> Hear her adventures
> SHIPWRECK and RAVAGES
> Hear her for Sixpence
> SAV-ED FROM SAVAGES

Although only one actress performs the piece, the narrative alternates between a third-person narrated script and Mrs Fraser's direct speech, both enclosed by a chorus refrain and underscored by the music. It allows for a sense of Mrs Fraser's subjective agency, while also placing her within the disorienting discourses and practices of an alien existence. In the first section the narrator relates Mrs Fraser's melancholic tale of shipwreck leading to the birth and drowning of the baby, while the lady establishes her identity by direct address, her voice juxtaposed with a whispering, sing-song, sea-sway refrain. The section ends with a note of melancholy, then a long pause.

Narration	Mrs Fraser	Chorus/refrain
List to the ship wreck		Stirling Castle
Mishap when reef struck		Eliza Fraser
Strangling embrace of the		
reef-ribboned sea		
Crew-all they leave her		
Cruel the lee shore		
Stranded in boats in the		
great griefless sea		
	'I was the wife of the Captain	
	I saved the life of the Captain'	
	'I was with child to the Captain	
	I gave birth to the child of the	
	Captain'	Stirling Castle
		Eliza Fraser

In the second section, 'The Savages', the pace of the music and the narration increases in an intensity of menace as the naked Frasers are stared at and jeered at, 'spat at and speared at'. Mrs Fraser's speeches, which recount the loss of her trunks of lace and linen, her disrobing by the natives and abandonment by the Captain, become more detached and shrill, while the six-word chorus ('in the land of the Kabi') reverberates, chant-like with tribal power. The Kabi come to life as the primitive of our fearful Western imaginings.

The tension of the drama builds to a climactic frenzy during the 'Corroboree' section. It opens to the slow deliberate beat of firesticks and pounding metal, over which is heard an exotic (to Western ears) recitative of Kabi names of people and places. The pace slows, then builds, slows and builds again towards the inevitable mating ritual. The Kabi names continue in a lingering, looping choral recitative which precedes and accompanies the mating-verse and shrill/thrill of the union of He-Ghost and She-ghost. This is punctuated by the breaking-point voice of an increasingly hysterical Eliza as the convict 'takes her in his swarthy arms':

> Had I been here in my English dress
> To tender you in your distress
> I could have brought you Midwifery
> Hygiene and Laundry
> Haute cuisine and Embroidery
> Hospital rules and good Husbandry
>   [*the sound of crashing metal*]
> I could have taught you to ballroom dance
> Delivered from your ignorance.

The music and the calling of place names intensify relentlessly to a hysterical level. The sounds are looped on an aural tape which brings the section to a close with Mrs Fraser's dramatic scream, discordant sounds and rhythms, and two final sombre drumbeats.

After a pause, a slow-paced, lyrical dream sequence follows. The musical score returns to the sonorous rhythms of nature. The buzz of a bee, the wind, a gentle flute and long warbling notes are introduced, underscored by an ear-piercing, high-pitched, one-note tone. Here the voice-over narration belongs to the woman and not an omniscient narrator: the pronouns shift from she to I ('As I lie in my distress / I dream of man in English dress'). Eliza's part reverts to the earlier dactylic verse rhythms of the narrator ('Tortures not hurting me / Now that the dream is me'); and the chorus re-echoes the corroboree chant, now in a gentler, ghostlike whisper of memory ('Cootharaba Cootharaba / Gather at the WaWa / Come to corroboree / She-Ghost to see') as the music lapses into a love song of gentle lyrical chords of string and flute, underscored by deep resonant piano chords below. Mrs Fraser clings to her sanity through the trancelike dream of mating with her English lover.

Sharp, surreal sounds introduce the epilogue, which takes the audience back to the show-booth performance in Hyde Park which opened the piece. Mrs Fraser is left to deal with her outer and inner, public and private states of woman and freak, victim and survivor – both subject and object in a complex physical and symbolic environment. The crude Cockney voice of the spruiker through a megaphone ('Come to the show now / Come to corroboree / Strange sight to see') is punctuated by a rude refrain with sexual innuendo ('ra-ra') as the Kabi chorus fades. Sounds drift off into a soft whistle and the audience contemplates the whole dramatic performance piece to the almost inaudible final sound of barely heard scratches on metal.

Blackman, like Josipovici, places an unbalanced Mrs Fraser in the public performance space of a sideshow where she is viewed as a freak. But Blackman's text, unlike that of the male artists, follows a chain of reputed historical events linked to crises of her identity – the loss of the baby, her trunks of valuables, her clothing and her husband's protection. It climaxes in a scene of sexual violation from which she escapes through fantasy into a utopian romance. The lover is not the convict of nationalistic versions, how-ever, but a 'proper' Englishman; the romance affords no voyeuristic pleasure to an eager but anxious audience. The woman (as split-subject) is saved from madness through what might be interpreted as dream therapy to a twentieth-century audience: her trancelike fantasy of romantic love and pat-ernal protection which becomes for her a form of utopian escape. When the piece was performed in 1978, as Sculthorpe's 'Eliza Fraser Sings', the com-poser adapted Blackman's epilogue, giving it a romantic, wistful close. Blackman is more sanguine, however, about the outcome. She makes no attempt to reconcile the race, class and gender divisions inherent in the story. She allows Mrs Fraser to remain caught within them. As Mrs Fraser's official rescuer returns her to civilisation, where she will be moulded to suit the demands of the age, the woman speaks her final disillusioned awareness: 'Aged in my agony / Exit from ecstasy / Wrecked in reality / Freak female property'. One could say that 'freak female property' is what the legendary Mrs Fraser has been since the time of the shipwreck and what she has remained in virtually all of her nineteenth- and twentieth-century recon-structions. Only the Sculthorpe–Blackman piece performs the plausible drama of a white woman caught in a harsh and alien colonial world as its victim and survivor. She accomplishes this by re-creating for the audience both the powerful threat of alienation from the self, its recovery within a world of fantasy and the ambivalent desires of fear and attraction to the primitive – in 'us'.

André Brink's Novel

André Brink's South African novel, *An Instant in the Wind* (1976), returns the story to a grand modernist narrative with South African inflections. Remark-ably, the English version appeared within a week of the publication of Patrick White's *A Fringe of Leaves*.[28] Brink recounts that he first learned of the story of

Mrs Fraser from the Thames and Hudson monograph *Sidney Nolan* which he came across in 1969. From the outset, the sight of the full-page colour-plate of Mrs Fraser as an 'animal-person', and the story of one of 'the devil's appearance [who comes from] out of the wilderness' . . . 'spooked' him. His initial impulse was to turn the tale into a contemporary account of a white woman stranded in the Angolan desert after an aeroplane crash, who is found by an escaped terrorist and returned to civilisation. But his research on eighteenth-century Afrikaans historical materials led him to turn the story into its present form.[29] This anecdote reminds us of the apocryphal nature of the story and how the dynamic between master and slave, nature and civilisation, freedom and captivity, structures for a white neo-colonial audience an interpretative framework for first-contact stories between white and black peoples. It also evokes for the white man the dream of paradise and woman's first betrayal, the legacy of a Christian cultural heritage.

Brink's novel concerns the fate of an Afrikaner woman, Elisabeth Larsson, the rebellious young wife of a fictitious Swedish naturalist and explorer, Erik Alexis Larsson. She is stranded in the interior of the veldt in 1749 after a fatal trekking accident, in which her husband succumbs to the environment which he has attempted to explore, map, name, classify and master – and dies. Left alone after her guide commits suicide and her Hottentot bearers desert her, she is found by a coloured runaway slave, Adam Mantoor. The two are reduced to a primitive existence. The pretences of race, class and culture fall away in their struggle for survival and, as occurs in White's novel, they are soon involved in an idyllic love affair. Although Elisabeth insists that the relationship will come to fruition in civilised society, she inevitably abandons Adam to the wilderness and submits to the demands of her social class when she is returned to civilisation. The novel ends here. Its prologue, however, written in the form of a historian's introduction, relates that a white party from the Cape hunted down and killed her slave rescuer. The prologue also contains the biographical information that, upon her return to the Cape, Elisabeth married an elderly neighbour. Two months later she gave birth to a child, whom the readers can presume is Adam Mantoor's son.

As was true of the initial reception of White's novel, South African reviewers searched for clues to the novel's authenticity. Brink prefaces his tale with a historian's speculation on the 'truth' of the story. In the preface he concocts personal histories for each of the major players from what he claims to have discovered in the Cape archival records and those of the London Missionary Society. The mock historian ponders the modern links to this colonial story. '*Who are you? who am I?*' (15) he asks, seeking modern answers to primordial dilemmas. Brink himself admits to a fascination with the eighteenth-century history of South Africa, when the country was a melting-pot of different cultures and races before it took on the racial and ethnic divisions of today. Although the events in the novel were wholly fictionalised, several reviewers believed that Erik Larsson's 'Journals', which begin the novel, and Elisabeth's 'Memoirs', which continue the story within the fiction, were authentic. One claimed to have found materials which reveal the 'facts' of the story in 'three folio volumes in the hands of the London Missionary Society'.[30] Another South African 'man of letters' quoted the fictionalised Larsson as a source of information concerning the relationship between white settlers and non-white indigenous people within South African litera-ture.[31] The critic continues, 'Brink begins his fictional reconstruction at the point where the runaway slave approaches Elizabeth [*sic*] alone and marooned in the bush after the disappearance of her husband.' In other words, the ruse allows readers to believe that the fatal trek may have occurred – but the love affair strains credibility to the degree that it can only be read within the borders of fiction.

Brink seems to have been delighted by the scores of researchers who approached the Cape archives in search of the authenticating documents. As Kossew suggests, Brink's framing of the novel within the guise of history may imply his larger purpose of enlightenment. He does not attempt to decon-struct the historical enterprise, nor does he subscribe to the fictionality of history. The novel pushes against the dominant forces of history, however, to provide a counter-history for South Africa, 'if not her-story, then at least their-story', with 'the crust of the [dominant coloniser's] history scraped off', but with the underlying philosophical structures of humanism intact.[32] Brink's fictionalised journey into the past becomes a quest for identity for the lost ones: women who have been subjected to men, slaves who remain sub-jected to masters. The novel aims to find a key in the past for understanding the present: '*Who are you? who am I?*', the questions of the privileged narrator, become questions of who are Elisabeth/Adam; the Audience/the writer; the master/the slave; the West/the world.

Elisabeth slips between her roles as both coloniser and colonised, master and slave. In her socialised life within Cape society she had been subjected to the patriarchal rule of her father and her husband; in archetypal terms, fol-lowing Kossew and other post-colonial critics, she is linked to both Prospero and Caliban (as well as the biblical Adam and Eve).[33] Like Prospero, she is part of the society which colonised, named, mapped and thus mastered the land. This identification links her character with those of her father and husband, who themselves are linked to God and His mission, begun by the creation of Adam in the biblical Garden of Eden. But also, like Caliban, she retains an essential rebelliousness which refuses to be enslaved by father, husband or country. In this her character is associated with that of the black slave, Adam Mantoor, and the fallen Eve in the biblical garden. In her rebel-lious acts of freedom Elisabeth challenges her father, the free settler, and her husband, the naturalist/explorer. That is, both socially and symbolically, she challenges the law of the Father: 'Naming, didn't you say, was your way of possessing a part of the earth' (65). On another level, however, she is also linked to the land (and the snake in the Garden) which 'devoured' her husband. In terms of the historical trajectory of the novel, her husband wandered alone into the bush and died of exposure. Elisabeth, guilty after the fact, wonders if her indifference to him may have been the cause of his death. In terms of the Cape society, she judges herself to be lacking in her wifely duties. In her 'natural' state of Edenic innocence with Adam, Elisabeth 'intuitively' submits to his dominance; she is passive to his active principle of survival (114–15). 'She was a landscape to be explored and possessed.' But she will also possess him, his body, and will become the cause of his death. In both the coloniser's world of civilisation and the slave territory of wilderness, woman functions as a metaphor for landscape: 'she bears the forest with her' (116). To Adam she becomes: 'Woman: the wilderness in which to lose oneself' (92). Like 'untamed nature' (41) she is treacherous and not to be trusted. As is often the case, there is a snake in this garden. The snake in the wilderness guarantees Adam's identity, his sense of belonging, and also his betrayal: Adam knows: 'love is the beginning of violence and betrayal' (101), and 'one is always betrayed' (68, 171). Thus, woman once again slips between her significations as creator and devourer, the source of man's origin and his betrayal.

The novel attempts to construct a memory of a world outside time and history, a pre-colonial, pre-lapsarian world of innocence and plenitude: Africa before colonisation. In that state Adam was named Aob. Aob is the name his mother gave him, the secret name she 'brought with her from that nameless land across the many mountains' (30). Adam Mantoor is his slave name. Although he knows from the native doctor that the poison which comes from the venom of the snake of the coloniser cannot be eradicated, he tells Elisabeth his secret name and asks her to call him Aob. Elisabeth demurs. To her he is and always will be Adam. She can only think of him as Aob for a brief instant when his body merges with hers in their acts of lovemaking. She tells him, 'If I called you Aob it would turn you into someone else, a stranger' (177). At the end of their journey together, as they approach civilisation and in desperation for what she is about to lose, she calls him Aob. She uses the name again in their final act of love in which he, for the first time, submits to her lovemaking. At this time, Elisabeth becomes the sea for Adam, the territory beyond the land, beyond naming – the force of nature, 'intense and wild'. And the question rises between them: 'Who are you? I have never known anyone better. Yet you are altogether strange to me' (249). The lovers exist in a state of pre-social alterity, an imagined state of mind beyond the restrictions of culture but not beyond the symbolic language of sexual difference. The love affair allows for an imaginary fusion between the sensual woman and the primitive other – a means of boundary dissolution wherein access to 'the primitive' becomes a means of access to 'the essential'.[34]

The novel also makes obvious reference to the political and racially charged situation in contemporary South Africa. Brink maintains that his purpose was to 'explore two different ways Africa can be experienced; and a consciousness of the nature of treason in human relationships'.[35] Although born in the Cape, his Elisabeth represents to Africa an imposed white culture, as did Ellen Gluyas Roxburgh in White's novel; his Adam is 'an Afrikaner' in the same sense that Jack Chance (without the racial conflations) was characterised as Australian, an underdog (white) native son within an Australian mythology of nation. Brink maintains 'he [Adam] is the Afrikaner after all'.[36] As in White's novel, illicit love crosses tabooed cultural boundaries (racial here as well as class-bound and, perhaps, more intense for that) and the woman's betrayal characterises the relationship. As in *A Fringe of Leaves*, love is represented as a natural and instinctual attraction which can overcome artificial social barriers. Elisabeth's love for Adam frees her from the sins of white cultural dominance which has enslaved her mind, as well as the social existence of the blacks since first colonisation in South Africa. Through that love Adam experiences his freedom, at least in the existential sense. The novel disturbs on the level of a lyrical romance. It does not have the emotional intensity of White's *A Fringe of Leaves*, nor does it examine to the same degree the savage instincts which White and Josipovici explored in the depths of civilised man. But like White's novel, it insists on the promise of a love which can unite humankind. In *An Instant in the Wind* that love is explored on both the geographic and psychic boundaries for man and woman. The love Adam feels is experienced as much for the land as for the woman. And the love of the land (imagined as the body of a woman) is what links Brink and gaoled fellow poet Breyten Breytenbach (to whom the novel is dedicated) to Adam, Adam to the Afrikaner culture, exiles everywhere to their homeland, while at the same time it establishes a symbolic place for Woman as she slips into the alterior space of the other. The dedication reads: 'For Breyten: such a long journey ahead for you and me'; the inscription is echoed by Elisabeth as she and Adam begin their trek back to civilisation and again in the final passage of the novel as Adam awaits his recapture by the white authorities:

> Come, he would think, breathless in the wind. The land which happened inside us no one can take from us again, not even ourselves. But God, such a long journey ahead for you and me. Not a question of imagination, but of faith. [250]

That 'faith' is the faith that love can override the racial conflict in South Africa; that men like Adam can exist on equal terms with men like Brink and Breytenbach. But that faith also expresses a Western desire: that Adam, his history, customs and culture, can be incorporated into the coloniser's body politic; his soil turned into Afrikaner soil.

The wind, in the title and also as recurring metaphor in the novel, signifies that which can blow away the artificial, inherited accretions of time and history to reveal life's essentials. For Elisabeth, love represents the essential life, free of cultural constraints. A violent storm presages the idyllic love affair through which Elisabeth experiences 'the overwhelming newness of her existence' (113), 'the way it may have been' (112) before the Fall. For Adam, the essential message is an existential one: man is born to be free. He knows the freedom of his being through choice – even if that choice is between freedom and loneliness in the wilderness, killing or not killing one's master on the farm, choosing to return to one's own sure death or remaining in exile, or choosing to explore suffering rather than be destroyed by it. In a passage which refers to the novel's title, Adam thinks, 'Suffering: it is like the sky through which a bird is flying. And only occasionally very rarely – an instant in the wind – it is allowed to alight on a branch or burning stone to rest: but not for long' (198). Love provides the instant of rest, the paradisiacal moment of mutual recognition, between Elisabeth and Adam:

> Just for an instant. Never more than an instant. Perhaps we can't bear more than an instant at a time. I remember. I shall try to go on. This terrible space surrounding us creates the silence in which, so rarely, preciously, I dare to recognise you and be recognised by you. [198]

There can be no Eden for more than an instant, then the suffering returns. That terrible suffering refers both to the black and white people who remain in South Africa as well as those white intellectuals and political activists who are forced to seek exile. Both Adam and Elisabeth are drawn back to the Cape, to the homeland they love. That irrational love pulls the heart beyond reason, just as it had pulled Brink and Breytenbach back from their exiles in Paris: 'the Cape, so remote now, so desirable beyond the grey monotony of those wintry days: yearning for it the way they'd yearned for the sea' (141). The choice, for Adam and Brink and Breytenbach in the terms of the novel, is a choice between 'liberty and loneliness' (73). In the end, what sustains Adam is an existential vision, a faith in the fact of one's existence: 'In the quiet persistence of suffering I discover again the desperate knowledge that I am. I am going on. Just that. The horizon remains unattainable, I have resigned myself to it. Nevertheless I am going on' (207). These didactic, rhetorical moments in the text turn the illiterate slave, Adam, into a noble Sisyphean figure, plodding on against impossible odds, buoyed by nothing but the faith of his existence: 'Rather than resist one must abandon oneself to it, allowing it to slowly burn into you: into everything inside you which has not yet existed, lending it consciousness: so that, painfully, in the process of being stripped of everything, one can give birth to oneself' (207). In the end, Brink takes up the mantle of the modernist artist. He transforms the

Mrs Fraser legend into Albert Camus's tale of *The Stranger*. The theme of the stranger lost in a landscape is not unlike Eldridge Cleaver's existential Black American examination of racial and sexual tensions in *Soul on Ice*. Brink quotes Cleaver in one of the novel's two epigraphs: 'It is lonely out here. We recognize each other. And, having recognized each other, is it any wonder that our souls cling together even while our minds equivocate, hesitate, vacillate and tremble?'

How is it possible for a mutual recognition to occur within a Western, humanist historical perspective and the South African context of colonisation? The novel promises a new day of 'truth' from within an Enlightenment view of history – white man's history. It forgets that there are other histories to be considered. This act of faith for the white man is only possible within a universalist philosophy. This philosophy incorporates woman and colonised peoples into its teleology of progress, a teleology in which women, natives and the land continue to be imagined as treacherous within the minds of men. Elisabeth and Adam may escape their ordeal in the wilderness through acts of survival, acts of will – but they cannot escape their colonisation within the narratives which construct them. The mutual recognition so desired by radical white settlers in the racially charged climate of contemporary South Africa, or radical white writers sympathetic to the political demands of formerly colonised peoples, cannot occur until they can be rid of the monster in the mirror, the snake in the garden, and other imaginary 'devils' which 'spook' them. In this dilemma Brink aligns himself with Nolan and White. He imagines the racial problem as a problem for common humanity. The white man speaks on behalf of blacks and woman, including them in his wide embrace. But that embrace may feel more like suffocation to the partner on the 'other' side.

Like Camus's *The Stranger*, to whom Edward Said makes reference in a similar vein in his *Culture and Imperialism*, Brink's novel can also be read as an act of domination, one which expresses a desire to possess South Africa. His existential guise allows the politics of the past and present to drop away in a poetic self-realisation in which Adam becomes an essence outside of time, history or interpretation. The communion with the land, like that of Adam to Elisabeth here, and Ellen to Jack Chance in *A Fringe of Leaves*, allows the characters/author/readers to partake in 'ceremonies of bonding with the territory'. Said suggests that these ceremonies ironically stimulate in today's reader queries about the need for such affirmations: 'When the violence of the [French, Afrikaner, English] past is thus inadvertently recalled, these ceremonies become foreshortened, highly compressed commemorations of survival, that of a community with nowhere to go.'[37] The equivocations, hesitations, vacillations and tremblings which Cleaver expressed in *Soul on Ice* and Brink affirmed in his novel's prologue, when read some twenty years after their first expressions, cause increasing unease. For contemporary readers, within the neo-, anti- and post-colonial contexts of white settler societies of South Africa, the United States or Australia today, such expressions of faith in the possibility of mutual recognition seem riven with complex and irreconcilable political and aesthetic contradictions.

Contexts of Reception

Although eventually published in ten different languages in Europe, America and England, in 1975 *An Instant in the Wind* was rejected by at least ten local publishers in South Africa. It was privately printed in Afrikaans and distributed to subscribers by post.[38] When the novel finally found a South African publisher, the first run sold out within six months of publication. In the heady days of apartheid, the novel was received as a political act of defiance designed to shock official taste. Now, in post-apartheid South Africa, a sanctioned film is planned. Given the repressive racial politics of the South African government, Brink, writing as an Afrikaner, offers a radical critique of his society. *An Instant in the Wind* is Brink's attempt to confront his country's ethnic divisions and policies of racial segregation within the limited and yet liberationist rhetoric of Enlightenment discourse. He means for his writing, like that of Breytenbach, to be read as an act of political engagement and resistance, as his dedication to Breytenbach makes clear. In a country where white writers have been subjected to constant threats and surveillance, writing a novel about an interracial love affair, even if set in the early days, can have dire consequences. Breytenbach had been gaoled when he returned to South Africa from his exile in Paris in 1975 with a forged passport. He served a seven-year prison sentence. Brink admits that 'I have for a long time been believing – sometimes hope against hope, as it were – that there was still a little glimmer of promise left.'[39] The novel needs to be read within the limits of its political and cultural context. At the same time, the theme of a love which can transcend all barriers forecloses a consideration of the sexual difference which confines women within a masculine economy of desire, or of a radical racial difference for black peoples beyond Western histories of colonisation. The novel argues its case within a humanist ideology of racial and cultural assimilation. In this it reinscribes difference even as it attempts to challenge white power. In other words, it is inscribed within its author's neo-colonial history.

The Novel as Enabling Myth

Brink's novel, transposing the story to a South African setting, returns us to the existential dimensions of interracial conflict studied in race and class terms in *A Fringe of Leaves*. A. J. Hassall has examined the Eliza Fraser story as depicted in Patrick White's novel, Sidney Nolan's paintings and André

Brink's novel within this framework. He shifts the focus beyond Australia to a more universalist perspective. For him the story, and its adaptations in the twentieth century, can be read as a post-colonial enabling myth within an international context. He writes:

> Nolan, White and Brink perceive in the stories a myth which embodies the archetypal confrontations between the European consciousness and the virgin continent, between the 'civilised' white settler and the 'natural' black inhabitant, between imprisonment and freedom, between woman and man on the edge of survival in the antipodean wilderness, and between suffering and the individual soul.[40]

He concludes that each of these artists fashions their confrontations as 'an enabling myth for their respective post-colonial societies'. That is, they portray colonial settlers conquering the physical, psychological, moral and political threats presented by the alien land and its people. In Hassall's article, Eliza Fraser, or Ellen Roxburgh/Elisabeth Larsson, becomes an Everyman character charting a post-colonial territory for modern white readers. This is an interpretation which readers who are culturally defined by their marginality may find difficult to accept. As the above analysis has shown, Mrs Fraser/Ellen Roxburgh/Elisabeth Larsson is a troublesome heroine, even within a modernist epistemology, straddling as she does both self and other categories which the novels struggle to keep intact. The central female character as Everyman cannot escape also becoming an Everywoman as other in the reconstructions. The rescuer/hero is represented as Everyman only as he loses his specific identity and stands on a collective humanist ground of mankind.

Troubling features of this critique surface when one deconstructs the hierarchies of gender, class and race which support the novels within a modernist framework. They become even more apparent when juxtaposed with the woman brought to life in the productions of Ondaatje or Josipovici, or the slave strangled and killed at the end of Brink's novel. Critics remain divided as to whether the novels of White and Brink succeed or fail on the basis of their final situations. In regard to *A Fringe of Leaves*, critics ask: Once Ellen Roxburgh has had her epiphany in the liminal environment of Fraser Island how can she return to civilisation? In regard to *An Instant in the Wind* they ask: Does the ending represent an 'opting out' – a distillation of history into myth, a situation where Western democratic political solutions are no longer viable?

No matter what readers might think of the vision of 'the essential life' conveyed by these novels, given the nature of masculine–feminine, Western and non-Western, self and other divisions which the texts uphold, even as they are challenged, the authors can do no more at the end than to settle their heroines into middle-class conformity where they, like the other women in their bourgeois world, will be absorbed. Therefore, at the end of *A Fringe of Leaves*, Ellen Roxburgh is left wondering 'whether she had served a purpose ever' (314). This leads some critics to conclude that she 'fails the test'. There is a paradox here, in that Ellen Roxburgh can only be a questing hero for mankind at the expense of her femininity. She can only transgress the boundaries of civilisation by slipping into the category of other through which she is constituted, along with peasants, convicts and Aborigines, albeit differently, in a partial, liminal and limited world. Like Elisabeth Larsson, as a colonial figure on the boundaries she cannot be retrieved as an emblem for an emerging post-colonial 'civilisation'. She can be Everyman as woman (and thus excused, even exalted, for her instinctual life, her passions, her intimacy with nature) but she is also sexed as female and tied to the social structures and the language of sameness and difference which keep women subjected to masculine prerogatives. She functions as a site of their desire – a desire for communion not only with Woman, or the feminine, but also with the land itself. Both women, in both novels, are caught within an impasse of difference.

These questions of difference have attended every reading of 'Eliza Fraser'. Each version recasts a myth of an originating event of first contact between white settlers and indigenous peoples. White and Brink imagine for their characters an idyllic Edenic world before the fall. In this space, the place of the 'natural', the 'instinctual' life, primitive and civilised characters can come together in a mutual drama of survival; lovers are not troubled by class or race divisions, a history of colonisation, nor a politics of oppression. Man and woman exist in a harmony, a complementarity in which the two merge into one – in a dream of a common humanity. That this dream can include within its horizons of national identity a Moreton Bay runaway convict and a Cape-town runaway slave attests to the seductiveness of the Western, humanist vision, at least for an audience of white readers. This is a vision of a universal, natural order beyond the constraints of the social world, or beyond the symbolic order of language; it has a compelling power which influences both social and psychic life. On a political level, it holds out a promise of a return to a society outside language and history, a 'real' world, imagined as beyond or underneath the artificial layerings of cultural inscription. On a psychic level, it satisfies the desire for harmony and wholeness imagined by the pre-social self in a dyadic relationship to the body of the mother, the space of Maternal bliss. In Christian terms, it holds out the promise of restoration to a pre-lapsarian Garden of Eden. This desire to return to a former plenitude operates within patriarchal, Christian, neo-colonial and post-colonial frameworks. It is a fantasy of return to a world before the violent rupture of sexual or racial difference. Such a dream is impossible. Within male-dominated Western culture, women's bodies are imagined as lack, as threatening enigma. Within a post-colonial world, still dominated by the politics of the Western metropolis, black bodies remain slaves to their own appearance. These bodies are sites of knowledge, sites of oppression. There is no nature outside culture; no woman or person of colour who is not always already inscribed as marginal, different and inferior within the politics of Western representation.

Difference is constituted on the body of the other within the relationship between male and female, black and white, coloniser and colonised. The cut between the two unequal and co-defining terms produces the rupture experienced socially and symbolically as sexual and racial difference. To engage in the fantasy of a return to wholeness effaces the memory of a violent rupture into difference (one constitutive of race, the other of gender, and both interrelated) which was the political, social and psychic work of 'first contact' and remains its legacy. Locating women on the side of nature and the instincts within the Edenic myth of origin, as the writers do with their different versions of a pre-lapsarian love idyll, preserves the category of the feminine within a masculine economy of representation. White imagines her as enigma; Blackman and Brink imagine her as a figure of nature-as-maternal-abundance. In this they preserve a space of a-cultural femininity for the pre-social subject, or the possibility of a return to an origin outside culture. But that enigma of penetration producing a blissful union can slip into an image of the monstrous or abject feminine, the Medusa (Nolan, Ondaatje and Josipovici). The maternal/abject woman becomes both the invention and the property of man (Blackman, Brink). Indigenous peoples caught in this imaginary and symbolic arena, a poetics within a politics of domination, become appropriated into Western categories of otherness. When they become emblems of mankind's primordial past (White, Brink) their identity is recuperated for 'us'. The fantasy effaces the violence at the origin of colonialism. To entertain a fantasy of wholeness for the family of man may assuage the coloniser's guilt. But it is yet another version of the white man's myth. It is another (perhaps *the*) grand incorporation of 'them' into 'us': the ultimate fantasy of the Self.

CHAPTER 9

And Now for the Movie: Popular Accounts

Nineteenth-century British audiences best remembered Mrs Fraser as a result of the sensational stories in the popular press; in the late twentieth century, in Australia at least, the release and circulation of the popular film *Eliza Fraser* (1976) produced a similar result. This film, with its attendant media publicity and mass audience appeal, had the power to supplant other knowledges of the event. This is evident, for example, in the newspaper reviews of the Blackman–Sculthorpe music theatre *Eliza Fraser Sings*, first performed in 1978. One review introduced its theme by commenting, 'with the recently made film of Eliza Fraser's traumatic shipwreck, capture by natives and subsequent rescue, her story is well known'.[1] The extent to which public knowledge of the event has been based on the film version became apparent to me when I travelled to Fraser Island in 1989 in the course of my research. I spoke to several tourists about my project. They had not encountered the Eliza Fraser legend in their travels (although a version is recounted in a glossy tourist publication, *Fraser Island*, and retold with relish by some tour operators); but they remembered the movie. One visitor remarked, 'Wasn't she an Englishwoman shipwrecked somewhere in Australia? Saw the movie. Susannah York. A bit of a tart as I remember.' Despite the fact that Patrick White's acclaimed novel and a reprint of Michael Alexander's history appeared in 1976, the same year as the film was released, the film has etched a memory of the *Stirling Castle* episode on the collective national consciousness. The making of the film was a first-class media event in Australia. At a cost of $1.2 million, it was Australia's first big-budget film. With overseas stars Susannah York and Trevor Howard, it attracted high-profile media attention, particularly in women's magazines, from the first day of filming.

The cultural dynamics of the Eliza Fraser story as a media event in the twentieth century parallel those which attended the nineteenth-century event, as discussed in Chapter 2. Like its nineteenth-century counterpart, this one activated the cultural wars between so-called 'high' and 'low-brow' culture: between the more academic concerns of a middle-class establishment press and the popular media's desire for sensational stories packaged for mass consumption. One issue at stake was the question of who had the right to speak for Australia, to define national identity for the late twentieth century. That question provoked just as many assertions and contestations of authority in the early 1970s in Australia as it had in the 1830s in England. The 1970s witnessed a complex array of shifting power relations in Australia between an old and new political order, partially brought about by the coming to power of the Whitlam Labor Government after twenty-three years of Liberal–Country Party rule. The era effected a significant shift in relations of power in Australia. One benchmark decision, which made these changes visible, was the conferring of citizenship rights for Aborigines and Torres Strait Islanders, granted for the first time in 1967. Another was the end to the White Australia immigration policy in 1973. In addition, acts against sex discrimination and race discrimination were passed by Parliament in 1975. Government policies, across the board, called for a re-evaluation of the nation's image and its political priorities. The Australian film industry, and the Australian Film Commission, established by the Whitlam government, supported a new generation of film-makers, whose films asserted brash, new forms of cultural nationalism.

The film *Eliza Fraser* appeared in the aftermath of these changes. The diversity of reactions that it provoked at the time give evidence that Australia was becoming more fluid and culturally diverse. In general, reviewers were hostile. Critics writing in the serious press questioned to what degree the film told the 'truth' – the truth of Australia's history as well as Mrs Fraser's 'true' story. In addition, film critics associated with the politics of the left berated the film, its director and scriptwriter, mainly on aesthetic grounds. The critics were embarrassed by its 'unabashed celebration' of an Ocker way of life. Even the tabloids were scathing. The public, however, supported the film, making it one of the most popular of the year. These diverse reactions sparked further nationalist questions in relation to who can or will speak for 'Australia'. Given the advance publicity, critics expected to see a 'great' Australian film, one which would respectfully and seriously represent Australia's colonial past. The pleasures, anxieties and desires of mass culture – the more pervasive elements of this film event in terms of popular culture – were subjected less to critical analysis. Nonetheless, the film raised important issues for Australia in the 1970s: issues of Australian national identity in opposition to a British heritage; of sexual deviance (particularly male homosexuality and woman's sexual excess) rather than of native savagery; of white cannibalism as opposed to Aboriginal cannibalism. It did so, however, in a way which parodied history, and turned tragedy into comedy and epic into melodramatic farce.

Although the political climate, structures of power, and ideologies of race and gender had changed significantly from the 1830s to the 1970s, the pattern of transposing fears of difference within the 'self' onto its 'others' had endured. In 1975 the position of the 'self' was occupied/contested by a newly emergent, imagined community of Australians broadly associated with the Whitlam era in politics. For the most part, however, the new voices were male and their concerns masculine. Feminists, Aborigines, New Australians, as well as gay rights and labour union activists, had a high profile during the period, registering their concerns for inclusion on a national political agenda. By and large, however, they were not attempting to *define* a nation so much as to find themselves located somewhere within its existing political and symbolic boundaries. The media conflict over the film *Eliza Fraser* provided a forum in which various segments of Australian society could express their vision of 'the nation'. Battle lines were drawn between those who liked the film and those who loathed it. Those who were identified as brash, adolescent, hedonistic Ockers, whose influence dominated the initial 1969–75 period of the new government-sponsored Australian film industry, were opposed by their serious, leftish bourgeois counterparts, who were about to effect a takeover. Both sides were anxious to include Aborigines in an Australian equation; both were hostile to neo-British pretensions at home and abroad. Sexual relations became a symbolic battleground, a terrain fraught with feminist and gay tensions as well as class-based ones. Like the media event's nineteenth-century predecessor, representations of these themes and their diverse audiences had more to do with shifting power relations than with an ostensible search for 'truth' or for an authentic national culture. The film *Eliza Fraser*, then, can be seen as a minor skirmish in a larger battle which continued throughout the 1970s.

The Role(s) of the Press

Public interest in the film from the outset was aided by the popularity of its overseas British stars, Susannah York and Trevor Howard. During the filming of *Eliza Fraser*, articles appeared in popular magazines like the *Women's Weekly*, often 'written on location'. They typically began by detailing the stars' impressions of Australia, and went on to relate something of the history of the nineteenth-century shipwreck. The articles generally kept public interest in the film alive. Their focus on the big-name (British) stars and a desire for their approval of 'things Australian' belied the assertive voice of Australian nationalism. Still, the articles commonly featured an emphasis on the nation's history through the story of Eliza Fraser, the shipwreck, and her alleged captivity. Typically, they 'got the history wrong', although their melodramatic renditions tended to support Mrs Fraser as the stalwart heroine of a truly tragic ordeal. 'How can a macabre story be a comedy?' one reporter asked. He then went on to recount the 'macabre' details: 'the ship-wreck, her child drowned at birth, her husband murdered before her eyes, a crew member roasted alive, the awful indignities suffered at the hands of the Aborigines'.

We can register now, but readers would not have known at the time that, with the exception of the shipwreck, all of these so-called 'events' were highly coloured versions of the histories, although all appeared in various news accounts about the film under the guise of 'truth'. But the problems of his-torical accuracy are more or less irrelevant in the evolution of a public consciousness about the film event. From the outset, the Eliza Fraser story had been shaped by an interplay between serious and popular accounts. In the article cited above, Tim Burstall, the director, answers the question: 'How can a macabre story be a comedy?' with his own outrageous version of 'the truth'. He justifies his comic treatment (somewhat ironically but with an uncanny reference back to the nineteenth-century controversy) with refer-ence to Mrs Fraser's veracity. 'She lied', he told the reporter, as if to indicate that this was excuse enough for turning the tragedy into a farce. She was 'an opportunist' who married again, 'toured England in a sixpenny sideshow attraction, and ended her days as a hale and hearty grandmother in New Zealand'.[2] The last phrase is an entirely new invention, Burstall's contri-bution of yet another fiction to be appended to the tale. These kinds of reports, farces in themselves, fed the (white) nation's hunger for knowledge of its own history. More importantly, the film, whatever its merits or defects in aesthetic or cinematographic terms, inserted an event, which had been represented solely within the 'high' cultural domains of Art, History, and Literature, into a more popular cultural arena.

The film also became a minor battleground for the unions which tried to intervene on behalf of the one hundred Aborigines who were taken to Fraser Island from Mornington Island for shooting on location. Actors' Equity insisted that the Aboriginal actors be treated equitably and paid equity wages, which was done, although Lindsay Roughsey, the Lardil tribal elder who plays Euenmundi in the Fraser Island episodes of the film, received a good deal less than other, featured, white actors. The union, however, did not manage to get the names of the Aboriginal actors (except for Roughsey), or even their clan or language affiliations, listed in the credits; they remain anonymous. The press, in an item headed 'Eliza Maligns the Blacks – Union', reported that the union was concerned that the film might 'damage Abor-iginal tribal customs, culture and habits' because 'films tamper with histori-cal facts'. The headline and the union concerns reported by the article employ a number of narrative strategies with regard to hierarchies of race and gender. These include an emblematic reference to a treacherous 'Eliza' who maligns the blacks; a paternalistic political gesture by the unions on behalf of the Aboriginal actors; and an enduring, white cultural interest in preserving the myth of Aboriginal authenticity, posited in the primordial past of traditional tribal culture. To the latter end, the union demanded that 'a competent historian' from the Anthropology Department at the Australian National University be hired as a consultant to the director.[3] Something of the sort must have occurred, although the action, if it was intended kindly towards the Aboriginal community, backfired badly. A month later, under the accusatory headline 'Lights, Cameras – but Aboriginals Forget Songs', the *Sydney Morning Herald* reported that the Aborigines were a 'major headache' to the film-makers. Burstall lamented that the first rehearsal of a corroboree was a 'dismal failure'. The young lads could not remember their traditional tribal songs and dances. When called upon to explain, the white Aboriginal consultant from Canberra, instead of defending the film event as an opportunity for the elders to teach the young their traditional dances after years of imposed assimilationist policies, blamed the problem on the laziness and ignorance of the Aboriginal boys. At least this was how the press chose to report her judgements. 'The trouble is that the young don't practise enough', she was reported as saying. 'They were too interested in Western music and culture.'[4] In other words, they were too Westernised and assimilated when they were supposed to be 'primitive' and 'authentic'. As with the nineteenth-century controversy, given the cultural dynamics provoked by the film, interest never flagged. The publicity, which itself provided extended grounds for cultural contestations, reached its peak at the time of the film's pre-Christmas holiday release in major cities across Australia.

As was fitting for a film of this calibre, the premiere was lavish. Champagne flowed as actors, directors, writers, crew, important invited guests and fans gathered in anticipation of a great, international, box-office success. Only the Aboriginal actors were missing. The budget could not stretch to fly them from Mornington Island to Melbourne for the festivities. Local blacks were called in to substitute, 'to give the premiere the right atmosphere'. (This may remind readers of the church service in Sydney, detailed in Chapter 2, which opened Mrs Fraser's subscription campaign. She did not attend but the surviving crew members sat in the aisles without their jackets, presumably for much the same reason – to lend an air of authenticity to the launch.) No one, not even the union, seemed to mind. In what strikes present-day readers as an incredible insensitivity to racial issues, the press reported that snubbed tribal elder Lindsay Roughsey was 'not angry, just sad'. He still thought 'the film company was wonderful'.[5] Nothing, it seemed, would spoil the celebration – except, unfortunately, the film itself. It flopped, at least with the critics. Reviews appeared under headings which revealed the critics' universal dismay: 'Eliza Goes to Pieces', 'Eliza's on the Rocks', 'Eliza Hits a Reef', 'Eliza Do Little' and 'Eliza Purple'. The last heading was a damning reference to Tim Burstall's 'beds and buttocks', Ocker sex-romp film *Alvin Purple* (1973) and its popular sequels which embarrassed the emerging radical establishment. Geraldine Pascall, a major film reviewer for the *Australian*, the country's leading national newspaper, reviewed *Eliza Fraser* as a 'bland, unexciting, pointless, limp, tasteless, clichéd, banal and boring' production.[6] There was a scandal, which had less to do with reports of a romance between the director and the leading actress which also were leaked to the press at the time, than with the profligate spending of public funds on what was deemed to be a vile and vulgar dramatisation.

Great Expectations: Ockers and their Knockers

It was not so much that the film was bad, but that expectations were high. Reviewers and other media commentators knew of and referred to Michael Alexander's history, Patrick White's novel and Sidney Nolan's paintings in their articles and reviews as preludes to the film. Despite hints, which had appeared in women's magazines and the popular press, of the film's transgressive treatment of history, the serious reviewers of the 'high' press were expecting a reverent, 'quality', historical reconstruction – not high adventure, parody and comic farce. Repeatedly, they expressed their dismay at the film which turned a 'human tragedy of epic proportions' into a slight 'comedy of terrors'.[7] In addition, the film widened a breach in the nationalistic culture wars between supporters of the raunchy, Ocker films like *Alvin Purple* and *Petersen* (both directed by Tim Burstall) and of the aesthetically pleasing period films like *Picnic at Hanging Rock* and *Caddie*, which had premiered that same year.

The film was neither Ocker nor authentic, although, like the Ocker films which preceded it, it was irreverent. Like them, it invited a mass audience to take pleasure in overturning the pretensions of 'high' culture, including its History. And like them, it represented the supposed nation's concerns as those of heterosexual, white men. This was an 'Eliza Fraser' reconstructed within the brash, strident and resolutely hedonistic nationalism of the present. The bourgeoisie took the high moral ground. They classified *Eliza Fraser*, along with the 1970s films *Alvin Purple* and *Barry McKenzie* and the long-running television series 'Number 96', the first television show to feature nudity, as 'coarse, vulgar rubbish'.[8] It would be a mistake, however, to see the warring forces, the Ockers and their knockers, as engaged in a dialectical debate. More accurately, the arguments, concerns and emotional commitments of each side were played off in a spiral of power in which both were fully implicated, 'upping the ante on each other'.[9] The stakes were high, however, and the exchange, which became quite heated, had a number of political consequences.

Judged as a failure in both artistic and commercial terms, the film was a turning point for the Australian Film Commission, Tim Burstall, and his company Hexagon Films. The AFC lost all of its substantial investment, not as a result of poor attendance figures, but because of poor box-office returns. This was due to the high budget for the film and its failure to sell to overseas distributors (deemed necessary from the outset to meet budget) despite its international stars. In 1975 the federal government had devised new funding policies which favoured aesthetic, 'quality' films over the embarrassing (to the Labor establishment at the time) Ocker variety. By 1976, Tim Burstall, the high-profile producer and director of a series of low-budget and lucrative films in the early 1970s, was considered to be out of step with the times. Failure to recoup production costs on *Eliza Fraser* led to the loss of his production company, Hexagon Films. He retaliated against hostile criticism with a series of angry public outbursts, calling the change in funding direction a 'bitter attack on the industry with its calls for "culture and quality" in film'. In typical larrikin fashion he remarked in defence of *Eliza Fraser*: 'The public wanted to see it as an epic. They didn't want to see their history portrayed on screen as basically bullshit, even though they know it is really the case.'[10] It was not so much 'the public', however, as the establishment left whose desires and expectations were thwarted by the film. 'The public' gave their support at the box office at the time. Subsequently, they have tuned-in for several television re-runs and continue to hire the video which has been in circulation for nearly two decades. Burstall's comment, however, reminds us that history itself is an object of public scrutiny. Mass audience enjoyment of the film's irreverent approach to history may be, in part, a product of history's perceived inaccessibility; its pretences of respectability; its reputation, in some quarters at least, as being 'basically bullshit'.

David Williamson, the scriptwriter and one of Australia's most popular young playwrights, did not escape the fallout from the film's bad reviews. One of the few writers in Australia willing to ride the boundaries drawn by the leading proponents in the nation's culture wars, his work included both popular filmscripts and serious plays. Prior to his collaboration with Tim Burstall on *Eliza Fraser*, he had written the plays and/or filmscripts *Stork* (1971), *The Removalists* (1972), *Don's Party* (1972), *Petersen* (1974, directed by Burstall) and *The Department* (1975). The establishment left had desires of claiming him, although feminists in its midst remained cool. His perceived forays into the Ocker camp caused concern, even outrage, amidst certain groups. In a 1990 television interview with comic Wendy Harmer, Williamson quipped that he experienced a form of 'female fascism' in the early 1970s. It caused him to live through 'twenty years of terror, afraid to write dramas about women who are less than wonderful', he said, for fear that pickets would greet him outside the theatre and 'kick him in the (mumble, mumble)'.[11] In his own defence, Williamson claims that his plays were far more critical of the extreme macho male competitiveness lying just under the skin of so-called 'mateship' than they ever were of women.[12] Nonetheless, feminist critics remained critical of his early plays, lamenting that he failed to portray women's characters with any depth or seriousness. Still, in some quarters he was celebrated for speaking of and for the nation. But, by 1975, 'the nation' and its expectations had changed.

Feminists were not alone in their dismay. Colin Bennett, the prominent film critic for the *Age* (Melbourne), queried if Williamson intended merely to reflect the base and hedonistic quality of life observed in the culture around him or to celebrate it? If the latter were the case, then the writer himself was '*as hollow a man without vision*' (emphasis in original).[13] Battered by the critics, who suggested he was 'out of his depth in period drama',[14] Williamson responded by passing the blame on to Burstall. Publicly, he commented that it was 'par for the course for any Burstall epic'. Privately, he wrote to a friend:

> The film isn't bad. It suffers from Burstall's inevitable heaviness – slow editing, hammering points home, slow pacing of dialogue scenes, etc., but it has a rather buoyant total feeling which I modestly attribute to myself (and the actors). The box office is very good but I really have resolved not to work with Burstall again. It's too depressing.[15]

And the box office was good. Although gross rentals brought 'minimal returns' (in film finance language this means less than 50 per cent of the budget), this was because the film had a million-dollar budget at a time when the average film production cost in Australia was about $300,000. Without overseas distribution, financial recovery of the investment was doomed, despite the film's popularity in Australia. And with *Eliza Fraser* the sun set on the era of Ocker films.

Tim Burstall and David Williamson's Film

From the opening scenes of a naked couple in bed surprised by a jealous husband at break of day, the film has all the makings of a *Boy's Own*, bedroom farce. The fact that the players in this scene were, at the time, immediately recognisable from popular films and television soaps, cues the viewer that the director is going for box-office appeal. In fact, Burstall skilfully cast actors whose roles in previous films and television serials would signify the nature of their characters in this one. Susannah York (Eliza Fraser) was well known as a saucy and seductive coquette from her *Tom Jones* role as Polly. Trevor Howard (Moreton Bay Commandant, Foster Fyans) was remembered for his portrayal of the overbearing and brutal Captain Bligh in *Mutiny on the Bounty*. Noel Ferrier (Captain Fraser) had played the pompous but vapid upper-class judge in several *Alvin Purple* productions. John Castle (Rory McBryde), the rakish womaniser caught by the gaze of the camera and the arrival of a jealous husband in the opening scene, was a popular television actor, known for his expressive sneer. Abigail (the mistress in the bed, who was mistaken for a wife) had played in the popular soap 'Number 96', where she had appeared in the nude, causing considerable public controversy. And John Walters (David Bracefell) had been cast as a handsome and likeable, underdog character in several television period dramas. Thus the key players had their characters established before they murmured their first lines. Other recognisable character-actors played the roles of a faithful first mate Brown, a wickedly duplicitous John Graham, and a rough lot of mutinous seamen: Darge, Youlden, Stone, Doyle and Hodge. Even Bruce McIvor, the gawky, adolescent star of *Stork*, whom in that film women found so incomprehensibly irresistible, was given a cameo role as a sentry easily distracted by the lures of Mrs Fraser as she aided Bracefell's midnight escape from Moreton Bay. Not only did Burstall choose his stars for mass audience appeal, their presence and portrayals in the film supplied the audience with an abundance of intertextual filmic and television references, overlaid with the adolescent, hedonistic sassiness associated with the Ocker push.

Despite the film's (ironic) full title, *The Faithful Narrative of the Capture, Sufferings and Miraculous Escape of Eliza Fraser*, this is not a film about Eliza Fraser, but one about a particular articulation of Australian nationalism. Like many other films produced in the early years of the new Australian cinema, *Eliza Fraser* measured an emergent national identity against an inglorious British past. The hero of this piece is the convict David Bracefell, who, along with an enamoured Eliza, stands out against the British colonial administrators, his gaolers at Moreton Bay. True to a romanticised version of convict offences and punishments, Bracefell has been gaoled for a slight crime. Formerly a sailor, he fell in love while on leave in Sydney and jumped ship to stay with his beloved, whereupon he was arrested and sent to Moreton Bay. In this film, as opposed to the legend, Eliza will not betray the good convict – although another woman may already have done so. Bracefell and Graham are introduced together as they enter the grey walls of the prison settlement, shackled in leg-irons, to await inspection by Foster Fyans, the sadistic Commandant. Fyans singles them out for 'special favours': a gratuitous flogging followed by onerous commissions in his service. Graham will act as an informant; Bracefell as a bedwarmer to the 'conscientious and exacting' head of command. In the early sequences of the film, then, the spectator's interest is aroused by the convicts' dilemma (sadistic, colonial rule) and the possibility of mateship (a defence against authority). These are coupled with the spectre of homosexuality (here perhaps a projection of Ocker male insecurity onto Fyans and, by implication, the sodomising British) which set the plot in motion. Bracefell, with a broad Aussie accent, acts the 'good mate'; by supporting Graham through his flogging ordeal, he invites the audience's approval of him and identification with him as a larrikin hero. The churlish Graham, with his Cockney snarl, fails to reciprocate the comradely gesture. Atypically, in terms of the myth of Australian nationalism, the film offers a spoof of mateship. Its sympathies may be Australian, but they derive their comic effects with regard to a number of national insecurities: about political power, homosexuality, excessive female sexuality, race relations, class struggle and authoritarianism, to name a few.

Eliza (Susannah York) acts as a foil for the men and a delightful spectacle for the audience. She functions, like the other, more instrumental, women in the film, as an alluring object of sexual exchange. Always a spectacular body, a site of visual pleasure, she moves the plot along. Together with Bracefell, she foils the Commandant – and contains the threat of homosexuality. Early in the piece we view her in the bedroom as she moves the audience through a typical comic romp of mistaken identities, managing to entertain, while at the same time keep hidden from each other, three amorous suitors. The first is David Bracefell, who has escaped the Commandant's quarters and his homosexual attentions, and whom the responsive Eliza takes to be Rory McBryde, with whom she had arranged a midnight assignation; the second is McBryde, who arrives late, weary from over-indulgence at the Commandant's dining table, and is unable to perform sexually; and the third is Captain Fraser, who appears unexpectedly from his separate quarters next door in his ridiculous nightshirt to apologise for his boorishness at dinner and warn his wife of Rory's 'weaknesses'. Spectators watch voyeuristically, like Bracefell, who cowers naked under the bed, and McBryde, who peers out nervously from behind a room divide, as the Captain attempts to seduce his unresponsive wife and the Commandant fumes at the loss of his bed companion. Thus, Eliza manages to unite four disparate men around herself: the brutal Fyans, the boorish Captain Fraser, the exploitative McBryde and the innocent convict Bracefell – who manages to gull them all.

New Encounters with the Natives

All is not sweetness and light in this film. It has a dark side – one which involves the viewer in an encounter between shipwreck victims and an inhospitable bush; white and Aboriginal culture, and the murderous instincts of desperate white men. At times the comedy hovers close to critical social commentary, particularly in its satire on the sadism of the colonial administration and in its subversion of dominant British colonial attitudes towards both the convicts and Aboriginal culture. The first encounter of the Frasers with their Aboriginal hosts calls attention to the latter theme. Captain Fraser responds to first contact with stereotypic fears of native savagery; his fears stand in marked contrast to Mrs Fraser's bemused interest. Their encounter with a small band of cautious but curious islanders (announced by the Captain's words, 'Cannibals, I knew it!') provides comic relief. The islanders chatter, examine and disrobe their specimens, kicking the Captain up the bum for their irreverent amusement and his poor judgement of the situation.

'I'm a British sea-captain,' he exclaims; 'I'm damned if I'll be ordered around by a savage!'

These comic scenes are juxtaposed against more sinister ones in which the mutinous seamen battle the hostile landscape, hunger and their own cannibalistic impulses. Their separate ordeal tests Captain Fyans's farewell warning to the Frasers: 'Nothing out there but hell swamps of heat, pestilence, reptiles and murderous savages.' The small band of desperate seamen confront the heat and pestilence in their struggle to find food and water. The reptiles, however, evade their incompetent, stalking gaze, and the murderous savages they confront are none other than themselves. They 'draw lots', taking action to reduce their number dramatically, thus enacting the macabre scene of white cannibalism, a facet of the original event which was examined by Michael Alexander in *Mrs Fraser on the Fatal Shore*. Somewhat incongruously, these scenes are juxtaposed with Captain and Mrs Fraser's encounters with 'the natives', as they are groomed for their respective roles at a corroboree. In one of the most comic scenes of the film, the rotund Captain, now acclimatised to native ways, prances through the camp, daubed in ochre and dressed in nothing but a lap-lap. In another comic scene, the Aborigines gracefully and patiently demonstrate their spear-throwing techniques to him. He attempts to mime their movements but he proves to be as inept at spear-throwing as Eliza is at food-gathering. As Karen Jennings writes:

> The characters of Captain Fyans (Trevor Howard), Captain Fraser (Noel Ferrier) and Rory McBryde (John Castle) articulate the dominant colonial discourse of the 'savagery' of both Aborigines and the lower classes. But . . . *Eliza Fraser* seeks to subvert these stereotypes. It does so by representing the Aborigines as dignified, assertive, strong and humorous in contrast to the white sailors and soldiers who are the film's real savages and cannibals. In this respect it is a conscious attempt to re-write populist histories of the real Eliza Fraser, whose husband was reputedly killed by Aborigines. In the film, Captain Fraser is killed by an Aboriginal hunting spear, but significantly it is thrown by a British soldier.[16]

Although the film neither romanticises nor ridicules the Aborigines, it does present them as childlike creatures of the senses, that is, through enduring European perspectives of the Noble Savage, here put to comic effect. Viewers largely perceive the islanders through other European characters in the film. If they sometimes appear dignified, strong, assertive and humorous, at other times they are also presented as primitive, menacing creatures of the senses, unable to rise above their momentary impulses and base desires. Through these contradictory representations, the film offers a critique of colonial attitudes and fears while it also re-enacts them.

Cinematographic techniques enhance the theme of otherness. Many scenes featuring the Aboriginal actors were shot in the dark, thus increasing the association of blackness with primitive menace. There is also an abundance of Aborigines in the film, chattering noisily as they surround the two miserable Europeans in a claustrophobic manner. They roam in anonymous bands, without names or individuality. Except for the corroboree scene, Aboriginal people are never seen in their own cultural context; they are represented only in their interactions with the white shipwreck victims. And the corroboree, carefully executed before the cameras, is an excessive ethnographic performance of 'Aboriginality'. In terms of the film as a whole, Aborigines form an anonymous presence in the background. As in Patrick White's novel, they are part of the hazards of the bush, and are easily accommodated. Nonetheless, both Eliza and Bracefell can cheerfully adapt to the demands of traditional Aboriginal society, Eliza temperamentally and Bracefell through his acquisition of bush survival skills. The sympathetic identification of Mrs Fraser and Bracefell with Aboriginal culture works in several directions. The pair provide for the audience a critique of colonial and racist stereotypes; at the same time their affiliation places women, the lower orders and the 'natives' together within a symbolic relationship of affinity. Thus, they both challenge and affirm categories of difference.

Excessive Femininity

If it might be said that Aborigines in the film perform themselves excessively in relation to the corroboree, so do the women in other scenes. They 'perform' their femininity as exoticism, marked for the viewer not by their primitive natures but by their sexual excess. The first woman, whose sleeping pose invites the viewer into the film, is played by Abigail, the television starlet whose previous claim to fame was for full-frontal nudity. In relation to Eliza Fraser, both the actress and the historical figure whose role she plays are constructed out of male fantasies of desire. In no scene in the film is Eliza featured on her own. Her place is to wait for, entertain, or otherwise be with, the men. This extends to her scene with the Aboriginal women as they prepare her for a marriage ceremony. In terms of dress, although always sexually provocative, she remains modestly attired, that is, on the white side of civilisation. Except for a brief moment when the women ceremonially paint her body, and again when she 'bathes' and swims naked in the luxuriant waters of Lake Waddy with her rescuer Bracefell, she remains clothed (albeit in an increasingly scanty petticoat) throughout the film. Her clothed body stands in opposition to the semi-nakedness of the Aboriginal women (and her husband and Bracefell), to which viewers have voyeuristic access during the sequences shot on Fraser Island. Frequent views of Bracefell's lithe and graceful body confound the film's ostensible anti-homosexual theme, at least in terms of viewers' pleasure.

Eliza's key scene comes late in the film, during her sideshow performance in old Sydney Town. Having been rescued from that 'fate worse than death' by the ubiquitous Bracefell, after losing her husband and succumbing to too many bizarre twists of plot, the attractive widow woos a Sydney circus audience with her tantalising tale of captivity. In these scenes, as Jennings suggests, she betrays her former acceptance of Aboriginal society by 'pandering to the prurient fascination/repulsion of the colonial settlers with her lurid sideshow tales of Aboriginal cannibalism and sexual menace'.[17] She feeds the eager fantasies of her rapt audience with a gruesome account of (near) forcible marriage to the 'cannibal chief', whom she enthusiastically describes as 'huge, black, powerful and menacing, with fire in his eyes that would brook no resistance'. The power of Susannah York's performance in these final scenes, in which she cynically exploits her Aboriginal hosts for commercial gain, confounds an easy reading of the film's critical social commentary.

Film critics have assessed the film *Eliza Fraser* and the character of the same name from a number of perspectives. Feminist film-maker Susan Dermody complains that the film trivialises women and Aborigines, all of whom are portrayed as mysterious, instinctual and tied to nature. Although the film offers a critique of racist stereotypes and beliefs through Mrs Fraser's characterisation, it also compromises its critique with its blend of comedy and horror, farce and adventure. Brian McFarlane disagrees, arguing that *Eliza Fraser* is the only film to treat a female figure from Australian history within a feminist ideology. With reference to the sideshow scene, he argues that the circus sideshow Eliza (and he means both the historical figure, who he believes survived her ordeal to take up a career as a raconteuse, and the character played by Susannah York in the film) 'assumes a stature that would otherwise have been denied her'.[18] Scriptwriter David Williamson concurs, arguing that Eliza Fraser negotiates and controls her own sexual availability throughout the film and exploits male sexual obsessions in the final sideshow scenes. For him, she is 'a cunning and intelligent woman who successfully negotiates male desire in her own interests'.[19] The positions of McFarlane and Williamson can be aligned with the 'positive images of women' arguments reliant on sociological approaches to women in film. Because the fictionalised Mrs Fraser has a dominant and ultimately successful social role in the film she can be read as a positive model for women. What these positions ignore, and why they are so strikingly opposed to Dermody's reading, is the degree to which 'Eliza' is constructed within the generic (literary and filmic) and cultural conventions of femininity. Her sexuality functions as a product of masculine desire; her success is measured within finely regulated terms of sexual difference. Even though at the end of the film Eliza Fraser emerges as a type of Australian hero (and this is a rare depiction of the historical Eliza in any fictionalised form), her ultimate 'success' is compromised. Like the plucky larrikin hero of other Ocker films, she rises from adversity to succeed in her own, covert schemes of personal and financial independence, despite the lustful advances of many suitors.[20] Thus, she gains the audience's approval as a plucky heroine, a suitable 'mate' for Bracefell. But she remains a suitable *mate*, a marriage partner. The traditional happy ending sets up the reunited couple to join the bourgeoisie. In the same gesture, Eliza is returned to woman's 'proper' maternal position as wife and mother. That is, she occupies the position of 'woman' contained within the generic conventions of the plot of a comedy of manners or bedroom farce. This filmic representation can hardly be said to place her within a 'feminist ideology', even in terms of a humanist politics, except as a complementary helpmate to man. Eliza Fraser's heroism, like the nobility afforded Aborigines in selective scenes, is contained within both masculine, bourgeois ideologies and voyeuristic filmic techniques which make her into a spectacle, an object of masculine fears and desires.

Overall, the film reinforces an assertive 1970s-style nationalism. Although in a satiric mode, it adheres to the pattern of the heroic (white) Australian native son battling against the British and the bush. The English upper-class authorities are represented as sadistic, conniving and sexually aberrant; the naval merchants as boorish, exploitative and/or deceiving; the working class as violent, depraved and duplicitous. All, except for Bracefell and Eliza, are incompetent in Australia's harsh and testing environment. The film betrays history, but that was its intention. It also reifies myth. As the brig sails over the horizon, the film draws to a close with an epilogue which reads: 'In fact history shows that it took eight months for Eliza to make her fortune. And history also shows that she returned with Captain Greene to New Zealand where they both lived happily ever after.' Kenneth Cook's novelistic version of the film asks, 'if you can't know the truth about history, what can you know the truth about?'[21] The film may be a send-up of history but at the same time it repeats, albeit often with a sharp irony, many dichotomous themes which structure traditional Australian narratives of nationhood: the uneasy relationships between Australia and England, convicts and their masters, the working class and middle class, Aborigines and Europeans, women and men. It challenges but also reinforces (white, male and middle-class) Australian mythologies of race, class and gender transplanted into the present. It might be argued, however, that the representation of Eliza as a figure of sexual excess may signal a crisis point in contemporary narratives of Australian nationalism. Our fascination with *her* enables us to disavow any guilty identification with the savagery, the cannibalism, the sadism, the authoritarianism, the fear of homosexuality and the exploitative race relations present in the film and also present in contemporary Australian cultural life.

Kenneth Cook's Popular Novel

Kenneth Cook's novel, *Eliza Fraser*, based on the film, more accurately could be called *The Life and Times of David Bracefell*. Bracefell is the privileged narrator, native informant and hero of the piece, supplanting the increasingly irrelevant Eliza Fraser. The novel continues the film's irreverent spoof of Australia's history. Like Eliza Fraser's captivity narrative of the nineteenth century, it is prefaced by an 'objective' editor's introduction. This one is by Kenneth Cook, and it guarantees the sincerity of the 'autobiographical' account, supposedly by Bracefell. The introduction engages the reader with a series of tantalising historical questions:

> Ever since 1836 when the ill-fated *Stirling Castle* was lost there has been considerable argument as to what happened to the survivors of the wreck. Was Captain Fraser killed by natives or was he the accidental victim of a plot to murder another man? Was the convict John Graham or the convict David Bracefell responsible for the rescue of Eliza Fraser? Who killed the First-Mate – natives or mutinous crew members? There was absolute evidence of cannibalism, but was it perpetrated by natives or by mutineers? Was Mrs. Fraser a respectable middle class woman or was she a hot-blooded beauty given to far from discreet peccadilloes with such disparate partners as a naval officer and an escaped convict? Was she an outrageous liar making capital out of her misfortunes or was she the courageous victim of almost unbelievable circumstances? [vii]

Kenneth Cook's satiric spoof of the tradition of captivity narratives and eighteenth-century realism promises to settle these questions. The narrative opens with the author's revelation of a recently discovered series of statements, made by David Bracefell, who, he maintains, married Mrs Fraser and moved to New Zealand where they lived as Captain and Mrs Greene. Cook parodies several narrative devices to legitimate David Bracefell's authority. In addition to the 'authenticity' of Bracefell's first-hand statements, he offers the collaboration of personal evidence from surviving members of the (fictitious) family as well as (authentic) documents from the archives of the Mitchell Library of Sydney. There are seven documents from the Mitchell Library presented in the appendix: they include a commemorative poem written by Captain Fraser to his wife after the wreck of the *Comet*; a sentimental poem written to the Captain by his sister; the traditional Irish ballad 'Moreton Bay'; and a Quaker description of Moreton Bay from 1836. In addition, there is George Lang's account of Aboriginal burial practices (which include cannibalism), derived from interviews with runaway convict Davis, who had lived as a 'white blackfellow' for over a decade and was rescued along with Bracefell by the Petrie rescue party in 1842; and Foster Fyans's letters to the Governor asking for a pardon for Graham (the convict rescuer of record). The final item is Lieutenant Otter's recommendation

of Graham to the Governor, which, in the course of the narrative, the fictitious Bracefell declares to be 'utter codswallop'. These documents are
somewhat inappropriately used to authenticate *Bracefell's* story as constructed in Cook's narrative; they frame the novel as a 'fiction of factual
representation' in a satiric mode.[22] Cook ironically utilises the tradition of
historical realism to feign a new performance of the genre. The comic effects
of the novel derive not only from this particular telling of the story but from
its miming of narrative strategies which have traditionally informed, structured and given a context to the developing genre, here turned into farce.
Readers familiar with the historical controversy concerning who rescued Mrs
Fraser, Graham or Bracefell, might derive additional pleasure from Cook's
transposition of heroism from Graham to Bracefell. At the same time, frequent references to 'natural' discourse give the text its 'authenticity'. Cook's
parody of historicism frames the novel in the ironic disguise of 'truth'.

The novel follows the flow of the film narrative, with few exceptions.
David Bracefell, the convict-hero and narrator of the novel, has a naive simplicity and a 'natural talent for native life' (97). As first-person narrator, and
as eye-witness of and participant in events depicted, he poses as an expert on
matters pertaining to Aboriginal law, habits and customs. In general,
Bracefell identifies with Aboriginal culture and against the European way of
life. His descriptions of Mrs Fraser derive their origins from a variety of other
sources, including the histories by John Curtis and Michael Alexander and
Patrick White's novel as well as the Williamson–Burstall film. But, as in the
film, the novel aims at mass-market appeal through an emphasis on Eliza
Fraser's sexuality. Mrs Fraser is perfection itself: 'unbelievably lovely . . .
[with a] strange combination of purity and wantonness, virtue and lust. She
made you think that rogering her would be a sort of spiritual exercise . . .
She was like a gazelle, and a good thirty years younger [than her boorish
husband]'(7).

More Titillating Visuals

These early descriptions of our heroine are complemented by front and back
cover illustrations on the inexpensive, paperback edition. It features selected
stills from the film version. On the front cover, a beautiful if somewhat
dishevelled Eliza, dressed in a tattered petticoat and corset, raises her head in
resistance to the cheek-fondling of an Aboriginal chief (Figure 13). Both
figures are framed within a fraying, historical parchment. On the back cover,
over the heading 'From the Violent, Bawdy Colonial Past comes A Rollicking
Tale of Lust and Adventure', three cameo shots from the film appear. One
features Eliza (Susannah York) minding an Aboriginal child who, like the
'Chief' on the front cover, raises his hand to Eliza's cheek. But here the child
sitting on her lap almost could be mistaken for a monkey raising an arm, his

Figure 13   Cover illustration, Kenneth Cook, *Eliza Fraser*, 1976.

dark head held back against her blonde hair in an intent gaze, as if preparing to pick a nit from her hair. The second cameo depicts Eliza smiling contentedly in bed atop her lover, Bracefell, her bare shoulder glowing in the golden light. The third cameo shows a red-coated soldier (popular television star, George Mallaby) about to engage in a duel with Rory McBryde, as the surly convict Graham looks on. Visually, they convey to the reader the familiar themes of sex and violence in an exotic setting. In this they mirror the cover illustration chosen for the 1976 reissue of Michael Alexander's *Mrs Fraser on the Fatal Shore*. It featured a resplendent Eliza/Susannah York on the cover, dressed in a low-cut, garnet silk gown; to her left and in the background, the remains of a wrecked ship, to her right three tribal Aborigines with spears and in ceremonial dress. Beneath the illustration the cover proclaimed: 'Shipwreck and scandal – the true story that shocked the world!' (Figure 14). Thus, twentieth-century versions of the story provide textual and visual supplements, primarily of sexual desire, to the sensational nineteenth-century accounts.

Bracefell's character, as constructed by Kenneth Cook, bears a close relation to the John Graham of Robert Gibbings's celebratory biography, although Graham acts as foil for Bracefell in Cook's account. Echoing Graham's reported testimony from Gibbings's *John Graham, Convict, 1824*, Bracefell describes the Frasers' treatment by the Aborigines in low-key, laconic terms: 'the natives didn't treat the Frasers any worse than they would have treated anybody else of supreme unimportance in their lives. They were fed and in a sense allowed to eat with the tribe, in strict order of social importance.' (74). Bracefell identifies himself with the natives, referring collectively to 'We wild men' (98) throughout the narrative. He suggests that Aborigines get bad press in white society from stories of liars like the mutinous seaman Darge (111) (referring with considerable anachronistic licence to Darge's reports of cannibalism which appear in Curtis, Alexander and some Queensland histories), as well as from circus publicity with its 'enormous posters of naked savages enthusiastically chewing away at white carcasses' (157).[23] Although Bracefell mouths the racist platitudes of colonial times concerning 'murderous savages' (94), the narrative makes clear that Aboriginal people possess wit, intelligence and survival skills wholly lacking in the white European society which, with some exceptions, acts with brutality, duplicity and ineptitude. Unlike other Australian accounts of the legend, nature here is beneficent – if one adapts to its demands. Although the penal colony is 'a cesspit' . . . [at the end of] the alimentary canal of creation' (16, 17), 'it's good country around Moreton Bay if you know how to live in it' (53), as do the Aborigines. While the mutineers face heat-exhaustion and starvation, the natives grow fat, living 'sumptuously' on native fruits, vegetables, honey and fish.

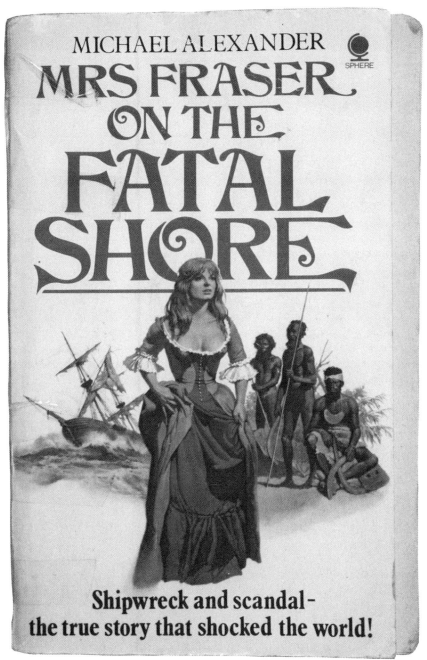

Figure 14 Cover illustration, Michael Alexander, *Mrs Fraser on the Fatal Shore*, 1976.
By courtesy of Michael Joseph, publisher.

In the character of Bracefell, Cook combines something of the naivety of a homespun bush philosopher with the knowledge of an ethnographer. Often the didacticism threatens the novel's farcical tendencies. For example, Bracefell describes his life thus:

> Life as a wild man suited me very well. It was much more pleasant and safer than anything I'd experienced before. There were no floggings and no cells for one thing. That wasn't because the aboriginals were lawless, it was just that the laws were so well worked out that it was almost impossible to break them. They had a very intricate social system that was part of the life of every member of the tribe and controlled who would marry whom . . . [etc., continued for two more pages, 113–15]

In opposition to the native way of life, Europeans are scoundrels, liars and cheats (except for David Bracefell): 'I suppose I'd been living with honest savages too long and I'd lost touch with the devious dishonesty of the white man' (127). The novel often points up the similarities between Aboriginal and European behaviour, as well as the differences. The Aboriginal and white men are alike in their venial pastimes: they lust after women; they derive pleasure from breaking taboos. But these are slight trespasses compared to the depravity of the white men. Although Fyans is 'a high priest bully' (23) and Fraser 'a pompous fat old bore of about sixty' (6), Bracefell saves his most serious condemnation for (the film version of) John Graham. He suggests towards the end of the novel that Graham not only spied on his mates but 'it is likely that he had taken [Bracefell's] place as Fyans's bed boy' (123) as well. Thus, Graham inherits the ultimate sign of otherness in this novel – a proclivity towards homosexuality. As Bracefell comments, 'Flogging, hanging, drawing and quartering . . . all were preferable to being raped by Fyans' (36). Thus, disguised by comedy and spoof, the novel displaces the fears about native cannibalism that had been expressed in nineteenth-century texts of Empire and the film's focus on Eliza's excessive sexuality, on to Graham, in typical Ocker fashion, with regard to overstated fears of homosexuality.

The Sodomising English

The novel and the film also construct homosexuality as the 'fate worse than death', worse even than the fantasies of interracial sexual violation reputedly faced by Eliza Fraser in the most sensationalised accounts. If one of the most common and emotively charged metaphors in the discourses of nationalism is the fantasy of homeland as the body of a woman threatened with violation, the worst insult to that enemy is sodomy. As the editors of *Nationalisms and Sexualities* claim, the representation of nationalism as a passionate, homosocial fraternity requires 'the identification, isolation and containment of male homosexuality'.[24] In the film and novel *Eliza Fraser* this threat is partially contained through a diversion of excessive sexuality on to Eliza Fraser, an insatiable and willing object of exchange between the men.

Fears and fantasies involving sodomy are not limited to Australia, although they recur with frequency in bush tales, anecdotes and jokes about 'outback' life (perhaps the pun has always been intended). One can trace within the discourses of nationalism in Australia a strong undercurrent of homophobia, generally discharged, as in the film and novel *Eliza Fraser*, against the British. It arises, however, not only in representations of sadistic British authorities like Foster Fyans in the days of penal settlement. There remains a lingering notion that Australia has 'played the patsy' for England throughout the course of its national development. This fear makes its way into films like *Breaker Morant* and *Gallipoli*.[25] It was evident, as well, in negotiations which took place in the past decade between Australia and Great Britain concerning who would meet the bill to clean up Maralinga (a vast tract of land in northern South Australia which was used in the 1950s by the British for atomic weapons testing, resulting in massive contamination of the land and massive dislocation and health problems for Aborigines living in the area).[26] The latent threat of sodomy (this time projected onto Aborigines as imagined aggressors of innocent white Australians) has emerged as an aspect of the national hysteria generated in response to the High Court's Mabo decision of 1992. The decision guaranteed Aboriginal and Torres Strait Island people limited rights to native title of Crown lands which they have constantly occupied or to which they have maintained an ongoing affiliation. The media quickly picked up the fears of white citizens, which were expressed as licence for Aborigines to lay claim to 'our own back yards', actions which would make Australia 'look bad' in the eyes of the world. These often reiterated phrases may displace the site of penetration from the male behind to the back garden but they barely mask the unconscious terror which the Mabo decision evoked for many white Australians – that they would be sodomised not by the British from afar, but by Aborigines in their own back yards.

Behind the rhetoric one detects the fantasy of a servile national body subject to penetration by its foes. This fantasy, which emerges from Australia's past in relation to British colonial authority, now affects white, neo-colonial relations towards Aboriginal people. In the recent media hysteria, however, Aborigines are positioned as the potential sodomisers of innocent, white Australians in this battle over ownership of the land. What is ironic is that these same newspapers, which now print letters expressing irrational fears of invasion of 'our own back yards', a decade ago defended the rapacious interests of the logging and mining companies and their incursions into Aboriginal lands and sacred sites – actions which required the intervention of the national government to contain. Those campaigns, which saw the Franklin River area of Tasmania, Kakadu National Park and Fraser Island become listed as World Heritage areas, were fought and won

rhetorically as battles amongst white men to protect and defend a com-
monly-owned land from environmental rape. Within a white Australian
erotics of nationalism, the battle lines have generally been drawn between
British (or more recently American or Japanese) aggressors and white Australian defenders of the land represented as a feminised body. Imagining
Aborigines as an aggrandising enemy to the body politic may seem new, but
versions of this representation of Aborigines (as the monstrous other) have
circulated within the narratives of nationhood since early colonial times. At
the same time, the fantasy counteracts more recent representations of Aborigines as sacred custodians of the land. Both forms of representation emerge
from Eurocentric frameworks of understanding and white settler anxieties
concerning national identity; both make 'their' problem 'our' problem,
'their' anger at white colonial dispossession 'our' terror of loss of face in the
eyes of the world. These eroticised narratives are not, of course, the only
mode of media representation. But they have the powerful effect of invoking
irrational fears. They are recirculated often enough to signal an ongoing
crisis of national affiliations and identities.

Overall, Cook's novel, like the Burstall–Williamson film, presents another
set of irreconcilable contradictions in its construction of race, class and gender categories. The novel gestures towards an Ocker brand of Australian
nationalism with its anti-British, anti-authority stance; at the same time it
accedes to the codes of middle-class conventionality. It represents the underdog as hero; at the same time it virtually excludes women, except as objects
of masculine desire. It sets up an affinity between Aboriginal life and convict
culture; at the same time it turns Aborigines into clowning mimics – almost
like 'us', but never quite the same. It provides a comic and farcical account
bearing virtually no relation to the dramatic historical event; yet for a
late-twentieth-century audience it is the way many Australians know 'Eliza
Fraser', if they know her at all.

Eliza Fraser and Australian Nationalism

Narrative supplements and comes to stand in the place of an event. The 'real'
Eliza Fraser cannot be rescued from these narratives, although they attract
their readers and viewers with their guises of history. Furthermore, history,
or academic knowledge, cannot be separated from mass or popular knowledge. Both forms of knowledge circulate together and reinforce each other
within different domains of cultural life. In these domains, 'Eliza Fraser'
becomes a locus for new ideological representations of Australian nationalism. The 1970s versions, which made a legend of the Eliza Fraser story,
reiterate several recurring preoccupations: in each of them Mrs Fraser's
sexuality is central. In each, the question 'Did she or didn't she?' arises: did
she have sex with the 'Chief' and/or her rescuer? In each, the indigenous
people provide an exotic context for a romance between the lost woman and

her underdog rescuer-hero. In terms of the dynamics of fear/desire, each of the texts exoticises the woman and the Aboriginal other and fetishises the body as a site of excess. Each turns the story into romance which enables the legend to rescue the convict as the underdog anti-hero of Australian nationalism. Many of the 1970s versions of the Eliza Fraser story also romanticise the 'primitive' in modernist terms and engage in fantasies of the penetration/ incorporation which call attention to the unstable boundaries of national identity. All promote the continued circulation of ideas about otherness within a variety of white masculine, neo-colonial contexts.

It is remarkable that the first revival of twentieth-century interest in the Eliza Fraser story occurred within a narrow band of time, between 1969 and 1976. Through drama, film, art and fiction, the event in Australia has become a part of an emerging nationalism associated in the early 1970s with the Whitlam era in politics. Within an international sphere it can be located as a part of the emerging discourses of post-colonialism and feminism, although the texts themselves also can be read as neo-colonial and anti-feminist accounts of national life which mask the implications of power and difference, as this analysis has suggested. The 1970s were a time of changing social relations between the sexes, and changing power relations between colonial, neo-colonial and post-colonial societies, colonised and colonising peoples. Yet Eliza Fraser, in her various forms, is seldom constructed as a hero or spokesperson for the dispossessed. Even when imagined as a figure who can broach the dangerous boundaries between white and Aboriginal culture, upper and lower class affiliations, nature and culture, reason and the instincts, she also continues to signify an older order of feminine difference. She is a troublesome other: quarrelsome, indulgent, overbearing and difficult in Alexander's history; sensual, alien, animal-like and tied to nature in Nolan's paintings; lusty, duplicitous, bold and fickle in Williamson and Burstall's film and Cook's novel. White's and Brink's constructions of the woman as boundary rider who transgresses cultural divisions and ultimately confounds them are more complex in their nationalist and modernist universalising terms. But they are equally insistent on the woman's sexuality, her instinctual nature, her links to the physical world. Except for the farcical film and novel, all reconstructions depict her as a betrayer of men.

These retellings and repetitions of the Eliza Fraser story occurred at a time when the women's movement was exerting considerable force within an international arena; when women's demands for political, social and economic equality were visible and widely reported; and when feminism began to challenge masculine perspectives, including those which link women to nature and men to culture. Yet, with the possible exception of Barbara Blackman's libretto, no feminist historian, artist, writer or critic took up the event. This is not to suggest that feminist interpretations favourable to Mrs Fraser would have escaped the discursive categories which locate Woman (and women) within masculine discourses, although they might have inverted or challenged them; nor that Eliza Fraser could ever be an easy heroine for our times, bound as she was by her own upper-class and racially charged colonial attitudes. The question here is not one of truth, but of who has the authority to speak, on behalf of whom and in what specific historical contexts. Her links with British colonial authority may have provided an obvious obstacle for Australian feminist writers addressing a nationalist tradition. But it is curious that no one, in Australia or abroad, attempted to present the story with a 1970s-style feminist hero. The materials which could have been used to fashion a feminist epic lay dormant. They include the story of a woman endowed with courage and fortitude who suffered extreme privations, including shipwreck, starvation, the birth and drowning of her child, the loss of her possessions, the shame and hardships of her own captivity, the death by spearing of her husband which she witnessed, numerous fatalities by other crew members, various forms of personal and sexual exploitation and possibly rape – and survived. But, with the exception of Barbara Blackman's short libretto, there are no feminist versions. On the contrary, the extant representations of Eliza Fraser and the shipwreck of the *Stirling Castle* reassert a femininity firmly inscribed within masculine systems of representation. Further, they tell 'her' story on 'his' behalf.

If one moves beyond feminist positions in regard to personal identity, further issues arise. The reiterated theme of betrayal in the male versions of the Eliza Fraser story calls attention to the ways in which Woman or the 'feminine' functions within discourses of otherness. Within the symbolic registers of language, woman is different from man/the masculine self (and thus inferior), or similar to man/the masculine self (and thus his complement). But she also signifies, within an imaginary and psychic realm for both men and women, the Maternal: she is an imaginary figure which represents the illusion of cosmic unity, the bliss of the pre-social mother–child union without division. Debased for being different from man (on whom he projects his fears) or reduced to his complement, his mirror image, she is also idealised to the degree that she allows access to fantasies of maternal bliss. One might posit that the inability for either men or women to achieve that desired state of unity signified by maternal bliss gives rise to and reinforces the theme of woman's betrayal. The feminine as a transgressive category in Western language and culture blurs the distinctions between self and other, inside and outside, the known and the unfamiliar. This highly ambivalent figuration leads to associations of Woman/women with duality, duplicity and, finally, betrayal. This theme is then played out within the discourses of Christianity, the structures of psychoanalysis, the quest motifs of romanticism, and the universalising myths of modernism, as well as the narratives of Empire and nation.

Taken together, these various representations of the Eliza Fraser story partake of mobile and fluid psychological, mythical, religious and political tendencies within an international context as well as an Australian national context. One effect is to resist the changing currents of history and reassert an ideology of white, male dominance and female submission within a British colonial and neo-colonial tradition. At the same time, these representations indulge the reader and viewer in one of the most significant fantasies of modern times. They depict a fantasy of Woman as a means of man's access to the essential, the eternal, to the attainment of a cosmic oneness through sexuality. The texts and paintings engage in a contradictory rhetoric of control of the body/politic and a desire for a dissolution of boundaries. The 1970s emanations of the Eliza Fraser legend, like other fantasies of a primitive or primal fantasies of pre-social wholeness, both 'test and affirm man's need to maintain separation, difference and control as attributes of masculinity',[27] and of his ('our') affiliations to national life. 'Eliza Fraser', then, can be read as a complex and contradictory category of meaning within national life. Her figuration slides between the boundaries of the psychic and social self. It reinforces, while it also challenges, the relationship between new settlers and the indigenous population. The legend, as well, makes visible the symbolic and sexual battleground in Australia between Ockers and the establishment left, straight and gay politics, popular and 'high' culture – and it can be adapted to question the boundaries between them. If one registers these multiple readings and possible positions, the various Eliza Fraser narratives confound and finally collapse the dichotomous understandings of culture in terms of familiar binary divisions: dominant/ marginal, universalist/nationalist, neo-colonial/post-colonial, masculine/ feminist, European/Aboriginal or radical/reactionary. Once one abandons the binaries as a structuring principle of analysis, attention can shift to an understanding of how the religious, the historical, the artistic, the political, the literary and the popular renditions can uphold and also unsettle cultural images and beliefs.

    In the last decade cultural commentators have begun to examine these issues again.[28] They suggest that narratives contain inherent contradictions which make it impossible for one to take up *a* position, either for or against them. Multiple positions and multiple readings are always possible, even demanded, if one is to register the conflicting network of power relations which constitute each text and the possible contexts of its reception. Each version of the story arises out of its particular historical setting and its specific locale. Its meaning can never be settled. Post-modern critique teases out the contradictions, examining what it is possible to say both within and against a particular reading, framework, discourse or tradition, in other words to unsettle the hegemonic project of modernist history. The consequences of the imperialist rupture which brought about the present (post)colonial condition also permeate our reception of the Eliza Fraser legend and its place(s) in national life.

CHAPTER 10

Oppositional Voices: Contemporary Politics and the Eliza Fraser Story

The most recent approaches to the Eliza Fraser story by artists in the 1990s in Australia give evidence of significant changes in attitudes and beliefs about what it means to be an Australian. The latest versions attest to a final collapse of faith in what has always been a fragile master narrative of Anglo-Australian nationalism, a collapse evident in the production of images and representations during the 1988 Bicentennial. Not only did the year signal a renegotiation of power relationships and notions of national identity between Aboriginal and non-Aboriginal Australians, it also prompted a new awareness of Australia's relationship to its northern neighbours. The fragile boundaries of identity were contested within both national and international arenas – and the mythical 'Eliza Fraser' story entered these circuits of meaning. She re-emerges in the work of Anglo-Australians in the 1990s in the form of a Noh play and a documentary film – in which 'Eliza' becomes the repository for white Australian guilt about its past relationship to black Australians. These new ways of presenting the Eliza Fraser story reinvent the categories of 'Aborigine' and 'Asian' in relation to white Australian culture. The most recent versions of the story are informed by, even as they transform, those of the past. In the Noh play and the film, the imagined ancient spiritual wisdom of Aboriginal and Oriental (and specifically, traditional Japanese) cultures fuse to provide a pre-text for national reconciliation. At the same time, presentations of a new 'Eliza' construct images of the nation with reference to a new Other – in this case an imagined community of racially united Australians juxtaposed against the country's Asian (and specifically Japanese) neighbours. The Anglo-Australian meanings associated with the categories 'Aboriginal' and 'Asian' remain unsettled and ambivalent.

The ambivalent and unsettled nature of the meanings of nationhood became publicly visible from the start of the Bicentennial in 1988. In the early dawn of Australia Day, more than 20,000 Aboriginal demonstrators and their supporters gathered from around the country to march through the streets of Sydney in order to protest against the official opening celebrations. In opposition to an official Australian desire to promote the day as a celebration of white settlement, they mourned it as the onset of the invasion of Aboriginal land. The marchers 'intruded' on the space of the official celebrants who had congregated at Botany Bay to re-enact the landing of the First Fleet, another contested 'first-contact' event. For many the protest, captured by television in the day-long coverage of Australia Day and beamed across the country, staged the end of at least one phase of the White Man's Story in Australia. No longer could the rhetoric of nationalism be contained within facile narratives of Australian identity played out as a family romance between England and Australia, a mother country and her native son, against the backdrop of an uninhabited land.

One of the more memorable attempts at image production to appear in response to the Bicentennial was the song 'Celebration of a Nation', promoted through a four-part serialised television clip which presented a variety of sanitised Australians singing the jingoistic song; another notable image was the red, yellow and black bumper sticker which read: 'White Australia has a Black History' which proliferated on cars, billboards, T-shirts, office doors and in homes across the country. The television promotion presented Australia as an exuberant, youthful outdoor culture, proud of its national indulgences (sun and surf, booze and beach girls, pristine outback landscapes) and tourist images (Ayers Rock, the Sydney Harbour Bridge and Opera House); boastful of its national unity in multicultural diversity (Australo-Asian fashion designers, Australo-Greek comedians, Aboriginal sportsmen, wheelchair athletes, the 'others' either singled out in close-up camera shots or discreetly placed on the margins of the singing throng). Critics of the Bicentennial feared that the promotion of such images might presage a chauvinistic, year-long, American-style festival of national narcissism, although the controversial bumper sticker confounded such an easy reading. Some Anglo-Australians continued to respond positively to the naive nationalism mirrored in the theme song. For others the year turned out to be a time to reflect critically on white Australia's black history: the 200th anniversary of white invasion and occupation of a land with a native population which had at least a 50,000-year history, juxtaposed against a contemporary population of conflicting and heterogeneous peoples. Within contemporary Australian culture, both Aboriginal and non-Aboriginal peoples are reconstructing the terms of their own and the nation's identity. Reciprocal self-representations emanating from within the two cultures bring multiple sets of understandings and imaginings to bear on what it means to be Australian. Each emanates from different historical and cultural locations; each is riddled with its own internal contradictions.

Subsequent events attest to the changing nature of power relationships between Aboriginal and non-Aboriginal Australians. One relates to Prime Minister Bob Hawke's Bicentennial promise of a Treaty of Reconciliation with Aboriginal and Torres Strait Island peoples, a promise which depends upon the efforts of the descendants of both settler and indigenous cultures to respond to each other ethically and morally, beyond the white Australian models of identity and difference. Another is the 1992 Mabo decision of the High Court on native land title, which overturned the doctrine of *terra nullius* which held that Australia had been empty, unowned and unoccupied prior to the arrival of the white colonisers. The decision has significance for a variety of reasons, not the least of which is that it acknowledges the validity of indigenous knowledges, oral traditions, kinship structures, law, and ongoing relationships with the land.

Another aspect of the Bicentennial was the insistence by the Prime Minister that Australia was geographically an Asian-Pacific nation and needed to identify culturally in these terms. From the outset it was clear that the motivations for a geopolitical redefinition were more economic than geographic or cultural. With the increasing dominance of Japan on the Australian stock exchange, the emergence of profitable new markets and trade links for Australia in South-East Asia, and the growing importance of Australia as a tourist destination for Asian travellers, Australia could no longer afford to maintain a 'Yellow Peril' mentality in relation to its northern neighbours. Business symposia, trade delegations, research collaboration, cultural exchanges and overseas student initiatives flourished, designed to increase understanding and to diminish irrational fears of 'Asia' within Australia and also to presage a greater economic presence for Australia within the Asian-Pacific region.

The push from Canberra to imagine Australia as a part of an Asian-Pacific community signalled further challenges to culturally produced meanings of nationhood. Annette Hamilton has studied the contradictory and ambivalent ways in which both Aborigines and Asians have been constructed within what she calls a National Imaginary.[1] She considers how those notions impact upon Australia's present economic and political realities. For her, the National Imaginary represents 'the means by which contemporary social orders . . . produce . . . images of themselves against others. An image of the self implies at once an image of the other, against which it can be distinguished'.[2] She attends to the ways in which contemporary images are informed by those of the past and become commodified and exchanged both within and outside national boundaries. Those commodified images, or projections of the nation's fears and desires, have allowed Anglo-Australians to neutralise their fears of difference through a multitude of imaginary appropriations of the other; which then seduce their producers into a trap of surface appearances. Hamilton suggests that the particularly fragile nature of white Australian identity, based on a short history of settlement, makes notions of nationhood particularly problematic within both national and international arenas.

In this book I have traced some of the complex and ambivalent Anglo-Australian appropriations and commodifications of images of Aboriginal otherness in relation to the past and present emanations of the Eliza Fraser story. Aboriginal people were imagined as 'savages' and 'primitives' in response to nineteenth-century settler desires of colonisation and fears of failure; they were divided into categories of 'good' and 'bad', or true and unauthentic, traditional and detribalised, within a twentieth-century history of white settlement. They have also been represented, in terms of twentieth-century modernism's attractions to a primitive essence as one in harmony with nature and in contact with the spirit world, as mystical – the repository of an ancient wisdom.

Australian constructions of 'Asians' are similarly complex and ambivalent. Nineteenth- century representations of the monstrous and devilish Asian of the gold-fields underwrites newer versions of the dangerous neighbours to the north who threaten to penetrate the fragile boundaries of the modern nation-state. The imaginary construction of the monstrous Asian, and specifically the Japanese, other reaches its peak in the aftermath of World War II, largely as a result of the bombing of Darwin and of Japanese atrocities suffered by Australian prisoners of war. Contemporary trends of Japanese economic investment in Australia prompt further unsettling fears of takeover in response to international economic and global forces which permeate the fragile boundaries of nationhood. Like Aboriginal resistance to frontier violence in the nineteenth century, the Asian presence also threatens notions of national identity, of secure masculinity, and it evokes fears for Anglo-Australians of failure, imagined as penetration/devourment. At the same time, the lure of the Asian as the mystical other beckons to those who desire an alternative Australian identity – an image promoted by 'new age' Australians scornful of the thin veneer of white Australian culture and disenchanted by the crass materialism and shallow secularism of contemporary bourgeois life. Hamilton, acknowledging that the nation's identity is changing and permeable, comments that although Aboriginal identifications might be incorporated into the nation's new sense of itself, Australians have been more circumspect in regard to their Asian others. Her optimistic predictions of Aboriginal identifications within a National Imaginary might be treated with some caution, however, given the obvious failure of Hawke's Treaty of Reconciliation and the hysteria generated by the media in response to the High Court's Mabo decision.

Allan Marett, the Noh *Eliza*

These changing cultural meanings and political realities have not been lost on the mythical Eliza Fraser. In 1989 Allan Marett, Senior Lecturer in Music at the University of Sydney, proposed and then produced an English version of a traditional, classical Japanese Noh play, *Eliza*, which was performed for students of Music and Theatre Studies at the University of Sydney before touring Japan. The program notes explain that the initial purpose of the undertaking was 'to allow students of Performance Studies, Music and Japanese to learn about Noh through participation, and to provide documentary materials for analysis by scholars and students'.[3] It is interesting that Marett chose the classical, ruling-class (samurai) dramatic form of the Noh play for his re-enactment of the Eliza Fraser story, rather than the more popular Kabuki, or the folk play from which Noh was derived. He represents 'Japan' to Australians through a particularly 'high' cultural form of Japanese drama. The production was made possible by the presence at the university of two visiting scholars from Japan, Richard Emmert and Akira Matsui, who trained the students in the techniques of movement, singing and instrumentation. Marett negotiated with the Adelaide Festival Centre Trust for a permanent loan to be made to the university of the Noh stage. The Festival Trust had commissioned its construction for a repertoire of Noh and Kyogen plays performed for the 1988 (Bicentennial) International Festival of Arts. These collaborative endeavours give evidence of the developing links between the arts, education and trade in fostering a new awareness of Australia's changing political realities.

The play *Eliza* was performed at the University of Sydney in 1989 as the third of three pieces. The first two introduced the audience to Noh theatre through abbreviated forms of Noh. One, *Maibayashi*, was a secular piece based on stories from the classical Japanese novel, *Tales of Genji*; the other, *Shimai*, was a traditional spiritual parable of enlightenment. As the program notes explain, the Australian play closely followed Noh conventions for text, music and dance. The notes also provide a summary of the ways in which the Eliza Fraser story has continued to circulate within Australia through the contemporary discourses of prose and poetry, film and music theatre. The notes also frame the story within the structure of a traditional Noh play; and they introduce a new guise for Eliza Fraser, this time as a bearer of white Australian guilt for the sins of the past.

> Like many Japanese Noh plays it was written against a backdrop of a number of literary and other sources. Australian novelists, composers, poets, film makers and ethnographers have treated the Eliza Fraser story in a variety of ways. Two major themes emerge, however: one, which sees Eliza as a victim – 'the poor white woman at the hands of the savages' – acts as a metaphor for our insecurities in the face of a hostile environment and an incomprehensible indigenous culture which is seen as threatening to 'civilised values'; a second which treats Eliza as a visionary figure – one who has been granted access to the spiritual power of the country by the indigenous custodians of the traditions of wisdom. This dichotomy is the source of the structure of Eliza.

Like many Japanese Noh plays it falls into two acts: the first focuses on a character trapped in the form of a ghost as the result of past deeds or mistaken views; in the second, the character, freed from its ghostly existence, is able to appear in its true form. Here, in Act 1, Eliza is trapped in the form of a ghost by the myth of Eliza-as-victim. Only when this myth is challenged is she freed (in Act 2) to testify to the true nature of her experiences among the Aborigines of Fraser Island.

Thus, the Noh *Eliza* becomes a site of reconciliation for the ambivalent ways in which fear and desire have motivated contradictory representations of Aborigines.

In the first act of the play, an old woman (or *shite*, main male character wearing the mask of a woman's face) appears before a traveller (*waki*, secondary character). Identifying herself only as a 'teller of stories', she emerges from a Hyde Park tent and tells of Eliza Fraser's captivity amongst savages. However, exaggerations begin to creep into her story, and the *waki*, who had been warned of her lies by a previous emanation of Eliza, begins to doubt her. The story-teller confesses to the *waki* that at first her stories were 'true' but as the public declared her 'mad' she began to embroider fictions to attract the sideshow crowds. When she told the truth, she was declared mad; when she constructed wild and brutal fantasies, she was considered sane. The she-ghost wants the *waki* to release her from the worldly attachment, the world of lies, which binds and punishes her. At the end of Act One, after the *waki* challenges the veracity of her stories, her 'front of falsehoods' fails and she disappears.[4] In the second act a youthful Eliza returns, a *shite* dressed in golden brocade robes and wearing the mask of a young woman, to perform a 'true' version of her visionary, spiritual experience on Fraser Island. To a corroboree with Aboriginal songs and rhythms Eliza becomes one with the dance of a totemic figure, Eaglehawk, and 'a single stick beat lights the way' out of the ground of lies the white ghosts have been compelled to tell. The play ends with the evocation of the ancient spiritual power of Aboriginal wisdom realised through song and dance.

As the notes indicate, 'Eliza' is a legendary figure brought to life by the stories which have been told about her in the nineteenth and twentieth centuries, stories which portray her either as victim or visionary. But 'Eliza' as a Noh play character is a figure who must confront the ghosts of her past, her worldly attachments, and her own 'past deeds or mistaken views' which cause her soul to walk the earth without rest. She must claim responsibility for her deeds and make restitution (even though her imaginary character and her deeds have been textually constructed with reference to the many layers of her historical and artistic representation). The 'Eliza' in this play *is* her history, her discursive production in Australia. On another level, 'she', or the accretion of 'lies' which white culture has perpetrated in relation to its rendering of first-contact stories, is 'us' – the personification of white settler culture in the form of a woman, sinning, untrustworthy, wily, deceitful and treacherous, who is capable of transformation. Through the play she/'we' undergo a journey of transformation. We gain enlightenment through a rendition of her story within a 'strange' Japanese cultural tradition with its own layering of class and gendered meanings. Because she is a legendary figure, she represents to the audience, at least in a transposition of Japanese religious and secular aesthetics, an aspect of themselves on the road to enlightenment. Although the spiritual dimensions of this 'lesson' would be reduced for most Australians by the unfamiliar aesthetics of the play and its explicit teaching purpose, the play conveys a strong and unmistakable moral message. It introduces an ethical dimension to the Eliza Fraser story which had not been present before. Despite the Japanese style, form and appearance of the stark stage, strange rhythms, and male actors in traditional masks and costumes who sing male and female parts to the accompaniment of a chorus with flute and drum, the play preys upon the conscience of white Australians. No doubt the play transmitted a telling message about Australia to a Japanese audience when it was performed abroad. At the same time, the evocation of 'Aboriginality' in a play which includes no Aboriginal performers, presented to a Japanese audience which itself has an imperialist history which has resulted in the exclusion of indigenous peoples from its National Imaginary, contains many cross-cultural ironies.

The figure of a woman as treacherous deceiver of men is a traditional theme in both Buddhism and in Japanese literature. In terms of Buddhist teachings, women cannot be truly liberated from their feminine nature; they must be reborn as men or sexually transformed at death.[5] At the close of the play, this Eliza is transformed into the male spirit of a totemic bird. There are a number of transformations being effected at the symbolic level: in Japanese terms, woman is transformed into man and walking ghost into primordial spirit; in Australian terms, a guilty white settler culture is transformed by and into the spiritual wisdom of indigenous peoples and reborn as a Dreamtime spirit. In both traditions, male fears and desires produce constructions of deceitful women (the debased 'other' in 'us') and imagine her ('our') spiritual and cultural transformation through the wisdom of the Buddhist priest or the spirit power of indigenous peoples. Curiously, 'we' become the mystical other of our imaginings. In response to similar themes in other contemporary constructions of white Australia's Aboriginal heritage, Hamilton comments:

> This posits the possibility of Aboriginal identity as THE Australian identity of the future, something not chosen by us but imposed on us by the land itself – perhaps, even, the product of a shared Dreaming. What the Aboriginal response to this new negotiation of meaning might be, as it enters into the circuits of cultural exchange is anyone's guess. One wonders if they really need such blessings.[6]

Some Aboriginal commentators have responded, vocally if not often in print, to white appropriations of the Dreaming, forcefully maintaining that white culture has *no* right to appropriate this material.

When the itinerant traveller ventures his opinion about the lies of Eliza Fraser, he speculates about the reason for her lies. He concludes that she was, in fact, a visionary with a spiritual attachment to the country and her journey was one of 'profound self-discovery'. That is, Patrick White's visionary Ellen becomes a Buddhist Eliza seeking transcendental wisdom. But like Ellen, her dreamtime visions were out of step with the times. Rather than be declared mad, this Eliza fed the fantasies of a public eager for her stories of savagery, 'just as we', the *waki* tells the audience, 'entangled in such myths of savagery, cut off from the wisdom of this land, are condemned to live as ghosts in this country'. By linking the story to treacherous women in both Western and Eastern traditions, the play continues to dramatise the symbolic, psychic and cultural treachery of women. In Noh plays there is often the suggestion that women in earlier times had shamanic or spiritual power, before their debasement; that debasement occurred partially through Buddhist teachings which equate desire and all of its earthly attachments with the feminine.[7] The dualistic nature of women's spiritual power and debasement are familiar within Christian teachings, as well. On a number of levels, then, 'we' also seem to be entangled in multiple myths of 'our' own construction.

Gillian Coote's Documentary Film

Although Marett's play may have had a limited impact within Australia due to its specific audience and didactic teaching purposes, knowledge of the perspective it conveyed expanded considerably when Gillian Coote took up the theme and form and used them as a framework for her documentary film, 'Island of Lies'. The film screened as a part of the Australian Broadcasting Corporation series *True Stories* in September 1991.[8] In the film Coote, as journeyer (*waki*), travels up the New South Wales coast to Fraser Island, tracing along the way the suppressed history of Aboriginal genocide in Australia's colonial history. The documentary opens with an invocation of noble wisdom from the Roman classical tradition, the following quotation from the philosopher Seneca:

> Why does no man confess his vices?
> Because he is yet in them:
> It is for a waking man
> to tell his dreams.

The epigraph is followed by a soundtrack narration accompanied by the music and visuals of the opening scenes from Marett's Noh play, creating a set of bizarre, complex and exotic cross-cultural reference points for this retelling of Australian history. In addition to the overlay of Noh music and episodic interludes, the dominant narrative of the film places 'Eliza' within an Australian nationalist discourse motivated by a Christian moral trajectory of sin, guilt, confession, redemption and reconciliation. 'Eliza lied about her knowledge of Aboriginal culture,' Gillian told me. 'People who lie or evade knowledge are punished. We are like Eliza.'

'Island of Lies' provides the viewer with a relentless and powerful examination of the blind spots of white Australian history, occlusions which obstruct the memory of white massacres of Aboriginal people. Early in the film the narrator provides questions which will guide the traveller on her quest: 'Will she encounter the ghosts of [white Australian] history? What secrets lie buried in the land? Who has the courage to break the silence? And will we be liberated by these encounters?' Coote employs a range of primary source materials used as 'natural evidence' to call forth a counter-memory of white settlement. These include visual and oral references to abandoned Aboriginal middens, hinges from fence posts used by settlers to trap Aboriginal groups prior to slaughter, the remains of skeletal bones buried in places with names like Slaughterhouse Creek, documentary film and oral histories of abusive practices towards Aboriginal children from the mission stations, anthropological maps containing the names and locations of Aboriginal territories obliterated by white surveyors' maps and replaced by crass commercial development.

Although the film unsettles notions of a unified (white) national identity, it also evokes some deep (and not always counter-hegemonic) emotional responses. The film chastises the crass materialism of contemporary Australian culture by appropriating aspects of Aboriginal and Japanese culture in order to reconcile contemporary white Australians to their violent frontier past. This process deserves closer analysis. As Coote drives north along the coastal road, the camera pans across a landscape which shows the signs of a 'progressive' history of white settlement – it moves from city to a 'pristine' wilderness to logging camps and lumber yards, electrical transmitters and power plants, as well as patches of fenced farmland. After passing a sign of new American capital investment in Australia, the ubiquitous McDonald's Restaurant with its giant figure of Ronald McDonald standing within the golden arches, Coote remarks that the land, no longer sacred, is now 'just another commodity available to the highest bidder'. Viewers are invited to ponder this remark as they watch a number of pointed visuals. The ancient land and its sacred origins have been overtaken by the debased remnants of modern capitalism. Soon the spectre of new forms of Japanese economic exploitation of Australian resources replaces the previous marks of white settler greed and American enterprise and exploitation. The first visual sign is a billboard advertisement directed to Japanese tourists for Hope

Island Resort, quickly replaced by another Japanese advertisement for Southern Cross Duty Free shops. The company name and the five stars of the Southern Cross are all that is readable in English on the massive board; the rest is in Japanese lettering. This scene is overtaken by a shot of a pagoda-style, neon-lit, Chinese take-away shop, then a directional map in Japanese which includes an arrow and the English phrase 'you are here' in the corner. Who is the you in these (un)familiar Asian-Australian settings? These film edits are followed by a scene of a young Japanese couple carrying a Ken Done shopping bag and walking by a real estate office. Beside them stands a kerb-side hoarding filled with Japanese writing with the English phrase 'we'll look after you' printed boldly at the bottom of the board. This is followed by a shot of a real estate display window featuring photographs of houses for sale in the price range of $200,000 to $700,000, with descriptions in Japanese, in case the Australian viewer wondered what was being promoted on the kerb-side chalkboard.

While other readings are possible and will be discussed below, this over-determined representation of Australia as a land, once sacred, which is now debased by crass commercial concerns imagines the land as a prostitute, 'available to the highest bidder'. The spectacle which accompanies this narrative leaves no doubt as to who the highest bidder is these days. These apparently casual narrative and visual references in the film have significant effects. They work both to provoke and to contain the threat of national/racial difference within contemporary Australia. If we remember Benedict Anderson's understanding of nationalism as an affiliation imagined as 'a deep, horizontal comradeship', the affiliation developed in and by the film is a comradeship between white and Aboriginal people standing together against a common enemy of foreign (and mostly Japanese) investment. Whereas novels and newspapers provided the materials which could produce affinities between peoples to create a sense of national unity in the nineteenth century, film and television are largely responsible for the production of this effect today. In this case, however, 'The People' is imagined as a united white and Aboriginal community, purged of racial differences. Yet this focus on national unity still requires an other to establish its identity. National identity cannot exist without difference. In the film the threat of difference (which threatens the boundaries of 'Australian' identity) is deflected onto the Japanese, the enemy to the nation in the forms of foreign investment and tourism. At the same time the film paradoxically pays homage to classical Japanese culture and the effacacy of Buddhist philosophies for a contemporary Australian audience.

At an earlier moment in the film, when Coote was talking to Len Payne about the Myall Creek massacre of Aborigines by white settlers, the camera had lingered on another site of Japanese terror. This time it was an imposing advertisement for a Charles Bronson film, *Kinjite*, meaning 'prohibited' or 'forbidden' in Japanese, and translated as *Forbidden Subjects* in English. The poster featured a dangerously alluring, nude woman (or an orientalist representation of Asian/Japanese type) lying prone across its lower border. Bronson stood above her, poised for action and clutching a revolver. Red Japanese writing beside the two figures ran the length of the poster's right side, announcing the film's Japanese title. This over-sized billboard film advertisement was featured on the side wall of the historical museum at Myall Creek to which Len had taken Gillian. The museum had refused to display the fence posts and hinges Len had found on his property, shameful artefacts of the white massacre of 1838. But its walls give evidence of other, less suppressed, external threats to national identity. And as Len and Gillian discuss a settler history of land appropriation at the entrance to the museum, the camera pans back from a close-up to mid-perspective to allow the bold red lettering of a sign behind them to come into focus. The sign reads 'Now open': does it refer to the museum – or the country? There are a number of 'forbidden subjects' which trouble this film. Some are well explored; others seem to do their work through visual cues which are best left understated.

'Island of Lies' also includes 'authentic' first-person accounts by white and Aboriginal speakers. They are mainly those of an Aboriginal woman, Ethel Richards, and a white man, Rollo Petrie, both descendants of Fraser Island families. As the film progresses, the two become emblems of a hope for a national reconciliation. Ethel and Rollo recollect to Coote their own memories and relate their knowledge of their family's history in the region, much of which has been silenced by settlers' fears. In terms of the Noh play which frames the film, they stand in the place of the ghost of Eliza Fraser and the cultural destruction that she/white settlement set in motion. The place of the Noh pilgrim priest is occupied by Coote, the film-maker. Like him, she finds 'no starting place, no places of pilgrimage' to trace an Aboriginal pre-contact history behind the facade of a Captain Cook monument or the place name, referred to ironically as her point of departure: 'Kurnell: Birthplace of a Nation'. The white people she encounters during her travels represent the present-day emanations of ghosts, like Eliza Fraser, for whom 'the front of falsehoods fails'. Their first-hand accounts lend an aura of authenticity to the film which gives it its oppositional political power. These oral recollections provide the viewer with incontrovertible evidence of a shameful past. At the same time, the local informants are woven into the symbolic texture of the film so that they become constituted as figures in a Christian morality play as well as seekers of enlightenment with reference to Noh traditions.

Coote journeys to three locations where Aboriginal massacres occurred in the nineteenth century: the three rivers district of New South Wales near Armidale, Myall Creek, and Fraser Island. In each place she encounters local descendants prepared to confront the ghosts of the past. The stories they tell of a settlement history of wanton murders and the retribution meted out by locals to white 'traitors' who try to tell the stories are, in the words of one settler, 'dreadful beyond expression'. His comment echoes in reverse the refrain from the nineteenth-century 'mournful verses' concerning the treatment of survivors of the *Stirling Castle*: 'To describe the feeling of these poor souls / is past the art of man.' Here, however, the 'poor souls' are the Aboriginal survivors, not the white colonial 'victims'.

The film works on the audience on several levels through its narrative elements, visual and aural cues and filmic techniques. It evokes both rational and emotive responses. Musical rhythms, guttural sounds, and songs, including several traditional Badtjala lullabies, and visual scenes from the Noh play, punctuate the documentary. They convey to a white audience a tone of high seriousness and ancient, brooding melancholy, accentuated by the sounds and rhythms of the didgeridoo as well as Aboriginal lullabies and hunting songs. Thus, two ancient cultures fuse into a primordial past: Aboriginal precontact culture and its imagined Japanese equivalent. Neither is accessible; both emanate from white, Western and Orientalist versions of a projected past fashioned as the ground for a future Australian community. The doublings redouble, enmeshing viewers in another return of the repressed (here, an emergence of white guilt over unacknowledged, unresolved frontier violence). What is strange (the Noh play, traditional Aboriginal culture) becomes knowable. What is redeemed (white Australians through the acknowledgment of the Noh play, Christian and Aboriginal senses of the sacred) provides the vehicle for absolving 'us' of a national guilt. That guilt is absolved through a series of binary constructions of sameness (identity) and difference. The film pays respect to the old traditional forms of Japanese culture and religion, even if they are represented through the ruling-class, samurai, cultural form of the Noh play. But the film also refers throughout to troubling signs in present-day Australia of an economically dominant and intrusive Japanese presence. The presence of an old (economically dominant) white Australian settler culture is equally troubling, but Rollo Petrie, the new white Australian figure of reconciliation, represents a redeeming quality for the nation, which now has a new Asian enemy. The redemption is imagined with reference to the enlightenment motif of Noh drama; at the same time, 'Japan' replaces the white oppressor as the enemy to national unity. Black and white citizens together forge a new community against the (suppressed) threat of a new invader. Thus, white viewers can project their guilt (which results from an admission of past exploitative and 'racist' actions) on to a modern, economically rapacious, Japan. But the suppressed filmic text enacts a new displacement of white national guilt. The guilt is re-enacted through a racist discourse in relation to modern Japanese investment, a division of ancient (good) and modern (bad) cultures, and a further appropriation of selected and modified Japanese and Aboriginal images to represent 'ourselves'.

'Lest We Forget'

More suppressions and displacements are transposed on to this tale of
Australia with reference to its Anzac Day rituals which are celebrated on two
markedly different occasions in the film. Anzac Day features in two segments
of 'Island of Lies'. In one, townsfolk gather for a typical Anzac Day ritual. As
the gathering sings the stirring anthem 'Lest We Forget', the camera pans to
the crowd, singling out an Aboriginal woman in an Akubra-style hat to which
is pinned the Union Jack and an Anglo-Australian woman bearing the badge
of reconciliation: 'White Australia has a Black History'. This scene is mirrored at the end of the film, when pilgrims gather to commemorate not
Anzac Day but the Myall Creek massacre in a similar ritualised celebration.
Again, both Aboriginal and non-Aboriginal mourners come together. But
this time the camera lingers on a white couple, a father and son, who stand
together, the father's hand resting on the son's shoulder. Together they
acknowledge Aboriginal deaths at the hands of white settlers. But within
nationalist mythologies Anzac Day valorises the sufferings of (white)
Australians in overseas wars. This symbolic celebration of manhood is a
significant myth of nation in which 'Japan' features as the avatar of violence
against white Australian soldiers overseas (although it should be remembered that Aboriginal soldiers also served in overseas wars – a fact largely
unacknowledged in nationalist accounts). In the ritual of reconciliation represented by the second Myall Creek ceremony, sorrow for Aboriginal people
suppresses reference to the ways in which Japan functions in traditional
Anzac Day rituals. The film suppresses a number of contradictory relations
between peoples from different racial, ethnic and cultural heritages. In the
terms of the film's nationalistic and Christian elements, the Myall Creek
celebrations represent all that has been forgotten or repressed, a past for
which the audience has not yet learned to mourn. The Myall Creek ceremony
signals a new departure for the nation, a new message to be passed down
symbolically from white father to son.

   The film also constructs a model of the classic quest by mythologising two
people: an Aboriginal woman, Ethel Richards, whose mother was descended
from the Badtjala people and who represents the remnants of the past; and a
white man, Rollo Petrie, the son of a white settler and industrialist,who represents the historical trajectory of White Australia. These two figures lend a
concrete historical drama to the film's quest motif. In the film, Gillian, the
pilgrim-traveller, approaches Ethel's present home in Brisbane, unsure
whether or not the Aboriginal woman will accompany the camera crew on
their journey north. To Gillian's delight, Ethel appears at the door. 'I've been
sick,' she says, 'so sick', as she envelops Gillian in a warm, maternal embrace.
She represents, in mythic terms, the sickness of 'true' country. The filmic
construction of this meeting underlines a strand of black/white loss within a

plot of reconciliation. Ethel is represented as an emanation of the ancient land, now reduced to the status of an itinerant Australian caught in then-etworks of white history. She piles her well-prepared sacks of blankets, parcels of food and clothing and assorted outback gear on to the pavement for Gillian to load into the four-wheel-drive vehicle. In humorous contrast to the plethora of ever-expanding parcels Ethel says, 'I can only travel light.' But on Fraser Island, and then again at Hervey Bay, she sheds the baggage of her hybrid heritage and is filmed running barefoot on the golden sands of static time. She becomes the shamanic figure of lost wisdom, the possessor of the holy grail – a vehicle for 'our' transformation and enlightenment.

Her companion on the journey is Rollo Petrie, an ageing, affable descend-ant of the original white settler family on Fraser Island, whose grandfather had been given land north of Brisbane to hold on behalf of the Undambi people. Rollo performs two roles – one as custodian of the Aboriginal land and the other as white settler. He defers his settler history to Ethel's ancient past. After the two have told their stories, he makes a pilgrimage into the rainforest to locate a satanay tree 'several thousand years old', which has miraculously escaped the loggers. He tells how he singled out this tree in his youth and always returns to it. He hopes to have his ashes spread under the tree after his death. On that sacred site, he reflects on the cultural and environmental destruction of the island and its people imposed by a brief but bloody history of white settlement. He stands in profile against the lush rainforest, his melancholic silence broken at last by the distinctive call of a whip-bird. The haunting sound parallels a familiar crack of the drum which punctuates the Noh play and aurally links the two ancient traditions, Abor-iginal and Japanese.

Later, as he and Gillian walk a rainforest track on Fraser Island, he reiter-ates the moral message of the film:

This was their country. Everything on it belonged to them and they belonged to it. We came on to a country and we think we own it and we take from it but we don't give back . . . We should have learned from them a little bit of the country or looking after our own country, [*pause*] looking after *the* country, not only our own country. No, I think it's very, very sad for us because we're losing this country. It's being undermined under our very noses. [*Noh whoop, and lingering drumbeat.*]

The call of the whip-bird, coupled with the Noh whoop and drumbeat, punctuates Rollo's reflections on the country which belongs to both white and Aboriginal peoples. These sounds fuse Ethel and Rollo, Anglo and Abor-iginal culture, Aboriginal and Japanese traditions into a vision of a sacred and desirable pre-colonial, pre-social world of harmony. The 'Japanese' effect of Noh music underscores his warning that 'we're losing this country'. At the same time, it sounds a new fear of foreignness; a sign that we will never escape our alienation/difference from ourselves.

The pause in Rollo's speech, when he says 'our own', and then corrects himself with '*the* country', is a significant moment in the film. At this moment, he assumes that Aboriginal and white people have equal claims to the land. The film suggests that they exist in the same time, space and history, which is white settler time, space and history.[9] The problem is that the time the film imagines is the progressive time of Western temporality; the space is the space of modern nationhood constructed both in the imaginary present and on the neo-colonial premise of difference. 'Ethel', now constructed as an atemporal emblem of Aboriginality (but through Noh, Arthurian quest motifs and Christian patterns of revelation), both is and is not in Western time, space – and history. That history of Australia was built on the notion of the land as *terra incognito, terra nullius* – unknown, untamed, unoccupied and open to the progressive mastery of colonisation. That process of colonisation relied upon the imagined absence of indigenous peoples, and also at the same time inscribed them in 'our' history as remnants of a static primordial past. Ethel's people were constructed as other to constitute 'Australia' within the history of the West. There is a slippage of meaning in the film, registered in part through Rollo's semantic alteration. This slippage reveals a gap, a disjunction between Ethel's story and Rollo's history, their separate and also interrelated heritage. Rollo shifts from the possessive pronouns 'their' and 'our own country' to the neutral article '*the*' country; in doing this he both acknowledges and occludes the nation's different pasts as he and the film text seek to include himself and Ethel, white and black Australians, in the 'deep, horizontal comradeship' of nation. This relatively minor speech act has enormous consequences. It smooths over contradictions, reconciles power relationships and disavows difference. If left to be explored, that disjunction might provide a site of interrogation where new histories of difference could emerge. Within the context of this film's narrative, the gap between 'Rollo' and 'Ethel' will be reconciled in an uneasy shuttle between a (historically determined) tainted present and a (timeless and inaccessible) sacred past (for him/'us', if not for her).

The way religion intrudes upon the stories of Ethel and Rollo is telling, given the moral and symbolic weight of the film. Rollo Petrie has no time for religion. He reports that the mission kids were 'flogged into submission', a tale concretised by his recollection of the scars on the back of Jindie, an Aboriginal companion of his youth. Jindie worked for and loved Rollo's mother, although she warned Mrs Petrie never to walk in front of her, fearing that her instinct for retaliation might lead her to harm the woman. Recounting the cruel and abusive treatment of Aborigines at the Mission, Rollo shakes his head in dismay and says, 'The missionaries have a lot to answer for.' In contrast, Ethel tells of how she loved to cook as an adolescent and had hopes of finding a job in a restaurant. She failed, being told that the business would suffer with the presence of a 'gin' behind the counter. She and her family lived in shanties on the edge of town, venturing in to do the only job Aboriginal women were allowed – domestic work in white households. But unlike Jindie, she says, 'I'm a Christian and Christians like to forgive and forget.' Her remark is interesting in a number of senses. It illustrates how Aboriginal culture is neither static nor primordial. Ethel is a product of post-contact religious training which she has incorporated into her subjective sense of what it means to be an Aboriginal Australian. The post-contact discourses of nationalism and Christianity form a part of her repertoire of responses to the conditions of modern life; she is embedded within a number of Aboriginal and non-Aboriginal mythic models, an important one of which has been, and continues to be, Christianity.

Her remark connects with an earlier recollection made by Geoff Bloomfield, author of the history of the massacre in three rivers area of New South Wales, *Balbalbora: the End of the Dancing.* He recounts how all the old hands knew about white massacres of Aboriginal people but the old Aboriginal man he knew in his youth would not talk about them because 'It's not the Christian thing to do.' Geoff, like Rollo Petrie, has little time for so-called Christians. He believes that the (white) Christians in the district caused him to lose his property after the publication of his book. 'They're [the whites] very savage out in these country places,' he says. These excerpts signal another troublesome moment in the narrative. They give evidence of the ways in which Christianity has different effects on and in the lives of Aboriginal and non-Aboriginal people. One effect is to silence judgement on others' oppressions through a belief in love; another is to give rise to anger and disgust from a position of non-belief. Although they are located differently and speak from different positions, both white and Aboriginal people, professed Christians and non-believers, have been indelibly marked by what Ray Evans and Jan Walker effectively called the 'double onslaught of Christianity and colonialism'.

In the film, Ethel and Rollo each register their own particular grievance in relation to Eliza Fraser. For Ethel, Eliza lied when she spread untrue stories of cannibalism about her people. Having been taught in white mission schools, Ethel is embarrassed by tales of cannibalism as it has been constructed within white Australian history, that is, as a mark of 'native' savagery. She seeks a 'true' past history without the cannibals; that is, she wants to imagine for her people a traditional past which conforms to the ethical dignity expected of Christian individuals, one inculcated by her religious upbringing. For Rollo, Eliza was an opportunist who played with the truth for her own financial advancement. Rollo is angered by her opportunism, an attribute which motivated his own family history. The Petrie family was central to the establishment of the timber industry in the area, which contributed, of necessity, to the destruction of the rainforest and the expulsion of island Aborigines. He is shamed by these actions of the settler past. He carries in his memory a sideshow 'Eliza' fashioned by local Queensland history. Both Ethel and Rollo confront their own ghosts of Eliza from within their own locations in a post-contact history. For both, Eliza Fraser's entrance into history signals the demise of Aboriginal culture in the region. Through their recollections, the film-maker posits a point of origin (the shipwreck episode) from which to trace an oppositional history of white appropriation of Aboriginal culture in Australia. That history forms the core of the film.

As a narrative of that horrible history unfolds, Rollo makes several gestures towards reconciliation – symbolically meaningful gestures which appeal to the emotions of a guilty white audience. On one occasion, he cups water from a clear island lake in his hands and offers it to Ethel, who drinks with gratitude. On another, he prepares a dinner of ah-wongs (shelled molluscs) which the pair have collected together on the beach. As they share their communion, the two gaze into a cleansing fire and dream new visions for the future. Ethel, who is seventy-seven, recalls her grandfather's story told to her as a child: 'The place is not ours now. But it will come back to us again', to a backdrop of a fiery sunset and the strains of a traditional Aboriginal lullaby. Confession, communion and the fires of purification prepare the pair for an apotheosis into a new community. Gestures such as these are significant symbols of reconciliation within a white imaginary; whether or not they presage a return of the land to Ethel's people is another matter.

The final scenes of the film return the viewer to Myall Creek. A Koori, Jim Miller, and an Anglo-Australian, Len Payne, conduct an Anzac Day-style celebration there in late June each year to mark the remembrance of two different inheritances derived from the shame and guilt of the Myall Creek massacre of 1838. With the solemnity of a religious ritual and the trappings of the Anzac ceremony, the pilgrims plant a commemorative tree, while the assembled mourners sing 'Lest We Forget' and place a wreath of remembrance in the shape and colours of the Aboriginal land rights flag at the site. Jim leads the pilgrims in a short Koori prayer which, in translation, means: 'We will always remember.' After this moment, heavy with cultural and national significance, the camera zooms in to a close-up shot of a yellow sun of chrysanthemums, and then out to reveal that it is the centre of the commemorative wreath, itself in the shape of the Aboriginal land rights flag. Ironically, the chrysanthemum is the national flower of Japan, and the sun is its flag's insignia. At this closing moment of the film, the sun blends with the red poppy (our Anzac flower) and other signifiers of exploitation and danger in the film – the blood on the land, the Japanese lettering on the billboards and the foreign film, the red pillars and calligraphy on the Asian restaurants, the Japanese real estate hoardings, and the 'Now open' sign which floated above the heads of Gillian Coote and Len Payne. These blood-red signs signal 'our' shame, 'our' exploitation of others in the past, but are also linked to Anzac and its associations of the Asian/Japanese threat to all Australians in the present.

The narrator reminds the viewers that a Noh ghost is released only when it takes responsibility for its lies. 'Only then can the *real* Eliza dance.' If not a marriage of two cultures, this drama of reconciliation between Ethel and Rollo on Fraser Island acts out a multi-faceted narrative of betrayal and redemption, herein located in the 'lies' of Eliza Fraser. The film's trajectory of loss, reconciliation and enlightenment comes to an uneasy close. Even though the director of the film is a woman, her placement within the film, as well as her modes of address to the audience, is that of the masculine subject of Australian history. In that story, white Australians achieve self-liberation through a repudiation of woman's lies, betrayal, sin and deception which mirror their own sins in relation to Aboriginal culture. A common identity of Aboriginal and non-Aboriginal Australians is posed, but it is measured with unspoken references to a new common enemy – the Japanese. Both 'Woman' and Aboriginal culture provide the imaginary 'Australian' with the means of liberation from the past. But the narrative sets up a new enemy, and new betrayals, for the future. What is registered in the image of the other is a reflection of the fears of the self.

Coote's film and Marett's play introduce a new ethos and a new responsibility into the discourse on Australian nationalism. They may be no more or less 'true' than the other stories, but they disrupt the codes of cultural meaning previously received and accepted. Both the play and the film prepare the ground for a new version of Australian history, one which acknowledges the hidden history of Aboriginal genocide and cultural dislocation brought about by white settlement. In attempting reconciliation, however, they link all peoples (black and white, Western and Oriental, males and females) to a common culture of universal humankind; and at the same time they manage to identify racial, class, ethnic and gendered differences which mark the internal and external, national and international boundaries of the nation. These recent representations partake of the contradictory impulses of a neo-colonial country existing in an international, 'post-colonial' world of mixed social, political and economic realities. As for Eliza, her mythical status has many disguises. In the words of contemporary critics of an English imperial past, 'We are living out the dotage of an imperial culture and our dreams are peopled by a good many ghosts.'[10]

Fiona Foley's Art: New Perspectives, New Departures

Given the uses white artists and writers have made of the Eliza Fraser story, how might it be possible for an Aboriginal commentator to make a difference? Is the search for a recoverable past behind the layers of colonial history the only approach possible? If one stands in a different cultural, political and subjective relationship to the story – specifically as a descendant of the Badtjala peoples of Fraser Island – the story and its accumulated meanings take on quite a different significance. Are alternate readings possible which reach beyond the distortions and appropriations of Western ideologies and values and alter their configurations for both Aboriginal and non-Aboriginal audiences?

The Eliza Fraser theme has been taken up in a variety of subtle and direct ways in the art work of Badtjala artist, Fiona Foley. Foley does something quite different with 'Eliza Fraser', something which calls our attention to the arbitrary nature of constructed boundaries of difference. She speaks not within the previously constructed systems of meaning but beside them – in a responsive, in-between space of reciprocal dialogue. In terms of her personal life's trajectory, she rides a number of boundaries which upset notions of a unified identity. Descended on her mother's side from the Badtjala people of Fraser Island (Thoorgine), and on her father's side from a politically active Australian Irish radical tradition, Fiona Foley has lived a complex modern-day existence. She was raised in the seaside town of Hervey Bay in Queensland, and has resided on Fraser Island and with several traditional communities in Arnhem Land. At present, she lives in Sydney where she works as a visual artist and curator. She was trained in Western art schools as well as in traditional Aboriginal environments, and her art has been internationally exhibited. It travelled to London (where she also studied for a time), New York and Kyoto, as well as to metropolitan centres throughout Australia. One of her paintings, showing a silver boat and fishing rings on a sea of deep blue, was chosen as the official poster for the 1994 Adelaide International Festival of Arts. She has been actively engaged in promoting Aboriginal art and culture in a number of contexts. In 1988 she helped to organise anti-Bicentennial activities. She delivered a powerful and moving speech on behalf of the dispersed people of Fraser Island during a Biennale Forum associated with the installation of two hundred Aboriginal burial poles at the Art Gallery of New South Wales.[11] She is one of the founders of Boomalli, an Aboriginal artists' co-operative based in Sydney which supports Koori artists. Known in metropolitan centres for her minimalist art, she has also worked as an artist-in-residence and exhibited with traditional Aboriginal artists from the Maningrida and Ramingining communities in Arnhem Land, working with them to create a new visual language for her art practice.

Although her ties to a traditional culture were ruptured due to the disintegration of the Badtjala people in the nineteenth century, Foley pays homage to kinship relationships and family influences in her artwork. Significant references are made, for example, to Wilf Reeves and Olga Miller in various paintings. Her great-uncle, Wilf Reeves, was an oral story-teller whose retellings of the creation myths of his people have been recorded and published in *The Legends of Moonie Jarl*, a book which was illustrated by her great-auntie Olga Miller (Wandi).[12] At the same time, Foley maintains that her art, like 'all Aboriginal art in this country, is political whether it is an abstract bark painting explaining the title deeds to land ownership or a recognisable symbol like the land rights flag in an oil painting'.[13] She recognises, however, that there are many reading publics comprised of people who will place different interpretations on her work. This multiplicity of readings emanates from diverse and contradictory cultural contexts which she both shares and resists.

In the catalogue for an exhibition which she also curated in 1992, Foley introduces herself in the following way:

As a Badtjala artist from Thoorgine (Fraser Island) a melancholy history of loss forms my memories.

> the OLD people
> oral history
> written text
> Eliza Fraser and the Sterling Castle [*sic*]
> a quarantine station
> the mission at Bogimbah
> eviction in 1904
> logging
> suffering and isolation
> sadness[14]

Through this listing she places herself within the discourse on Eliza Fraser as one directly affected by the *Stirling Castle* incident. That incident stirs her memory, inflects her life history, and motivates her art practice. Foley maintains that all of her art is 'about' Fraser Island (or Thoorgine, a name she traces to the island for the Badtjala people) in one way or another. She refers to the Eliza Fraser story in a number of paintings and exhibitions, particularly in ten paintings and an installation which were exhibited together in 'By Land and Sea I Leave Ephemeral Spirit' which opened at the Roslyn Oxley9 Gallery in Sydney in 1991. The design on the cover of the catalogue for that exhibition (Figure 15) featured a blackened space overlaid with a full moon in the upper right-hand corner and a reproduction of the head of Mrs Fraser, taken from John Curtis's contemporary sketch in *The Shipwreck of the Stirling Castle* (Figure 7), lying on its side and bordered with dots in the lower left foreground. The head and moon are separated by an indeterminate form. It could be read as a totemic reference, a rib-bone from the dugong, an elongated amphibian creature, or a snake – perhaps related to the serpent Yindingie, spirit guide to the Badtjala people sometimes called the rainbow serpent.[15] That design, like the cover illustration for this book, 'Eliza

FIONA FOLEY

By Land and Sea I Leave Ephemeral Spirit

30 JANUARY TO 16 FEBRUARY 1991

ROSLYN OXLEY9 GALLERY
SOUDAN LANE (OFF 27 HAMPDEN STREET) PADDINGTON NSW 2021
TEL (02) 331 1919 FAX (02) 331 5609

Figure 15 'By Land and Sea I Leave Ephemeral Spirit', by Fiona Foley. Catalogue of exhibition at the Roslyn Oxley9 Gallery, Sydney, 1991.
By permission of the artist.

Heads for Trouble I', has a strong sense of boundaries, contrasts and ambiguities: an in-between space between land and sea, light and dark, past and present, spirit and form, comedy and tragedy, oral histories and written texts. Elements of a projective past for both Mrs Fraser and a pre-contact culture can be discerned in the paintings, emerging as shadow figures which mediate the bounded space. In the cover illustration chosen for this book, five black figures, Badtjala warriors perhaps, can be discerned emerging from the dark, brooding, starlit sky while Mrs Fraser's overturned head is sharply outlined in the foreground of ochre-coloured, flattened sand. As in Aboriginal myth, the stars themselves might be said to hold the spirits of the Badtjala warriors.

Foley's art practice contains considerable ambiguity which confounds an easy reading. Who, for example, is the 'I' in the title: 'By Land and Sea I Leave Ephemeral Spirit'? If one 'reads' the catalogue illustration with its head of Eliza Fraser prominent in the foreground, one could assume the 'I' was Eliza Fraser. On the other hand, the 'I' in the title of an exhibition usually refers to the artist herself. In a humanist sense, Fiona Foley's spirit, one which emanates from her complex cultural, historical and experiential background, is everywhere apparent in the paintings. The 'I', however, remains a floating signifier with indeterminate meaning. The action implied in 'I leave' is similarly ambiguous. What is it that is being left? It could refer to traces of a colonial presence (that connected with Mrs Fraser) and those of a pre-contact past (that connected to the Badtjala people) as well as to the artist's understandings of representations of the event (her bequest to us). In terms of Foley's art, a possible reading is that, although the artist pays homage to and mourns the loss of a pre-colonial past, she does not seek its recovery. The spirit/ghosts conjured by her creative endeavours are ephemeral. They appear everywhere, last a short time, and are left behind – not to fashion a future but to inhabit the recesses of personal and communal memory. Still, to the degree that her name registers 'Aboriginality', the 'I' can be read as the abiding presence of an Aboriginal heritage (pre- and post-contact). It remains as a part of her personal, her people's pre-contact and the country's post-contact existence. The reference is to a spirit (a ghost, one's soul) which is ephemeral (appearing everywhere for a short time, not lasting) and which the 'I' leaves (to be left behind, to omit, to leave alone without interference, to surrender, to bequeath); it suggests that the artist is striving towards multiple meanings, multiple identities and addressing multiple audiences. Her art, like that of a number of contemporary Aboriginal artists working from communities dispersed by white histories of colonisation, would seem to 'both represent and dismantle referential signs of identity fixed by colonialist, nationalist and transnationalist discourses'.[16] This art aims not to essentialise identity but to call attention to the ways in which identity is produced with reference to difference. It aims 'to identify *different histories*, local positions and agendas [in which] the viewer/reader becomes the sub-ject' (emphasis mine).[17]

Fiona Foley's 'Eliza Fraser' paintings have a number of recurring aesthetic and political motifs which signify a history of white appropriation of Fraser Island and Aboriginal culture. They too can be read from a number of pos-itions. The rat trap, which recurs in several of Foley's works (see Figures 16–18), is a particularly disturbing image. In several paintings the rat trap bears the markings of an Aboriginal land rights flag, hovering on the border between past and present. In one it takes the ambiguous form of a black rectangle placed in the foreground of the painting on the sand. The black rectangle can be read as a stick of dynamite, a blackened votive candle, or even an iconic reference to other Australian artists' motifs: the black rec-tangle as an inverted reference to Nolan's Ned Kelly head or the dark rectangle in the paintings of Imants Tillers, in which it signifies an indeter-minability of meaning. The photographic reproduction of Mrs Fraser's face, taken from the sketch drawn in 1837 in preparation for John Curtis's *The Shipwreck of the Stirling Castle*, appears in a number of the paintings. In 'Eliza's Trap', the cut-out image of her face appears with distorted eyes and mouth placed to the left and above a horizontal border of coloured sand mounds which create a boundary between sand and sky. An installation entitled 'Eliza's Rat Trap' features seven rat traps, painted in the red, yellow and black contrasts of the Aboriginal land rights flag, lined up like religious icons on the wall with fourteen white votive candles placed on the floor below them. The centre trap contains a collage photograph of Eliza's head caught in its spring. (She/we, white invaders, become vermin in this counter-hegemonic reference to the Eliza Fraser legend.) Another painting features a dead, dried convolvulus flower in the place where Mrs Fraser's head might be expected to be found. (The convolvulus vine is a traditional symbol for Fraser Island, where it grows prolifically. It may have been the vine used by Mrs Fraser to make her 'fringe of leaves'.) In one painting Foley replaces Mrs Fraser's head/the dried flower with a cross made of postage stamps bearing the portrait of Queen Elizabeth II opposite a land rights flag. The images are not necessarily traditional nor derivative, but common objects found and utilised within frontier society. Some are physical, some symbolic, some sin-ister, some violent, some ironically patriotic, but all are reminiscent in one way or another of usage on a white colonial frontier of insecurity. They are objects, both symbolic and practical, through which settler society fought an enemy whose presence it disavowed; an enemy which nonetheless continued to respond creatively to colonisation through struggle and resistance. Through these objects the artist brings signs of the past into a politics of the present. Eliza Fraser's invasion into Foley's projective past lends new political

Figure 16 'Mrs Fraser Heads for Trouble III', by Fiona Foley, 1981.
By permission of the artist.

Figure 17 'Eliza's Trap', by Fiona Foley, 1991.
By permission of the artist.

and social contexts to the legend and the physical environment of Fraser
Island (Thoorgine). The paintings provide a space in which the viewer can
make new connections with familiar objects, connections not only to the
artist's suffering, isolation and sadness on behalf of the Badtjala people, but
also to her anger as a response to the colonial enterprise.

The paintings make a strong impact, whether read separately or together.
The images which refer to remnants of a violent frontier – Mrs Fraser's head,
the rat trap, the dried flower, the postage stamps – are ready-made emblems
of Western culture reproduced in the art works in a way which deconstructs
their common associations. These images work against available meanings
and also call attention to their history, their embeddedness, within power
relations of the past.[18] The rat trap is perhaps the most onerous image. A
common but debased household object, it is utilised to kill common but
debased domestic vermin. When Foley allows Mrs Fraser's head to be caught
in the trap, she registers a new and sinister reading of the story, a challenge to
all previously received Western versions of the event. The 'trap' can also be
read, colloquially, as one's foul mouth, as in the Cockney expression 'shut
your trap', perhaps a reference to the story of Aboriginal captivity attributed

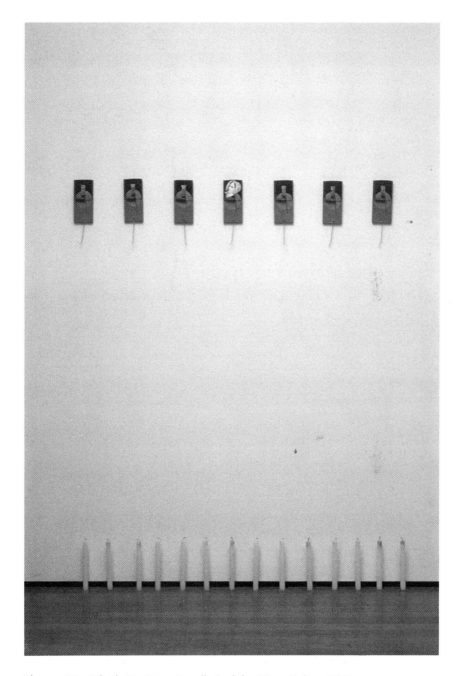

Figure 18 'Eliza's Rat Trap Installation', by Fiona Foley, 1991.
By permission of the artist.

to Mrs Fraser and reiterated repeatedly by white Australians. When Eliza's face appears in the rat trap as a part of a series of red, black and yellow plaques on a wall underlined by candles, it calls attention to the homage, bordering on religious, which has been paid by a dominant white Australian culture to a white cultural icon of colonialism. It may also signal a message to white viewers: we are to see ourselves as the vermin, the betrayers of an Aboriginal heritage, whose broken necks and severed heads represent 'white culture' in a contemporary rendering of 'us' through an Aboriginal imaginary.

From an Aboriginal perspective, the rat trap can register further levels of meaning. White colonisation 'trapped' Badtjala peoples, not only by the presence of the coloniser but also by the establishment of reserves, missions and quarantine stations on Fraser Island. The religious iconography, too, slides between the borders of Western/Aboriginal signification. Western Christianity brought an end to the language, rituals and ceremonies of the Badtjala peoples. The Bogimbah Mission, referred to in Foley's list of memories of loss cited above, was a particularly nasty 'trap'. Plagued by mosquitoes, it was inaccessible to the mainland which could nonetheless be seen across the Great Sandy Strait. Thus, it was literally a location of both physical and cultural dispossession. Eliza Fraser's invasion into Fiona Foley's projective past lends new political, symbolic and social contexts to the story and the physical environment of Fraser Island (Thoorgine). The paintings provide a space through which the viewer can make new connections with familiar objects. Through them the artist comments ironically on notions of Western progress and the effects of colonialism in terms of her differently registered constructions of race, gender, nationalism and identity.

The Christian cross composed of postage stamps, which appears opposite an Aboriginal flag, calls attention to objects of everyday life which reinforce the tension between the Christian settler society's loyalty to England and patriotism to Australia while also displacing a recognition of Aboriginal concerns. Foley relates that her great-uncle Wilfie (Moonie Jarl) was a stamp collector.[19] Her symbols and images pay tribute to her kinship ties as well as convey cultural or political meanings. The full moon is sometimes painted a sombre black, at other times vulval and suffused with light; it brings a feminine, intuitive image to the paintings. Many of the landscape paintings comprise recurring Aboriginal colours of red and yellow ochre and charcoal; they place the artist/the viewer in a space of dispossession which is also a militant, political Aboriginal space of reclaiming, which her paintings seek to renegotiate and claim differently within the history of the present. A number of paintings combine Aboriginal motifs with signs of Australian colonialism. One features three sea ah-wongs, another a dried purple flower from the convolvulus vine, native to Fraser Island. Each image is bordered/protected/closed off by dots, as is the widow's cap of Mrs Fraser in another painting; the dots, suggestive of the artistic, cultural and political borders between Western and Aboriginal perspectives. The dead flower when placed on the horizon line of a painting might be read as a reference to Mrs Fraser's 'fringe of leaves'; the blossom, which once protected her feminine identity, is now dried and flattened by time. The four paintings entitled 'Thoorgine Country' re-territorialise the land through an ironic use of images, symbols and aesthetic perspectives; they also call attention to the naming of 'Fraser Island', a gesture of naming which paid homage to the Frasers and their ordeal while at the same time eradicating the Aboriginal place/space. The homeland of Fiona Foley's people was renamed as an Australian place and space on the map called Fraser Island. The renaming represents an imposition of Western culture, a historical production of space, an act of bringing together language and landscape, politics and identity, of taking power by linguistic displacement.[20]

A number of the paintings in the exhibition 'By Land and Sea I Leave Ephemeral Spirit' might be read, in part, as the artist's response to Sidney Nolan's paintings. Foley's division of the canvas into two halves, of sand/desert and sky is similar to Nolan's in the 'Ned Kelly' series ('The Pursuit', 'The Encounter', 'Ned Kelly'). Nolan, commenting on the strong horizon line in his 'Ned Kelly' paintings, explained: 'I wanted a clear ambiguity for this was the tranquil scene for subsequent violence.'[21] The phrase reverberates ironically when thought of in terms of the horizon of Foley's landscapes. In addition, both artists present the viewer with expressionistic, childlike, 'untutored' use of figures and signs in which the work is reduced to a few elements. One of Foley's paintings, 'Fraser Island Lost in Space', repeats several motifs from Nolan's 'Ned Kelly' and 'Mrs Fraser' series. A perspectival painting comprised of three receding rectangles, it frames its interior beach scene inside a vacant blue-black rectangle (rather than the gun-barrel frame for Nolan's 'Mrs Fraser', Figure 1) reminiscent of Ned Kelly's mask, inside which appears an elongated and flattened beach landscape. When read as an ironic reflection on white perspectives (aesthetic and political), it calls attention to the Eurocentric biases of Nolan's personal myth, as well as underdog myths of Australian nationalism and the flattened perspectives within a Western art aesthetic. Another painting which might be seen as reflecting the concerns of the earlier artist, but with an ironic juxtaposition of colour and mood, is the sombre painting 'Thoorgine Country IV', which is reminiscent of Nolan's 'Lake Wabby'. Instead of Nolan's wide expanse of cloudy blue sky and white sand framed by rainforest foliage, Foley's painting features a pitch-black sky, blue-black waters and dunes of burnt orange. Two crows face each other in the dunes on the left, while a long dead, ghostly white tree stands alone in the burnt orange sands on the right. This scene of sterility and death contrasts sharply with the magical optimism of an Edenic garden represented in Nolan's earlier painting. At the same time, the 'black crows' may be read as an ironic reference to Aboriginal people – facing each other on a barren landscape, deliberating on what to do with what they have left of their country.

When Foley returned from her residency as an artist in Arnhem Land in 1991, she exhibited her work with that of two Maningrida artists, Terry Gandadila and Dale Yowingbala, in an exhibition entitled *The Concept of Country*. For that exhibition she constructed an installation, 'Lost Badtjalas, severed hair'. In this, photographs of four Badtjala people, three men and one woman (the woman featured again in 'Givid Women and Mrs Fraser' shown in a 1992 exhibition), are framed along a wall and intersected by wooden poles from Maningrida from which a container of the artist's hair is suspended. Foley has brought together the images of Mrs Fraser's head, the three men and single anonymous woman in the photographs, and the rat traps in at least three exhibitions. The photographs had been known to the artist through the cherished private records of her family as well as through their use as illustrations in ethnographic texts; she came across them again in the archives of the John Oxley Library in Brisbane. Although much is known about the legendary Eliza Fraser, not even the name of the Badtjala woman nor the dates of the photographs were recorded in the archives. The repetitious use of these images confronts the viewer with an indeterminate locus of meaning that also makes reference to the absence of recorded aspects of the artist's cultural heritage. The installation might be read as an ironic contrast between a Western disinterest in a pre-colonial Aboriginal cultural heritage and its knowledge, juxtaposed against the widespread attention paid to Eurocentric versions of the Eliza Fraser story. But the inclusion of the artist's hair gives it extra poignancy, as one art critic has commented:

> These pictures express the dilemma that confronts many Aboriginal people who are attempting to discover their heritage. Essentially racist documents, the emanations of scientific or anthropological discourses, are often the only remnants of their largely forgotten histories. A work such as 'Lost Badtjalas, severed hair' functions both as a statement of these limitations and as an act of reclamation. By presenting them through a frame comprised of wooden poles from Maningrida, Foley states boldly that her ancestors, whose human significance had been reduced to scientific specimens, have been re-territorialised. The inclusion of her own hair is a symbolic gesture that reflects the ambiguity of the photographs. [The traditional Aboriginal symbolism of mourning invoked by the hair can be read as an expression] of Foley's own feeling of deculturation, an assertion of power and an act of mourning.[22]

By juxtaposing the rat trap, the photographs, the Maningrida poles and the artist's hair, Foley takes objects out of their ordinary or expected contexts, which include everyday life, the museum archive, traditional culture, memory and personal history. Through her art practice, she repositions and recycles these objects into a politics of the present. Her position relative to the paintings represents both an interrogation of, and an identity with, the present. It provides a space for a new articulation of social identities occluded by a history of Western illusions of cultural unity.

The border in Foley's art takes on added meaning in this context. The border itself is important both as a conceptual territory and a visual subject in contemporary art practice, as the recent theme of the Ninth Biennale of Sydney, 'The Boundary Rider', attests. A border defines national, racial, gendered and class boundaries and identities. It also marks a site of exclusion and discrimination. In Foley's art, known icons of cultural identity recirculate across the borders of identity and difference. They demand new modes of reading. Foley returns to that space on the border, that liminal environment between land and sea, where an episode of first contact occurred in 1836. Instead of attempting to fix its meaning, as every other commentator has endeavoured to do, she disturbs the sand, digging beneath the sureties of a white colonial history, allowing for sudden shifts and displacements to take place at the border's edge. In her art, no meaning is fixed; the present is not determined by the past. If one reads the border as a negative locus, a place where anything might happen, where meanings can shift depending on one's position, then that border can be a place where 'the promise of difference takes shape'.[23] That difference is one beyond the space of marginality, of inferiority, of anonymity required by the gendered, class-bound, and anxious white colonial histories of the past. It can register the possibilities of reconciliation, but it also signals an Aboriginal anger at the appropriating politics and practices of the invading white culture.

Foley's art practice might be seen as taking place in a liminal 'in-between' cultural space of difference; the artist is in dialogue with, but stands apart from, the concerns of Western historiography. Since its first appearance, the Eliza Fraser story has provided a multitude of opportunities for the reiteration of colonial perspectives within neo-colonial contexts; but it is also a story amenable to the articulation of new stories of difference. Western feminists also traverse those troublesome borders that Fiona Foley exposes for the metaphorical 'Eliza'. At this historical rupture it may prove more productive to examine the newly exposed terrain in order to register the networks of power which have been hidden as they surface in new contexts; to attend to signs of rational and affective displacements in a complex post-contact history of white affiliations and group identities; to decentre concerns with 'race' and gender; and to re-engage with Aboriginal perspectives in a way that attempts not to rewrite history but to extend an intercultural dialogue which recognises the full subject status of both Aboriginal and non-Aboriginal people.

Conclusion

The shipwreck of the *Stirling Castle* occurred as an indeterminate liminal event in 1836. Mrs Fraser herself became a *cause célèbre* precisely because the borders of identity within England/Empire and between Empire and the imperial world were shifting. With the end of slavery in the colonies, the Empire needed another context in which to carry out a 'rescue' mission – to preserve 'civilisation' against the incursion of the 'barbarian'. At home (that is, in England which represented itself as Empire), the management of the event helped to contain the threat. But the various representations of Mrs Fraser's story also functioned to constitute class, regional and ethnic differ-ences. She became a public figure and her story a performance of Empire, especially through the sensational stories of her 'captivity' and press reports of her London trial. The discourses of science and sentiment which attended the event furthered the rise of bourgeois subjectivity, the cult of the 'angel in the house' domesticity, and the division of life into public and private spheres. Mrs Fraser's representation of herself (and others' representations of her) in Liverpool and London as 'a poor widow woman without a farthing' gave occasion for the settlement at Sydney to assert an identity on behalf of the residents of New South Wales. This was perhaps one of the earliest times in which the phrase 'the national character' was invoked in relation to injur-ies felt by transposed Britons in the colony. At the time of the event, there were conflicting accounts of the shipwreck, the 'mutiny' and behaviours of Mrs Fraser herself, the Captain, ship's officers, crew and servants – all of whom overstepped the boundaries of their race/class/gender identities in the liminal environment of ocean and 'untamed' land. Doubts remained about the nature of the 'captivity' and rescue, as well as about possible occurrences of cannibalism (both indigenous and white), betrayal, and the nature of a lady's virtue. With no clear heroes available amongst the sur-vivors, it was uncertain as to who had the right to speak for whom in representing the event. It found its first privileged narrator in the figure of John Curtis.

Intermittently for nearly 160 years, historians have attempted to contain, contest, order and disassemble the 'truth' about the event. Yet the docu-mentation remains shrouded in mystery. So far, not even the most basic data about Mrs Fraser's place of birth, the nature of her life before the shipwreck or after the rescue, or information about the date and circumstance of her death have come to light. These gaps have motivated the anxieties and desires of a host of writers, artists and commentators and have provided ample room for fantasies, projections and interpretative supplementation. In Australia, the story has helped to legitimise the white settler's presence in the colony where it was invoked to demonstrate the superiority of settler culture over the indigenous population. The aftermath of the event promoted exploration, mapping, surveying and renaming of the land and constructing histories of white Australia which knew itself in relation to its Aboriginal others – all acts of Western appropriation necessary to the foundation of the modern nation-state.

In the period between 1969 and 1976, the Eliza Fraser story became embedded within a 1970s-style nationalism both in Australia and overseas. Sidney Nolan, Patrick White, Peter Sculthorpe, Barbara Blackman, David Williamson, Tim Burstall and Kenneth Cook all adapted the story to various nationalist ends in Australia, where the local version of David Bracefell's rescue became a part of a mythologised, anti-British nationalist history. The revisions of Michael Ondaatje, Gabriel Josipovici and André Brink took the story into a broader, Western neo-colonial arena. In each case the new versions challenged the seemingly fixed hierarchies of race, class and gender; at the same time they retained self and other categories, but filled them with new, ambiguous and contradictory meanings. Those revisions imagined Eliza Fraser as an object of both fear and desire. Fantasies of her feminine difference, her sexual excessiveness, recur in the writings of various male artists. Fantasies of her excessive sexuality, and her spectacular body, have become the locus for the (feminine) Other, one which protects the interests of Western homosociality and provides an erotic investment for the romance of nationalism. Eliza and her convict/slave rescuer have become emblems within a number of nationalist histories in opposition to the dictates of an outmoded imperialism. But in locating the pair in the pre-lapsarian garden and identifying them with maternal plenitude, the timeless land and the instincts, new versions of the story reinforce older dynamics of neo-colonial power within the psychological frameworks of modernism and the philosophies of liberal humanism.

The latest reincarnations of 'Eliza' by Allan Marett and Gillian Coote in the 1990s recontextualise the story, this time in keeping with shifting political forces within Australia and new global economic realities which ambivalently tie Australians to the Asian-Pacific region. Marett and Coote provide oppositional readings and a new ethical and moral stance for Eurocentric white Australians to consider in relation to their blindness to the history of racial oppression and genocide within the country. At the same time, their versions also invoke the promise of plenitude for Aboriginal and non-Aboriginal Australians together. They attempt to discover the 'real' behind the accumulations of social attitudes and cultural customs. But they also reinforce self and other categories, locating an enemy this time (as a threat from) beyond (in Japan), rather than within the borders of the country. Each version insists on its boundaries between the self and its others.

Fiona Foley offers a different approach to the story, one which crosses over the borders of national identity and difference and invites a multitude of responses. Her retelling invites the viewer to reopen the case, to think again, not to determine ultimate meanings but to allow a recognition of different (and perhaps) irreconcilable contexts, political agendas and realities to be exposed.

We are all stuck in our histories. As Jane Gallop remarks, the place where we are *stuck* is also where we are attached.[24] In Australia, our subjectivities, whether derived from Aboriginal, Eurocentric or Asian-Pacific contexts, are attached to our situated neo-colonial histories. Forms of nationalism, arising out of the contexts of imperialism, colonialism and neo-colonialism, have impacted on Western and non-Western peoples differently. 'Australia', even in Benedict Anderson's terms of an imagined community, has never been a unified country. Texts perform defining acts of nationalism. The 1970s witnessed a shift in how (white) Australians understood themselves and their relationship to Britain, a shift signalled by the politics of the Whitlam Labor government and sacking of Gough Whitlam in 1975. In the 1990s, the country is still enmeshed in the politics of nationalism, a politics tied to the domination of the West over the rest of the world. The republican debate, the Mabo ruling, and the spaces between them open up new possibilities for discourses and practices of nation formation. They also provide new contexts for a repetition of neo-colonial acts of domination.

The categories of race, class and gender have been the most powerful and enduring sites on which identities have been constructed in the West for the last two hundred years. The various fictions of 'Eliza Fraser' have borne witness to the important work of representation in attempting to contain national anxieties about difference; the textual strategies they employ reveal the operations of power and resistance. The versions presented and the readings attempted throughout this study indicate that the dilemma of how to define the nation can never be settled, although the desire is passionately felt and must be, of necessity, constantly contested. In present-day Australia, relations between Aboriginal and non-Aboriginal Australians and questions of land title and ownership remain the most pressing problems. The ways in which 'race' has been invoked in the Eliza Fraser story and in the wider society, the ways in which 'race' and sexuality continue to haunt the Australian imaginary, suggest that white Australian culture has only begun to confront the effects of its own Eurocentric constructions.

The nationalist debate promises to intensify as Australia attempts to refashion itself as a republic. Cultural contestations on issues of identity and difference promise to become more marked. There are still forbidden subjects. At the same time, cultural identities are not seamless. Ruptures, contradictions, discontinuities abound. One thing is clear from the Eliza Fraser stories. The 'real' Eliza Fraser is not there. She never has been. Neither are the Aboriginal 'natives'. Both are fictions; neither has a voice in these narratives. They are displaced by white man's concerns, dispersed to the margins within the narratives, and/or located within projections of his fears and fascinations. From the moment of the initial event, different positions have been available from which to contest the master narratives. Although meaning circulates around different nodes of power/knowledge at different times, in no narrative can it be ultimately determined or unified. This investigation has uncovered contestations at every point – in the everyday life experience of the shipwreck survivors, in the academic histories and the creative representations of the event, in the repositionings of different audiences over time. There are contestations between the Captain and crew, the crew and Mrs Fraser, her mulatto steward and the mutineers, the island people and the shipwreck survivors, the convict rescuer(s), the publics of Empire and colony, metropolis and province, Commonwealth and nation, British and Australian historians, regional and national perspectives, national and global contexts, black and white perspectives, Western and non-Western inflections. They all differ, they all are also tied to their own affiliations to landscape, to their own different race, class and gendered boundaries of identity and difference.

I indicated at the beginning of this study that recent feminist, post-modern and/or post-colonial critiques introduce different questions and different strategies of analysis. They focus not on the truth of history but on how the concept of history is produced; not on its coherence but on the limits of a text's historical field; not on truth but on ambivalent knowledges and desires; not on the production of identities but on their dispersal. Now that I reach the end of my journey I hope that this study has shed further light on these areas and located readers in another 'in-between' space where new understandings of difference can be articulated. There is no end to the story(ies) – but there is considerable scope for new perspectives and new departures in the complex and non-unified dimensions of a (post/neo/anti-)colonial world.

Notes

Preface

1 'Critical Dilemmas: Looking for Katharine Susannah Prichard', *Hecate* 10, 2 (1984), 49.

2 I discovered this story on the back of a postcard sold on Fraser Island which featured the Rainbow Sands. It may be a modern 'legend' manufactured for tourists, as I could discover no Aboriginal source for it.

1 Her Story/History: The Many Fates of Eliza Fraser

1 The twentieth-century representations of the legend have been critically examined by J. S. Ryan, 'The Several Fates of Eliza Fraser', *Journal of the Royal Historical Society of Queensland* 11, 4 (1983), 88–112; Jim Davidson, 'Beyond the Fatal Shore: The Mythologization of Mrs Fraser', *Meanjin* 3 (1990), 449–61; Yolanda Drummond, 'Progress of Eliza', *Journal of the Royal Historical Society of Queensland* 15, 1 (February, 1993), 15–25; and myself in 'Australian Mythologies: The Eliza Fraser Story and Constructions of the Feminine in Patrick White's *A Fringe of Leaves* and Sidney Nolan's "Eliza Fraser" Paintings', *Kunapipi* 11, 2 (1989), 1–15. In addition to these studies, a historical biography of Eliza Fraser is being prepared by Yolanda Drummond, a New Zealand writer, which promises to include the New Zealand connection. (Eliza reputedly migrated to New Zealand with her second husband in the 1840s, although no records have been found to confirm this. Her son James settled there, where his descendants still live.) A master's thesis on the history of the Cooloola area, which includes Fraser Island, is in preparation by Elaine Brown through the History Department, University of Queensland.

2 For a critique of the discourses of colonialism as they produce 'the other', see Homi Bhabha, 'The Other Question: Difference, Discrimination and the Discourse of Colonialism', in *Literature, Politics and Theory*, ed. Francis Barker (London: Methuen, 1986), 148–72.

3 The quotation marks around the word 'race' apply to usage of the term in general, although they will not be used throughout the text. They are employed here in the first instance to register the fact that 'race' is a problematic term. Within the discourses of natural science, the term has been used to designate essential

characteristics of biological and/or genetic origin. Within the discourses of colonialism, it signifies differences shared by people marked by their inferiority to the white race. In terms of the Great Chain of Being, these people were placed within the 'zero order of civilisation'; in terms of evolutionary hierarchies, presently attributed to Social Darwinism, they occupied the lowest rungs on the ladder of life-forms on a scale of human evolution from savage to civilised. Far from a natural or real phenomenon, the term 'race' is an apparatus of power, a category of containment employed to construct cultural notions of inferiority and superiority.

4 For an insightful explication of this perspective see Robert Young, *White Mythologies: Writing History and the West* (London: Routledge, 1990), 1–19. For a discussion on the nexus between power and knowledge, see Michel Foucault, 'Truth and Power', in *Power/Knowledge: Selected Interviews and Other Writings, 1972–1977*, ed. Colin Gordon, trans. Colin Gordon *et al.* (New York: Pantheon, 1980), 109–33.

5 There is little ethnographic information about the indigenous peoples of Fraser Island, or Thoorgine or K' Gari (pronounced 'Gurree') as it is called by their present-day Badtjala (or Butchella) descendants. For the name, see Shaun Foley, *The Badtjala People* (Hervey Bay: Aboriginal Corporation Inc., 1994); Olga Miller, *Fraser Island Legends* (Brisbane: Jacaranda Press, 1993). The records which do exist are fragmentary and often contradictory; see Ian McNiven, 'Ethnohistorical Reconstructions of Aboriginal Lifeways along the Cooloola Coast, Southeast Queensland', *Proceedings of the Royal Society of Queensland*, 102 (August 1992), 5–24. The island itself extends some 122 kilometres from north-north-east to south-south-west and varies from 5 to 25 kilometres in width. It is located off the coast of Hervey Bay in south-east Queensland. Norman Tindale, in *The Aboriginal Tribes of Australia* (Berkeley: University of California Press, 1974), suggests that the island was one of the most densely inhabited areas of Australia in pre-contact times. In 1938 L. P. Winterbotham, the honorary curator and founder of the Anthropology Museum at the University of Queensland, interviewed Gaiarbau, a survivor of the rainforest people north of Brisbane, from whom he gained a knowledge of the territories, languages and customs of the indigenous peoples of south-east Queensland. In the 1950s Tindale, through Winterbotham, conducted further interviews with Gaiarbau. On the basis of Gaiarbau's testimony and previous anthropological work by Winterbotham, Tindale constructed his map of Aboriginal languages, 'hordes' and territories in the Great Sandy Region. He speculates that three separate groups of interrelated people within the Kabi-Kabi (Gabi-Gabi) language group occupied the island and adjacent mainland areas. He designates several bands – identified as 'hordes' or small tribes – with distinct territorial affiliations: the Ngulungbara to the north; the Badjala in the centre and mainland territory extending across the Great Sandy Strait and to Bauple Mountain; and the Dulingbara to the south of the island and the adjoining Cooloola sandmass. Possibly numbering about 2000 at the time of the shipwreck of the *Stirling Castle*, they probably made seasonal movements between the island and the mainland in the coastal and lake districts of the Cooloola region. F. J. Watson (following Matthew, *Two Representative Tribes of Queensland*, London: T. Fisher Unwin, 1910) published *Vocabularies of Four Representative Tribes of South-East Queensland* (Brisbane: Royal Geographical Society of Queensland, 1944), in which he suggests that the whole group belonged to one great Kabi nation which occupied the catchment areas of the Burrum, Mary, Noosa, Maroochy and Mooloolah

Rivers and all land between. If these speculations are accurate, this would mean that the *Stirling Castle* party, after having been wrecked on the Swain (or Eliza) Reef some 400 kilometres north-east of Fraser Island, drifted for some six weeks to the south-west before landing at Orchid Beach on the north of Fraser (then The Great Sandy) Island. The party landed in the territory of the Ngulungbara; they were assigned to and lived with small groups of Badtjala people, and passed through Badtjala and Dulingbara territory on the mainland. Immediately before her rescue Mrs Fraser was taken south to Fig Tree Point on Lake Cootharaba where a local group, possibly headed by Euenmundi, were hosting a coroboree attended by other Kabi peoples. These points of contact are illustrated in Map 2. In addition to the cited works of Matthew, Tindale, and Watson, see Peter K. Lauer, 'Report of a Preliminary Ethnohistorical and Archaeological Survey of Fraser Island', *Occasional Papers in Anthropology* (Brisbane: University of Queensland Anthropological Museum, 1977) and McNiven, 'Ethnohistorical Reconstructions'. For a discussion of these territories in relation to the Eliza Fraser story and the cultural history of the island, see the cited works of Lauer and McNiven; John Sinclair, *Fraser Island and Cooloola* Sydney: Weldon Publishing, 1990), and Elaine Brown, 'Nineteenth-Century Cooloola: History of Contact and Environmental Change' (MA thesis, History Department, University of Queensland, 1995).

6 The term 'native' needs to be placed within a historical context. It was used within British imperial and colonial discourses as an all-embracing term to designate persons of inferior race and status. More recently, this signification has been challenged and the term has been rescued to some degree by indigenous peoples throughout the world, as in 'native' Amer-Indians, for instance. In Australia in 1992 the High Court ruling in regard to land rights and native title revived the term in a new context, one which signals its use by Aborigines and Torres Strait Islanders to designate their ongoing territorial and land affiliations. The use of the term in this study is not intended to subscribe to nineteenth-century racist under-standings but rather to refer to territorial groups encountered by Mrs Fraser and the other survivors when the survivors' precise location is in doubt or unknown.

7 I use the term within quotes to indicate that although Eliza Fraser and subsequent narrators viewed the event as a captivity, from another perspective it could be seen as her survival. She was not held captive. The time she spent on the island, although harsh from her perspective, nonetheless paralleled that of other female members of her host group.

8 Lieut. Charles Otter, letter to his sister in England, 1836, quoted in John Curtis, *The Shipwreck of the Stirling Castle* (London: George Virtue, 1838), 186.

9 On liminality, see Victor Turner, *The Forest of Symbols: Aspects of Ndembu Ritual* (Ithaca, NY: Cornell University Press, 1967), 94ff. Turner adapts Arnold van Gennep's 'liminal phase' from his *Rites de Passage* to examine liminality as an in-between or transitional state of marginality. In this state the subject experiences considerable ambiguity, being on the threshold between past and future cultural realms and meanings. The shipwreck victim in an alien environment can be said to experience a similar set of dilemmas – reduced to a 'slave' status, necessarily silenced and submissive, and exiled from any semblance of community.

10 Some of these issues are taken up by Henry Reynolds, *The Other Side of the Frontier* (Ringwood, Vic.: Penguin, 1982); Paul Carter, *The Road to Botany Bay: An Essay in Spatial History* (London: Faber & Faber, 1987); and Debbie Bird Rose, *Hidden Histories: Black Stories from Victoria River Downs, Humbert River and Wave Hill Stations* (Canberra: Aboriginal Studies Press, 1991).

11 See Benedict Anderson, *Imagined Communities: Reflections on the Origin and Spread of Nationalism* (London: Verso, 1991); and Homi Bhabha, ' "Race", Time and the Revision of Modernity', *Oxford Literary Review* 13 (1991): 193-219.

12 Reynolds, *The Other Side*, 98.

13 Armitage (in Watson, ed., n.d., p. 96) records the song which makes reference to Cook's voyage and translates it as follows: 'These strangers, where are they going? Where are they trying to steer? They must be in that place *thoorvour* [a dangerous shoal], it is true. See the smoke coming in from the sea. These men must be burying themselves like the sand crabs. They disappeared like the smoke.'

14 See J. G. Steele (ed.), *Explorers of the Moreton Bay District, 1780–1830* (Brisbane: University of Queensland Press, 1972), 84-5; and Steele (ed.), *Brisbane Town in Convict Days, 1824–1842* (St Lucia: University of Queensland Press, 1975, reprinted 1987), 12.

15 Robert Darge, one of the *Stirling Castle* survivors from the pinnace, reported to John Curtis that 'there was a general, deep-rooted hatred in the breasts of the natives to white men'. He attributes this hatred to the fact that 'the natives were sometimes wantonly fired upon by the soldiers and constabulary'. He relates that one of the natives of his tribe had been shot by whites and had lost his leg as a result, causing enmity between himself and his fellow kinsmen since he was unfit for hunting and fishing. See Curtis, 223.

16 See Robert Darge's account of his treatment in Curtis, 220-4.

17 Ann Curthoys refers to the problems of inclusion of Aboriginal perspectives (which can lead to further Western appropriations) in her article 'Identity Crisis: Colonialism, Nation and Gender in Australian History', *Gender and History* 5, 2 (Summer, 1993), 165-76. Peter Lauer in his anthropological survey of Fraser Island refers extensively to the text of John Curtis, *The Shipwreck of the Stirling Castle*. But he makes no attempt to reconcile survivors' testimonies with the counter-histories he gleaned from their texts which enabled him to document Aboriginal customs, languages and practices. See his 'Report', cited above.

18 Elaine Brown and Yolanda Drummond: see note 1, above.

19 Yolanda Drummond has located a copy of the book by Robert Gibbings, *John Graham, Convict, 1824*, in the possession of one of Eliza Fraser's descendants in New Zealand which contains a marginal note, written by a great-grandson. In response to Gibbings's contention that Mrs Fraser had lived all her life in the Orkney Islands, he responds: 'Wrong. She came from Ceylon where her parents lived.' See 'Progress of Eliza', *Royal Historical Society of Queensland Journal* 15, 1 (February, 1993), 16.

20 Michael Alexander, *Mrs Fraser on the Fatal Shore* (London: Michael Joseph, 1971, reprinted 1976), 18 and Neil Buchanan and Barry Dwyer, *The Rescue of Eliza Fraser* (Noosa, Qld: Noosa Graphica, 1986), 1.

21 I use the term 'post-colonial' to refer to the historical situation of nationhood after the formal structures of colonial authority and administration have been dismantled. Australia, however, is not a post-colonial nation if one takes the term to mean that it has moved beyond the political and ideological effects of colonialism. It remains neo-colonial in that its political, economic and social practices and the ways in which it represents itself continue to be tied to the ideologies, oppressions and effects of its colonial past.

22 See Jane Mackay and Pat Thane, 'The Englishwoman', in *Englishness: Politics and Culture, 1880–1920* (London: Croom-Helm, 1986), 191-229. Although the article studies the construction of the stereotype of 'the Englishwoman' in the service of

Empire at a later period, the authors' assertions that the category had no fixed nationality but was rather 'a conduit of the very essence of the race' has relevance here.

23 For a further explication of the Lacanian subject and its implications within feminist theory, see Elizabeth Grosz, *Jacques Lacan: A Feminist Introduction* (Sydney: Allen & Unwin, 1991), 147–87. For a discussion of the relation of psychoanalysis to politics and the split subjectivity of the social and psychic subject, see Joan Copjec, 'Cutting Up', in Teresa Brennan, *Between Psychoanalysis and Feminism* (London: Routledge, 1989), 227–46; and Jacqueline Rose, 'Introduction: Feminism and the Psychic' and 'Femininity and its Discontents', in *Sexuality in the Field of Vision* (London: Verso, 1986), 1–25, 83–103.

24 See Michel Foucault, 'Nietzsche, Genealogy, History' in *Language, Counter-Memory, Practice*, ed. Donald F. Bouchard, trans. Donald F. Bouchard and Sherry Simon (Ithaca, NY: Cornell University Press, 1977), 139–64. The ideas that writing supplements language, that absence resides at the origin of things, and that the desire for presence and certitude motivates belief in the face of endless deferrals are derived from Derrida. See Jacques Derrida, 'Plato's Pharmacy', in *Dissemination*, trans. Barbara Johnson (London: Athlone Press, 1981), 97–115.

25 Etienne Balibar, 'Introduction', in E. Balibar and I. Wallerstein, *Race, Nation, Class: Ambiguous Identities*. (London: Verso, 1991), 19.

26 Curthoys, 66.

27 Debbie Bird Rose, 'Worshiping Captain Cook', *Social Analysis* (Summer 1994), 46.

28 See, for example, Marcia Langton, '*Well, I heard it on the Radio, and I Saw it on the Television*' (Canberra: Australian Film Institute, 1993); Simon Ryan, 'A Word with the Natives: Dialogic Encounters in Journals of Australian Exploration', *Australian and New Zealand Studies in Canada* 8 (1993), 71–83; Jane Belfrage, 'The Great Australian Silence: Inside Acoustic Space', in *Proceedings from the 'Bring a Plate' Feminist Cultural Studies Conference*, ed. Ruth Barkan, *et al.* (Melbourne: University of Melbourne, 1994, (forthcoming); Jackie Huggins and Kay Saunders, 'Defying the Ethnographic Ventriloquists: Race, Gender and the Legacies of Colonialism', *Lilith* (Summer 1993), 60–70; and the work of Paul Carter, previously mentioned.

29 Benedict Anderson, *Imagined Communities: Reflections on the Origin and Spread of Nationalism* (London: Verso, 1983), 15.

30 *Ibid.*, 16.

31 Andrew Parker, Mary Russo, Doris Sommer and Patricia Yeager (eds), *Nationalisms and Sexualities* (London and New York: Routledge, 1992), 5.

32 Anderson, 16, 40.

33 Mary Louise Pratt, *Imperial Eyes: Travel Writing and Transculturation* (London and New York: Routledge, 1992). I realise that Pratt's analysis involves contrasting the discourses of science with those of the sentimental novel – a different, albeit related, genre from that of sensational captivity stories in the popular press. But the effects of the circulation of the Eliza Fraser story within the contexts of academic and popular knowledge can be related productively to Pratt's analysis of the intersections between academic (scientific) and popular (sentimental) knowledges. These ideas will be taken up in subsequent chapters.

34 See also Jon Stratton, *Writing Sites: A Genealogy of the Postmodern World* (Sydney: Harvester, 1990), 230ff; and Christina Crosby, *The Ends of History: Victorians and 'The Woman Question'* (London: Routledge, 1991), 2–5.

35 See E. P. Thompson, *The Making of the English Working Class* (London: Gollancz, 1983); and Lenore Davidoff and Catherine Hall, *Family Fortunes: Men and Women of the English Middle Class, 1780–1850* (London: Hutchinson, 1987).

36 Catherine Hall, *White, Male and Middle Class: Explorations in Feminism and History* (London: Routledge, 1992), 208.

37 See Henry Reynolds, *Frontier: Aborigines, Settlers and Land* (Sydney: Angus and Robertson, 1987). Reynolds maintains that these ideologies precede contact, frame 'knowledge', and inform subsequent political action. In the 1870s Social Darwinism provided the ideological and political justification for the extermination of Aborigines on the frontier.

38 A Lady Long Resident of New South Wales [Charlotte Barton], *A Mother's Offering to her Children* (Milton, Qld: Jacaranda, 1977, reprint of 1841 edn), 170.

39 *Ibid.*, 177. This account was also published in the *Sydney Gazette* in 1841. It is discussed in Elaine Brown's MA thesis, 'Nineteenth-century Cooloola: History of Contact and Environmental Change' (History Department, University of Queensland, in progress).

40 W. H. Traill, *A Queenly Colony* (Brisbane: Gregory, Government Printer, 1901).

41 For a historical account of the fate of escaped convicts in the area, including that of Graham and Bracefell, see John Sinclair, *Fraser Island and Cooloola* (Sydney: Weldon, 1990), 54–5.

42 Henry Stuart Russell, *The Genesis of Queensland* (London: Vintage Books, 1888, reprinted Toowoomba, 1989), 257–8.

43 Charles Barrett, 'White Woman among Cannibals', in *White Blackfellows: The Strange Adventures of Europeans Who Lived Among Savages.* (Melbourne: Hallcraft, 1948), 79.

44 Richard White, 'The Imagined Community: Nationalism and Culture in Australia', in *Stories of Australian Art* (London: Commonwealth Institute, Australian Studies Centre, 1988), 36.

45 Richard Brantlinger comments that in the 1830s the battle against slavery may have been won by the abolitionists but, paradoxically, the war against racism was lost. Similarly, in the 1970s, the battle against homogeneous conceptions of Australian culture may have been won, but the war against racism had hardly begun. See Brantlinger, *Rule of Darkness: British Imperialism, 1830–1914* (Ithaca, NY: Cornell University Press, 1988), 175.

46 See for example, Edward Said, *Orientalism* (New York: Pantheon Books, 1978), the pioneering study of how the imperial West has discursively constructed the Orient; Michel Foucault, *The History of Sexuality*, trans. Robert Hurley, vol. 1 (London: Allen Lane, 1979) for an analysis of the production of sexualities in the nineteenth century; Louis Henry Gates, Jr, 'Editor's Introduction: Writing "Race" and the Difference it Makes', *Critical Inquiry* 12 (1985), 1–20, for a discussion on 'race' as a historical construction; Christina Crosby, *The Ends of History: Victorians and 'The Woman Question'* (London: Routledge, 1991) for a study of the othering of women in nineteenth-century histories and literature; Homi Bhabha (ed.), *Nation and Narration* (London: Routledge, 1990) for a discussion of the ambivalent nature and function of national discourses; and Robert Young, *White Mythologies – Writing History and the West* (London: Routledge, 1990) for a deconstructive history of European colonialism. In addition, the various writings of the French feminists, particularly Hélène Cixous and Luce Irigaray, provide post-modern philosophical critiques of phallogocentrism, or the ways in which systems of representation subject women to a relationship of dependence on men. Of particular relevance is Hélène Cixous, 'Sorties', in Hélène Cixous and Catherine Clement, *The Newly Born*

Woman, trans. Betsy Wing (Minneapolis: University of Minnesota Press, 1986), 63–75, which analyses the politics of othering in colonial and patriarchal contexts and the political/libidinal economies of desire; and Luce Irigaray, 'This Sex which is Not One', trans. Claudia Reeder, in *New French Feminisms*, ed. Elaine Marks and Isabel DeCortivron (Amherst, Mass.: University of Massachusetts Press, 1980), 99–106, in which Irigaray examines feminine difference beyond masculine representations. She gestures towards the alterity of the Other and the (im)possibility of a female imaginary, and feminine desire.

47 This position, with regard to Aboriginality, is discussed by Stephen Meucke, 'Where are the Aboriginal Intellectuals?', *Australian Book Review* 148 (February–March 1993), 25–9; Ann McGrath, '"Beneath the Skin": Australian Citizenship, Rights and Aboriginal Women', in *Women and the State*, ed. Renate Howe, Melbourne, LaTrobe University Press, 1993, 99–114; Jan Pettman, 'Whose Country is it Anyway? Cultural Politics, Racism and the Construction of Being Australian', *Journal of Inter-cultural Studies* 9, 1 (1988), 1–24; and Ann Curthoys, 'Feminism, Citizenship and National Identity', *Feminist Review* 44 (Summer, 1993), 19–38, and in 'Identity Crisis . . .', cited above.

2 Eliza Fraser's Story: Texts and Contexts

1 See Carolyn Porter, 'History and Literature: "After the New Historicism"', *New Literary History* 21, 2 (Winter, 1990), 259–60.

2 In relation to the intersubjective constructions of 'Aboriginality', see Marcia Langton, *'Well, I Heard it on the Radio, and I Saw it on the Television'* (Canberra: Australian Film Institute, 1993), 31–6.

3 Porter, 260.

4 See E. P. Thompson, *Making of the English Working Class* (London: Gollancz, 1967); Catherine Hall, *White, Male and Middle Class: Explorations in Feminism and History* (London: Routledge, 1992); and Peter Hulme, *Colonial Encounters: Europe and the Native Caribbean, 1492–1797* (London: Methuen, 1986).

5 In addition, modern readers may be amused to find that in September 1837, a minor announcement appeared to say that an English engineer had crossed the channel to elicit French government support for his scheme to build a channel tunnel from Dover to Calais with costs, estimated at one million pounds, to be shared by the French and English governments. Needless to say, the scheme failed to eventuate.

6 See Michael Alexander, *Mrs Fraser on the Fatal Shore* (London: Michael Joseph, 1971), 102–4. These stories are attributed to Robert Hodge, the only survivor of the pinnace party which had abandoned the longboat. He was rescued by crew of the schooner *Nancy*, and returned to Port Macquarie before reaching Sydney on 10 August 1836.

7 Foster Fyans, letter to the Colonial Secretary (6 September 1836), cited in Robert Gibbings, *John Graham, Convict, 1824* (London: J. M. Dent, 1956), 107.

8 Jane Mackay and Pat Thane define the woman's role in Empire in these terms in their essay 'The Englishwoman', in *Englishness: Politics and Culture, 1880–1920* (London: Croom-Helm, 1986), 191–229. Although they deal with a later period when English imperialism had reached its peak, their discussion of the 'white woman's burden' has relevance for the ways in which Mrs Fraser was represented within the contexts of Empire.

9 'Mrs. Fraser's Narrative', reproduced in Neil Buchanan and Barry Dwyer, *The Rescue of Eliza Fraser* (Noosa, Qld: Noosa Graphica, 1986), Appendix 7, 35. Subsequent quotations are taken from this source.

10 Harry Youlden, 'Shipwreck in Australia', *The Knickerbocker* 41, 4 (1853), 291.

11 See Youlden, 291–300.

12 John Curtis, *The Shipwreck of the Stirling Castle* (London: George Virtue, 1838), 49–50.

13 See Andrew Hassam, ' "Our Floating Home": Social Space and Group Identity on Board the Emigrant Ship', *Working Papers in Australian Studies*, 76 (London: University of London, Sir Robert Menzies Centre for Australian Studies, 1992), 3.

14 Hassam, 7.

15 Present-day readers are aided by the historical reconstructions of Michael Alexander. See 33–4, 101–7.

16 From John Graham's log, quoted in Gibbings, 98.

17 Alexander, 106.

18 Youlden, 300.

19 Details reported here concerning Greene's activities have been taken from Yolanda Drummond's unpublished paper, 'Two Women', sent to me with personal correspondence (3 May 1991).

20 See Hugh Edwards, *Australian and New Zealand Shipwrecks and Sea Tragedies* (Sydney: Mathews/ Hutchinson, 1978), 53; Curtis, 376 (illus.); and Alexander, 105. Curtis takes up the story of this wreck in the second half of his book.

21 Jim Davidson, 'Beyond the Fatal Shore', *Meanjin* 3 (1990), 450–1.

22 See Robert McNab, 'Wreck of the *Stirling Castle*', in *The Old Whaling Days: A History of Southern New Zealand from 1830 to 1840* (Auckland: Golden Press, 1913), 149–56.

23 Anon., *Wreck of the Stirling Castle.* (London: J. Catnach of Seven Dials, 1837) reproduced in Alexander, 13–14.

24 Quoted in Alexander, 14.

25 See Anna Clark, 'Queen Caroline and the Sexual Politics of Popular Culture in London, 1820', *Representations* 31 (Summer 1990), 51.

26 Anon., 'Disastrous Wreck of the Ship "Stirling Castle," Bound from Sydney, N.S.W., to Singapore', *Alexander's East India Colonial Magazine* 14, 82 (1837), 258.

27 This is the report challenged by Michael Alexander who believes that its improbability screens a repressed memory of white cannibalism. See Alexander, 102–4.

28 Buchanan and Dwyer, 42.

29 Richard Slotkin, *Regeneration through Violence: Mythology of the American Frontier, 1600–1860* (Middletown Conn.: Wesleyan University Press, 1973), 94–5.

30 Carroll Smith-Rosenberg, 'Captured Subjects/Savage Others: Violently Engendering the New American', *Gender and History* 5, 2 (Summer 1993), 179.

31 See Richard VanDerBeers, 'A Surfeit of Style: The Indian Captivity Narrative as Penny Dreadful', *Research Studies* 39, 4 (December 1971), 303.

32 This same formula, he suggests, attends conversion and emigration narratives as well as the later black slave narratives.

33 Homi Bhabha, 'Introduction', in Bhabha (ed.), *Nation and Narration*, 5.

34 See Slotkin, 247–59, and also Robert Berkhofer, *The White Man's Indian: Images of the American Indian from Columbus to the Present* (New York: Knopf, 1978), 71–111.

35 See Leslie Fiedler, *Return of the Vanishing American* (London: Jonathan Cape, 1968), and note his analysis of 'radical' miscegeny: 'Between them ... women and Indians make for us a second, home-grown definition of what we consider the Real West, the West of the West, as it were; a place to which white male Amer-

icans flee from their own women into the arms of Indian males, but which those white women, in their inexorable advance from coast to coast, destroy', 53.

36 Andrew Lattas, personal communication, 16 February 1994. See also Louis Bredvold, *The Natural History of Sensibility* (Detroit: Wayne State University Press, 1962); and Suzanne Clark, *Sentimental Modernism: Women Writers and the Revolution of the Word* (Bloomington: Indiana University Press, 1991). Bredvold maintains that the novel of sensibility peaked in the latter half of the eighteenth century when genius and virtue were seen as closely related – the spontaneous 'excellences of human nature' (66). Clark argues that by the Victorian era, as gender and class divisions solidified, sensibility was more often aligned with the feminine in a category which included the excesses of passion. She writes, 'There is a development from sympathy, from a conception of passion as the basis of sociability, into a conception of passion as hypochondria and hysteria – that is a turn from pathos as a rhetorical asset to pathos as not only diseased, and isolated, but feminised' (21). She concludes that the development of the gothic novel signifies an ambivalence of the place of the emotions in social life.

37 See Pauline Turner Strong, 'Captivity in White and Red: Convergent Practice and Colonial Representation on the British-American Frontier', in *Crossing Cultures: Essays in the Displacement of Western Civilisation*, ed. Daniel Segal (London: University of Arizona Press, 1992) 33–104, for a feminist analysis of historical contexts and symbolic representations for the American captivity narrative.

38 Roland Barthes, *Mythologies*, trans. Annette Lavers (London: Jonathan Cape, 1972), 109.

39 Berkhofer, 28–30.

40 Terry Goldie, *Fear and Temptation: The Image of the Indigene in Canadian, Australian, and New Zealand Literatures* (Kingston, Ontario: McGill–Queen's University Press, 1989), 17.

41 Abdul R. JanMohamed, 'The Economy of Manichean Allegory: The Function of Racial Difference in Colonial Literature', *Critical Inquiry* 12, 1 (1985), 63.

42 *History of the Captivity and Providential Release therefrom of Mrs. Caroline Harris* (New York: Perry and Cooke, 1838) 3.

43 See June Namias, *White Captives* (Chapel Hill: University of North Carolina Press, 1993), 36–41.

44 *Narrative of the Capture, Sufferings, and Miraculous Escape of Mrs. Eliza Fraser* (New York: Charles Webb and Sons, 1837), 1.

45 For a detailed structural analysis of this idea with specific reference to the literary tropes of wildness through history see Haydon White, 'The Forms of Wildness: Archaeology of an Idea', in *The Wild Man Within: An Image in Western Thought from the Renaissance to Romanticism*, ed. Edward Dudley and Maximillian E. Novak (Pittsburgh: University of Pittsburgh Press, 1972), 3–39.

46 The identification of the woman captive with the Biblical Daniel in the lion's den repeats a mythical motif which can be traced back to the first American woman's captivity narrative, that of Mrs Mary Rowlandson. For a fuller discussion see Smith-Rosenberg, 177–84. The melodramatic rhetorical embellishments are familiar devices contained in the sentimental literature of the time. For a fuller discussion see VanDerBeers, 299–302, and Namias, 36–44.

47 Strong, 62, 74, 79.

48 Roy Harvey Pearce, 'The Significances of the Captivity Narrative', *American Literature* 19 (1947–8), 18.

49 See Priscilla Wald, 'Terms of Assimilation: Legislating Subjectivity in the Emerging Nation', *Boundary 2* 19, 3 (Fall 1992), 77–104.

50 Michael Paul Rogin, *Ronald Reagan, the Movie and other Episodes in Political Demonology* (Berkeley: University of California Press, 1987), 147, quoted in Wald, 82.

51 Wald, 87.

52 See James Levernier and Hennig Cohen (eds and comps), *The Indians and Their Captives* (Westport, Conn.: Greenwood Press, 1977), 267.

53 Mary Louise Pratt, *Imperial Eyes: Travel Writing and Transculturation* (London and New York: Routledge, 1992), 86.

54 Smith-Rosenberg, 179.

55 Smith-Rosenberg, 181.

56 Smith-Rosenberg, 184.

57 By the 1830s there was a common format, a stereotypical narrator and a stylised narrative in the American captivity genre. The illustration which accompanies the Eliza Fraser narrative would be repeated a year later with the publication of the captivity of Mrs Caroline Harris, and Mrs Harris, like Mrs Fraser, would be introduced as a 'Frail Flower' type. See June Namais, *White Captives* (Chapel Hill: University of North Carolina Press, 1993), 38–9.

58 Kay Schaffer, *Women and the Bush: Forces of Desire and the Australian Cultural Tradition* (Sydney, New York and London: Cambridge University Press, 1988), 8–15.

59 Benedict Anderson, *Imagined Communities: Reflections on the Origin and Spread of Nationalism* (London: Verso, 1983, repub. 1991), 16, 145.

60 Bhabha, 'DissemiNation: Time, Narrative, and the Margins of the Modern Nation' in *Nation and Narration*, 302.

3 John Curtis and the Politics of Empire

1 *The Times* (London), 19 August 1837, 6.

2 Michael Alexander, *Mrs Fraser on the Fatal Shore* (London: Michael Joseph, 1971), 129.

3 Personal research and discussion with the reference and bibliographic librarians, British Museum, London, March, 1989.

4 Alexander, 154.

5 See Suzanne Clark, *Sentimental Modernism* (Bloomington: Indiana University Press, 1991), 7, 23–30; R. F. Brissenden, *Virtue in Distress* (London: Macmillan Press, 1974), 18–20, 68–80; and L. I. Bredvold, *The Natural History of Sensibility* (Detroit: Wayne State Press, 1962).

6 See Lynette Finch, *The Classing Gaze* (Sydney: Allen and Unwin, 1993), for a discussion of how the discursive construct of the working class was articulated as a 'knowable, measurable and recognisable category', a distinct class emerging out of its wider association with the lower orders, 9–10.

7 Harry Youlden, 'Shipwreck in Australia', *The Knickerbocker*, 41, 4 (1853), 20. Curtis did not interview Youlden. He reported, on the basis of Darge's testimony, that Youlden had been left to starve in the bush and was later rescued and returned to Sydney in a debilitated condition but that he had subsequently died of a heart condition at the age of 24. See John Curtis, *The Shipwreck of the Stirling Castle* (London: George Virtue, 1838), 230.

8 Curtis, i, ii, iv, vi.

9 Curtis, 216.

10 Curtis, 373.

11 For conflicting interpretations as to the role of the Society, the government and the missions in protecting Aboriginal life and rights to possession of the land, see Henry Reynolds, *Dispossession: Black Australians and White Invaders* (Sydney: Allen

and Unwin, 1989); and A. G. L. Shaw, 'British Policy towards the Australian Aborigines, 1830–1850', *Australian Historical Studies* 99 (October 1992), 265–85. For an analysis of colonial policy as it constructs 'the Aboriginal Other' at different historical moments see Jon Stratton, 'A Question of Origins', *Arena* 89 (1989), 134.

12 Raymond Evans, 'The Pattern of European Conquest' in Raymond Evans, Kay Saunders and Kathryn Cronin, *Race Relations in Colonial Queensland: A History of Exclusion, Exploitation and Extermination* (St Lucia: Queensland University Press, 1975, revised edn 1988), 51.

13 The emergence of frontier violence and story of the Nundah missionaries is more complex than this little narrative suggests. See Evans, Saunders and Cronin; Raymond Evans and Jan Walker. '"These Strangers, Where Are They Going?": Aboriginal–European Relations in the Fraser Island and Wide Bay Region, 1770–1905', *Occasional Papers in Anthropology* 8 (1977); and Roger Milliss, *Waterloo Creek* (Ringwood, Vic.: McPhee Gribble, 1992), 489–92.

14 Quoted in Evans and Walker, '"These Strangers . . ."', 77. Again, this is a simplified version of events which are detailed in the Evans and Walker paper.

15 This is Henry Reynolds's contention. See *The Law of the Land* (Ringwood, Vic.: Penguin, 1987), 149.

16 Anon., *'Eliza and her Black Man'* (London: Bedborough Printers, n.d.). It is difficult to know whether or not readers of this ballad at the time of publication would link it to their memory of the Eliza Fraser story, although the references to an Australian captivity and a trial by the local mayor would seem to point in this direction.

17 For further discussions of the ways historical memory is bound up with imaginative desires and pleasures of a mass cultural audience, see Carolyn Porter, 'History and Literature: "After the New Historicism"', *New Literary History* 21, 2 (Winter 1990), 359–64; and Anna Clark, 'Queen Caroline and the Sexual Politics of Popular Culture in London, 1820', *Representations* 31 (Summer 1990), 47–68.

18 See Paul Carter, *Living in a New Country: History, Travelling, Language* (London: Faber and Faber, 1992).

19 See Kate Darian-Smith, 'The White Woman of Gippsland: A Frontier Myth', in Kate Darian-Smith, Roslyn Poignant and Kay Schaffer, *Captured Lives: Australian Captivity Narratives*. (London: University of London, Sir Robert Menzies Centre for Australian Studies, 1993), 14–34.

4 Policing the Borders of Civilisation: Colonial Man and His Others

1 For a study of rhetorical figures in colonial writing see David Spurr, *The Rhetoric of Empire: Colonial Discourse in Journalism, Travel Writing and Imperial Administration* (Durham and London: Duke University Press, 1993). For a study of the 'primitive' as a trope of colonialism/modern life see Marianna Torgovnick, *Gone Primitive: Savage Intellects, Modern Lives* (Chicago: University of Chicago Press, 1990).

2 Torgovnick, 6.

3 These stories concerned the behaviours of the mutinous crew on the pinnace, which may not have been known to Curtis nor any of the survivors in London at the time of publication.

4 John Curtis, *The Shipwreck of the Stirling Castle* (London: George Virtue, 1838) 147. Subsequent references will be taken from this text, with page numbers cited parenthetically.

5 Curtis, 149.

6 Yolanda Drummond notes this extraordinary coincidence and suggests that the the whole story was concocted by Captain Greene during the return voyage to England. She also attributes the emphasis on Divine Providence, which creeps with regularity into sensational versions of the tale, to Greene. See Yolanda Drummond, 'Progress of Eliza Fraser', *Royal Historical Society of Queensland Journal* 15, 1 (February 1993), 20–1.

7 See Paula J. Byrne, *Criminal Law and Colonial Subject: New South Wales, 1810–1830* (Melbourne: Cambridge University Press, 1993).

8 See for example *The Times* (London), 16 July, 3 August 1837; 30 July, 25 August, 3 September 1838.

9 Robert Gibbings, *John Graham, Convict, 1824* (London: J. M. Dent, 1956; first publication New York: Faber and Faber, 1937), 105. This account is an oppositional history on behalf of the Irish, written to restore the reputation of Graham. It was prepared for the sesquicentennial anniversary of the First Fleet's arrival.

10 The time Graham had to serve before release was also complicated by a second crime, committed in Sydney, for which he was sent to Brisbane; and by his absconding from the penal settlement at Moreton Bay during the administration of the brutal commandant Logan.

11 Michael Alexander, ed., 'Hans Staden among the Cannibals of Brazil', in *Discovering the New World, Based on the Works of Theodore de Bry* (London: London Editions, 1976), 63.

12 At the same time women were involved publicly with men in Chartist agitation as well as in strikes, protests, demonstrations and boycotts. There were separate female Chartist and anti-slavery associations, as well, in which women mounted successful public campaigns. See Anne Clark, 'The Rhetoric of Chartist Domesticity: Gender, Language, and Class in the 1830s and 1840s', *Journal of British Studies* 31, 1 (January 1992), 76.

13 Quoted in Catherine Hall, *White, Male and Middle Class: Explorations in Feminism and History* (London: Routledge, 1993), 174.

14 Johannes Fabian, *Time and the Other: How Anthropology Makes its Object* (New York: Columbia University Press, 1983), 17–18.

15 See Spurr, 'Classification', 61–75.

16 Peter Hulme, *Colonial Encounters: Europe and the Native Caribbean, 1492–1797* (London: Methuen, 1986), 14.

17 Andrew Lattas, 'Savagery and Civilisation: Towards a Genealogy of Racism', *Social Analysis* 21 (August 1987), 40.

18 Thomas Carlyle for the Eyre Defence Committee (1849) quoted in Hall, 282.

19 See for example, 'Gossip from a Clerical Visitor' (report of the minister, Thomas Atkins, of his visit to Moreton Bay from November 1836 to January 1837) and 'The Reverend Christopher Eipper Describes the German Mission' (1841) in *Brisbane Town in Convict Days: 1824–1842*, ed. by J. G. Steele (St Lucia: University of Queensland Press, 1987).

20 Lattas, 46.

21 Personal communication with the late Gerry Langevad, July 1991.

22 Annual report of the District of New South Wales, 1822, Wesleyan Mission House, B.T. Series 1, Box 52, 1215, quoted in Lattas, 40.

23 See Henry Reynolds, 'The Land, the Explorers and the Aborigines', in *Through White Eyes*, ed. Susan Janson and Stuart MacIntyre (Sydney: Allen and Unwin, 1990), 120–97; Ray Evans and Kay Saunders, 'Preface to the 1988 Edition', Ray Evans, Kay Saunders and Kathryn Cronin, *Race Relations in Colonial Queensland*, xi-xix (St Lucia: University of Queensland Press, 1988); Deborah Bird Rose, *Hidden Histories: Black Stories from Victoria River Downs, Humbert River and Wave Hill Stations* (Canberra: Aboriginal Studies Press, 1991), esp. chapters 3 and 5; and Byrne, *Criminal Law and Colonial Subject*.

5   Cannibals: Western Imaginings of the Aboriginal Other

1 *The Times* (London), (23 August 1837), 6.

2 Anon., 'Wreck of the Stirling Castle' (London: J. Catnach of Seven Dials, 1837).

3 As was mentioned in Chapter 2, John Curtis, *The Shipwreck of the Stirling Castle* (London: George Virtue, 1838), provides the reader with several descriptions of Aboriginal life which assume that the natives were cannibals and that Mrs Fraser was a victim of their brutal savagery. He also includes reports by Baxter and Hodge of reputed cannibalistic behaviours. But their testimonies leave many questions unresolved, as this chapter will demonstrate. Curtis's scientific conjectures are based on pseudo-ethnographies of observations of Eora Aborigines from the Port Jackson area north of Sydney, the people of New Holland and South Sea Islanders, far from the Cooloola region. Robert Gibbings, *John Graham, Convict, 1824* (London: J. M. Dent, 1956) is a celebration of the Irish convict which creates a sense of Graham's heroism by juxtaposing his actions against the natives' murderous impulses. In relation to the treatment of Mrs Fraser, however, he observes flatly that the natives meant no malice to Mrs Fraser: 'She was merely a gin, whether returned from the dead or otherwise' (77). Michael Alexander, *Mrs Fraser on the Fatal Shore* (London: Michael Joseph, 1971) reports on unreferenced evidence that 'the Aborigines of Fraser Island were known [by whom, on what evidence and when?] to be exceptionally cruel' (54) although he notes that with the exception of Mrs Fraser's narratives, other crew members report favourable and fair treatment during their time on the island (36). Later he suggests, in a patronising way, that Eliza may have exaggerated her sufferings (52). His knowledge of Aboriginal–European relations appears to be limited and based on subsequent fictional accounts. For example, he speculates that 'friendly intercourse had been established with neighbouring tribes, even to the extent of Aborigines prostituting their women to convicts out on working parties' (25). He also says that 'there is sufficient evidence . . . that the Aborigines were cannibals', or, 'if they did not hunt men specifically, like their cousins [note the presumption of 'the same'] in New Guinea and Borneo, they were not, it would appear, above eating an enemy . . .' (37). In the end, Alexander's text is ambivalent on the issue, allowing the reader to come to whatever conclusions s/he desires. In the appendix to his comic spoof of a novel *Eliza Fraser* (1976), Kenneth Cook includes a report of the Reverend George Lang, lodged in the Mitchell Library. This contains the testimony of Davis (or Duramboi), a 'white blackfellow' who lived in the Cooloola area with Aborigines for over a decade and was returned to white society in 1842, on Aboriginal burial customs. The report includes a section on ritual burial ceremonies, including the flaying, burning and consumption of bodies according to strict custom. This macabre 'authenticating' document in a bawdy spoof of white history for modern readers strikes one as a singularly inappropriate inclu-

sion, designed further to sensationalise the fiction of sex and savagery in Australia's colonial past. Queensland historians Evans and Walker '"These Strangers Where Are They Going?" Aboriginal–European Relations in the Fraser Island and Wide Bay Region, 1770–1905', *Occasional Papers in Anthropology* 8 (1977) attempt an anthropological reconstruction of the *Stirling Castle* episode sympathetic to an Aboriginal perspective. Admitting that the survivors suffered 'intense privations' (44), Evans and Walker surmise that their punishments probably came from the natives' frustration with 'their seemingly obtuse uselessness' coupled with anger over soldiers shooting at and wounding their people further south (45). The account attempts to explain a rationale for Aboriginal behaviours, assuming that the islanders took them to be the ghosts of their dead relatives and (at the same time) foreign invaders intent on killing. They conclude that 'their ordeal and their cultural incompetence and confusion before the demands of Aboriginal society provide an ironic preview of the ways Aborigines themselves would soon be made to suffer as a bewilderingly new social order, not of ghosts but of ambitious, purposeful men and women, was imposed on them' (45). Buchanan and Dywer, *The Rescue of Eliza Fraser* (Noosa Heads, Qld: Noosa Graphica, 1986) include a section in their appendix entitled 'The Kabi-Kabi and their Treatment of the Castaways in Perspective' which attempts to present an Aboriginal perspective. Without mentioning cannibalism or human sacrifice, they maintain that although the Kabi enjoyed a 'fierce reputation' (46) and may have had their sport with the shipwreck victims, in the main the *Stirling Castle* survivors were treated in a humane fashion and attempts were made to assimilate them into a native way of life. 'It was not so much systematic ill treatment of the castaways by savage natives, as their inability to cope in a foreign environment' (47).

4 See, for example, Haydon White, 'The Forms of Wildness: Archaeology of an Idea', in *The Wild Man Within: An Image in Western Thought from the Renaissance to Romanticism*, ed. Edward Dudley and Maximillian E. Novak (Pittsburgh: University of Pittsburgh Press, 1972), 3–39; W. Arens, *The Man-Eating Myth: Anthropology and Anthropophagy* (Oxford: Oxford University Press, 1979); Michael Taussig, *Shamanism, Colonialism, and the Wild Man: A Study in Terror and Healing* (Chicago: University of Chicago Press, 1986); Andrew Lattas, 'Savagery and Civilisation: Towards a Genealogy of Racism', *Social Analysis* 21 (August 1987), 39–58; Gananath Obeyesekere, 'British Cannibals: Contemplation of an Event in the Death and Resurrection of James Cook, Explorer', *Critical Inquiry* 18 (June 1992), 630–54; and Maggie Kilgour, *From Communion to Cannibalism: An Anatomy of Metaphors of Incorporation* (Princeton: Princeton University Press, 1993).

5 See Deborah Bird Rose, 'Worshiping Captain Cook', *Social Analysis* 34 (December 1993), 43–50.

6 See Taussig, 105.

7 Curtis, *The Shipwreck of the Stirling Castle*, 103. Subsequent references will be taken from this text and page numbers cited parenthetically.

8 Michel de Certeau, *Practice of Everyday Life* (Berkeley: University of California Press, 1984), 154.

9 Taussig, *Shamanism*, 105–7, 127.

10 Kilgour, 17.

11 Johann Reinhold Forster, *The 'Resolution' Journal of Johann Reinhold Forster, 1772–1775*, ed. Michael E. Hoare, 4 vols (London, 1982) 4:676, cited in Gananath Obeyesekere, 'British Cannibals: Contemplation of an Event in the Death and Resurrection of James Cook, Explorer', *Critical Inquiry* 18 (Summer 1992), 649.

12 Michael Alexander, *Mrs Fraser on the Fatal Shore*, Appendix I, 159. Subsequent quotations are taken from this source and will be cited parenthetically.
13 Marianna Torgovnick supplies an explanation of these practices. She writes, 'In New Guinea, the practice of collecting heads had a clearly defined social value, with none of the idiosyncratic, macabre overtones it acquired in the West. Collected heads were a fact of life, often a familiar element of decor. The heads collected sometimes belonged not just to slain enemies but to cherished ancestors. The Asmat of New Guinea, for example, traditionally sleep on their fathers' skulls as a means of drawing strength from ancestors.' See Torgovnick, *Gone Primitive: Savage Intellects, Modern Lives* (Chicago: University of Chicago Press, 1990), 148.
14 See Cameron Forbes, 'Islands in the Storm', *Australian Weekend Review*, 26–27 June 1993, 1.
15 Obeyesekere, 'British Cannibals', 641.
16 *Ibid.*, 635.
17 Kilgour, *From Communion to Cannibalism*, and Peggy Reeves Sanday, *Divine Hunger: Cannibalism as a Cultural System* (Cambridge: Cambridge University Press, 1986) also examine the symbolisation of cannibalism in terms of unconscious fantasies of incorporation resulting from childhood experiences of bonding with and separation from the mother which are common to all humanity, Kilgour from a literary and Sanday from an anthropological perspective.
18 Obeyesekere, 643–6.
19 *Ibid.*, 638.
20 *The Times* (London), 24 August 1937, 4; Alexander, 54.
21 Youlden, 'Shipwreck in Australia', *The Knickerbocker* 41, 4 (April 1853), 299.
22 *The Times* (London), 25 August 1837, 3.
23 *Ibid.*, 23 August 1837, 7.
24 See Alexander, 55, 129. In the first instance Alexander speculates that the natives constructed an exhibition for Baxter; later he suggests that the whole account as it appeared in the sensational stories may have been 'a fantasy of [Eliza's] confused mind, [or] a nightmare dredged up from travellers' tales told by her husband'.
25 Anon., *Tales of Travellers* (London: Mark Clark, 1838), 387.
26 See Peter Lauer, 'Report of A Preliminary Ethnohistorical and Archaeological Survey of Fraser Island', *Occasional Papers in Anthropology*, 8 (Brisbane: University of Queensland Anthropological Museum, 1977), 19.
27 Curtis, 103.
28 Obeyesekere, 643.
29 Both events are recounted in Constance Campbell Petrie, *Tom Petrie's Reminiscences of Early Queensland* (Brisbane: Watson, Ferguson and Co., 1904), 266, 35. The Petrie family arrived in Australia in 1831 on board the *Stirling Castle* when Tom Petrie was an infant. They moved to Brisbane in 1837, where Andrew Petrie took up the position of superintendent of works, or chief engineer, for the area. The family lived 'bush' from that time and Tom grew up with virtually the sole companionship of Aboriginal children.
30 The holdings of Aboriginal skeletal remains and other objects of their material culture in museums throughout the world was one of the ways in which the Australian Aborigine became an anthropological specimen of 'primitivism' to the nineteenth-century public and the scientific community. It is estimated that as late as 1989 in Australia, public museums possessed holdings of some 100,000 items, including 'ancestral remains held for scientific purposes, archaeological

material, photographs, genealogies, archival documents, anthropological field notes, recordings of language and song, and thousands of metres of ethnographic film – all dealing with Aboriginal cultures and history', and valued at some $400,000. Although the burial remains and some significant ritual holdings recently have been passed into the hands of their traditional owners, historically these collections have been deemed as Crown property and thus beyond the possession or control of Aboriginal peoples. Museum practice is one of the on-going indirect and covert mechanisms of what Adrian Marree calls 'internal colonialism' in Australia and Professor Yarwood refers to as a 'friendly form of genocide' through which the rightful Aboriginal inheritors are dispossessed of and alienated from their own cultural property. See Marree, 'Museums and Aborigines: A Case Study in Internal Colonialism', *Australian-Canadian Studies* 7, 1–2 (1989), 63–80.

31 See Brian Simpson, *Cannibalism and the Common Law* (Chicago: University of Chicago Press, 1985), discussed in Obeyesekere, 639–40.

32 Obeyesekere, 643.

33 Marcus Clarke, *His Natural Life* (Ringwood, Vic.: Penguin, 1970), 559.

34 The story of Cox and Pearce is treated in some detail in Robert Hughes, *The Fatal Shore* (London: Collins Harvill, 1987), 219–26. It should be noted, however, that neither histories of early convict days, nor accounts of Tasmania's history, nor any Australian encyclopedia which I could locate in university libraries and archives in Adelaide in 1993, mention these events. Despite the significant historical reconstructions which have occurred since the 1970s and the plethora of historical publications in the wake of the Bicentenary, it appears that the taboo on white cannibalism as a fit subject of Western history remains strong. Even the belated discovery of 'proof' of this common practice can produce provocative headlines around the world. On the very day I prepared this manuscript an article appeared in the local press which claimed that there is strong evidence that the crew of a British vessel wrecked in Canada's Arctic region in 1847 ate their dead mates, although rumours to this effect, which shocked Britons of the day, were dismissed at the time. See 'Explorers May Have Eaten Comrades', *Advertiser* (Adelaide), 13 June 1994, 11.

35 See for example, Edward K. Said, *Culture and Imperialism* (London: Chatto and Windus, 1992). Said reports in his study that 'only in the nineteenth century did European historians of the Crusades begin *not* to allude to the practice of cannibalism among the Frankish knights, even though eating human flesh is mentioned unashamedly in contemporary Crusader chronicles' (16).

36 See Alexander, Appendix III, 'Missionaries Come to Moreton Bay', 163–4.

37 Henry Stuart Russell, *Genesis of Queensland* (London: Vintage Books, 1888, reprinted Toowoomba, 1989), 255–6.

38 Russell, 'Mr. Russell's "Excursions in Australia"', *Journal of the Royal Geographic Society* (London) 15, 2 (1845), 312–13.

39 See also Simon Ryan, 'A Word with the Natives: Dialogic Encounters of Australian Exploration', *Australian and New Zealand Studies in Canada* 8 (1993), 71–83.

40 Russell, 261.

41 Petrie, *Reminiscences*, 18–19.

42 See also Arens, 26–8, 158, and Sanday, 47–8 ff., on cannibalistic rituals and the maintenance of phallic masculinity.

43 See Michael Pickering, 'Cannibalism amongst Aborigines? A Critical Review of the Literary Evidence', unpublished PhD thesis (Australian National University, 1985); and Noel Loos, *Invasion and Resistance* (Canberra: Australian National

University Press, 1982). In relation to reports of cannibalism in the Cooloola area of Queensland, see Peter Lauer, 'Report of a Preliminary Ethno-historical and Archaeological Survey of Fraser Island', *Occasional Paper* 8 (Brisbane: University of Queensland Anthropology Museum, 1977), 13–14; George Lang's report of the testimony of James Davis (Duramboi), Mitchell Library Papers; and Petrie, *Reminiscences*, 18–19.

44 David Bowman, 'Yes, and Lasseter's Reef Lives On', *Australian Society* (September 1991): 14–15. See also Raymond Evans, Kay Saunders and Kathryn Cronin, *Race Relations in Colonial Queensland* (St Lucia: University of Queensland Press, 1988), 72–3, 210–13 ff.

45 Quoted in Bowman, 14.

46 There are a number of references to the survivors being taken out into the bay and dumped overboard, behaviours which the survivors interpreted as cruel and sadistic. Olga Miller's retelling of some Fraser Island legends puts a different slant on these occasions. She retells the myth of a man turned into a catfish by Yindingie, messenger of the god Beeral, when he was teaching the men how to swim. Swimming skills were essential to these coastal people. Miller comments at the end of the myth that 'My brothers and sisters and I were all put over the side of the dinghy some distance from shore at the age of six months. We swam naturally. I used to crawl to the beach before I could walk.' See Miller, *Fraser Island Legends* (Brisbane: Jacaranda Press, 1993), 20–1.

47 Peter Lauer discusses the grooming and healing practices of Fraser Island groups, including the plucking of body hairs and painting of the body. Firebrands may have been applied to survivors with ulcerated skin and also in an attempt to remove body hairs. Sand may have been applied to Mrs Fraser's post-partum body for cleansing or for protection from the sun. See Lauer, 11–12.

48 See Petrie, throughout; Evans and Walker, 44–5; Buchanan and Dwyer, 45–7.

49 Ebenezer Thorne, *Queen of the Colonies*, 337, cited in Elaine Brown's MA thesis, 'Nineteenth-century Cooloola: History of Contact and Environmental Change' (History Department, University of Queensland) in progress.

50 Rose, 46–7.

51 Obeyesekere, 650.

52 See George Lang, letter to his uncle upon the occasion of the white massacre of natives (31 March 1858), reproduced in the appendix to Evans, Saunders and Cronin, *Race Relations*, 375–8; and Petrie, 149 ff. Lang, at least, was not always consistent in his sympathies. Later, as a journalist, he wrote the pamphlet 'Queensland' (1864) which contained rumours of the cannibalistic sacrifice of young girls at the Bon-yi feast, reported earlier in the chapter.

53 Cited in Evans, Saunders and Cronin, *Race Relations*, 47.

6 Modern Reconstructions: Michael Alexander and Sidney Nolan

1 Michael Alexander, *Mrs Fraser on the Fatal Shore* (London: Michael Joseph, 1971; 2nd edn, 1976). Future quotations are taken from the 1971 edition and page numbers are cited parenthetically.

2 Interview with Michael Alexander and Michael Luke (London, 6 October 1992). See 'Hans Staden Among the Cannibals of Brazil', in *Discovering the New World, Based on the Works of Theodore de Bry*, ed. Michael Alexander (London: London Editions, 1976), 90–121. Hans Staden was a German seaman who visited the coast of South America in the sixteenth century on a Portuguese trading ship. The narrative of his adventures with the Tupinamba Indians contains sensational accounts of

man-eating savages, interspersed with lurid woodcuts, often referred to by various commentators. See W. Arens, *The Man-Eating Myth* (Oxford: London, 1979), 22–30.

3 Kenneth Clark, Colin MacInnes, and Bryan Robertson, eds, *Sidney Nolan* (London: Thames and Hudson, 1961).

4 Similar volumes on the art of Arthur Boyd, William Dobell and Russell Drysdale were to follow.

5 Sir Raphael Cilento, 'All Tempests to Endure' (1966), unpublished manuscript, later renamed 'The Convict and the Captain's Lady', held at the Fryer Library, Brisbane.

6 Information supplied on inner front dust-jacket of the 1971 edition of *Mrs Fraser on the Fatal Shore*.

7 *Ibid.*

8 For a detailed examination of the evidence on which Alexander bases his narrative see Yolanda Drummond, 'Progress of Eliza Fraser', *Journal of the Royal Historical Society of Queensland* 15, 1 (February 1993), 15–25.

9 Jill Ward, 'Patrick White's *A Fringe of Leaves*: History and Fiction', *Australian Literary Studies* 8 (1978), 404.

10 See Drummond, 16.

11 J. S. Ryan, 'The Several Fates of Eliza Fraser', *Journal of the Royal Historical Society of Queensland* 11, 4 (1983), 103.

12 Kenneth Cook, *Eliza Fraser* (Melbourne: Sun Books, 1976), 7.

13 Anne Summers, *Damned Whores and God's Police* (Ringwood, Vic.: Penguin, 1975).

14 See, for example, Barry Dwyer and Neil Buchanan, *The Rescue of Eliza Fraser* (Noosa Heads, Qld: Noosa Graphica, 1986), 15–16.

15 Drummond, 21.

16 Cilento, draft ms, 'All Tempests to Endure'. All subsequent quotations come from this text and page numbers are cited parenthetically.

17 Clark, MacInnes, and Robertson, *Sidney Nolan*. The lavish production, striking cover painting and exotic introduction, along with the contention that Nolan came from an Irish working-class family 'with no artistic traditions of any kind' (10), no doubt added to the popular reception and appeal of Nolan and his paintings.

18 The Viking edition, as 'vulgar' as the Alexander and Cook (re)publications to come (1976), featured an elegant Eliza amidst African huts in an alien, threatening landscape. See David Marr, *Patrick White: A Life* (Sydney: Random House, 1991), 569.

19 Stephen Spender, 'Introduction', in *Sidney Nolan: 'Leda and the Swan' and Other Recent Works, 16 June–16 July 1960* (London: Mathieson Gallery, 1960); also quoted in the catalogue introduction to *Nolan's Fraser*, Robyn Bondfield (Brisbane: Queensland Art Gallery, 1989).

20 Nicholas Rothwell, 'Nolan: The Artist in Exile Begins his Long Journey Home', *Weekend Australian*, 15–17 August 1989, 6. This is a curious comment, since Nolan would have known as a result of his trip that Mrs Fraser was not from the Orkneys, as the locals are quick to point out, although it was her home and the place of her departure for Australia in 1836. In a curious twist of fate, however, Nolan was bound to the place in another way. Adams makes the connection in his story of Cynthia Nolan's suicide. Cynthia was Nolan's second wife (and the estranged sister of John Reed, to whom she bore an uncanny resemblance); they married in 1948, shortly after the collapse of his association with the artists' community, Heide. He reports that Cynthia Nolan's mother had died when Cynthia was four

years old. Her curiosity about her mother's background led her to Somerset House in London on the last day of her life, where she carried out some archival research. Nolan never saw her alive again. He received a telegram under his door that evening, which read: 'OFF TO THE ORKNEYS IN SMALL STAGES. LOVE CYNTHIA' which Nolan took to be an indication of a lead into her mother's background. But Cynthia did not go to the Orkneys; she was found dead in a local hotel room the following day. See Brian Adams, *Sidney Nolan: Such is Life* (Melbourne: Hutchinson, 1987), 228–9.

21 Jane Clark, *Sidney Nolan: Landscapes and Legends – A Retrospective Exhibition, 1937–1987* (Sydney: International Cultural Corporation of Australia, 1987), 91.

22 Robert Melville, ed. and intro. to Sidney Nolan, *Paradise Garden* (London: R. Alistair McAlpine, 1971), 7.

23 These alternative readings have been suggested by other curators and art historians. Felicity St John Moore, curator and modernist art historian, suggests that Nolan used a similar process in his portrayal of Ned Kelly, 'taking the mythical centaur and giving it an original but literal and *legend-related* twist' (emphasis in original). The theme of humiliation as conveyed through Mrs Fraser's alien and less than human pose is also suggested by the curator of the Darmstadt exhibition in his catalogue essay. See below.

24 Melville, 9.

25 Christopher Heathcote, 'Nolan: An Art Transformed', *Age*, 30 November 1992, 14.

26 Adams, 67.

27 Rothwell, 6.

28 The fictitious 'Ern Malley' and his fabricated poems were the subject of an elaborate hoax devised by two university students, James McAuley and Harold Stewart, in 1944 while they were in the Army. McAuley and Stewart invented a classic Australian but undistinguished past for their poet: son of a deceased English father, raised by his mother in working-class suburban Sydney, he had worked as a garage mechanic and insurance salesman. They also invented a naive sister, Ethel, who sent three of her deceased brother's poems, including the polished 'Dürer: Innsbruck, 1495', to Max Harris, seeking his advice on their merits. He responded with enthusiasm, asking if more poems were available; they were promptly dispatched. With the exception of the first carefully crafted but oblique poem 'Dürer: Innsbruck, 1495', the poems had been cobbled together on one afternoon (or so the story goes) from bits of Shakespeare, the *Concise Oxford Dictionary* and a book of quotations. Harris soon published them with great fanfare in an elaborate edition of *Angry Penguins*, the literary journal sponsored by the Reeds and illustrated by Sidney Nolan. The hoax was designed by McAuley and Stewart to counteract the disturbing influences of modernism in art exemplified by the Heide group and its journal. To the delight of the public and embarrassment of the Heide group, the Australian press published the story of how Harris, Nolan and the Reeds had been duped, a story which seriously jeopardised the journal's credibility and strained relationships all around. In an additional and particularly parochial move, Max Harris was called to court in Adelaide and convicted on charges of publishing obscene material. The group felt betrayed. See Michael Heyward, *The Ern Malley Affair* (St Lucia: University of Queensland Press, 1993).

29 Albert Tucker, *Faces I Have Met* (Melbourne: Century Hutchinson, 1986), 12. In the introduction to the volume, Richard Haese comments, 'if Sunday was the animating and binding presence at Heide, as Tucker surely believes, it was a

presence with which he was never comfortable, and these images of Sunday verge on the daemonic ... [while] her friends regarded her as someone of unique beauty and presence' (7). It is Haese who refers to Sunday's gaze in the portrait as 'guardian-like' (6).

30 Janine Burke, a feminist writer and art historian, provides a very different interpretation of Sunday Reed in her biography of Joy Hester. Hester was the only female artist to be a member of the Heide group. A close friend of Sunday Reed, she married Albert Tucker and lived at Heide through the turbulent period of Nolan's separation. Burke saw Sunday Reed as 'the most influential woman in Melbourne's radical cultural life ... who saw and readily supported the younger artists whose talents she quickly recognised'. Burke continues, 'She was a powerful personality, articulate, sophisticated, well-read, highly sensitive and imaginative.' Burke's research led her to conclude that Sunday Reed developed and generously supported the talents of the younger artists, although she could sometimes be mean, selfish and domineering. See Burke, *Joy Hester* (Richmond, Vic.: Greenhouse, 1983), 45.

31 Melville, 1.

32 *Ibid.*, 6-7.

33 Heather Brown, 'Nolan's Journey to Paradise', *Australian Weekend Magazine*, 21 October 1989, 23, 18.

34 *Ibid.*, 24.

35 Anne-Marie Willis, *Illusions of Identity: The Art of Nation* (Sydney: Hale and Iremonger, 1993), 53-8. See also my comments in *Women and the Bush* (Melbourne: Cambridge University Press, 1988), in relation to Paul Hogan and Henry Lawson.

36 Colin MacInnes, 'Introduction', in *Sidney Nolan: Catalogue of an Exhibition ...* (London, Whitechapel Art Gallery, 1957), 9. The representation parallels sketches of the artist's life from Adams' biography and the Thames and Hudson monograph. It is repeated in the background publicity which announced the 1989 exhibition 'Nolan's Fraser' at the Queensland Art Gallery and regional centres.

37 Brown, 18.

38 Heathcote, 14.

39 B. R. [Bryan Robertson], 'Preface', in *Sidney Nolan: Catalogue of an Exhibition ...* (London, Whitechapel Art Gallery, 1957), 4.

40 MacInnes, 14.

41 Barrie Reid, 'Nolan in Queensland: Some Biographical Notes on the 1947-48 Paintings', *Art and Australia* (September 1967), 447. Nolan's paintings had been represented in this way by John Reed as well. In the catalogue of the exhibition 'The Formative Years: 1940-1945' he wrote: 'I believe that one of his major achievements has been to reveal to us in paint the very essence of the Australian landscape – something which no painter had previously been able to do', Catalogue essay, 'The Formative Years: 1940-1945' (Melbourne: Museum of Modern Art of Australia, 1961).

42 See my discussion of these approaches to national identity in *Women and the Bush*, 87-9.

43 Clarke, MacInnes, and Robertson, 74 (catalogue description) and 22 (introductory essay by MacInnes).

44 Richard Haese, *Rebels and Precursors: The Revolutionary Years of Australian Art* (Melbourne: Allen Lane, 1981). Like all attempts to unify disparate developments, this one has been contested. Bernard Smith argues that this approach obscured earlier movements in Australian art and neglected the importance of social realist artists. See Smith, *Australian Painting, 1788-1990* (Melbourne: Oxford University Press,

1991), chapter 8, 'Rebirth, 1939–1950'. Peter Herbst maintains that there were fissures within the Heide group not taken up by Haese and also that other important artistic activities were made peripheral in Haese's depiction of the centrality of Heide. See Herbst, 'Introduction', in *The Boxer Collection: Modernism, Murrumbeena and Angry Penguins* (Canberra: Australian Government Printing Service, 1981), 4–16. Neither of these critics mentions the importance of earlier modernist women artists, Margaret Preston, Thea Proctor and Grace Cossington-Smith, all of whom blended modernist and nationalist themes and aesthetics in innovative ways in Sydney a generation before Heide came into being. Humphrey McQueen maintains that if there was a modernism in Australia between the wars, Margaret Preston was *it* (144). He reports that John Reed, however, dismissed her art as merely 'decorative', a move designed to posit the superiority of the Angry Penguins' modernism (143). See McQueen, *The Black Swan of Tresspass: The Emergence of Modernist Art in Australia to 1944* (Sydney: Alternative Publishing Cooperative Limited, 1979). McQueen defines modernism as '*a range of responses to a nexus of social-artistic-scientific problems*' (xiii, emphasis his) which could be marshalled by both conservative and radical forces to strengthen their positions. As Anne-Marie Willis comments, 'the desire for this paradoxical *tradition* of artistic non-conformity precedes its "discovery", which is in fact an invention', 54.

45 Robert Hughes, as well, subscribes to this perspective. In his study *The Art of Australia* (Harmondsworth: Penguin, 1966) he comments that the Angry Decade was crucial in the history of Australian painting. Not only did the paintings bring about a magical rediscovery of the Australian landscape, they 'laid a common ground of myth, attitude, and symbolic technique on which the younger post-war figurative painters . . . have taken root.' He concludes that the decade produced 'a short-lived but identifiable local tradition, *where no overseas traditions can be grasped*' (emphasis mine, 166).

46 Most notable were the works of Bernard Smith and Robert Hughes. See Smith, *Place, Taste and Tradition: A Study of Australian Art Since 1788* (Sydney: Ure Smith, 1945) and *Australian Painting*; and Hughes, *The Art of Australia*.

47 Haese, 264.

48 'The Antipodean Manifesto', written by Bernard Smith, was a controversial essay which appeared in the catalogue of the Antipodean Exhibition of 1959, which included the work of the Heide group of artists. The manifesto argued for a distinctive form of national art which was both Australian and universal, and sprang from the artist's ability to create and transform myths for the deepened enlightenment of his society. See Haese, 264–5.

49 Rothwell, 2.

50 Bernd Krimmel, Catalogue essay *Sidney Nolan Exhibition* (Darmstadt, 1971). I am grateful to Gordon Collier, Professor of Commonwealth Literature at the University of Giessen, who brought the exhibition and catalogue essay to my attention and kindly provided a translated synopsis of its contents. See also Werner Kruger, 'Sidney Nolan in Moderna Museet Stockholm', *Art International* 20 (April–May, 1976), 31–4.

51 A reference to the testimony of the white blackfellow Duramboi (James Davis) as recorded by John Dunmore Lang after his return to Brisbane in 1842. Duramboi had absconded from the penal settlement at Moreton Bay and lived for over thirteen years with local Aborigines. His testimony is reproduced in the appendix to Kenneth Cook's novel, *Eliza Fraser* (1976).

52 Publicity circulated and displayed in galleries at the time of the exhibition 'Nolan's Fraser', Queensland Art Gallery, 1989.

53 Brown, 8–9.
54 For a fuller analysis of this article and attendant issues, see Andrew Lattas, 'Primitivism, Nationalism and Individualism in Australian Popular Culture', in *Power, Knowledge and Aborigines*, ed. Bain Atwood and John Arnold (Melbourne: Latrobe University Press, 1993), 45–58. My discussion is indebted to insights in this article and a longer unpublished version, which were generously supplied to me by the author.
55 Cynthia Nolan, *Outback* (London: Methuen, 1961).
56 Adams, 112.
57 Quoted in Brown, 10–11.
58 *Ibid.*, 10.
59 Critical understandings of the symbolism in Nolan's 'In the Cave' in the 1970s posited quite another interpretation of the relation between white and Aboriginal culture. MacInnes maintained that the X-ray figure of 'Mrs Fraser' represents a remnant of Australia's primordial past from which the convict emerged as the figure of the future. But it can also function as an icon of a more primal myth of merging, of boundary transgression.
60 Lattas, 57. Meaghan Morris has also addressed this problem of 'allochronism', a term borrowed from Johannes Fabian, and applied to an Australian political context. The concept formed the basis for her talk at the Adelaide International Festival of the Arts, Artists' Week Talk, 9 March 1992.
61 Lattas, 56.
62 These complex metaphors which explore dimensions of the inside/outside dichotomy in Western discourse are examined in depth by Maggie Kilgour in *From Communion to Cannibalism: An Anatomy of Metaphors of Incorporation* (Princeton: Princeton University Press, 1993). In her conclusion she writes that the recurring fantasy of a world in which everything is imagined as being inside has 'been the dream underlying the hope of the scientific mastery of nature, as well as various forms of imperialism; it has also been the nightmare underneath the gothic, which acknowledges the more infernal side of incorporation' (238).

7   Patrick White's Novel, *A Fringe of Leaves*

1 David Marr, *Patrick White: A Life* (Sydney: Random House, 1991), 377–8.
2 Marr also reports that Reeves was the first Aboriginal person that White had ever talked to, although he had already created the character of Alf Dubbo. Reeves was also the uncle of Fiona Foley, the Badtjala artist who has adapted the story in a series of paintings and installations. Foley's art is discussed in Chapter 10.
3 Marr, 413. The story goes that Patrick White and Sidney Nolan enlisted Peter Sculthorpe as the composer and Sir Robert Helpmann as the choreographer for their proposed Opera House performance. The four creative artists travelled to Fraser Island together in the mid-1960s to plan the piece. The meeting was a disaster, ending in a débâcle which strained relations between the four men. Three of them would subsequently create their own new versions of the Eliza Fraser story. Private correspondence with Barbara Blackman Veldhoven (4 November 1992). See also Michael Hannan, *Peter Sculthorpe: His Music and Ideas, 1929–1979* (St Lucia: University of Queensland Press, 1982), 111.
4 Marr, 541.
5 *Ibid.*, 378.
6 The first to document the parallels between the (then known) history and depictions in White's novel was Jill Ward. Her articles compared White's novel with the

accounts of Mrs Fraser's captivity related by Michael Alexander in *Mrs Fraser on the Fatal Shore*. Her research has provided a touchstone for later critics, although, as Ann Rebecca Ling points out with hindsight, her research was limited and her conclusions unreliable. See Jill Ward, 'Patrick White's *A Fringe of Leaves*: History and Fiction', *Australian Literary Studies* 8 (1978), 402–18, and 'Patrick White's *A Fringe of Leaves*', *Critical Quarterly* 10, 3 (Autumn 1977), 77–81; Ann Rebecca Ling, '*Voss* and *A Fringe of Leaves*: Community and Place in the Historical Novels of Patrick White', MA thesis, English Department, University of Queensland, 1983, 40–52.

7 The filmscript 'The Dreamtime of Mrs Fraser', written by Michael Luke, had been circulating in Sydney in the early 1970s. Luke had applied for funds from the newly formed Australian Film Commission. His plans collapsed when the AFC funded Tim Burstall's production, *Eliza Fraser*.

8 White, 'Patrick White Speaks on Factual Writing and Fiction,' *Australian Literary Studies* 10 (1981), 100.

9 White, *Flaws in the Glass* (London: Jonathan Cape, 1981), 104.

10 The title of an influential essay published in *Patrick White Speaks* (Sydney: Primavera Press, 1989) which will be discussed below.

11 Patrick White, *A Fringe of Leaves* (Harmondsworth: Penguin, 1976), 335. Subsequent citations will be taken from this edition of the novel, and page references will be cited parenthetically.

12 See for example, Brian Kiernan, *Patrick White* (London: Macmillan, 1980), 126–35; and L. T. Hergenhan, *Unnatural Lives* (St Lucia: University of Queensland Press, 1983), 154–5.

13 See, for example, Hena Maes-Jelinek, 'Fictional Breakthrough and the Unveiling of "Unspeakable Rites" in Patrick White's *A Fringe of Leaves* and Wilson Harris's *Yorokon*', *Kunapipi* 2, 2 (1980), 33–43; and Diana Brydon, ' "The Thematic Ancestor": Joseph Conrad, Patrick White and Margaret Atwood', *World Literature Written in English*, 24, 2 (1984), 386–79.

14 Brydon, 389–395.

15 *Ibid.*, 391.

16 I am thankful to Gordon Collier for his perceptive reading of this chapter and, in particular, for his critical understanding of this important dimension of White's work. See Collier, *The Rocks and Sticks of Words: Style, Discourse and Narrative Structure in the Fiction of Patrick White* (Philadelphia and Amsterdam: Rodopi Press, 1993).

17 Quoted in Marr, 277.

18 See *Ibid.*, 69.

19 For a fuller analysis of landscape and the quest motif, see Patricia Morley, 'Patrick White's *A Fringe of Leaves*: Journey to Tintagel', *World Literature Written in English* 21, 2 (1982): 303–15.

20 *Ibid.*, 304.

21 Title of a book by Richard Poirier, which explores the failed quest of Huckleberry Finn in terms of fictional style and this modernist conception of a world beyond culture. See Poirier, *A World Elsewhere: The Place of Style in American Literature* (New York: Oxford University Press, 1966).

22 A. P. Riemer, 'Landscape with Figures – Images of Australia in Patrick White's Fiction', *Southerly* 42 (1982), 20.

23 Riemer, 32.

24 Morley, 310.

25 See Dennis Haskell, 'A Lady Only by Adoption – Civilization in *A Fringe of Leaves*', *Southerly* 47, 4 (1987), 437.

26 Edward W. Said, *Culture and Imperialism* (London: Chatto and Windus, 1992), 228.

27 Veronica Brady, 'A Properly Appointed Humanism: Australian Culture and the Aborigines in Patrick White's *A Fringe of Leaves*', *Westerly* 2 (June 1983): 61–8.

28 Brady, 'Patrick White and Literary Criticism', *Australian Book Review* 133 (August 1991), 9.

29 L. T. Hergenhan, *Unnatural Lives* (St Lucia: University of Queensland Press, 1983), 160, 165.

30 There may be other readings which I have missed, but there are three articles by non-Australian critics which structure their analysis around a discussion of cannibalism: Canadian critic Terry Goldie, 'Contemporary Views of an Aboriginal Past: Rudy Wiebe and Patrick White', *World Literature Written in English* 23, 2 (1984), 429–39, repr. in Goldie, *Fear and Temptation: The Image of the Indigene in Canadian, Australian, and New Zealand Literature* (Kingston: McGill University Press, 1984), 194–214; European critic Maes-Jelinek, 'Fictional Breakthrough . . .'; and Canadian critic Morley, 'Journey to Tintagel'.

31 Goldie, 432, 438.

32 *Ibid.*, 435. The word 'inexhaustible' occurs in the novel in reference to the sexuality of Aboriginal women, or the lubra in the mind of Jack Chance. It is interesting in the light of the observations of Brian Simpson and Gananath Obeyesekere, discussed in Chapter 5, that white survivors of shipwreck looked to non-white survivors as first victims, drawing on their fantasies of libidinal potency of dark peoples. Perhaps this 'dark bond' of primal fantasy, which evokes libidinal desires in relation to non-white women as well as men, can be traced through Goldie's narrative as well.

33 Maes-Jelinek, 38.

34 *Ibid.*, 39.

35 Marianna Torgovnick, *Gone Primitive: Savage Intellects, Modern Lives* (Chicago: University of Chicago Press, 1990), 173.

36 See White, 'The Prodigal Son', quoted in Marr, 277, 327–8.

37 Andrew Lattas, original paper, 3, an abridged version of which appears as 'Primitivism, Nationalism and Individualism in Australian Popular Culture', in *Power, Knowledge and Aborigines*, ed. Bain Atwood and John Arnold (Melbourne: La Trobe University Press, 1993), 45–58.

38 John Rickard, 'Manning Clark and Patrick White: A Reflection,' *Australian Historical Studies*, 98 (1992), 122.

39 Patricia Morley, 'Under the Carpet: Vanity, Anger, and a Yearning for Sainthood (Essay Review)', *Antipodes* 6, 1 (1992), 45.

40 John Docker, 'Review of *Patrick White: A Life*', *Australian Historical Studies* 99 (1992), 347–8.

41 Lattas, original, 19.

42 Lattas, 'Primitivism', 51 ff.

8 A Universal Post-colonial Myth? Representations Beyond Australia

1 See Michael Hannan, *Peter Sculthorpe: His Music and Ideas, 1929–1979* (St Lucia: University of Queensland Press, 1982), 111–24.

2 Marianna Torgovnick, *Gone Primitive: Savage Intellects, Modern Lives* (Chicago: University of Chicago Press, 1990), 8, 253.

3 *Ibid.*, 151.

4 Michael Ondaatje, *The Man With Seven Toes* (Toronto: Coach House Press, 1969). All quotations will be taken from this source and line numbers will be cited parenthetically.

5 See Julia Kristeva, *The Powers of Horror: An Essay on Abjection*, trans. by Leon Roudiez (New York: Columbia University Press, 1982).

6 See Torgovnick, 53.

7 See Sigmund Freud, 'The Medusa's Head': 'To decapitate equals to castrate. The terror of the Medusa is thus a terror of castration that is linked to the sight of something. The hair upon the Medusa's head is frequently represented in works of art in the form of snakes, and these once again are derived from the castration complex. It is a remarkable fact that, however frightening they may be in them-selves, they nevertheless serve actually as a mitigation of the horror, for they replace the penis, the absence of which is the cause of the horror. This is a con-firmation of the technical rule according to which the multiplication of penis symbols signified castration.' Quoted in Laura Mulvey, 'Fears, Fantasies and the Male Unconscious, or "You Don't Know What is Happening, Do You, Mr. Jones?"', *Spare Rib* (1972), reprinted in *Visual and other Pleasures* (Bloomington, Ind.: Indiana University Press, 1989), 6.

8 This discussion makes use of the Lacanian notion of desire which focuses on desire as an impossible state of being, rather than an object. For a discussion of desire and the relationship of psychoanalysis to politics see Joan Copjec, 'Cutting Up', in *Between Feminism and Psychoanalysis*, ed. Teresa Brennan (London: Routledge, 1989), 227–46.

9 See Roslyn Poignant, 'Captive Aboriginal Lives', in Kate Darian-Smith, Roslyn Poignant and Kay Schaffer, *Captured Lives: Australian Captivity Narratives* (London: University of London, Sir Robert Menzies Centre for Australian Studies, 1993), 41.

10 Poignant, 9.

11 Gabriel Josipovici, 'Dreams of Mrs Fraser', *Steps: Selected Fiction and Drama.* (Manchester: Carcanet, 1990), 155. Subsequent quotations will be taken from this source.

12 Harold Hobson, 'Book Learning: Review of *Dreams of Mrs Fraser*', *Sunday Times* (London), 13 August 1972, 34.

13 Josipovici, 164.

14 Michel Foucault, *The History of Sexuality*, vol. 1 (Harmondsworth: Penguin, 1981; first published 1976), 63.

15 Hobson, 34.

16 Josipovici, 172.

17 *Ibid.*, 169, 170.

18 Personal correspondence with Gabriel Josipovici, 14 October 1991.

19 Michel de Montaigne, 'On Cannibals', in *The Complete Works of Montaigne*, trans. Donald M. Frame (Stanford: Stanford University Press, 1958). For a discussion of the fictive uses of barbarism, wildness and savagery in the works of Montaigne and Levi-Strauss, see Haydon White, 'The Forms of Wildness: Archaeology of an Idea' in *The Wild Man Within: An Image in Western Thought from the Renaissance to Romanticism*, ed. Edward Dudley and Maximillian E. Novak (Pittsburgh: University of Pittsburgh Press, 1972), 3–39.

20 Hannan, 25.

21 *Ibid.*, 190.

22 Tape of interview with Barbara Blackman Veldhoven, 4 November 1992.

23 Judith Newton, 'Family Fortunes: "New History" and "New Historicism"', *Radical History Review* (Winter 1989), 19.

24 Torgovnick, 246.

25 Barbara Blackman, '*Eliza Surviver: The Sorrowful Adventures of a Lady* – A Text for Music Theatre', *Quadrant* 21, 4 (April 1977), 34–9.

26 Blackman, 35.

27 Torgovnick, 246.

28 André Brink, *An Instant in the Wind* (London: Fontana, 1983; first published in Afrikaans in 1975; first English version published by W. H. Allen, London, 1976). Subsequent references to the text will use the 1983 version. Page numbers will be cited parenthetically in the text.

29 André Brink, 'A Bit of Wind around at the Moment', trans. for Kay Schaffer from Afrikaans by Jenny McDonogh, *Rapport* (South Africa), 6, 3 (1976), 24–5. See also Jim Davidson, 'An Interview With André Brink', *Overland* 94/95 (May 1984), 28.

30 Hjalmar Thesen, 'A Moving and Poignant Story: Review of *An Instant in the Wind*', *Eastern Province Herald*, 10 November 1976, 7.

31 Referred to by Brink in 'A Bit of Wind', 25.

32 Sue Kossew, *Pen and Power: A Post-colonial Reading of the Novels of J. M. Coetzee and André Brink*, (Atlanta and Amsterdam: Rodopi Press, forthcoming). I am grateful to Sue Kossew for making a draft of her PhD thesis available to me. Although her research and mine follow similar lines of inquiry, I am indebted to her close readings of the novel and her analysis of the differences between Brink's counter-history (*An Instant in the Wind*) and John Coetzee's more deconstructive readings of history in his fiction (*Dusklands* and *Foe*). The prior quotation is taken from Kossew's thesis, 78; the later quotation comes from the preface to *An Instant*, 15.

33 Kossew, 81. See also Gayatri Chakravorty Spivak, 'Three Women's Texts and a Critique of Imperialism', *Critical Inquiry* 12, 1 (1985), 243–61; and Peter Hulme, *Colonial Encounters: Europe and the Native Caribbean, 1492–1797* (London: Methuen, 1986), 187, 89–136.

34 See Torgovnick, 150–1.

35 Brink, 'A Bit of Wind', 25.

36 *Ibid.*

37 Edward W. Said, *Culture and Imperialism* (London: Chatto and Windus, 1992), 223.

38 Welma Odendaal, 'They had to Swallow their Words', *The Star* (Johannesburg), January 1978, 6.

39 Davidson, 28.

40 A. J. Hassall, 'The Making of a Colonial Myth: The Mrs Fraser Story in Patrick White's *A Fringe of Leaves* and André Brink's *An Instant in the Wind*', *Ariel* 18, 3 (1987), 4.

9   And Now for the Movie: Popular Accounts

1 Peter Burch, 'New Music Theatre is a Must', *Sydney Morning Herald*, date and page unknown. Clipping supplied by Barbara Blackman Veldhoven.

2 Tim Burstall, interview with Lenore Nicklin, 'On location – With Love and Ochre', *Sydney Morning Herald Weekend Magazine*, 8 May 1976.

3 Anon., 'Eliza Maligns the Blacks – Union', *Telegraph* (Sydney), 22 April 1976.

4 Ralph Sharman, 'Lights, Cameras – But Aboriginals Forget Songs', *ibid.*, 26 May 1976.

5 Anon., 'So Sad over Film Snub', *ibid.*, 26 December 1976, 11.

6 The adjectives are culled from the article and do not appear in this exact sequence. Geraldine Pascall, 'Eliza's on the Rocks', *Australian*, 18 December 1976. The newly formed Australian Film Commission had invested $250,000 in the film, money which was never recovered by box-office receipts.

7 Keith Connolly, 'Review of *Eliza Fraser*', *Cinema Papers* (1977), 362.

8 See Tom O'Regan, 'Cinema Oz: The Ocker Films', in *The Australian Screen*, ed. Tom O'Regan and Albert Moran (Ringwood, Vic.: Penguin, 1989), 77–80.

9 Dana Polan makes a similar point, à la Foucault, in his analysis of the cultural production of the concept of 'professors'. See 'Professors', *Discourse* 16, 1 (Fall 1993), 39.

10 O'Regan, 82, 97.

11 David Williamson, interview with Wendy Harmer, 'In Harmer's Way', ABC television, 19 March 1990. In fact Williamson's fears were not entirely overstated. Pickets did protest the depiction of a dominant/submissive lesbian relationship in one of Williamson's plays at La Mama in the late 1970s and the play was stopped.

12 Williamson, private correspondence, 8 March 1994. In relation to the charge that Williamson personally led the Ocker-dominated male club, or saw himself as 'storyteller to the tribe', he responded that he has always been uneasy with Burstall's macho bluster, never drank with the famous Melbourne male arts mafia, and referred to all writers as 'storytellers to the [wide rather than narrowly defined] tribe'.

13 Quoted in O'Regan, 81.

14 Eric Reade, *History and Heartburn: The Saga of Australian Film, 1896–1978* (Sydney: Harper and Row, 1979), 254.

15 Brian Kiernan, *David Williamson: A Writer's Career* (Melbourne: William Heinemann, 1990), 258.

16 Karen Jennings, *Sites of Difference: Cinematic Representations of Aboriginality* (Melbourne: Australian Film Institute, 1993), 27.

17 *Ibid.*, 27.

18 Brian McFarlane, *Australian Cinema, 1970–1985* (London: Secker and Warburg, 1987), 164.

19 Williamson, personal correspondence.

20 Susan Dermody, 'Action and Adventure', in *The New Australian Cinema*, ed. Scott Murray (Melbourne: Nelson, 1980), 82–3.

21 Kenneth Cook, *Eliza Fraser*, based on the original screenplay by David Williamson (Melbourne: Sun Books, 1975), 1. Subsequent quotations will be taken from this edition of the novel and page numbers will be cited parenthetically.

22 See Haydon White, *Tropics of Discourse: Essays in Cultural Criticism* (Baltimore: Johns Hopkins Press, 1978), 121–34.

23 Although the circus was not a feature of Eliza Fraser's times, in the 1880s circus impresario Robert Cunningham abducted three groups of Aborigines, including several from Fraser Island. They toured in the United States and Europe with the Barnum and Bailey circus, where they were displayed as 'exhibits' and 'curiosities' along with other indigenous people, exotic plants and animals. See Roslyn Poignant, 'Captive Aboriginal Lives: Billy, Jenny, Little Toby and their Companions', in Kate Darian-Smith, Roslyn Poignant and Kay Schaffer, *Captured Lives: Australian Captivity Narratives* (London: University of London: Sir Robert Menzies Centre for Australian Studies, 1993), 35–57.

24 See Andrew Parker, Mary Russo, Doris Sommer and Patricia Yeager (eds), *Nationalisms and Sexualities* (London and New York: Routledge, 1992), 6. The editors make reference to a similar evocation of this eroticised narrative of nationalism which occurred during the Gulf War, when Americans told the world how Sadam Hussein had raped the innocent women and children of Kuwait. The most popular book of the campaign carried the title *The Rape of Kuwait*. In keeping with the fantasy, US bombers inscribed the message 'Bend Over Saddam' on the ordinance dropped on Iraq prior to bombing.

25 For an analysis of displaced homosexuality in the film *Gallipoli*, see Barbara Creed, 'Feminist Film Theory: Reading the Text', in *Don't Shoot Darling: Women's Independent Film-making*, ed. Annette Blonski, Barbara Creed and Freda Freiberg (Sydney: Greenhouse, 1987), 298.

26 For an analysis of media projections of the British as boys' school 'bullies' and 'asses' affecting a 'lickspittle' servitude on the part of Prime Minister Menzies, see Graeme Turner, 'Semiotic Victories: Media Constructions of the Maralinga Royal Commission', in *Australian Cultural Studies: A Reader*, ed. John Frow and Meaghan Morris (Sydney: Allen and Unwin, 1993), 180–91.

27 Marianna Torgovnick, *Gone Primitive: Savage Intellects, Modern Lives* (Chicago: Chicago University Press, 1990), 151.

28 See for example Homi Bhabha, 'The Other Question: Difference, Discrimination and the Discourse of Colonialism', in *Literature, Politics and Theory*, ed. Francis Barker, *et al.* (London: Methuen, 1986), 148–72; four essay by Gayatri Chakravorty Spivak, 'Can the Subaltern Speak? Speculations on Widow Sacrifice', in *Marxism and the Interpretation of Culture*, ed. by Cary Nelson and Lawrence Grossberg (London: Macmillan, 1988) 271–313; 'Subaltern Studies: Deconstructing Historiography' and 'A Literary Representation of the Subaltern: A Woman's Text from the Third World', in *In Other Worlds: Essays in Cultural Politics* (New York and London: Routledge, 1988) 197–221 and 241–68; 'The Post-colonial Critic', in *The Post-Colonial Critic: Interviews, Strategies, Dialogues*, ed. Sarah Harasyn (New York and London: Routledge, 1990) 67–74; Edward W. Said, *Culture and Imperialism* (London: Chatto and Windus, 1992); Alan Lawson and Chris Tiffin (eds), *De-Scribing Empire* (London and New York: Routledge, 1994); and essays in the following collections: *Us/Them: Translation, Transcription and Identity in Post-Colonial Literary Cultures*, ed. Gordon Collier (Atlanta and Amsterdam: Rodopi, 1992); *Nationalisms and Sexualities*, ed. Andrew Parker, Mary Russo, Doris Sommer, and Patricia Yeager (New York and London: Routledge, 1992); *Colonialism and Culture*, ed. Nicholas B. Dirks (Ann Arbor: University of Michigan Press, 1992); and *Writing Women and Space*, ed. Alison Blunt and Gillian Rose (New York and London: Guildford Press, 1994).

10 Oppositional Voices: Contemporary Politics and the Eliza Fraser Story

1 See Annette Hamilton, 'Fear and Desire: Aborigines, Asians and the National Imaginary', *Australian Cultural History* 9 (Summer 1990), 14–35. I also discuss imaginary constructions of otherness within discourses of national identity in *Women and the Bush: Forces of Desire and the Australian Cultural Tradition* (Melbourne: Cambridge University Press, 1988).

2 Hamilton, 'Fear and Desire', 15.

3 'An Evening of No Drama: Eliza', directed by Akira Matsui and Richard Emmert, written by Allan Marett, music by Richard Emmert, choreography by Akira

Matsui. Program Notes, Theatre Services Unit and Department of Music, University of Sydney, 1989.

4 Program notes, 'Eliza', Tokyo productions (28–29 May 1990).

5 See Diana Y. Paul, *Women in Buddhism: Images of the Feminine in Mahayana Tradition* (Berkeley: University of California Press, 1979, rev. edn 1984).

6 Hamilton, 23.

7 See Carmen Blacker, *The Catalpa Bow: A Study of Shamanistic Practices in Japan* (London: George Allen and Unwin, 1975), 19–22.

8 Gillian Coote, producer, writer and director, 'Island of Lies', shown on *True Stories*. ABC TV, March 1991. Documentary distributed by Ronin Films.

9 See Homi K. Bhabha, '"Race", Time and the Revision of Modernity', *Oxford Literary Review* 13 (1991), 208–9.

10 Janet Batsleer, *et al.* (eds), *Rewriting English* (1985), quoted in Peter O. Stummer, 'Perceptions of Difference: The Conceptual Interaction of Cultures in Literary Discourse', in *Them/Us: Translation, Transcription and Identity in Post-Colonial Literary Cultures*, ed. Gordon Collier (Amsterdam and Atlanta: Rodopi, 1992), 307.

11 See Jennifer Isaacs and Rosemary Crumline, *Aboriginality: Aboriginal Art and Spirituality* (St Lucia: University of Queensland Press, 1989), 42.

12 Moonie Jarl [Wilf Reeves], *The Legends of Moonie Jarl*, illus. Wandi [Olga Miller] (Brisbane: Jacaranda Press, 1964).

13 *Ibid.*

14 Fiona Foley, 'Author's Introduction', *Tyerabarrowaryaou: I Shall Never Become a White Man*, curated by Fiona Foley and Djon Mundine (Sydney: Museum of Contemporary Art, 1992), 15.

15 See Moonie Jarl, 6–8, 21.

16 Charles Merewether, 'Fabricating Mythologies: The Art of Bricolage', in *The Boundary Rider: Ninth Biennale of Sydney*, ed. Anthony Bond (Sydney, 1992), 20. Merewether discusses artistic practices employed by South American post-modernist artists. But his analysis of post-modern forms of artistic address has relevance for Foley's work and that of a number of other Aboriginal artists, including artist Gordon Bennett; writer and critic Mudrooroo; and film-maker Tracey Moffatt.

17 Merewether, 21.

18 This tendency to utilise everyday objects in collage or montage paintings has been remarked upon by Merewether, 21.

19 Fiona Foley has a closer relation to the world of stamp collecting, being a designer herself. She was one of four Aboriginal artists whose designs were selected to illustrate postage stamps in 1993 to commemorate the Year of Indigenous Peoples. The 45-cent stamp with her design featuring a black cockatoo and black and red feathers was issued in July 1993.

20 For an analysis of the significance of these dynamics of mapping and naming in the colonial encounter, see Mary Hamer, 'Putting Ireland on the Map', *Textual Practice* 3, 2 (Summer 1989), 3–16.

21 Quoted by Elwyn Lynn, Catalogue essay, *Sidney Nolan's Ned Kelly*. Canberra: Australian National Gallery, 1985.

22 Martin Thomas, 'Aborigines Restore Engagement to Art', review of *The Concept of Country*, exhibition by Terry Gandadila, Dale Yowingbala and Fiona Foley, Ivan Dougherty Gallery, *Sydney Morning Herald*, 22 June 1991, 43.

23 See Stephen Bann, 'A Hole in the Wire', in *The Boundary Rider*, ed. Anthony Bond (Sydney, 1992), 24. Bann examines the play of frontiers and boundaries in contemporary art practice in terms of writings on utopian thought by the French

writer Louis Marin. Bann explains: 'For him, the abiding characteristic of Utopian thought (since its modern emergence with Sir Thomas More's treatise) has been the conceptualization of a space between frontiers: a *neutral place*, a locus whose characteristics are semiotically negative, whose specificity consists in being neither one or the other, *neither* this edge nor the other . . . a negative locus in which the promise of difference can take place.' That being said, it remains the case, as a discerning friend remarked after reading this passage, that the 'border', taken literally in physical, material and political terms, is *not* a place where anything can happen. The invading white settler culture is not likely to 'go home'.

24 Jane Gallop, *Around 1981* (New York and London: Routledge, 1992), 9.

Bibliography

Adams, Brian. *Sidney Nolan: Such is Life*. Melbourne: Hutchinson, 1987.

Alexander, Michael. *Mrs Fraser on the Fatal Shore*. London: Michael Joseph, 1971; 2nd edn, 1976.

Alexander, Michael, ed. 'Hans Staden among the Cannibals of Brazil.' In *Discovering the New World, Based on the Works of Theodore de Bry*: 90–121. London: London Editions, 1976.

Anderson, Benedict. *Imagined Communities: Reflections on the Origin and Spread of Nationalism*. London: Verso, 1991.

Anon. [A.B.]. 'Love which is itself a mere instant in the wind: review of *An Instant in the Wind*.' *Natal Witness*, 23 October 1980: 1.

Anon. [T.D. and I.C.H.]. 'Wild White Men.' In *Australian Encyclopedia*: 303–8. Melbourne: Collins, 1984; 2nd edn.

Anson, Stan. 'The Postcolonial Fiction.' *Arena* 96 (March 1991): 64–6.

Armitage, E. 'Corroborees of the Aborigines of Great Sandy Island', in F. J. Watson (ed.), 'Vocabularies of four representative tribes of South-Eastern Queensland'. Supplement to *Journal of the Royal Geographic Society of Australia* (Queensland) XLVIII, 34.

Arens, Werner. *The Man-Eating Myth : Anthropology and Anthropophagy*. Oxford: Oxford University Press, 1979.

Ashcroft, Bill, Gareth Griffiths, and Helen Tiffin, eds. *The Empire Writes Back: Theory and Practice in Post-Colonial Literatures*: 155–239. New York: Routledge, 1989.

Ashcroft, W. D. 'Intersecting Marginalities: Post-colonialism and Feminism.' *Kunapipi* 11, 2 (1989): 23–35.

'Australia's Greatest Crisis Since 1975.' *Advertiser* (Adelaide), 11 June 1993: 14.

Balibar, Etienne, and Immanuel Wallerstein, *Race, Nation, Class: Ambiguous Identities*: 37–67. London: Verso, 1991.

Bann, Stephen. 'A Hole in the Wire.' In *The Boundary Rider*, ed. Anthony Bond: 25–8. Sydney, 1992.

Barker, F., P. Hulme, M. Iverson, and D. Loxley, eds. *Europe and Its Others*. Colchester: University of Essex, 1985.

Barrett, Charles. 'White Woman among Cannibals.' In *White Blackfellows: The Strange Adventures of Europeans Who Lived among Savages*: 67–79. Melbourne: Hallcraft, 1948.

Barthes, Roland. *Mythologies*. Trans. Annette Lavers. London: Jonathan Cape, 1972.

[Barton, Charlotte] A Lady Long Resident of New South Wales. *A Mother's Offering to Her Children*. Milton, Qld: Jacaranda, 1977; reprint of 1841 edn.

Belfrage, Jane. 'The Great Australian Silence: Inside Acoustic Space.' In *Proceedings from the 'Bring a Plate' Feminist Cultural Studies Conference*, ed. Ruth Barkan, *et al.* Melbourne: University of Melbourne, forthcoming.

Berkhofer, Robert F., Jr. *The White Man's Indian: Images of the American Indian from Columbus to the Present*. New York: Knopf, 1978.

Bhabha, Homi K. '"Race", Time and the Revision of Modernity.' *Oxford Literary Review* 13 (1991): 193–219.

Bhabha, Homi K. 'DissemiNation: Time, Narrative and the Margins of the Modern Nation.' In *Nation and Narration*, ed. Homi Bhabha: 291–320. London: Routledge, 1990.

Bhabha, Homi K. 'Introduction: Narrating the Nation.' In *Nation and Narration*, ed. Homi K. Bhabha: 1–7. London: Routledge, 1990.

Bhabha, Homi K. 'The Other Question: Difference, Discrimination and the Discourse of Colonialism.' In *Literature, Politics and Theory*, ed. Francis Barker: 148–72. London: Methuen, 1986.

Bhabha, Homi K. 'Signs Taken For Wonders: Questions of Ambivalence and Authority Under a Tree Outside Delhi, May 1817.' In *Europe and Its Others*, ed. Francis Barker, Peter Hulme, Margaret Iverson, and Diana Loxley: 89–106. Colchester: University of Essex, 1985.

Bhabha, Homi K. 'Sly Civility.' *October* 34 (1985): 71–80.

Bhabha, Homi K. 'On Mimicry and Man: The Ambivalence of Colonial Discourse.' *October* 28 (March 1984): 125–33.

Bhabha, Homi K. 'Representation and the Colonial Text: A Critical Exploration of Some Forms of Mimeticism.' In *The Theory of Reading*, ed. Frank Gloversmith: 93–122. Brighton, Sussex: Harvester Press, 1984.

Bhabha, Homi K., ed. *Nation and Narration*. London: Routledge, 1990.

Blacker, Carmen. *The Catalpa Bow: A Study of Shamanistic Practices in Japan*. London: George Allen and Unwin, 1975.

Blackman, Barbara. 'Eliza Surviver.' *Quadrant* 21, 4 (April 1977): 31–9.

Blunt, Alison and Gillian Rose, eds. *Women, Writing and Space*. New York and London: Guilford Press, 1994.

Bondfield, Robyn. *Nolan's Fraser*. Brisbane: Queensland Art Gallery, 1989.

Bottomley, Gillian. *From Another Place: Migration and the Politics of Culture*. Melbourne: Cambridge University Press, 1992.

Bowman, David. 'Yes, and Lasseter's Reef Lives On.' *Australian Society* (September 1991): 14–15.

Brady, Veronica. 'Patrick White and Literary Criticism.' *Australian Book Review* 133 (August 1991): 9–11.

Brady, Veronica. 'A Properly Appointed Humanism: Australian Culture and the Aborigines in Patrick White's *A Fringe of Leaves*.' *Westerly* 2 (June 1983): 61–8.

Brantlinger, Richard. *Rule of Darkness: British Imperialism, 1830–1914*. Ithaca, NY: Cornell University Press, 1988.

Brantlinger, Richard. *The Spirit of Reform: British Literature and Politics, 1832–1867*. Cambridge, Mass.: Harvard University Press, 1977.

Bredvold, L. I. *The Natural History of Sensibility*. Detroit: Wayne State University Press, 1962.

Brink, André. 'A Bit of Wind Around at the Moment.' *Rapport* (South Africa).

Brink, André. *An Instant in the Wind*. London: Fontana, 1983.

Brissenden, R. F. *Virtue in Distress*. London: Macmillan Press, 1974.

Brown, Elaine. 'Nineteenth-century Cooloola: History of Contact and Environmental Change.' MA thesis. History Department, University of Queensland, in progress.

Brown, Heather. 'Nolan's Journey to Paradise.' *The Weekend Australian Magazine* 21–22 October 1989, 8–24.

Brydon, Diana. '"The Thematic Ancestor": Joseph Conrad, Patrick White and Margaret Atwood.' *World Literature Written in English* 24, 2 (1984): 386–97.

Buchanan, Neil, and Barry Dwyer. *The Rescue of Eliza Fraser*. Noosa Heads, Qld: Noosa Graphica, 1986.

Burger, Angela. *Fraser Island*. Privately published by the author, 1986.

Burke, Janine. *Joy Hester*. Richmond, Vic.: Greenhouse, 1983.

Tim Burstall (director) and David Williamson (screenplay). *A Faithful Narrative of the Capture, Sufferings and Miraculous Escape of Eliza Fraser*. Sydney: Hexagon Films, 1976.

Byrne, Paula J. *Criminal Law and Colonial Subject: New South Wales, 1810–1830*. Melbourne: Cambridge University Press, 1993.

Carter, Paul. *Living in a New Country: History, Travelling and Language*. London: Faber and Faber, 1992.

Carter, Paul. *The Road to Botany Bay: An Essay in Spatial History*. London: Faber and Faber, 1987.

Chatwin, Bruce. *Songlines*. London: Jonathan Cape, 1987.

Cilento, Sir Raphael. 'The Convict and the Captain's Lady', or 'All Tempests to Endure.' Brisbane, 1966. Unpublished manuscript held at the Fryer Library, Brisbane.

Cixous, Hélène. 'Laugh of the Medusa.' Trans. Keith Cohen and Paula S. Cohen. *Signs: A Journal of Women and Culture* 1, 4 (June 1976): 875–93.

Cixous, Hélène. 'Sorties.' Trans. Betsy Wing. In *The Newly Born Woman*, ed. Hélène Cixous and Catherine Clement: 63–75. Minneapolis: University of Minnesota Press, 1986.

Clark, Anna. 'Queen Caroline and the Sexual Politics of Popular Culture in London, 1820.' *Representations* 31 (Summer, 1990): 47–68.

Clark, Anne. 'The Rhetoric of of Chartist Domesticity: Gender, Language and Class in the 1830's and 1840's.' *Journal of British Studies* 31, 1 (January, 1992).

Clark, Jane. *Sidney Nolan: Landscapes and Legends: A Retrospective Exhibition, 1937–1987*. Sydney: International Cultural Corporation of Australia, 1987.

Clark, Kenneth, Colin MacInnes, and Bryan Robertson. *Sidney Nolan: Landscapes and Legends*. London: Thames and Hudson, 1961.

Clark, Suzanne. *Sentimental Modernism*. Bloomington: Indiana University Press, 1991.

Clarke, Marcus. *His Natural Life*. Intro. and ed. Stephen Murray-Smith. Ringwood Vic.: Penguin, 1970 [first serialised 1870–2 in *Australian Journal*].

Collier, Gordon. *The Rocks and Sticks of Words: Style, Discourse and Narrative Structure in the Fiction of Patrick White*. Philadelphia and Amsterdam: Rodopi, 1993.

Collier, Gordon, ed. *Us/Them: Translation, Transcription and Identity in Post-Colonial Literary Cultures*. Atlanta and Amsterdam: Rodopi, 1992.

Connolly, Keith. 'Review of Eliza Fraser.' *Cinema Papers* (April 1977): 362–63.

Cook, Kenneth. *Eliza Fraser*. Melbourne: Sun Books, 1976.

Coote, Gillian. *Island of Lies*. Film produced by Tony and Gillian Coote Pty Ltd. Sydney: Ronin Films, March 1991.

Copjec, Joan. 'Cutting Up.' In *Between Feminism and Psychoanalysis*, ed. Teresa Brennan: 227–46. Sydney: Routledge, 1989.

Creed, Barbara. 'Feminist Film Theory: Reading the Text.' In *Don't Shoot Darling: Women's Independent Film-making*, ed. Annette Blonski, Barbara Creed, and Freda Freiberg: 280–313. Sydney: Greenhouse, 1987.

Crosby, Christina. *The Ends of History: Victorians and 'The Woman Question'*. London: Routledge, 1991.

Curthoys, Ann. 'Feminism, Citizenship and National Identity.' *Feminist Review* 44 (Summer, 1993): 19–38.

Curthoys, Ann. 'Identity Crisis: Colonialism, Nation and Gender in Australian History.' *Gender and History* 5, 2 (Summer, 1993): 165–176.

Curtis, John. *The Shipwreck of the Stirling Castle*. London: George Virtue, Ivy Lane, 1838.

Darian-Smith, Kate, 'The White Woman of Gippsland: A Frontier Myth.' In *Captured Lives: Australian Captivity Narratives*, ed. Kate Darian-Smith, Roslyn Poignant and Kay Schaffer: 14–34. London: University of London, Sir Robert Menzies Centre for Australian Studies, 1993.

Darian-Smith, Kate, Roslyn Poignant, and Kay Schaffer. *Captured Lives: Australian Captivity Narratives*. London: University of London, Sir Robert Menzies Centre for Australian Studies, 1993.

Davidoff, Lenore, and Catherine Hall. *Family Fortunes: Men and Women of English Middle Class, 1780–1850*. London: Hutchinson, 1987.

Davidson, Jim. 'Beyond the Fatal Shore: The Mythologization of Mrs Fraser.' *Meanjin* 3 (1990): 449–61.

Davidson, Jim. 'An Interview With André Brink.' *Overland* 94/95 (May 1984): 24–30.

de Certeau, Michel. 'Heterologies: Discourse on the Other.' Trans. Brian Massumi and Wlad Godzich. In *Theory and History of Literature*, vol. 17. Minneapolis: University of Minnesota Press, 1986.

de Certeau, Michel. *Practice of Everyday Life*. Berkeley: University of California Press, 1984.

de Montaigne, Michel. 'On Cannibals.' Trans. Donald M. Frame. In *The Complete Works of Montaigne*. Stanford: Stanford University Press, 1958.

Dermody, Susan. 'Action and Adventure.' In *The New Australian Cinema*, ed. Scott Murray: 79–95. Melbourne: Nelson, 1980.

Derrida, Jacques. 'Plato's Pharmacy.' Trans. Barbara Johnson. In *Dissemination*: 97–115. London: Athlone Press, 1981.

Derrida, Jacques. *Of Grammatology*. Trans. G. C. Spivak. Baltimore: Johns Hopkins University Press, 1976.

Dirks, Nicholas B. 'Introduction: Colonialism and Culture.' In *Colonialism and Culture*, ed. Nicholas B. Dirks: 1–26. Ann Arbor, Michigan: University of Michigan Press, 1992.

'Disastrous Wreck of the "Stirling Castle", bound from Sydney N.S.W. to Singapore.' *Alexander's East India and Colonial Magazine* 14, 82 (1837): 258–63.

Docker, John. 'Review of *Patrick White: A Life*.' *Australian Historical Studies* 99 (1992): 347–8.

Drummond, Yolanda. 'Progress of Eliza Fraser.' *Journal of the Royal Historical Society of Queensland* 15, 1 (February 1993): 15–25.

Drummond, Yolanda. 'Two Women.' 1991 (unpublished).

Edwards, Hugh. *Australian and New Zealand Shipwrecks and Sea Tragedies*. Sydney: Mathews/Hutchinson, 1978.

'Eliza and Her Black Man.' Bedborough Printers (London). Handbill, nd.

'Eliza Maligns the Blacks – Union.' *Telegraph* (Sydney), 22 April 1976.

Evans, Ray, Kay Saunders, and Kathryn Cronin. *Race Relations in Colonial Queensland: A History of Exclusion, Exploitation and Extermination.* St Lucia, Qld: University of Queensland Press, 1988.

Evans, Raymond, and Jan Walker. '"These Strangers, Where Are They Going?"'. Aboriginal-European Relations in the Fraser Island and Wide Bay Region 1770–1905.' *Occasional Papers in Anthropology* 8 (1977): 39–105.

'An Evening of No Drama: Eliza.' *Program Notes.* Sydney: Theatre Services Unit and Department of Music, University of Sydney, 1989.

'Explorers May Have Eaten Comrades.' *Advertiser* (Adelaide), 13 June 1994: 11.

Fabian, Johannes. *Time and the Other: How Anthropology Makes its Object.* New York: Columbia University Press, 1983.

Fiedler, Leslie. *Return of the Vanishing American.* London: Jonathan Cape, 1968.

Foley, Fiona. 'Author's Introduction.' In *Tyerabarrowaryaou: I Shall Never Become a White Man,* 20 pp. catalogue for exhibition curated by Fiona Foley and Djon Mundine. Sydney: Museum of Contemporary Art, 1992.

Foley, Shaun. *The Badtjala People.* Hervey Bay: Thoorgine Educational and Cultural Centre, Aboriginal Corporation Inc., 1994.

Forbes, Cameron. 'Islands in the Storm.' *Australian Weekend Review* 26–27 June 1993: 1.

Foucault, Michel. *Power/Knowledge: Selected Interviews and Other Writings, 1972–1977.* Compiled and ed. Colin Gordon. New York: Pantheon, 1980.

Foucault, Michel. 'Nietzsche, Genealogy, History.' Trans. Donald F. Bouchard and Sherry Simon. In *Language, Counter-Memory, Practice: Selected Essays and Interviews,* intro. and ed. Donald F. Bouchard: 139–64. Ithaca, New York: Cornell University Press, 1977.

Foucault, Michel. *The History of Sexuality, Vol. 1.* Trans. Robert Hurley. Harmondsworth: Penguin, 1976.

Foucault, Michel. *The Archaeology of Knowledge.* Trans. Alan Sheridan. New York: Pantheon Books, 1970.

Gallop, Jane. *Around 1981.* New York and London: Routledge, 1992.

Gates, Henry L., Jr. 'Editor's Introduction: Writing "Race" and the Difference it Makes.' *Critical Inquiry* 12 (1985): 1–20.

Gibbings, Robert. *John Graham, Convict, 1824.* London: J. M. Dent, 1956.

Goldie, Terry. *Fear and Temptation: The Image of the Indigene in Canadian, Australian, and New Zealand Literatures.* Kingston, Ontario: McGill-Queen's University Press, 1989.

Goldie, Terry. 'Contemporary Views of an Aboriginal Past: Rudy Wiebe and Patrick White.' *World Literature Written in English* 23, 2 (1984): 429–39.

Griffiths, Gareth. 'Imitation, Abrogation and Appropriation: The Production of the Post-Colonial Text.' *Kunapipi* 9, 1 (1987): 13–20.

Grosz, Elizabeth. *Jacques Lacan: A Feminist Introduction.* Sydney: Allen and Unwin, 1990.

Gunew, Sneja. 'Feminism and Difference: Valedictory Thoughts on the Australian Scene.' *Australian Women's Book Review* 5, 2 (June, 1993): 40–44.

Gunew, Sneja. 'PMT (Post-modernist tensions): Reading for (multi)cultural Difference.' In *Striking Chords: Multicultural Literary Interpretations,* ed. Sneja Gunew and Kateryna Longley, 36–46. Sydney: Allen and Unwin, 1992.

Gunew, Sneja. 'Denaturalizing Cultural Nationalisms: Multicultural Readings of "Australia".' In *Nation and Narration,* ed. Homi Bhabha: 99–120. London: Routledge, 1990.

Gunew, Sneja. 'Australia 1984: A Moment in the Archaeology of Multiculturalism.' In *Europe and Its Others*, ed. Francis Barker *et al.*, 178-93. Colchester: University of Essex Press, 1985.

Gunew, Sneja. 'Framing Marginality: Distinguishing the Textual Politics of the Marginal Voice.' *Southern Review* 18, 2 (1985): 142-57.

Haese, Richard. 'Introduction.' In Albert Tucker, *Faces I Have Met*: 1-8. Melbourne: Century Hutchinson, 1986.

Haese, Richard. *Rebels and Precursors: The Revolutionary Years of Australian Art*. Melbourne: Allen Lane, 1981.

Hall, Catherine. *White, Male and Middle Class: Explorations in Feminism and History*. London: Routledge, 1992.

Hamer, Mary. 'Putting Ireland on the Map.' *Textual Practice* 3, 2 (June 1989): 3-16.

Hannan, Michael. *Peter Sculthorpe: His Music and Ideas 1929-1979*. St Lucia, Qld: University of Queensland Press, 1982.

Harmer, Wendy, interview with David Williamson, 'In Harmer's Way.' ABC television, 19 March 1990.

Haskell, Dennis. 'A Lady Only by Adoption – Civilization in *A Fringe of Leaves*.' *Southerly* 47, 4 (1987): 433-42.

Hassall, A. J. 'The Making of a Colonial Myth: The Mrs. Fraser Story in Patrick White's *A Fringe of Leaves* and André Brink's *An Instant in the Wind*.' *Ariel* 18, 3 (1987): 3-38.

Hassam, Andrew. '"Our Floating Home": Social Space and Group Identity on Board the Emigrant Ship.' *Working Papers in Australian Studies*, No. 76. London: University of London, Sir Robert Menzies Centre for Australian Studies, 1992.

Heathcote, Christopher. 'Nolan: An Art Transformed.' *Age* (Melbourne), 30 November 1992: 14.

Herbst, Peter. 'Introduction.' *The Boxer Collection: Modernism, Murrumbeena and Angry Penguins*: 4-16. Canberra: Australian Government Printing Service, 1981.

Hergenhan, L. T. *Unnatural Lives*. Brisbane: University of Queensland Press, 1983.

Heyward, Michael. *The Ern Malley Affair*. St Lucia: University of Queensland Press, 1993.

History of the Captivity and Providential Release therefrom of Mrs. Caroline Harris. New York: Perry and Cooke, 1838.

Hobson, Harold. 'Book Learning (Review of *Dreams of Mrs. Fraser*).' *Sunday Times* (London), August 1972: 46.

Huggins, Jackie, and Kay Saunders. 'Defying the Ethnographic Ventriloquists: Race, Gender and the Legacies of Colonialism.' *Lilith* (Summer, 1993): 60-70.

Hughes, Robert. *The Fatal Shore*. London: Collins Harvill, 1987.

Hughes, Robert. *The Art of Australia*. Harmondsworth: Penguin, 1966; rev. edn. 1970, reprinted 1980.

Hulme, Peter. *Colonial Encounters: Europe and the Native Caribbean, 1492-1797*. London: Methuen, 1986.

Hulme, Peter. 'Polytropic Man: Tropes of Sexuality and Mobility in Early Colonial Discourse.' In *Europe and Its Others* vol. 2., ed. Francis Barker, Peter Hulme, Margaret Iverson, and Diana Loxley. Colchester: University of Essex, 1985.

Irigaray, Luce. 'This Sex which is Not One.' Trans. Claudia Reeder. In *New French Feminisms*, ed. Elaine Marks, and Isabel DeCortivron: 99-106. Amherst, Massachusetts: University of Massachusetts Press, 1980.

Isaacs, Jennifer, and Rosemary Crumline. *Aboriginality: Aboriginal Art and Spirituality*. St Lucia, Qld: University of Queensland Press, 1989.

JanMohamed, Abdul R. 'The Economy of Manichean Allegory: The Function of Racial Difference in Colonialist Literature.' *Critical Inquiry* 12 (1985): 59–87.

Jarl, Moonie (Wilf Reeves). *The Legends of Moonie Jarl*. Brisbane : Jacaranda Press, 1964. Illus. Wandi [Olga Miller].

Jennings, Karen. *Sites of Difference: Cinematic Representations of Aboriginality*. Melbourne: Australian Film Institute, 1993.

Josipovici, Gabriel. 'Dreams of Mrs. Fraser.' First performed in London, Royal Theatre (Upstairs), August 1972. Playscript published in *Steps: Selected Fiction and Drama*: 155–73. London: Carcanet, 1989.

Kiernan, Brian. *David Williamson: A Writer's Career*. Melbourne: William Heinemann, 1990.

Kiernan, Brian. *Patrick White*. London: Macmillan, 1980.

Kilgour, Maggie. *From Communion to Cannibalism: An Anatomy of Metaphors of Incorporation*. Princeton: Princeton University Press, 1993.

Kossew, Sue. *Pen and Power: A Post-colonial Reading of the Novels of J. M. Coetzee and André Brink*. Atlanta and Amsterdam: Rodopi Press, forthcoming.

Kossew, Sue. 'Pen and Power: A Post-colonial Reading of the Novels of J. M. Coetzee and André Brink.' PhD thesis, School of English, University of New South Wales, 1993.

Krimmel, Bernd. Catalogue Essay. In *Sidney Nolan Exhibition*. Darmstadt, 1971.

Kristeva, Julia. *The Powers of Horror: An Essay on Abjection*. Trans. Leon Roudiez. New York: Columbia University Press, 1982.

Kruger, Werner. 'Sidney Nolan in Moderna Museet Stockholm.' *Art International* 20 (April-May 1976): 31–34.

Lacan, Jacques. 'The Mirror Phase.' *New Left Review* 51 (1968): 71–77.

Langevad, Gerry. *Some Original Views around Kilcoy, Book 1: The Aboriginal Perspective*. University of Queensland, Anthropology Museum Papers, 1997.

Langton, Marcia. *Well, I Heard it on the Radio, and I Saw it on the Television*. Canberra: Australian Film Institute, 1993.

Lattas, Andrew. 'Primitivism, Nationalism and Individualism in Australian Popular Culture.' In *Power, Knowledge and Aborigines*, ed. Bain Atwood, and John Arnold: 45–58. Melbourne: Latrobe University Press, 1993.

Lattas, Andrew. 'Primordiality and Australian National Identity: The Politics of Otherness.' Unpublished paper (September 1988): 1–17.

Lattas, Andrew. 'Savagery and Civilisation: Towards a Genealogy of Racism.' *Social Analysis* 21 (August 1987): 39–58.

Lauer, Peter K. 'The Museums' Role in Field Work: The Fraser Island Study.' *Occasional Papers in Anthropology* 9 (1977): 31–72.

Lauer, Peter K. 'Report of A Preliminary Ethnohistorical and Archaeological Survey of Fraser Island.' *Occasional Papers in Anthropology*, 8 (1977): 1–38. Brisbane: University of Queensland Anthropological Museum.

Levernier, James and Hennig Cohen, eds and comps. *The Indians and Their Captives* Westport, Conn.: Greenwood Press, 1977.

'A Life: Sir Sidney Nolan.' Narrated and interviewed Peter Ross. ABC television documentary, 13 January 1993.

Ling, Ann Rebecca. '*Voss* and *A Fringe of Leaves*: Community and Place in the Historical Novels of Patrick White.' M.A. thesis, English Department, University of Queensland, 1983.

Loos, Noel. *Invasion and Resistance*. Canberra: Australia National University Press, 1982.

Luke, Michael. 'The Dreamtime of Mrs Fraser.' Filmscript. London: Acorn Pro-
    ductions, 1970.
MacInnes, Colin. 'Introduction.' In *Sidney Nolan: Catalogue of an Exhibition of Paintings
    from 1947 to 1957 held at the Whitechapel Art Gallery, London: June to July 1957.*
    London: Whitechapel Art Gallery, 1957.
Mackay, Jane, and Pat Thane. 'The Englishwoman.' In *Englishness: Politics and Culture,
    1880–1920*: 191–229. London: Croom-Helm, 1986.
Maes-Jelinek, Hena. 'Fictional Breakthrough and the Unveiling of "Unspeakable
    Rites" in Patrick White's *A Fringe of Leaves* and Wilson Harris's *Yurokon.' Kunapipi*
    2, 2 (1980): 33–43.
Marett, Allan. 'Talking about Eliza: Cross Cultural Perspectives on the Relationship
    Between Performance and Discourse.' Unpublished lecture delivered at Hong
    Kong University, 1992.
Marett, Allan. *Eliza.* Tokyo production: May 1990.
Marett, Allan. *Eliza: An English Noh Play.* Directed by Richard Emmert and Akira
    Matsui. Sydney: 1989.
Marr, David. *Patrick White: A Life.* Sydney: Random House, 1991.
Marree, Adrian. 'Museums and Aborigines: A Case Study in Internal Colonialism.'
    Australian–Canadian Studies 7, 1–2 (1989): 63–80.
Matthew, J. *Two Representative Tribes of Queensland.* London: T. Fisher Unwin, 1910.
McFarlane, Brian. *Australian Cinema, 1970–1985.* London: Secker and Warburg, 1987.
McGrath, Ann. '"Beneath the Skin": Australian Citizenship, Rights and Aboriginal
    Women', in *Women and the State*, ed. Renate Howe: 99–114. Melbourne:
    Latrobe University Press, 1993.
McNab, Robert (ed.). 'Wreck of the "Stirling Castle".' In *The Old Whaling Days: A
    History of Southern New Zealand from 1830–1840*: 149–56. Auckland: Golden
    Press,   1913.
McNicoll, D. D. and Bryce Hallett. 'Sir Sidney Leaves Art World an Awesome Legacy.'
    Australian, 30 November 1992: 4.
McNiven, Ian. 'Ethnohistorical Reconstructions of Aboriginal Lifeways along the
    Cooloola Coast, Southeast Queensland.' *Proceedings of the Royal Society of Queens-
    land* 102 (August 1992): 5–24.
McQueen, Humphrey. *The Black Swan of Trespass: The Emergence of Modernist Art in Aus-
    tralia to 1944.* Sydney: Alternative Publishing Cooperative Limited, 1979.
Melville, Robert. 'Disquieting Muse.' In Sidney Nolan, *Paradise Garden*, ed. Robert
    Melville: 5–9. London: R. Alastair McAlpine Publishing, 1971.
Merewether, Charles. 'Fabricating Mythologies: The Art of Bricolage.' In *The Boundary
    Rider: Ninth Biennale of Sydney*, ed. Anthony Bond: 20–4. Sydney: Ninth Biennale
    of Sydney, 1992.
Meucke, Stephen. *Textual Spaces: Aboriginality and Cultural Studies.* Sydney: University
    of New South Wales Press, 1992.
Meucke, Stephen. 'Where are the Aboriginal Intellectuals?' *Australian Book Review* 148
    (February 1993): 25–9.
Miller, Olga. *Fraser Island Legends.* Brisbane: Jacaranda Press, 1993.
Milliss, Roger. *Waterloo Creek.* Ringwood, Vic. McPhee Gribble, 1992.
Morley, Patricia. 'Patrick White's *A Fringe of Leaves*: Journey to Tintagel.' *World Litera-
    ture Written in English* 21, 2 (1982): 303–15.
Morley, Patricia. 'Under the Carpet: Vanity, Anger, and a Yearning for Sainthood.'
    Essay Review. *Antipodes* 6, 1 (1992): 45–6.
Morris, Meaghan. Artists' Week Talk. Adelaide: Adelaide Festival of Arts, March
    1992.

Mudrooroo, Narogin. *Writing from the Fringe: A Study of Modern Australian Literature.* Melbourne: Hyland House, 1990.

Mulvey, Laura. 'Fears, Fantasies and the Male Unconscious or "You Don't Know What is Happening, Do You, Mr. Jones?"' In *Visual and Other Pleasures*: 6–13. Bloomington: Indiana University Press, 1989.

Namias, June. *White Captives.* Chapel Hill: University of North Carolina Press, 1993.

Narrative of the Capture, Sufferings, and Miraculous Escape of Mrs. Eliza Fraser. New York: Charles Webb and Sons, 1837.

Nicklin, Lenore. 'On Location – With Love and Ochre', *Sydney Morning Herald Weekend Magazine*, 8 May 1976.

Nolan, Cynthia. *Outback.* London: Methuen, 1961.

Nolan, Sidney. *Paradise Garden*, ed. Robert Melville. London: McAlpine, 1971.

Obeyesekere, Gananath. *The Apotheosis of Captain Cook: European Mythmaking in the Pacific.* Princeton, NJ: Princeton University Press, 1992.

Obeyesekere, Gananath. 'British Cannibals: Contemplation of an Event in the Death and Resurrection of James Cook, Explorer.' *Critical Inquiry* 18 (Summer, 1992): 630–54.

Odendaal, Welma. 'They Had to Swallow Their Words.' *The Star* (Johannesburg), 16 January 1978: 6.

Ondaatje, Michael. *The Man With Seven Toes.* Toronto: Coach House Press, 1969.

O'Regan, Tom. 'Cinema Oz: The Ocker Films.' In *The Australian Screen*, ed. Tom O'Regan, and Albert Moran. Ringwood, Vic.: Penguin, 1989.

Parker, Andrew, Mary Russo, Doris Sommer, and Patricia Yeager, eds. *Nationalisms and Sexualities.* London and New York: Routledge, 1992.

Pascall, Geraldine. 'Eliza's on the Rocks.' *The Australian* (Canberra), 18 December 1976: 25.

Paul, Diana Y. *Women in Buddhism: Images of the Feminine in Mahayana Tradition.* Berkeley: University of California Press, 1979; rev. edn. 1984.

Pearce, Roy. 'The Significances of the Captivity Narrative.' *American Literature* 19 (1948): 1–20.

Petrie, Constance Campbell. *Tom Petrie's Reminiscences of Early Queensland.* Brisbane: Watson, Ferguson and Co., 1904.

Pettman, Jan. 'Whose Country is it Anyway? Cultural Politics, Racism and the Construction of Being Australian.' *Journal of Inter-cultural Studies* 9, 1 (1988): 1–24.

Pickering, Michael. 'Cannibalism amongst Aborigines? A Critical Review of the Literary Evidence.' PhD dissertation, Australian National University, 1985.

Poignant, Roslyn. 'Captive Aboriginal Lives.' In *Captured Lives: Australian Captivity Narratives*, by Kate Darian-Smith, Roslyn Poignant, and Kay Schaffer: 35–57. London: Sir Robert Menzies Centre for Australian Studies, 1993.

Poirier, Richard. *A World Elsewhere: The Place of Style in American Literature.* New York: Oxford University Press, 1966.

Polan, Dana. 'Professors.' *Discourse* 16, 1 (Fall, 1993): 28–49.

Porter, Carolyn. 'History and Literature: "After the New Historicism"', *New Literary History* 21, 2 (Winter, 1990), 253–81.

Pratt, Mary Louise. *Imperial Eyes: Travel Writing and Transculturation.* London and New York: Routledge, 1992.

Reade, Eric. *History and Heartburn: The Saga of the Australian Film, 1896–1978.* Sydney: Harper and Row, 1979.

Reed, John. 'The Formative Years: 1940–1945.' Catalogue essay. Melbourne: Museum of Modern Art of Australia, 1961.

Reid, Barrie. 'Nolan in Queensland: Some Biographical Notes on the 1947–48 Paintings.' *Art and Australia* (September 1967): 446–7.

'Review of André Brink's *An Instant in the Wind*.' *Unisa English Studies* 23, 1 (April 1985): 69.

Reynolds, Henry. 'Land Without Owners: *Terra Nullius* in Australian Politics and History.' Paper given at *Significant Others: Second Conference of the Australian Cultural Studies Association*, December 1992.

Reynolds, Henry. 'The Land, the Explorers and the Aborigines.' In *Through White Eyes*, eds. Susan Janson and Stuart MacIntyre, 120–97. Sydney: Allen and Unwin, 1990.

Reynolds, Henry. *Dispossession: Black Australians and White Invaders*. Sydney: Allen and Unwin, 1989.

Reynolds, Henry. *Frontier: Aborigines, Settlers and Land*. Sydney: Allen and Unwin, 1987.

Reynolds, Henry. *The Law of the Land*. Ringwood, Vic.: Penguin, 1987.

Reynolds, Henry. *The Other Side of the Frontier: Aboriginal Resistance to the European Invasion of Australia*. Ringwood, Vic. Penguin, 1982.

Reynolds, Henry, and Noel Loos. 'Aboriginal Resistance in Queensland.' *Australian Journal of Politics and History* 22 (1976): 214–26.

Rickard, John. 'Manning Clark and Patrick White: A Reflection.' *Australian Historical Studies* 98 (1992): 116–22.

Riemer, A. P. 'Landscape with Figures – Images of Australia in Patrick White's Fiction.' *Southerly* 42 (1982): 20–38.

Robertson, Bryan. 'Preface.' In *Sidney Nolan [Catalogue of an Exhibition of Paintings from 1947 to 1957 held at the Whitechapel Art Gallery, London: June to July 1957]*. London: Whitechapel Art Gallery, 1957.

Rogin, Michael Paul. *Ronald Reagan, the Movie and Other Episodes in Political Demonology*. Berkeley: University of California Press, 1987.

Rose, Deborah Bird. 'Worshiping Captain Cook', *Social Analysis* 32 (December 1993): 43–50.

Rose, Deborah Bird. *Hidden Histories: Black Stories from Victoria River Downs, Humbert River and Wave Hill Stations*. Canberra: Aboriginal Studies Press, 1991.

Rose, Jacqueline. *Sexuality in the Field of Vision*. London: Verso, 1986.

Ross, Peter. 'Nolan at Sixty.' ABC television documentary, 1992.

Rothwell, Nicholas. 'Nolan: The Artist in Exile Begins His Long Journey Home.' *Weekend Australian* 15–17 August 1989: 6.

Russell, Henry Stuart. *The Genesis of Queensland*. London: Vintage Books, 1888.

Russell, Henry Stuart. 'Mr. Russell's "Excursions in Australia".' *Journal of the Royal Geographic Society* (London), 15, 2 (1845): 310–20.

Ryan, J. S. 'The Several Fates of Eliza Fraser.' *Journal of the Royal Historical Society of Queensland* 11, 4 (1983): 88–112.

Ryan, Simon. 'A Word with the Natives: Dialogic Encounters in Journals of Australian Exploration.' *Australian and New Zealand Studies in Canada* 8 (1993): 71–83.

Said, Edward W. *Culture and Imperialism*. London: Chatto and Windus, 1992.

Said, Edward W. *Orientalism*. New York: Pantheon Books, 1978.

Sampson, David. 'Black and White: *A Fringe of Leaves*.' *Meridian* 2, 2 (October 1982): 109–15.

Sanday, Peggy Reeves. *Divine Hunger: Cannibalism as a Cultural System*. Cambridge: Cambridge University Press, 1986.

Schaffer, Kay. 'Colonizing Gender in Colonial Australia: The Eliza Fraser Story.' In *Writing, Women and Space*, ed. Gillian Rose and Alison Blunt: 117–40. New York: Guilford Press, 1994.

Schaffer, Kay. 'Captivity Narratives and the Idea of "Nation".' In *Captured Lives: Australian Captivity Narratives*, by Kate Darian-Smith, Roslyn Poignant, and Kay Schaffer: 1–17. University of London: Sir Robert Menzies Centre for Australian Studies, 1993.

Schaffer, Kay. 'Australian Mythologies: The Eliza Fraser Story and Constructions of the Feminine in Patrick White's *A Fringe of Leaves* and Sidney Nolan's Eliza Fraser Paintings.' In *Them and Us: Translation, Transcription and Identity in Post-Colonial Litarary Cultures*, ed. Gordon Collier: 371–83. Amsterdam and Atlanta: Rodopi Press, 1992.

Schaffer, Kay. 'The Eliza Fraser Story and Constructions of Gender, Race and Class in Australian Culture.' *Hecate: Women/Australia/Theory [Special Issue]* 17, 1 (1991): 136–49.

Schaffer, Kay. 'Trial By Media: The Case of Eliza Fraser.' *Antipodes* (US), (1991): 114–19.

Schaffer, Kay. *Women and the Bush: Forces of Desire in the Australian Cultural Tradition.* Melbourne: Cambridge University Press, 1988.

Schaffer, Kay. 'Critical Dilemmas: Looking for Katharine Susannah Prichard', *Hecate* 10, 2 (1984), 45–52.

Sculthorpe, Peter. *Eliza Fraser Sings*. Musical composition with libretto by Barbara Blackman. Commissioned by the Canadian Lyric Arts Trio, first performed in Sydney and Melbourne and recorded for transmission on ABC radio in 1978.

Sharman, Ralph. 'Lights, Cameras – But Aboriginals Forget Songs.' *Telegraph* (Sydney), 26 May 1976.

Shaw, A. G. L. 'British Policy towards the Australian Aborigines, 1830–1850.' *Australian Historical Studies* 99 (October 1992): 265–85.

Shipwreck of Mrs. Fraser and Loss of the Stirling Castle. London: Dean and Munday, 1837.

Simpson, Brian. *Cannibalism and the Common Law.* Chicago: University of Chicago Press, 1985.

Sinclair, John. *Fraser Island and Cooloola.* Sydney: Weldon, 1990.

Slotkin, Richard. *Regeneration through Violence: Mythology of the American Frontier, 1600–1860.* Middletown, Conn.: Wesleyan University Press, 1973.

Smith, Bernard, *Australian Painting 1788–1990.* Additional chapters by Terry Smith. Melbourne: Oxford University Press, 3rd edn. 1991.

Smith, Bernard. *Place, Taste and Tradition: A Study of Australian Art Since 1788.* Sydney: Ure Smith, 1945.

Smith-Rosenberg, Carroll. 'Captured Subjects/Savage Others: Violently Engendering the New American.' *Gender and History* 5, 2 (Summer, 1993): 177–95.

Smith-Rosenberg, Carroll. 'So Sad over Film Snub.' *Telegraph* (Sydney), 26 December 1976: 11.

Spender, Stephen. 'Introduction.' In *Sidney Nolan: Leda and the Swan and Other Recent Works.* London: Mathieson Gallery, 1960.

Spivak, Gayatri Chakravorty. 'Acting Bits/Identity Talk.' *Critical Inquiry* 18, 4 (June 1992): 770–803.

Spivak, Gayatri Chakravorty. 'The Post-colonial Critic.' In *The Post-colonial Critic: Interviews, Strategies, Dialogues*, ed. Sarah Harasym: 67–74. New York and London: Routledge, 1990.

Spivak, Gayatri Chakravorty. 'Poststructuralism, Marginality, Postcoloniality and Value.' In *Literary Theory Today*, eds. Peter Collier, and Helga Geyer-Ryan: 219–44. Ithaca: Cornell University Press, 1990.

Spivak, Gayatri Chakravorty. *In Other Worlds: Essays in Cultural Politics.* New York and London: Routledge, 1988.

Spivak, Gayatri Chakravorty. 'Can the Subaltern Speak? Speculations on Widow Sacrifice.' In *Marxism and the Interpretation of Culture*, ed. Cary Nelson, and Lawrence Grossberg, 271–313. London: Macmillan, 1988.

Spivak, Gayatri Chakravorty. 'A Literary Representation of the Subaltern: A Woman's Text from the Third World.' *In Other Worlds: Essays in Cultural Politics*: 241–68. New York and London: Routledge, 1988.

Spivak, Gayatri Chakravorty. 'Subaltern Studies: Deconstructing Historiography.' *In Other Worlds: Essays in Cultural Politics*: 197–221. New York and London: Routledge, 1988.

Spivak, Gayatri Chakravorty. 'Three Women's Texts and a Critique of Imperialism.' *Critical Inquiry* 12, 1 (1985): 243–61.

Spurr, David. *The Rhetoric of Empire: Colonial Discourse in Journalism, Travel Writing, and Imperial Administration.* Durham and London: Duke University Press, 1993.

Steele, J. G., ed. *Brisbane Town in Convict Days: 1824–1842.* St Lucia: University of Queensland Press, 1975, reprinted 1987.

Steele, J. G. *Explorers of the Moreton Bay District, 1780–1830.* St Lucia: University of Queensland Press, 1972.

Stratton, Jon. *Writing Sites: A Genealogy of the Postmodern World.* Sydney: Harvester, 1990.

Stratton, Jon. 'A Question of Origins.' *Arena* 89 (1989): 133–51.

Strong, Pauline Turner. 'Captivity in White and Red: Convergent Practice and Colonial Representation on the British–American Frontier.' In *Crossing Cultures: Essays in the Displacement of Western Civilization*, ed. Daniel Segal: 33–104. Phoenix: University of Arizona Press, 1992.

Stummer, Peter O. 'Perception of Difference: The Conceptual Interaction of Cultures in Literary Discourse.' In *Them/Us: Translation, Transcription and Identity in Post-Colonial Literary Cultures*, ed. Gordon Collier: 307–17. Amsterdam and Philadelphia: Rodopi, 1991.

Summers, Anne. *Damned Whores and God's Police.* Ringwood, Vic.: Penguin, 1975.

'Sunday Afternoon with Peter Ross: Interview with Sir Sydney Nolan.' ABC, 17 April 1992.

Taussig, Michael. *Shamanism, Colonialism, and the Wild Man: A Study in Terror and Healing.* Chicago: University of Chicago Press, 1986.

Thesen, Hjalmar. 'A Moving and Poignant Story: Review of *An Instant in the Wind*,' *Eastern Province Herald* (Port Elizabeth), 10 November 1976: 7.

Thomas, Martin. 'Aborigines Restore Engagement to Art.' *Sydney Morning Herald*, 22 June 1991: 43.

Thomas, Nicholas. *Colonialism's Culture: Anthropology, Travel and Government.* Melbourne: University of Melbourne Press, 1994.

Thompson, E. P. *The Making of the English Working Class.* London: Gollancz, 1967.

The Times (London). 16 July, 3, 19, 23, 25 August 1837; 30 July, 25 August, 3 September 1838.

Tindale, N. B. *The Aboriginal Tribes of Australia.* Berkeley: University of California Press, 1974.

Torgovnick, Marianna. *Gone Primitive: Savage Intellects, Modern Lives.* Chicago: Chicago University Press, 1990.

Traill, W. H. *A Queenly Colony*. Brisbane: Gregory, Government Printer, 1901.

Trinh T. Minh-ha. *Woman, Native, Other*. Bloomington: Indiana University Press, 1989.

Tucker, Albert. *Faces I Have Met*. Vic.: Century Hutchinson, 1986.

Turner, Graeme. 'Semiotic Victories: Media Constructions of the Maralinga Royal Commission.' In *Australian Cultural Studies: A Reader*, ed. John Frow and Meaghan Morris: 180–91. Sydney: Allen and Unwin, 1993.

Turner, Victor. *A Forest of Symbols: Aspects of Ndembu Ritual*. Ithaca, NY: Cornell University Press, 1967.

'US Chill for André Brink Novel.' *Cape Times* (Cape Town), 2 March 1977: 9.

VanDerBeers, Richard. 'A Surfeit of Style: The Indian Captivity Narrative as Penny Dreadful.' *Research Studies* 39, 4 (December, 1971): 297–306.

Wald, Priscilla. 'Terms of Assimilation: Legislating Subjectivity in the Emerging Nation.' *Boundary 2* 19, 3 (September 1992): 77–104.

Ward, Jill. 'Patrick White's *A Fringe of Leaves*: History and Fiction.' *Australian Literary Studies* 8 (1978): 402–18.

Ward, Jill. 'Patrick White's *A Fringe of Leaves*.' *Critical Quarterly* 10, 3 (1977): 77–81.

Watson, F. J. *Vocabularies of Four Representative Tribes of South-East Queensland*. Brisbane: Royal Geographical Society of Queensland, 1944.

White, Haydon. *Tropics of Discourse: Essays in Cultural Criticism*. Baltimore: Johns Hopkins Press, 1978.

White, Haydon. 'Forms of Wildness: Archaeology of an Idea'. In *The Wild Man Within: An Image in Western Thought from the Renaissance to Romanticism*, ed. Edward Dudley and Maximillian E. Novak: 3–39. Pittsburgh: University of Pittsburgh Press, 1972.

White, Patrick. *Flaws in the Glass*. London: Jonathan Cape, 1981.

White, Patrick. *The Twyburn Affair*. New York: Penguin Books, 1981.

White, Patrick. 'Patrick White Speaks on Factual Writing and Fiction.' *Australian Literary Studies* 10 (1981): 99–101.

White, Patrick. *A Fringe of Leaves*. Harmondsworth: Penguin, 1976.

White, Patrick. 'The Prodigal Son.' In *Patrick White Speaks*. Sydney: Primavera Press, 1989. First pub. *Australian Letters* 1, 3 (1958): 39–40.

White, Richard. 'The Imagined Community: Nationalism and Culture in Australia.' In *Stories of Australian Art*: 35–45. London: Commonwealth Institute, Australian Studies Centre, 1988.

Willis, Anne-Marie. *Illusions of Identity: The Art of Nation*. Sydney: Hale and Iremonger, 1993.

'Wreck of the *Stirling Castle*'. In *Tales of Travellers*. London: Mark Clark, 1838.

'Wreck of the Stirling Castle: Horrib Treatment of the Crew by Savages.' London: J. Catnach of Seven Dials, 1837.

Youlden, Harry. 'Shipwreck in Australia.' *The Knickerbocker* 41, 4 (1853): 291–300.

Young, Robert. *White Mythologies: Writing History and the West*. London: Routledge, 1990.

Index

Throughout this index, EF indicates Eliza Fraser.